£4199

The Scottish Enlightenment
and the Militia Issue

The Scottish Enlightenment and the Militia Issue

JOHN ROBERTSON
St Hugh's College, Oxford

JOHN DONALD PUBLISHERS LTD.
EDINBURGH

ISBN 0 85976 109 6

Exclusive distribution in the United States of America and Canada by Humanities Press Inc., Atlantic Highlands, NJ 07716, U.S.A.

The publishers acknowledge the financial assistance of the Scottish Arts Council in the publication of this volume.

Printed in Great Britain by Bell and Bain Ltd., Glasgow

Acknowledgements

In the dozen years over which this book has been researched and written, first as a doctoral thesis and again in its present, revised form, I have incurred many debts, which it is a pleasure to acknowledge.

Before all, I owe thanks to Hugh Trevor-Roper, Lord Dacre of Glanton, who supervised the thesis and advised on its revision. His friendly guidance and ever instructive judgement, with its keen sense of the important in Scottish history, have been a constant support and inspiration. A second major debt is to Istvan Hont, who has combined friendship and good counsel with the sort of penetrating yet sympathetic criticism which provides the strongest of encouragements to persevere. Two direct contemporaries in the field, Alexander Murdoch and Richard Sher, have helped throughout, commenting generously on my thesis, passing on stray references, and providing me with the invaluable opportunity to debate and clarify my arguments. Among already established scholars, Nicholas Phillipson was generous with hospitality, time and ideas in the earlier stages of research and writing. As an examiner of my thesis he also made a helpful suggestion about the potential importance of Lord Belhaven, whom I had hitherto overlooked through concentrating on Fletcher: though he may not agree with the use I have made of the suggestion, its value will be evident. To my other examiner, Blair Worden, I also owe much. I appreciated contrasting early words of enouragement from Quentin Skinner and Duncan Forbes, and later I enjoyed stimulating discussions with David Kettler. More impersonally, the books of J. G. A. Pocock and A. H. Williamson have made fundamental contributions to my understanding of the militia issue and of Scottish political consciousness.

My first book provides a welcome opportunity to thank my history teachers at Trinity College, Glenalmond, John Barry, David Graham-Campbell and David Kent, and my undergraduate tutors at Wadham College, Oxford, Cliff Davies and Pat Thompson. Balancing discipline and tolerance, they made history a commitment. It was at Wadham that I began my research, assisted by a Senior Scholarship, while the thesis was written at Christ Church, where I was a Research Lecturer between 1975 and 1980. I am most grateful to the Dean, Canons and Students of Christ Church for that opportunity to do my work free of almost all commitments, yet in stimulating company. But perhaps the happiest of these institutional acknowledgements is to St Hugh's College, Oxford, where I hold my present teaching appointment. To the Governing Body I am grateful for the grant of a term's sabbatical leave, during which the final version of the book was begun; but I am still more grateful to my colleagues and undergraduates for the atmosphere, at once pleasant and challenging, in which I work.

The greater part of my research was done in the Bodleian, the National Library of Scotland and the Scottish Record Office, whose staffs are constantly helpful and where the environment is a standing inducement to scholarship. Elsewhere I would like particularly to thank Miss Catherine Armet, archivist at Mount Stuart, whose kind assistance made it possible for me to consult the papers of the third Earl of Bute; I am grateful to the present Marquess of Bute for permission to cite from them. I am likewise grateful to the National Galleries of Scotland for permission to reproduce on the cover the portrait of Andrew Fletcher and the Tassie medallions of David Hume and Adam Smith. Mrs Mary Aldworth has typed both the thesis and the book, assisted with the latter by Mrs Joy Johnson: gratitude is due not only for their work, but for the resigned good humour with which they have accepted the uneven progress of my writing. John Tuckwell of John Donald was encouragingly quick to accept the thesis for publication, and has since been judiciously tactful in awaiting its revision.

My parents, Lewis and Elspeth, and my brother Mark have never failed in interest, confidence and encouragement. Maxine Berg, my wife, has now lived with this book for quite long enough: besides adding to our happiness with two splendid daughters, Frances and Gabriel, she has by her goading, patience and love enabled me to reach the end, and I am deeply grateful.

Contents

Abbreviations

NLS   National Library of Scotland
SRO   Scottish Record Office
BL   British Library
PRO   Public Record Office
EUL   Edinburgh University Library
DNB   *Dictionary of National Biography*
Halkett & Laing S. Halkett & J. Laing,
                Dictionary of Anonymous and Pseudonymous Literature of Great Britain (Edinburgh 1882–88)

1

The Significance of the Militia

To explain why Scotland should have produced so distinguished a branch of the eighteenth-century European Enlightenment presents historians with a remarkable opportunity. On the one hand, later eighteenth-century Scotland was a society transformed. For long, as David Hume could describe it to Edward Gibbon, 'the rudest, perhaps, of all European nations; the most necessitous, the most turbulent and the most unsettled',[1] Scotland had appeared at the end of the seventeenth century to be facing economic collapse and political breakdown. Yet within a hundred years the country achieved a level of economic development and political stability that enabled it to participate fully in the joint British enterprise of industrial revolution and empire. The Scottish Enlightenment, on the other hand, was distinguished precisely for its interest in 'the progress of society'. The principles of human nature, the material, moral and institutional causes of (and hindrances to) social development — to these David Hume and Adam Smith, William Robertson and Adam Ferguson, Lord Kames, Thomas Reid and John Millar devoted their philosophical, political, economic and historical enquiries. There can be little doubt that it was Scotland's own social transformation which inspired this distinguishing interest of the Scottish Enlightenment.[2] But just how did Scottish thinkers understand and generalise from their society's particular experience? One approach to the answer, I wish to argue in this book, lies in the issue of a militia, a subject of keen debate in eighteenth-century Scotland. In the context of Scottish experience, the militia was an issue which could not but have powerful social and political resonances. At the same time, as an issue central to one of the most fertile traditions of European discourse about politics, the militia presented the thinkers of the Scottish Enlightenment with the opportunity for far-reaching intellectual reflection.

What made the militia issue significant in the particular Scottish context was the nation's distinctive martial heritage. Since the high middle ages — to recede no further — both the social structure and the national identity of Scotland had been closely bound up with military prowess. In part, the martial character of Scottish social structure was the common legacy of European military feudalism. Though belated, the introduction of feudalism into Scotland in the twelfth and thirteenth centuries had been remarkably clear-cut. With active royal encouragement, the classic form of feudal 'knight service' had been accepted by new Anglo-Norman and old Scottish families alike; and these in turn had developed the system on their own lands, in the Highlands as well as the Lowlands. Traditional, pre-existing 'Lordship' was thus defined and strengthened anew in feudal terms; while among the lesser vassals there emerged the distinct and scarcely less important class of lairds.[3]

But the copy-book imposition of feudalism was not alone responsible for the martial quality of Scottish society. Alongside 'knight-service' there had survived an older form of military organisation, the 'Scottish service', by which the earls raised infantrymen from among the common people. Put to the test of battle at the turn of the thirteenth and fourteenth centuries, this 'Scottish service' proved the better adapted to Scotland's circumstances: while the feudal host was routed at Dunbar in 1296, it was from the Scottish service that Wallace was provided with his followers, and Bruce drew the victors of Bannockburn. As a consequence, the later middle ages saw the increasing modification of feudal military relations, and the development of other types of martial connection that embraced all levels of the local community. Bruce himself began the process in the aftermath of his victory, revising feudal obligations to align them with the more plebeian form of service.[4] Further dilution of the legal framework of feudalism occurred in the fifteenth century, with the development of new forms of tenancy: in particular, the introduction of feuing enabled the lairds to acquire a more independent landed base. What simultaneously ensured that this weakening of feudalism meant no softening of martial character was the widespread adoption in the period of voluntary bands of 'manrent' between lords and their followers — bands which themselves were usually based on the still more enduring ties of kinship. Extending down through the local communities, these obligations of band and kinship confirmed and reinforced the continuing primacy of armed lordship in Scottish society. The result was a society strikingly atavistic, but with a cohesion which should not be under-estimated. The justice of the local communities of late mediaeval Scotland might still be that of the dark-age blood-feud; but they appear to have avoided the social conflict common elsewhere in Europe.[5]

Even so, Scotland's martial social structure was not in itself unusual. Military feudalism was a European phenomenon; and the obligations of bond and kinship, in variant forms, were the response of many late mediaeval societies to uncertain times. It was the combination of a martial social structure with a martial national identity which rendered Scotland distinctive. The reliance on a martial identity was necessitated by the weakness of Scotland's political institutions. Scotland was without the self-sustaining organs of government, central and local, which developed early in mediaeval England or France. Instead the country owed its emergence as an independent kingdom in the twelfth and thirteenth centuries almost entirely to the vigour of its kings; and the military feudalism they imposed on society was, under the crown itself, the only tangible expression of national unity. Defeat at Dunbar underlined the precariousness of an identity on such foundations: an independent kingdom, in G. W. S. Barrow's words, 'was no more and no less than a kingdom which could defend itself by arms'.[6] In the event, the Scots proved equal to this challenge: the persevering campaigns of Wallace and Bruce culminated in 1314 in a victory at Bannockburn so decisive that it justified for ever the claim to a national identity. Soon after, that identity received further, ideological affirmation in the Declaration of Arbroath's eloquent proclamation of the 'Community of the Realm of Scotland' in 1320.[7] But all the ideological pride and sophistication of that Declaration could not disguise the reality that Scotland was a community by arms alone: and as such, it remained an inherently unstable community. Over the next hundred and fifty years its history proved to be a sorry catalogue of violence and confusion, as repeated royal minorities and the ambitions and hatreds of over-mighty families, Douglases and Stewarts, reduced it to near anarchy. Nevertheless, the anarchy was at least martial; and with the help of English indifference, the nation's hard-won identity survived. The last years of the fifteenth century actually saw it gain new strength, when astute Stewart kingship secured not merely Scotland's independence of England, but recognition in Europe at large. As Scottish literary culture shared in the continental movement of humanism and flowered at court, patriotic Scots even began to imagine that distinction in letters might be added to prowess in arms to form joint marks of national identity.[8]

The century of the Reformation in Scotland brought major changes, both to social structure and to national identity: but in neither of these spheres was the importance of the martial actually displaced. The changes were a combination of the institutional and the ideological. For the first time, Scotland acquired in the sixteenth century institutions, the Reformed Kirk and the central law courts (both the Court of Session and the College of Justice), capable of imposing themselves on the social structure. These institutions still of course rested on a limited social base, the professional interests of the ministers and lawyers in alliance with the newly independent lairds; and their authority over the local communities was gradual in developing. Nevertheless their emergence offered a first challenge to the simple, uninstitutionalised ties of lordship and kinship which had hitherto held those communities together. Institutional developments were accompanied, moreover, by a vigorous ideological drive to undermine and absorb those older loyalties. The ministers of the Kirk championed a new moral discipline; the lawyers urged the rule of law over the feud; and together they subjected the local communities to the novel terror of the witch-hunt.[9]

Perceptions of the national identity were likewise the subject of change and complication in the sixteenth century. Institutional developments, not only those of the Kirk and the central courts, but the emergence of a rudimentary government bureaucracy and the acquisition of new authority by the Estates, at last gave the nation's claim to independence some constitutional substance. Ideology opened up still grander possibilities. In the sweeping perspective of the Apocalypse, Arthur Williamson has argued, the national identity came to be thought of in terms transcending mere independence from England. Probably the most far-reaching of such reformulations of Scotland's identity was that of John Napier of Merchiston: on his reading of the *Book of Revelations,* Scotland was to be seen as one of the seven surviving ancient kingdoms (England being but another) which would together destroy the Roman Antichrist. The more widely held view was less ambitious: as John Knox recognised, the relative historical weakness of Scottish ecclesiastical and political institutions made it impossible for Scotland to rival England's claim to be an 'Elect Nation'. But what the Reformation did make possible, Knox believed, was a new joint relationship with England in a greater, imperial union of 'Britain'. When James VI travelled south in 1603 to become James I, this was his ideological priority. He might soon be disillusioned; but now it was English insularity that was blocking the expansive aspirations of Scotland.[10]

All the institutional enterprise of the Kirk and the Courts, all the historical vision of Napier and Knox could not, however, undermine the continuing importance of arms for Scottish society and nationhood. The very Reformation itself required the armed assistance of the nobility and lairds to succeed. The first Band of the Lords of the Congregation in 1557; the second band of 1560 and the insurrection (albeit with English assistance) which followed; the deposition of the Queen in 1567: all were organised through the band, the pervasive instrument of Scottish lordship.[11] Nor did martial energies subside when the Reformation was secure. Instead Scotsmen poured overseas to take advantage of the religious revolts and wars of continental Europe. By the end of the sixteenth century there was a Scottish contingent of several thousand in the Dutch army; and the Thirty Years' War in the early seventeenth century brought further opportunities for mercenary service in the armies of Sweden. More secular ideologists than Napier and Knox did implicitly recognise this reality. The humanist George Buchanan would justify Mary's deposition with a radical general theory of resistance in *De Jure Regni apud Scotos,* and seek in his *History of Scotland* to refurbish the mediaeval idea of the 'Community of the Realm' as Scotland's 'ancient constitution': but the key terms of his argument betray the traditional rough-and-ready resorts of the Scottish nobility, acting in the absence of institutional constraints.[12] Equally revealing, the radically minded David Hume of Godscroft wrote the history of the deeds of one leading family, the House of Douglas, as if it was the equivalent to the history of Scotland.[13] Even the Jacobean unionist Sir Thomas Craig felt compelled by English slights to assert that Scotland's particular contribution to a British empire would be her distinction in arms and letters.[14]

The still deeply martial character of Scottish society and nationhood is clearly evident in the upheaval of the Civil War in the mid-seventeenth century. The National Covenant of 1638 might proclaim Scotland's unique relationship with the Almighty — and at the same time implicitly commit the nation to a programme of imperial union with England. The Kirk might mobilise, discipline and witch-hunt as never before. But the constitutional ideology of the Covenanters was that of Buchanan, of the community in arms; and the strength of their rebellion lay in their armies. Eagerly the mercenaries came home, and the Covenanters made particular efforts to obtain their services. For the rest, men were raised ostensibly by national levy, but almost certainly with the aid of lordship in the localities.[15] The outcome was of a pattern with Scotland's past. Once again the nobility professed to fight for the community of the realm — none more vehemently than Montrose, after as well as before he turned Royalist; and once more it is evident that ideals did but gloss the imperatives of family rivalry — Montrose actually basing his campaign for the King on clan feuds against the Campbells.

The Civil War was nonetheless also a turning point. Thereafter, beginning in the Lowlands but eventually extending to the Highlands, political and social developments combined to weaken the martial strain in Scottish life. Paradoxically, one agent of change was the militarisation of government itself. Having experienced the influence which the Covenanting clergy were able to exert over their own followings, the nobility were at last prepared to accept a large measure of central royal authority. From the Restoration the crown was thus able to maintain a small standing army; and in 1663 the Scottish Estates voted a Militia Act in which they acknowledged 'his Majesty's royal prerogative and undoubted right of the sole power of the raising, arming and commanding of his subjects', and offered the King twenty thousand foot and two thousand horse, armed and furnished with forty days' provision, 'to march to any part of his dominions of Scotland, England or Ireland for suppressing of any foreign invasion, intestine trouble or insurrection, or for any other service wherein his Majesty's honour, authority or greatness may be concerned'.[16] Such enthusiasm for armed royal authority, however, did not survive the use to which these forces were put by Charles II's minister, the Earl (later Duke) of Lauderdale, and by James Duke of York and afterwards VII of Scotland. Deployed not only to harry plebeian Covenanters, but to aid and abet factional quarrels among the nobility, the army became a major source of grievance against the Restoration regime; and the fall of James in 1688 brought the experiment of armed government to an abrupt end. With every historical justification, the Claim of Right issued by the Scottish Estates in 1689 denounced as a particular violation of 'the laws and liberties of the Kingdom', the 'levying or keeping on foot a standing army in time of peace'.[17]

While the arbitrary use of military power after the Restoration thus began to discredit the martial strain in the conduct of Scottish politics, still more important was to be the undermining of its social foundations. Changes in estate organisation — the shift from multiple to single tenancies, the introduction of longer and written leases, the payment of rent in money — indicate a growing emphasis on economic exploitation of the land; conversely they almost certainly indicate a declining interest in the retention of a military following.[18] Increasingly too the Lowland Scottish nobility appear to have been taking their model of behaviour from England, and to have renounced direct action in favour of the law as a means of settling disputes.[19] But it is uncertain how extensive and fast was the change before the Revolution in 1688: the raising in 1678 of the so-called 'Highland Host', in which independent Highland bands recruited by specially commissioned noblemen were combined with noble-led units of Lowland militia, suggests that the old ways were not yet redundant.[20] The end of lordship in Scotland is a subject still virtually unexplored; the assertion of Gordon Donaldson that 'it would have seemed ludicrous by 1688 should a landlord in Lowland Scotland have proposed to call out his dependents either to pursue a feud or to challenge the crown', awaits confirmation.[21]

If not by 1688, then certainly by 1707, however, it seems clear that the social structure and political life of Lowland Scotland were no longer predominantly martial in character. During the debate over the Union, as we shall see, even the historically well-entrenched place of martial achievement in the national identity came under fire, critics decrying it as a mark of a barbarous past. Adherents of the martial identity fought back to effect, winning widespread acceptance of the view that pride in the nation's military achievements was one of the best assurances of continuing 'independence' within the Union. But, the Jacobites among them apart, the weapons and purposes of those who so argued were purely ideological. In practice, Scotland was no longer militarily independent. The regiments in Scotland were part of the British establishment, and Scottish gentlemen were absorbed — in disproportionate numbers — into the officer corps of the British army.[22] The national militia instituted at the Restoration, with its opportunities for the display of aristocratic influence in the localities, was meanwhile neglected. There was no provision for its renewal in the Treaty of Union, and in 1708 a bill at Westminster to rectify the omission was apparently blocked by the last use of the royal veto. Simultaneously, Lowland magnate power was weakened by changes in Scotland's civil administration — the abolition of the Estates, the strengthening of the offices of local government, the growing prestige of the Edinburgh law-courts. Ever-quickening social change, the now self-conscious commitment of landowners to 'improvement' and the revolution of manners, completed the dissolution of the old martial order.

Only in the Highlands did traditional ways last into the eighteenth century. There the Civil War had given fresh purpose to the fighting instincts of clanship. The hereditary enemies of the Campbells had been mobilised in the service of the Royalist Montrose; and the Covenanters' unprecedented assault on Gaelic culture had served only to provoke vernacular poets to fresh celebrations of the martial feats and feuds of their chiefs.[23] The War over, the Highlanders had proceeded to reap the reward for their Royalism by being accorded a prominent role in the armed forces of the Restoration government. At the same time economic change was still little felt, so that there were few internal pressures for demilitarisation. The Highlanders thus remained unaffected by the disillusionment with martial ways that was growing so fast in the Lowlands, and were in a position to resist the hostile pressures increasingly exerted on them by government and Lowland society after 1688. Even if there was no longer an authorised outlet for their martial proclivities within Scotland, Highlanders continued to serve abroad as mercenaries in the Dutch and French armies until the mid-eighteenth century. Meanwhile clanship survived at home in conjunction with the cause of Jacobitism, each exploiting the other for mutual preservation. In a period of less than forty years the alliance staged two aborted risings (in 1708 and 1719) and two full-scale rebellions (in 1715 and 1745); yet perhaps its persistence was as much a measure of the demilitarisation of the Lowlands as of the continuing martial vigour of clanship. When confronted finally with English professional soldiers at Culloden in 1746, the Highland army disintegrated. Outright repression, disarming legislation and the abolition of hereditary jurisdictions then completed the destruction of their society and cause so efficiently that within eleven years the Highlanders too could safely be absorbed, complete with the newly invented kilt, into the British army. From the wreck of the last vestiges of the old martial order a new role for the Scot thus promptly emerged: the tartan soldier as the cutting edge of the British empire.

Just at this moment, when martial achievement seemed for all practical purposes no longer to matter, and to have become simply a heritage of memory and myth, sudden new anxieties over the defence of Scotland made the nation's military organisation a subject of open debate. Incorporating union with England might have removed one territorial threat, but it had perhaps also made Scotland more vulnerable to others. Enemies of Britain might now regard Scotland's long coastline as the weak link in the island's defences, and land forces there either as a diversion or as a full-scale invasion. However exaggerated, such fears became widespread during the Seven Years' War; and they were raised again twenty years later during the American War. In response, there occurred a series of agitations between 1759–62, and between 1775–83, in support of a demand for the re-establishment of a Scottish national militia. Advanced in the form of parliamentary bills, the demand for a militia was a means of exerting pressure on the London government to guarantee Scottish security. But in appealing for the support of the Scottish political community — the county landowners and, to a lesser extent, the burgh oligarchies — the advocates of a militia by no means limited their case to the immediate military situation. At stake, it was claimed, were matters as large as the nature of Scotland's relation to England within the Union, and the proper structure of Scottish landed society in an age of improvement. Even though the case for a militia was by no means unchallenged, and the agitations repeatedly failed in their object, simply by forcing critics to respond to their claims, the militia enthusiasts were successful in generating a debate on Scotland's whole experience of social and political transformation. In effect the militia issue called upon the Scots to reconsider the two themes historically embodied in their martial heritage, the structure of landed society and the national identity, in the light of their eighteenth-century achievements of political stability and economic development.

Simultaneously, the general problem of national defence and military organisation presented itself as central to the Scottish Enlightenment's enquiry into 'the progress of society'. In several cases, direct personal connections can be established between the Scottish militia issue and the Enlightenment enquiry. The framing of the demand and organising of the agitations can be traced to a particular group of Edinburgh literati, the 'Moderates', led (on this occasion) by the Reverend Alexander Carlyle and Adam Ferguson. The active involvement of these literati was of double significance. The debates themselves were conducted with unusual intellectual sophistication; and at the same time the concerns articulated in them can be found again, developed and generalised, in a deliberately theoretical work such as Adam Ferguson's *Essay on the History of Civil Society*, published in 1767, shortly after the first round of agitation. Two other important members of the Enlightenment, David Hume and Adam Smith, were not, on the available evidence, active participants in the Scottish militia debates. But the general problem of military organisation, and the concept of a militia in particular, occupied an important place in their social and political thinking; and their discussions of the subject were recognised by Ferguson and Carlyle as having definite — and challenging — implications for the cause of a militia in Scotland. In short, the late eighteenth-century demand for a national militia would appear to have placed the thought of the Scottish Enlightenment in a direct relationship with Scottish experience.

It would nevertheless be a mistake to interpret the significance of the militia issue for the Scottish Enlightenment as but a straightforward reflection of Scotland's martial heritage. Vital though the Scottish experience was in stimulating and directing the Enlightenment's interest in the issue, what Scotland could not provide were the intellectual resources with which to pursue the interest: these had to come from the common

stock of European political thought.[24] Since the Renaissance, the forms of
military organisation and the particular merits of a militia had been a
subject of recurrent discussion among Italian and English political thinkers, and their discussion has been conducted in the terms of an increasingly defined intellectual tradition. That discussion, and the intellectual
tradition which developed with it, must now be interposed between
Scottish Enlightenment thinking and Scotland's martial heritage. For it
was from that wider, European context that the militia derived its
intellectual significance.

The origins of European discussion of the militia may be traced to the
city-states of northern Italy, and in particular to Florence, during the later
middle ages. Employing their mercantile wealth to subordinate their rural
hinterlands, these cities had early checked the development of feudal
military power; but the same wealth, by bringing to the cities social
instability as well as subject territory, had also encouraged the neglect of
their traditional form of defence, a militia of citizens, and reliance instead
on hired and frequently foreign mercenaries. By the late fourteenth
century, the change was causing the cities' humanist literati acute concern.
Inspired by Petrarch, they denounced the mercenaries as agents of
northern barbarism, enhancing Italy's historic vulnerability to the interference of foreign powers. Convinced of the perpetual validity of the
classical concept of the armed citizen, they struggled to renew the militia
ideal in a form appropriate to the growing social and political sophistication of the cities. In the early fifteenth century, hopes were pinned upon
the nobility: the Florentine Leonardo Bruni's *De Militia* (c.1422) appealed
to the example of the Roman knights. By the opening of the sixteenth
century the issue had become critical, as the new infantry armies and
artillery of Germany, France and Spain swept across Italy, overwhelming
the Florentine republic. In response came the most resonant of all
affirmations of the militia ideal — the radical, vernacular appeal to the
example of the ancient Roman *popolo armato* in the *Discorsi* and *Arte della
Guerra* of Machiavelli.[25]

The terms in which Machiavelli and his humanist predecessors argued
the cause of the militia were, with differences of emphasis, broadly the
same. They belonged among a body of concepts which together were
sufficiently coherent and systematic to become — if not yet in the writings
of the humanists, then certainly in the aftermath of Machiavelli — a
distinct tradition of intellectual discourse. Following J. G. A. Pocock, I
shall henceforth describe this as the 'civic tradition'.[26] Of classical and
ultimately Aristotelian origin, the concepts of the civic tradition were
developed by the Florentines to define the institutional, moral and material
conditions of political community, understanding political community as
the free participation of all citizens in public life. The first condition of
political community was the existence of regular institutions. These should
be formally established by a constitution; and the constitution should be

framed so as to distribute the several legislative, executive and judicial functions of government among citizens in a manner which satisfied and harmonised the citizens' various aspirations and capacities. The Florentine thinkers agreed, however, that institutions alone would be insufficient unless activated by a moral will to participate: it was essential that citizens should demonstrate public spirit or 'virtue' in carrying out their duties. The concept of virtue itself was increasingly politicised: while the Latin *virtus* of the humanists might still cover the range of classical and christian moral values, Machiavelli's vernacular *virtù* expressed only unceasing, single-minded devotion to the political life. Finally, there was a general recognition among the Florentines that the cultivation of virtue was in turn dependent on a third, material condition: the citizens must be economically independent or autonomous. This did not mean, the humanists in particular insisted, that citizens need adhere to a Spartan ideal of poverty; but it did require that they abstain from direct, personal involvement in economic activity, which should be left to a class of 'servants'. Citizenship, in other words, must be restricted, excluding those actively engaged in service. Thus defined, the institutional, moral and material conditions of political community were interlocking: only if all three were met would citizens be able to realise the highest civic ideal of liberty — the liberty 'to' participate in political life.

Within this framework, the concept of a militia had a privileged place. Obliging every citizen to bear arms, the militia focused all the conditions of political community. As an institution, it was the country's defence against external enemies; but it also served an important unifying function within the community, the common obligation of military service offsetting the inequality in the roles allotted citizens in civil life. At the same time, the militia required the fulfilment of both the moral and the material conditions of political community. Virtue was a quality citizens needed to display as much in war as in civil affairs, while economic independence was essential if citizens were to be free to take up arms whenever required. Altogether, participation in the militia was the simplest and in the last resort the most important expression of the citizen's political liberty.

Defining the conditions of political community, the Florentine formulation of the civic tradition simultaneously identified political community's antithesis. Counterposed to the civic concept of regular, constitutional government was the irregular, strictly unconstitutional state of despotism or tyranny. A despotism was a state which lacked the institutions to prevent the arbitrary exercise and abuse of power: under such a regime the people were effectively reduced to the condition of 'slaves'. Central to this antithesis of political community, moreover, was the contrasting distribution of arms. Instead of a militia, a despot was characteristically reliant on mercenary soldiers. Possessing neither material independence nor virtue, mercenary soldiers remained untouched by the normal ties of civil association: they had no commitments other than self-preservation and loyalty to their leader. By their very existence, therefore, they embodied the subversion of political liberty. The process by which such a state of despotism became established (unless it was simply imposed by conquest) was denominated in the civic tradition as 'corruption'. Corruption occurred through citizens putting their private, material interests before the public good, and thus declining the pursuit of virtue: of this process there was no surer indication than a willingness among citizens to entrust their defence to mercenary soldiers. Understood in these terms, it should be noted, corruption was virtually synonymous with change: while the cultivation of virtue — even the hyperpolitical Machiavellian *virtù* which entailed constant conflict and expansion — was still essentially directed at the preservation and renewal of the fabric of the political community, corruption was a genuinely dynamic, transforming force. Dissolving the moral commitment of citizens to participate, it led to the neglect of institutions and ended in the loss of political liberty.

If such, in abstract, was the civic tradition in its original, Florentine formulation, it is important to note that from the first it overlapped with two other sets of ideas.[27] Unless the civic tradition is distinguished from these, the intellectual significance of the militia issue may be lost. On one side, there was a close relation with the political cause of republicanism. Both the humanists and the Machiavelli of the *Discorsi* were ardent champions of the republican against the princely form of government; and this commitment could well be expressed in civic constitutional principles. It was always difficult in civic terms to see how a single ruler could be prevented from becoming arbitrary and despotic, dependent for his security upon mercenary soldiers. Yet republicanism and the civic tradition should not simply be regarded as synonymous. Republicanism was a practical political cause, by no means exclusively dependent on the civic tradition for intellectual support; (it also evolved a strong juristic foundation). The civic tradition, on the other hand, was an intellectual discourse on politics; and in its terms it was not altogether impossible — as Aristotle had indicated — to regard monarchy as a constitutional form of government, or to envisage — as did Machiavelli in *Il Principe* — a prince using a militia to win the allegiance of his subject citizens. As we shall see, it became increasingly necessary, and intellectually feasible, to argue the case for a militia on civic principles without presupposing the political framework of a pure republic.

The second set of ideas with which the civic tradition overlapped lay among the less political, more moral and cultural strains of thought that co-existed within the broad movement of humanism. Initially, indeed, it is a matter of debate whether it is legitimate to distinguish a consciously 'civic' perspective in *quattrocento* humanism, so imbued were the Florentine literati with the cultural ideals of Petrarch and, behind them, with the moral teachings of Cicero, themselves an adaptation of the Stoic philosophy. Following Petrarch, the humanists' critique of mercenaries was as

much cultural as political; and even as they advocated a militia, they held it
a commonplace that a man of virtue was proficient no less in letters than in
arms. Even after Machiavelli's assault on Ciceronian values, the intellectual
distance between the civic tradition and Stoic–Ciceronian moral philosophy
remained short: the two can often be found mixed in the work of a single
thinker. Nevertheless, it is quite as important to maintain a distinction
between the civic tradition and Stoic–Ciceronian moralism as it is to
differentiate civic principles from republicanism. As the humanists at least
made clear, the case for a militia required the fulfilment of institutional as
well as moral and material conditions. Machiavelli's *Discorsi*, with their
impassioned evocation of the armed citizen of ancient Rome, made the
point still more strongly: there was an inseparable connection between the
institution of a militia and the cultivation of a specifically political *virtù*. It
was precisely that connection, however, that Ciceronian moralism, by its
relative indifference to political institutions and dilution of the political
quality of virtue, tended to undermine. Wherever such moralism subsequently intruded, it will be seen that the significance of the militia was
compromised.

There is a further reason for discriminating between the civic tradition
and Stoic–Ciceronian moral philosophy. The latter was always intellectually janus-faced, associating not only with the civic tradition, but also with
the very different jurisprudential traditions of natural and Roman law.
Whatever the overlap with Ciceronian moralism itself, between the civic
and those jurisprudential traditions there was a definite conceptual gulf. In
the jurisprudential perspective, society, not the political community, was
the universal element; the possession of rights, not the pursuit of virtue,
was the condition of association between men; and liberty was consequently understood as the private, juristic freedom 'from' authority, rather than
as the public, political liberty 'to' participate.[28] The existence of such a
gulf between the civic and the jurisprudential traditions did not necessarily
place them in conflict. In relation to arms in particular, it was possible for
separate civic and jurisprudential arguments to run in parallel: the bearing
of arms might be presented simultaneously as a public duty and a private
right, as an expression of the citizen's liberty to participate and as a
guarantee of the individual's freedom from authority. But given two such
contrasting overall perspectives, the civic political and public, the jurisprudential social and private, the possibility of a direct conflict was ever-
present. In the case of arms, the individual's right and freedom might also
be construed in a way antithetical to the civic — as a right not to bear
arms, as a freedom from military conscription. As we shall see, such a
jurisprudentially based argument was to provide perhaps the most fundamental challenge to the militia concept in the eighteenth century.

After Machiavelli, the further development of the civic tradition —
understood as a distinct intellectual discourse on the lines I have described
— and of the militia concept was due, once again, to the challenge of a new

military phenomenon. This was the standing army, which became common throughout Europe in the seventeenth century. The standing army embodied no very original strategic conception: it was simply built upon the superiority of infantry established by the Swiss and Spanish at the start of the sixteenth century. Nor did it signal an immediate change in composition and recruitment. The Dutch and Swedish forces in the early seventeenth century, the French later in the same century, and the British well into the eighteenth century regularly included sizeable contingents of mercenaries. What was so distinctively novel about the standing army was, first, its discipline, and, second, its close relation to the state which organised and financed it. Its discipline subjected soldiers to a degree of regulation and supervision hitherto regarded as quite incompatible with military honour — and in so doing set a menacing example of authority to civilian populations. Still more important, however, was the strengthening of the state involved in the creation of a bureaucracy to manage the armies, in the increase of taxation to maintain them and (by the eighteenth century) in the conscription of men to serve in them. In Russia the army of Peter the Great was founded upon and proceeded to reinforce a transformation in the entire pattern of social and political obligations. In Brandenburg-Prussia the military administration effectively subordinated and then absorbed the civil. In France the great armies of Louis XIV ensured the consolidation and extension of the administrative centralisation begun in the early seventeenth century, and at once required and enforced ever high taxation. In Britain acceptance of a standing army was ultimately dependent upon the Financial Revolution, probably the least oppressive but most effective of all the military-related additions to a state's resources. In short, wherever it emerged in the hitherto loosely articulated political world of feudal and early modern Europe, the standing army was a wonderful concentrator of power.[29]

As such, the standing army did not want for intellectual justification. The late sixteenth-century adaptation of the Stoic values of resignation and submission by the Fleming Justus Lipsius, combined with the jurists' reinforcement of the concept of sovereignty, supplied more than enough cover for both the new armies and the enhancement of state power they entailed.[30] But while the flexible moral philosophy of Stoicism could be accommodating, there was no place at all for the standing army within the stricter framework of the civic tradition. Institutionally, morally, materially, the standing army represented the complete negation of the civic ideal of political community.

It was particularly in England that the attempt was made to renew the civic tradition and its concept of a militia in the face of this challenge. There the emergence of a standing army was late, sudden and wholly unexpected. Throughout the sixteenth century England had diverged from the continental pattern by relying for defence upon a refurbished national militia; in the mid-seventeenth century, exploiting the resulting weakness in state power, the English confidently launched into civil war on the simple basis of raising county levies. From this conflict, however, there shortly emerged the extraordinary historical anomaly of a standing army, the New Model, which, after a rapid process of self-politicisation, actually overturned the monarchy and instituted a republic. Confronted with such a paradox, all parts of the political spectrum hastened to demand the re-institution of a militia; and the most ambitious and original of these appeals was one emanating from the republican left and framed in the terms of the civic tradition — James Harrington's *Commonwealth of Oceana* (1656).

Harrington's major innovation was to adapt civic concepts to the historical circumstances of an agrarian society. On this basis, he envisaged the reconstitution of the newly established English Republic (the Commonwealth of Oceana) as a genuine political community. The natural citizens of the Republic, he argued, were the county freeholders: with the decline of the 'Gothic' military aristocracy, these held the political 'balance' in English society. If their position was now secured by an Agrarian Law, regulating the possession of landed property, the free-holders would provide the Commonwealth with a lastingly stable social foundation. At the same time, the Republic should reform its constitution by introducing a strict rotation of offices and, the most urgent priority, by organising all the freeholders into a militia. By thus compelling every citizen actively to participate and practise virtue the Republic would make itself a political community fit to withstand its enemies and the forces of corruption alike.[31] In their immediate, practical context, of course, such hopes foundered on the impossibility of reconciling the twin supports of the republic, the Army and the county communities; and the prospect of rendering England into Oceana disappeared with the dissolution of the Republic between 1658 and 1660. But the Republic's failure did not discredit Harrington's arguments. Both a political commitment to a militia and an interest in the intellectual discourse of the civic tradition were to survive the restoration of the monarchy in 1660.

The reconstitution of the English militia was in fact one of the earliest measures of the Cavalier parliament after the Restoration: in acts which were almost as assertive of royal authority as their Scottish equivalents, the parliament indicated that such a force need be no threat to the monarchy. With the local operation of the militia still in the hands of the gentry, however, the crown very quickly showed its own preference for a smaller but more reliable standing army on the continental model.[32] Ever-increasing in size, this royal army was little less unpopular than its republican predecessor; and from the late 1660s it was the subject of continuous criticism within and without parliament. Tories joined radical Whigs in a loose 'Country Party' opposition, and once again it was the left which brought to the anti-army case the intellectual strength of the civic tradition. The radical Whigs, headed by Henry Neville, the translator of

Machiavelli, explicitly repeated Harrington's arguments, but now they joined his analysis of the conditions of citizenship in an agrarian society to a more familiar historical perspective in which a militia of freeholders became part of the ancient Saxon constitution of England. In this way they were able to adapt the case for a militia to the circumstances of a mixed monarchy rather than a republic. With the Revolution of 1688, their cause appeared to have triumphed: the Declaration of Right denounced the maintenance of a standing army in peacetime without consent of parliament as contrary to law, and a thorough reform of the militia was expected to follow.[33] In the event, the triumph was deflected by the simultaneous outbreak of the Nine Years' War, during which the size of the army rose to extraordinary new levels, approaching one hundred thousand men. But when the war ended in 1697, the opposition immediately brought the issue to a head, throwing themselves into a single-minded attempt to disband William's army. The ensuing 'Standing Army Controversy' of 1697–8 saw the dangers of a standing army repeatedly displayed, the benefits of a militia urged again and again in its stead. It was perhaps the most thorough single debate on forms of military organisation to occur in early modern Europe, and a clear demonstration of the continuing intellectual vitality and relevance of the civic tradition.[34]

It was, moreover, at this point that the experience of Scotland was at last brought into the debate, and subjected to analysis in the terms of the civic tradition. Hitherto Scottish military organisation had been too primitive to be relevant, while, perhaps because of this, it seems that the civic tradition remained unknown in Scottish political thought. Humanism, of course, had early penetrated Scottish intellectual life: Buchanan had drawn heavily on Stoic–Ciceronian moral philosophy, and the ideal of combining distinction in arms and letters, as we saw, had been taken over by the nation as a whole. But no one had yet cast the Scots for citizenship of a political community constituted on strict civic principles, or made a case for a Scottish militia.[35] That was now the contribution of Andrew Fletcher of Saltoun. In 1697 Fletcher was the author of the most original intervention in the English Standing Army Controversy, depicting the danger through a remarkable historical analysis of the progress of corruption throughout Europe. A year later Fletcher turned his attention to Scotland, and sketched a plan for separate Scottish and English militias under joint British command. Immediately, moreover, he proceeded to link the demand for a Scottish militia with further proposals for the reform first of Scotland's social structure and then of Scotland's constitution. Without radical social changes to ensure the independence of the landowning class, without the strengthening of the nation's independent political institutions, without a national militia to be a school of virtue, Fletcher insisted, there would be no future for a free, independent Scotland; with such reforms, however, Scotland would set an example to the whole of Europe. In effect, Fletcher was calling upon the Scots to renounce the martial social order and national identity they had inherited from the past, and to reconstitute themselves as a proper political community on civic principles.

At the time, Fletcher's fellow-countrymen were provoked rather than persuaded by his proposals. Alternative schemes of many social and political varieties were canvassed in the intensive debate which preceded the Union; and the passing of the Act of Union itself represented a clear defeat for Fletcher's vision. Nevertheless, Fletcher had already achieved something of the utmost significance. After his intervention, debate on the social and political condition of Scotland, both in his own time and in the later period of the Enlightenment, would be conducted in the terms he had laid down. Nowhere is this clearer than in the subsequent eighteenth-century debate on the Scottish militia. Without Fletcher's challenge to the Scots to confront their martial heritage with the principles of the civic tradition, the militia issue, if raised at all, must have remained devoid of intellectual significance; and the connection it made possible between Scottish experience and the thought of the Scottish Enlightenment would have been, in a strict sense, inconceivable.

It is with an extended discussion of Fletcher's writings that the account of the militia issue in eighteenth-century Scotland accordingly begins in the following chapter. The same chapter also examines the immediate response to Fletcher's challenge in the Union debate, when two contrasting views of the Scottish martial heritage were articulated: these would subsequently underlie different approaches to the militia issue later in the century. The renewal of interest in the issue during the early period of the Enlightenment is examined next, in Chapter 3. Though scattered and generalised, David Hume's reflections on forms of military organisation can be seen to represent one major development of Fletcherian arguments, albeit radically transforming their implication. But a quite different approach was adopted by the group of 'Moderate' literati — and it was these who emerged as the champions of a new Scottish militia. Two narrative chapters, 4 and 5, then consider in detail the terms in which the Moderates made their case for a Scottish militia, and the course of the successive agitations they inspired. The narrative is followed in Chapter 6 by an assessment of the militia advocates' achievement in using the issue to win support for their reassertion of the traditional view of Scotland's martial identity and social order. With Chapter 7 the study returns to the thought of the Enlightenment, and examines the treatment of forms and purposes of military organisation in the theoretical writings of Adam Ferguson and Adam Smith. In their work, it will be argued, can be seen the 'intellectual consequences' of the different approaches to the militia issue developed since Fletcher: where Ferguson elaborated the approach adopted by the Moderate group, Smith pursued still further the line of argument developed by Hume. The very different arguments which resulted throw fresh light on the two thinkers' respective contributions to the Scottish

Enlightenment's enquiry into 'the progress of society'; at the same time, they suggest an implicit disagreement over the propriety of the current demand for a Scottish militia. Feared by the militia's advocates, the existence and extent of such disagreement is confirmed in the final chapter, which takes its title from the last pamphlet contribution to the debates: *Reasons Against a Militia for Scotland* (1783). It there becomes clear that the arguments of Hume and Smith pointed Scotland in a direction quite contrary to that urged by the Moderate advocates of a militia.

Constructed on this plan, my study of the militia issue is designed to take advantage of the remarkable opportunity to relate the intellectual to the social in the explanation of the Scottish Enlightenment. As such is now the ambition of many, however, it may help to specify a little more fully the particular approach I have in mind. Through an account of the militia issue, my object is to build a bridge between the experience of Scottish society and the thought of the Scottish Enlightenment. The metaphor is deliberately chosen: the building of a bridge presupposes that the two sides to be joined, the social and the intellectual, remain some distance apart. My approach should thus be distinguished from the more comprehensively 'social' approach to the explanation of the Scottish Enlightenment presently being pursued by a number of other scholars, outstanding among them being Nicholas Phillipson. At its boldest, this approach would virtually assimilate the intellectual to the social, presenting the thought of the Scottish Enlightenment as the straightforward 'cultural' or 'ideological' reflection of the experience of Scottish society.[36]

By bridging rather than attempting to assimilate the social and the intellectual, I hope to avoid two dangers. The first is the excessive domestication of the Scottish Enlightenment which is liable to result from interpreting it as an episode, however distinguished, in Scottish culture. Without denying the importance of their interrelation, there is, it seems to me, a distinction to be drawn between the enlightening of Scotland and the Scottish Enlightenment, between, in Trevor-Roper's phrase, the 'camp-followers' and the 'real intellectual pioneers'.[37] The camp-followers may have contributed largely to the enlightening of Scotland; but the Scottish Enlightenment, as a branch of the greater European Enlightenment, was the achievement of the pioneers, the thinkers of European stature. To explain the Scottish Enlightenment, it is therefore essential that the work of the pioneers be studied in some degree independently of the Scottish context, and be considered in the broader setting of European thought and experience. The second danger I wish to avoid follows from the first. In being domesticated, the Enlightenment may also be tamed. For it is precisely when the connection between Scottish society and Enlightenment thought is drawn too close, when the wider, European context of the Enlightenment is neglected, that any potentially critical implications of Enlightenment thought for Scottish society itself are most likely to be missed. Fully to appreciate the significance of the Scottish Enlightenment, therefore, it is necessary not only to distance its thought from the purely Scottish context, but also to be alert to the consequent possibility of conflict between them. More than simply a cultural or ideological expression of Scottish social experience, the thought of the Scottish Enlightenment might even have an ideological implication at odds with that experience.

The desire to avoid the twin dangers of domesticating and taming the Scottish Enlightenment has shaped what follows. Although the militia issue attracted the attention of major Enlightenment thinkers and camp-followers alike, I have deliberately not assimilated the two. As the outline of the chapters has indicated, consideration of Enlightenment thinking on the issue, first in Hume's *Essays,* and later in Ferguson's *Essay on Civil Society* and Smith's *Wealth of Nations,* has been kept apart from the narrative account of the Scottish militia debates. Even when the writings of the Enlightenment seem most to have articulated Scottish concerns, I have sought first to consider them in their own, general terms. At the same time, it is very much the theme of this study that some of the Enlightenment thinkers were arguing along lines which, however general in expression, yet reflected critically on Scottish experience. In particular, the relative unimportance of political institutions as compared with moral values and the system of ranks in ensuring the cohesion of society, while a central feature of Scottish historical experience, was not universally taken for granted in the Enlightenment's discussion of the militia issue. That a militia must involve consideration of a society's institutions as well as its values was a lesson passionately taught by Andrew Fletcher before the Union, and repeated later, in the Enlightenment, by both David Hume and Adam Smith: and what they held true for the progress of society in general was also, by implication, true for Scotland in particular. Even in post-Union, enlightened Scotland, it would seem, the absence of their own political institutions was not something that thinking Scots could afford to accept without question.

NOTES

1. Letter of 18 March 1776: *The Letters of David Hume,* ed. J. Y. T. Greig, two volumes (Oxford 1969), II, p. 310.

2. H. R. Trevor-Roper, 'The Scottish Enlightenment', *Studies on Voltaire and the Eighteenth Century,* LVIII (1967).

3. G. W. S. Barrow, *The Anglo-Norman Era in Scottish History* (Oxford 1980), Ch. 5.

4. Barrow, *Anglo-Norman Era,* Ch. 6, and the same author's *Robert Bruce and the Community of the Realm of Scotland* (Edinburgh 1976), pp. 100–2, 122–3, 296–8, 402–6.

5. Jenny Wormald, *Court, Kirk and Community. Scotland 1470–1625* (London 1981), Chs. 2–3.

6. G. W. S. Barrow, *Kingship and Unity. Scotland 1000–1306* (London 1981), quotation from p. 162.

7. Barrow, *Robert Bruce*, pp. 424–30.

8. Wormald, *Court, Kirk and Community*, Chs. 1, 4.

9. Wormald, *Court, Kirk and Community*, Ch. 10.

10. A. H. Williamson, *Scottish National Consciousness in the Age of James VI* (Edinburgh 1979), Ch. 1.

11. Jenny Wormald, '"Princes" and the Regions in the Scottish Reformation', in N. Macdougall (ed.), *Church, Politics and Society: Scotland 1408–1929* (Edinburgh 1983).

12. H. R. Trevor-Roper, 'George Buchanan and the Ancient Scottish Constitution', *English Historical Review*, Supplement 3 (1966); R. A. Mason, '*Rex Stoicus*: George Buchanan, James VI and the Scottish Polity', in J. Dwyer, R. A. Mason and A. Murdoch (eds.), *New Perspectives on the Politics and Culture of Early Modern Scotland* (Edinburgh 1982). See also R. A. Mason, 'Covenant and Commonweal: the Language of Politics in Reformation Scotland', in Macdougall (ed.), *Church, Politics and Society*, on the secular, traditional character of the propaganda of the earlier Congregation movement of 1559–60.

13. Williamson, *Scottish National Consciousness*, pp. 133–4.

14. Sir Thomas Craig, *De Unione Regnorum Britanniae Tractatus*, ed. C. S. Terry, *Scottish History Society*, LX (Edinburgh 1909), Ch. viii.

15. David Stevenson, *The Scottish Revolution 1637–44* (Newton Abbot 1973), pp. 129–31, 189–90; and *Scottish Covenanters and Irish Confederates. Scottish–Irish Relations in the mid-Seventeenth Century* (Belfast 1981), pp. 75–83. But the recruitment and composition of the armies have not been studied in detail.

16. 'Act for Raising a Militia', 1663, repr. in *English Historical Documents VIII: 1660–1714*, ed. A. Browning (London 1953), pp. 610–11.

17. *A Source Book of Scottish History III: 1567–1707*, eds. W. C. Dickinson and G. Donaldson (Edinburgh 1954), p. 201. Other violations alleged in the Claim of Right included the use of army officers as judges overriding hereditary jurisdictions, and the general disarming of Protestants in favour of Catholics.

18. I. Whyte, 'The Emergence of the New Estate Structure', in M. L. Parry and T. R. Slater (eds.), *The Making of the Scottish Countryside* (London 1980).

19. N. T. Phillipson, 'Lawyers, Landowners, and the Civic Leadership of Post-Union Scotland', *Juridicial Review*, 21 (1976), pp. 106–7.

20. J. R. Elder, *The Highland Host of 1678* (Glasgow 1914).

21. Gordon Donaldson, *Scotland James V–James VII* (Edinburgh 1971), p. 401. Rosalind Mitchison, *Lordship to Patronage. Scotland 1603–1745* (London 1983), Ch. 4, confirms a general decline in the power of lordship, but not the specific disappearance of martial proclivities.

22. J. Hayes, 'Scottish Officers in the British Army 1714–63', *Scottish Historical Review*, XXXVII (1958).

23. A. I. Macinnes, 'Scottish Gaeldom 1638–51: the Vernacular Response to the Covenanting Dynamic', in Dwyer, Mason and Murdoch (eds.), *New Perspectives on Early Modern Scotland*.

24. The same is of course true in general of the enquiry into 'the progress of society': Trevor-Roper, 'The Scottish Enlightenment', *Studies on Voltaire*, LVIII, p. 1643.

25. C. C. Bayley, *War and Society in Renaissance Florence. The De Militia of Leonardo Bruni* (Toronto 1961).

26. J. G. A. Pocock, 'Civic Humanism and its role in Anglo-American Thought', in his collection *Politics, Language and Time* (London 1972); *The Machiavellian Moment. Florentine Political Thought and the Atlantic Republican Tradition* (Princeton 1975). I have chosen to use the term 'civic tradition' rather than Pocock's alternatives of 'civic humanism' and 'Machiavellian tradition' because, important though the humanists and Machiavelli were to its formulation, the tradition was not to remain fixed in the form they gave it. See also the opening paragraphs of my 'The Scottish Enlightenment at the Limits of the Civic Tradition', in I. Hont and M. Ignatieff (eds.), *Wealth and Virtue. The Shaping of Political Economy in the Scottish Enlightenment* (Cambridge 1983).

27. J. H. Hexter, 'Republic, Virtue, Liberty, and the Political Universe of J. G. A. Pocock', in his *On Historians* (London 1979), pp. 292–303; Quentin Skinner, *The Foundations of Modern Political Thought. Volume I: The Renaissance* (Cambridge 1978), Part ii.

28. J. G. A. Pocock, 'Virtue, Rights and Manners. A Model for Historians of Political Thought', *Political Theory*, 9 (1981). My own use of the term 'tradition' to describe both the civic and the jurisprudential discourses, but not the discourse of Stoic–Ciceronian moral philosophy, is meant to be indicative. Civic and jurisprudential principles formed more or less coherent and systematic conceptual structures; and jurisprudence had the added advantage of a recognised corpus of texts and commentaries. Stoic–Ciceronian moralism was altogether more loosely articulated: hence its ability to overlap with each of two such distinct discourses as the civic and the jurisprudential.

29. Michael Howard, *War in European History* (Oxford 1976), Ch. 4; John Keegan, *The Face of Battle* (Harmondsworth 1978), pp. 176–7 — for sheer rhetorical effect; S. E. Finer, 'State and Nation-building in Europe: The Role of the Military', in C. Tilly (ed.), *The Formation of National States in Western Europe* (Princeton 1975). The revisionism of Geoffrey Parker, 'The Military Revolution 1560–1660 — a Myth?' in his *Spain and the Netherlands 1559–1659* (Glasgow 1979), does not affect the central point about the standing army's enhancement of state power and consequent impact on society.

30. Gerhard Oestreich, *Neostoicism and the Early Modern State* (Cambridge 1982).

31. James Harrington, *The Commonwealth of Oceana* (1656), repr. in J. G. A. Pocock (ed.), *The Political Works of James Harrington* (Cambridge 1977): Pocock, 'Historical Introduction' to *The Political Works of Harrington*, Chs. 1–4, and *The Machiavellian Moment*, pp. 384–400; on the wider debate on the New Model: L. G. Schwoerer, *'No Standing Armies!' The Anti-Army Ideology in Seventeenth Century England* (Baltimore and London 1974), pp. 51–71.

32. J. R. Western. *The English Militia in the Eighteenth Century. The Story of a Political Issue 1660–1802* (London and Toronto 1965), pp. 3–51.

33. Henry Neville, *Plato Redivivus* (1681), repr. in Caroline Robbins (ed.), *Two English Republican Tracts* (Cambridge 1969), pp. 125, 134–5; Schwoerer, *'No Standing Armies!'*, pp. 95–154; Pocock, *The Machiavellian Moment*, pp. 406–20.

34. Schwoerer, *'No Standing Armies!'*, pp. 155–87; and see further below, pp. 26–30.

35. Williamson, *Scottish National Consciousness*, pp. 89–90, 96, 115–16, suggests avenues by which the civic tradition might have made its way in the late sixteenth century, but apparently did not.

36. Nicholas Phillipson's interpretation has so far been developed in three pioneering general essays and several more particular studies; a full, book-length study, to be entitled *The Pursuit of Virtue*, is awaited. The three general essays are: 'Towards a Definition of the Scottish Enlightenment', in A. Fritz and D. Williams (eds.), *City and Society in the Eighteenth Century* (Toronto 1973); 'Culture and Society in the Eighteenth Century Province: the Case of Edinburgh and the Scottish Enlightenment', in L. Stone (ed.), *The University in Society*, Vol. II (Princeton 1975); and 'The Scottish Enlightenment', in R. Porter and M. Teich (eds.), *The Enlightenment in National Context* (Cambridge 1981). Individual studies will be referred to at appropriate points below.

A rather different social interpretation has been developed by Richard Sher, in *Church and University in the Scottish Enlightenment: The Moderate Literati of Edinburgh* (Princeton and Edinburgh 1985). For Sher the mainstream of the Scottish Enlightenment is to be reached through the ideology of the Moderates. I am most grateful to him for arranging for me to read a typescript of his work.

37. Trevor-Roper, 'The Scottish Enlightenment', *Studies on Voltaire*, LVIII, p. 1639.

2

The Challenge of Andrew Fletcher

Andrew Fletcher, laird of Saltoun in East Lothian, was an alarming, fascinating figure. A man of temper and violence, he disturbed contemporaries little less by his incorruptible honesty. If not an unbeliever, his cast of mind was resolutely secular. He combined severity in personal taste with cosmopolitanism of the intellect: he was a constant traveller and lifelong bibliophile. But it was politics that provided the essential thread of his life. Born in 1653, he was returned a member of the Convention of the Scottish Estates in 1678, and elected again to the Estates proper in 1681. There he vigorously opposed the policies of Lauderdale and the Duke of York, not least the use to which they were putting the Scottish militia; and as a Commissioner of Supply in his county he did all he could to obstruct its levying. For his pains, Fletcher was forced into exile, first in England, where he seems to have associated with Whig opponents of the Duke of York's succession, and then in Paris and Holland. In 1685 he landed with Monmouth in the West, only to return prematurely (and no doubt fortunately) to exile after a fatal quarrel with a fellow-rebel over a horse. Having travelled in disguise through Spain and fought the Turk in Hungary, Fletcher was back in England with William in 1688. Restored to Scotland, and eventually to his estate of Saltoun, Fletcher did what he could to radicalise the Revolution Settlement. But not being a member of either the Convention or the subsequently elected Estates, he was to make little impact until the late 1690s.[1]

A Discourse concerning Militias and Standing Armies; with relation to the Past and Present Governments of Europe and of England in particular, printed in London in 1697, was, as far as is known, Fletcher's first publication.[2] As its title declared, the pamphlet set the problem of militias and standing armies in a broad historical perspective. There was perhaps, Fletcher began, nothing in human affairs so unaccountable as the way in which the greater part of mankind allowed itself to be abused in the name of government. Instead of heeding 'those excellent rules and examples of government which the ancients have left us', the generality of all ranks of men were 'cheated by words and names', continuing to believe that they enjoyed liberty as long as the ancient terms and outward forms of government were preserved. Of this there was a striking instance in 'the alteration of government which happened in most countries of Europe about the year 1500'.

For about eleven hundred years before then, Fletcher believed, the monarchies established by the Gothic conquerors of the Roman Empire had been limited, because the sword had remained securely in the hands of the kings' subjects, the barons and their vassals. After 1500, however, the 'balance' of those monarchies had been disturbed, as princes put themselves in possession of the sword, by means of 'standing mercenary forces kept up in time of peace, absolutely depending on them'. Thereby the monarchies were changed into tyrannies, since all governments are tyrannical 'which have not in their constitution a sufficient security against the arbitrary power of the prince'. Fletcher traced this alteration, which he emphasised was not 'the contrivance of ill-designing men', to a combination of events: the revival of ancient learning, and the inventions of printing, the compass and gunpowder (the three inventions which sixteenth-century writers had singled out as unknown to the ancients). Treating these events less as causes than as symbols of more fundamental developments, Fletcher then proceeded to explain, in a brilliant few paragraphs of historical analysis, that the sixteenth century had seen 'a total alteration in the way of living, upon which all government depends'. To a renewed desire for the arts and luxuries of the ancients, made possible by the rediscovery of ancient learning and the invention of printing, the compass had enabled Europe to add the luxury of Asia and America. Not without benefit in themselves, such expensive new tastes proved fatal to liberty, as the barons compounded the military service of their vassals for rent, and the people neglected military exercise. Princes were left free to raise their own armies by taxation; and with gunpowder making war 'a constant trade to live by', and soldiers depending for subsistence and preferment directly on the prince, the power of the sword transferred decisively from subject to monarch.

By good fortune, England in particular had been largely exempt from this European pattern. The power of the barons had indeed gone; but with virtually no continental possessions to defend after 1500, England's monarchs had had no excuse to maintain standing forces. Events since the accession of Charles I, however, suggested that this isolation might not last. He himself had sought to become absolute, 'though somewhat preposterously; for he attempted to seize the purse before he was master of the sword'. Charles II had been more successful: his guards had been an insuperable obstacle to the efforts of the 'Country Party' to anticipate the Revolution. Even though the policies of James II had then provoked the nation to the last degree, and had alienated a great part of his army, it still required a foreign force to save England in 1688. Now the present King wished likewise to maintain mercenary forces in peace time: 'wise and active' as he was, there was no more reason to depend on his good will. There was no military need to continue the army, for France was exhausted by war and persecution; if a conflict was to break out over the Spanish Succession, England should fight it at sea. The decisive consideration, however, remained the security of England's liberties: and there could be none against 'a standing army of mercenaries, backed by the corruption of a Nation, the Tendency of the way of living, the Genius of the Age, and the Example of the World'.

A mercenary army, Fletcher argued, was 'exactly calculated to enslave a nation'. Composed of men who made a trade of war, and who depended upon heavy and perpetual taxation for their maintenance, it formed a united and powerful interest in the nation, prompt to embroil the state in war and a useless burden in peace. The manners of mercenary soldiers were a further hazard. The officers were almost wholly devoid of honour and ever ready to cheat and oppress their inferiors; under such leadership, the men soon became debauched. The officers of the English army might still, Fletcher allowed, be an exception in their conduct: but what if they were then to exploit public gratitude by having themselves returned to parliament? A militia, by contrast, was 'the chief part of the constitution of any free government'. The militia of ancient Rome, 'the best that ever was', made her mistress of the world; the Lacedemonians' militia secured their liberty for eight hundred years; the modern Swiss militia rendered that people at present the freest, happiest and best defended in all Europe. It was true, Fletcher acknowledged, that monarchs had lately used every means to discredit the militia, and that most men now believed it could not be made serviceable. But, he contended, the discipline and courage of the English people had been proved as recently as the Civil War: the battle of Naseby had been won by an army which included virtually none with foreign service, while the King's army contained above a thousand. If the present English militia was defective, it was only because it did not exercise the whole people, and because men of property shunned the service. It only required parliament to remedy these faults for England to have a perfectly adequate and safe defence.

A year later, in 1698, Fletcher re-issued his pamphlet in Edinburgh, under the new title *A Discourse of Government with relation to Militias*.[3] The second edition contained a few revisions, and, more important, additional material on two subjects. In the first place, the pamphlet was now addressed to the particular experience of Britain as a whole, Scotland as well as England. It was, Fletcher observed, a further reason for England's not needing standing armies after 1500 that Scotland had been unable to afford one. The Scots too had preserved their ancient liberties at a time when they were disappearing thoughout Europe. It was true that in the mid-sixteenth century Mary of Guise had proposed a tax for mercenary soldiers, while her daughter Queen Mary, who looked upon the slavery of the people as the freedom of kings,[4] had succeeded in maintaining a few guards. But the former had been dissuaded by the proud remonstrance of three hundred lesser barons, declaring that their forefathers had themselves defended the nation; and the latter's guards were soon abolished. Now, however, the arbitrary designs of the English-born Stuarts had encroached upon Scotland's 'ancient limited and legal monarchy' no less than upon England's. If the present King maintained his mercenaries, the two countries would stand together in danger of succumbing to 'a French fashion of monarchy'. The Scots therefore were as much in need of a universal militia as the English: and that the commonalty of Scotland still possessed the necessary military capacity was demonstrated by the actions of Montrose during the Civil War, when most of his forces were but the tenants and vassals of the family of Gordon.[5]

The second new feature of the 1698 edition of Fletcher's pamphlet was its inclusion of specific proposals for remodelling the militias of Britain. By way of preface to these, Fletcher elaborated at greater length his reasons for holding the universal military service of freemen desirable in modern society:

> That the whole free people of any nation ought to be exercised to arms, not only the example of our ancestors . . . and that of the wisest governments among the ancients; but the advantage of choosing out of great numbers, seems clearly to demonstrate. For in countries where husbandry, trade, manufactures, and other mechanical arts are carried on, even in time of war, the impediments of men are so many and so various, that unless the whole people be exercised, no considerable numbers of men can be drawn out, without disturbing those employments, which are the vitals of the political body. Besides, that upon great defeats, and under extreme calamities, from which no government was ever exempted, every nation stands in need of all the people, as the ancients sometimes did of their slaves. And I cannot see why arms should be denied to any man who is not a slave, since they are the only true badges of liberty; and ought never, but in times of utmost necessity, to be put into the hands of mercenaries or slaves . . . .[6]

Fletcher also acknowledged his proposals to be novel in so far as the models left by ancient authors gave little guidance on the training of the people in peacetime. But he hoped that his plan would at least resemble their 'excellent institutions' in forming the minds as well as the bodies of men for 'military and virtuous actions'.[7]

Fletcher's major proposal was for the establishment of four mobile camps, three in England and one in Scotland, in which all the young men of the two countries would be required to serve on reaching the age of twenty-two. Those with the means to support themselves would serve two years, those who had to be maintained at public expense one. In the camps Fletcher would have the youth taught the use of arms and the martial arts, and trained in marching, foraging, battle order and fortification. To ensure that these skills were not subsequently lost, he then supplemented the proposal for permanent camps with provisions for continuing local exercises fifty times a year, and a larger, week-long summer camp. If necessary a small proportion of the militia might be improved still further by active service overseas: Fletcher acknowledged that there were apparently no militias comparable with those exercised in actual war, as the barons' had been in their feuds, and Rome's in its perpetual wars. Fletcher's proposals, however, were by no means restricted to military training: the whole way of life in the camps was to be strictly regulated. The diet of all ranks would be frugal in the extreme; only plain coarse clothes were to be worn; and Sunday was firmly set aside for historical reading and moral declamation. Both clergy and women were banned from camp; and homosexuality was to be punished by death. In general, punishments were to be more rigorous than those of civil law, while rewards ought to be honorary. Thus would the camps, Fletcher hoped, be 'as great a school of virtue as of military discipline', the youth learning 'greater and better things than the military art, and more necessary too, if anything can be more necessary than the defence of our country'.[8]

Fletcher concluded both editions of his militia pamphlet with a vehement peroration on the awful consequences of continuing a standing army. That of *A Discourse of Government*, however, is particularly remarkable for its estimate of the respective qualities of the Scots and the English:

> ....the Scots, who have for so many ages, with such resolution, defended their liberty against the Picts, Britons, Romans, Saxons, Danes, Irish, Normans and English, as well as against the violence and tyranny of so many of their own princes; ....the English, who, whatever revolutions their country has been subject to, have still maintained their rights and liberties against all attempts; who possess a country, everywhere cultivated and improved by the industry of rich husbandmen; her rivers and harbours filled with ships; her cities, towns, and villages enriched with manufactures; where men of vast estates live in secure possession of them, and whose merchants live in as great splendour as the nobility of other nations; .... Scotland, which has a gentry born to excel in arts and arms; .... England, which has a commonalty, not only surpassing all those of that degree which the world can now boast of, but also those of all former ages, in courage, honesty, good sense, industry, and generosity of temper; in whose very looks there are such visible marks of a free and liberal education; which advantages cannot be imputed to the climate, or to any other cause, but the freedom of the government under which they live....[9]

It is clear that even if the Scots as well as the English enjoyed a free government, in other respects there was a vast gulf between the two nations. The Scots had only the history of their martial achievements and their gentry's hereditary excellence in arts and arms to show for their freedom; the English had all the benefits of wealth and social stability.

To assess and interpret Fletcher's militia pamphlet, it must obviously be set in context. Its first context was the English Standing Army Controversy of 1697–8. In itself this controversy is not the concern of the present study; but comparison with its major themes helps to elucidate important features of Fletcher's general argument. Following the Peace of Ryswick in 1697, the Country Party alliance united once again in an attempt to force the disbandment of the army. While the Tories, skilfully led by Robert Harley, made the running in parliament, where they succeeded in carrying the reduction of the army's numbers to a mere seven thousand, the radical Whigs or 'Commonwealthmen' launched a propaganda onslaught on the whole concept of a standing army. The most productive of these anti-army writers was John Trenchard, one of the group started by Henry Neville which met at the Grecian Club and regarded itself as heir to the legacy of James Harrington. Trenchard's two principal contributions were *An Argument shewing that a Standing Army is Inconsistent with a Free Government, and Absolutely Destructive to the Constitution of the English Monarchy* (1697) and *A Short History of Standing Armies* (1698). A second member of the same group, the more intellectually minded Walter Moyle, is generally supposed to have assisted Trenchard. John Toland was a third notable contributor to the controversy with *The Militia Reform'd* (1698): he perhaps represented a more radical group of republicans which met at the Calves Head. The controversy, however, was by no means one-sided: faced with the radical onslaught, the Court Whigs rallied support for William's army. One of the Whig Junto, John, Lord Somers, contributed his own carefully argued *Letter Ballancing the Necessity of keeping a Land Force in Times of Peace: with the Dangers that may follow on it* (1697). But the most vigorous defences of the army came from the hired pen of Daniel Defoe. He replied directly to Trenchard's pamphlets, and in addition he inverted the title of the first of them to produce his own *An Argument Shewing that a Standing Army, with Consent of Parliament, is Not Inconsistent with a Free Government* (1698).[10]

The principal subjects of controversy were two: on the one hand, strategy and the nature of modern war, and on the other, the constitutional implications of the rival forms of military organisation. On the issue of strategy, the anti-army writers maintained that, as an island, England should rely primarily on its navy; if there had to be an English interest in Flanders, German mercenaries could be hired to do the fighting there. Should the navy be bypassed by an invading force, all that was required for the defence of English soil itself was a universal militia of the propertied.[11] A detailed plan for such a militia was outlined by Toland: it was to involve weekly training and annual camps (three in the provinces and one in the metropolis).[12] Generally, however, the anti-army writers saw little problem in the nature of modern warfare: in Trenchard's view, military exercises were now simpler than they had been among the ancients.[13] The defenders of the standing army seized on such simple-mindedness. According to Defoe, it was imperative that there be a British army ready to fight in Flanders, to ensure that war did not reach British soil at all. As for 'that black swan', a militia, Defoe was contemptuous. War, he insisted, was now a trade, needing both discipline and experience, and hence requiring that people make it 'their whole employment'.[14] Somers went still further, arguing that 'regular troops' had always been superior to militias. Sparta, Athens and Thebes, Macedon and Rome, the Saracens and the Turks had successively had the better of their enemies as long as their troops were regular and disciplined. Particularly striking was Somers' analysis of the Roman example:

> While the Romans were but a militia, tho they were the best that ever was [cf. Fletcher's identical observation, above p. 24], they made war on their neighbours, who were weaker than they, with great advantage; but when Hannibal came against them with a trained army, they fell before him upon every occasion, till a long war had taught them that art, and then they not only beat him out of Italy, but forced Carthage to a submission. Nothing stood before the Roman Armies, as long as they were kept under discipline, but when all the order of War was broke, and they became a militia, the Northern Nations in Europe, as well as the Saracens in the East, over ran the Roman Empire.[15]

As the very titles of the pamphlets indicate, however, the central issues of the Standing Army Controversy were constitutional. Trenchard introduced each of his major pamphlets with clear statements of the radical Whig view of the English constitution. In this perspective, a blend of civic and ancient constitutional principles, England was cast as a mixed monarchy. Taking its form from the 'Gothic balance' which had anciently existed between king, lords and freeholders, mixed monarchy entailed a strict balance between the three estates of crown, nobility and people, meeting in parliament, and a clear separation between legislature and executive. It also assumed an identity of interest between government and governed, secured through the people's free choice of their legislators in the House of Commons. With such a constitution, Trenchard then argued, a militia of the propertied classes was the only compatible form of military organisation. It would embody in itself the balance which existed between the three estates in parliament, and it would reinforce the identity of interest between government and the people. A standing army, however, gave the crown an instrument of power wholly outwith the constitution: possessed of such a force, the king could with impunity interfere in elections, coerce parliament and command the purse. As Trenchard put it simply, 'sovereignty and the sword march hand-in-hand': a standing army, the examples of history showed again and again, replaced liberty with slavery.[16]

In response, Somers declined to confront the constitutional issue directly, contenting himself with more shrewd criticism of the classical precedents popular with anti-army writers. Sparta and Rome, he pointed out, had been pure military republics, without luxury or even trade: as such their example was irrelevant to sophisticated modern societies such as England.[17] Defoe, however, directly disputed Trenchard's interpretation of the English constitution. There had never been, Defoe argued, a 'Gothic balance'. In reality the Gothic model of government had been a baronial tyranny, enslaving the common people; those who regretted its overthrow ought to reflect on the 'liberties' enjoyed by the commons in Poland, where it still existed. Far from reproducing any Gothic balance, Defoe went on, parliament was historically the institution by which the English people had been able to check the power of the barons. The true balance of the constitution, Defoe maintained, was the people's control of the purse, exercised, with the people's tacit consent, by their representatives in parliament. If therefore parliament gave its express consent to a standing army, there was no reason to suppose such a force inconsistent with free government.[18] In effect Defoe was countering Trenchard's civic and ancient constitutional view of England as a mixed monarchy with an alternative view based on the principles of parliamentary sovereignty: in response to Trenchard's pejorative identification of an army and sovereignty, Defoe would make a positive case for the subordination of an army to the sovereignty of parliament. As yet the case was no more than an outline; but Defoe's contribution to the Standing Army Controversy marks an important step in the gradual rise of the doctrine of parliamentary sovereignty and the eclipse of the rival theory of mixed monarchy.

There is no doubt which side Andrew Fletcher was on in the Standing Army Controversy. The radical Whigs welcomed *A Discourse concerning Militias and Standing Armies*; and it is quite probable that Fletcher, a frequent visitor to the metropolis, was personally acquainted with them.[19] The closeness of Fletcher's connection with the London radicals must however remain uncertain for want of evidence; his own sardonic comment in a pamphlet of 1701 that the opposition to William III consisted of no more than 'a weak, unpaid and disorderly militia party' conveys a distinct sense of distance.[20] Scepticism is reinforced by a close comparison of Fletcher's arguments with those of other anti-army writers. Certainly there was much common intellectual ground between them. Both Fletcher and Trenchard argued, in terms identifiably deriving from the civic tradition, that a militia in which all free men participated was the proper counterpart for a balanced, free constitution; both regarded a mercenary army as the harbinger of despotism and slavery. Yet despite these essential affinities, Fletcher cannot be assimilated to the English anti-army writers on intellectual any more than political grounds: his adaptation of the concepts of the civic tradition was distinctive and original.

The key to Fletcher's originality, as Pocock was the first to observe, lies in the unique historical perspective in which he set the problem of military organisation.[21] It was a perspective quite distinct from that adopted by either Trenchard or Defoe. Unlike Trenchard's, Fletcher's history of government was not a mere catalogue of examples, good and bad: it described a process of development, whose consequences extended into the present, and could not arbitrarily be set aside in the name of any previous, superseded model. No more, however, was Fletcher's history, like both Trenchard's and Defoe's, the story of a purely insular, English experience. The account of the alteration in government since 1500 was European in scope: if England had hitherto been an exception to the continental pattern, there could be no assumption that it would continue thus for ever. With this historical perspective, at once developmental and comparative, Fletcher was in a position to develop an independent argument, transcending the simple antagonism between the views of Trenchard and Defoe, on each of the major issues in the controversy.

On the one hand, for all his invocation of the example of classical and Gothic militias, Fletcher fully accepted that the nature of warfare was now radically different. War, he agreed with Defoe, had become a trade, and required — as his plan for a new militia prescribed — intensive training, strict discipline and, if possible, battle experience. Fletcher was even prepared to accept the new economic order which was responsible for war becoming a trade. Whether or not the specialisation of economic activity in modern society was to be regarded as part of the process of 'corruption', Fletcher certainly recognised it as irreversible. So doing, however, he appears to have regarded economic specialisation as a further argument against a standing army and in favour of a militia. Acknowledging that the occupations of men in countries with husbandry, trade and manufactures were many and varied, Fletcher yet refused to accept that this justified making war itself a separate, specialist occupation; rather he argued that only if there was universal military training could any considerable number be withdrawn from service without prejudicing vital branches of employment.

In presenting the constitutional case against the army, on the other hand, Fletcher was not reliant upon those notions of a Gothic balance so dear to Trenchard. However he approved the barons' military limitation of royal power — and we shall see that Fletcher was no admirer of a feudal nobility in other respects — he accepted that the Gothic order had almost everywhere disappeared for good. Furthermore, Fletcher's understanding of the historical process of European corruption since 1500 meant that he did not, like Trenchard, conceive of the standing army simply as an external threat to a free constitution. Rather, Fletcher's perspective made it possible to see the emergence of such armies as historically interdependent with the growth of modern systems of public finance: the two were integral parts of the post-Renaissance European state. Far more sophisticated than Trenchard's, Fletcher's historical analysis thus made it clear that simple reiteration of the doctrine of mixed monarchy, however ancient and English, was no adequate response to the danger of a standing army. Yet at the same time, Fletcher's analysis also probed the weaknesses of Defoe's opposite but equally anglocentric argument for parliamentary sovereignty. The mere principle of parliamentary consent, by which Defoe set such store, must be a thin shield against the corrupting pressures of the modern military-financial nexus: it was all too probable, indeed, that the members of parliament would themselves be corrupted, their 'sovereignty' then enhancing rather than checking government's arbitrary power.

There was of course a further respect in which Fletcher's contribution to the Standing Army Controversy was distinctive: its explicit inclusion of Scotland within the scope of the argument. The implication of Fletcher's references to Scotland in *A Discourse of Government*, moreover, was that its predicament in relation to standing armies should by no means be thought to be the same as England's. That the danger was actually still greater in his own country, Fletcher made quite clear in another publication in 1698, the first of *Two Discourses concerning the Affairs of Scotland* which he addressed particularly to the members of the Scottish Estates or parliament.

Faced with the government's intention to maintain in peacetime Scottish forces almost as large as those it had had in the recent war — some thirty thousand men — Fletcher did not repeat the arguments that a standing army was inconsistent with liberty and incompatible with the established constitution. He explicitly set such considerations aside, pausing only to deny that support for the late King James and the disorders of 'a few wretched Highlanders' gave the government any serious cause for alarm. Instead, Fletcher simply objected that Scotland was unable to pay: 'such forces are not to be maintained, without increasing the poverty of this country, and reducing it at length to utter desolation'. Scotland's present poverty reflected its ill-fortune in having been virtually the only part of Europe conveniently situated for trade which had not applied itself to commerce; and this, Fletcher believed, was 'partly through our own fault, and partly by the removal of our Kings into another country'. The bad consequences of the regal union with England were all too plain in the government's present determination to maintain the size of the Scottish army. It was one thing to treat Scotland, and particularly the Highlands, as a 'seminary' for the army of Flanders during the war. But now, in time of peace, Scotland was simply being exploited to defend 'two of the richest nations in the world; nations that have manifested their unwillingness to let us into the least co-partnership with them in trade'. If the eighty-four thousand pounds proposed to maintain the Scottish forces (a sum utterly disproportionate to that which England, many times richer and with a larger population, was required to pay) were applied instead to Scotland's husbandry, manufactures and trade, it would vastly enrich the nation. So saying, however, Fletcher did not forget that Scotland's poverty was also its own fault. He directly confronted the legacy of Scotland's historic martial tradition:

> It is not the least misfortune of this country, that the younger sons of the nobility and gentry have in all times had their inclinations debauched to an idle, for the most part criminal, and almost always unprofitable sort of life; I mean that of a soldier of fortune. Their talents might have been much better employed in trade and husbandry to the improvement of their country, and increase of their patrimony.[22]

The predicament of Scotland, it is clear, provides a second context for *A Discourse of Government with Relation to Militias,* a context very different from that of the metropolitan Standing Army Controversy. Of the urgency of Scotland's predicament by 1698 there is no doubt: in that year the country's economic and social backwardness came to a crisis. Even as Fletcher wrote the *Two Discourses concerning the Affairs of Scotland,* the fate of the Scots' expedition to Darien, and with it apparently the country's entire commercial future, hung in the balance, while at home a succession of harvest failures had brought severe shortages and suffering to the common people. Passionately though he exhorted the Scottish parliament to provide immediate support for the one and relief from the other, however, it is clear that Fletcher was already looking beyond the present emergency. As if anticipating the failure of purely remedial measures — by 1700 Darien was lost and Scotland's population had been reduced by between, perhaps, 5 to 15%[23] — Fletcher insisted upon the long-term, structural roots of the crisis.

If the Darien venture was now so vital, it was because the Scots had previously neglected their many opportunities for trade.[24] The numbers and distress of the poor, while certainly exacerbated by the harvest failures, had long defied attempts at remedy: vagabondage, Fletcher believed, had become endemic among a large proportion of the labouring class.[25] The 'principal and original source' of the country's poverty, however, was the mismanagement of agriculture. The letting of lands at exorbitant rates, compounded by the practice of requiring rent in kind, Fletcher argued,

> makes the tenant poorer even than his servant whose wages he cannot pay; and involves in the same misery, day-labourers, tradesmen, and the lesser merchants who live in the country villages and towns; and thereby influences no less the great towns and wholesale merchants, makes the master have a troublesome and illpaid rent, his lands not improved by enclosure or otherwise, but...everywhere run out and abused.[26]

To break this chain of national immiseration, Fletcher proposed that parliament enact a series of radical reforms. Trade should be promoted by raising a new land tax and applying its proceeds as credit for a national trading company.[27] Poverty and vagabondage should be 'eliminated' by subjecting the entire labouring class of Scotland to a regime of domestic servitude. Every man of a certain estate, Fletcher suggested, could be obliged to maintain, educate and employ a proportionate number of servants and their families, in return for the power to sell them when he ceased to have work for them to do. (Still more drastic measures, however, would be required in the Highlands, where everyone was a vagabond: Fletcher wanted the entire population, the people and their masters, transplanted into the Lowlands.) Finally, Scottish agriculture should be transformed by a programme of virtually compulsory investment. Great proprietors should be obliged to sell lands which they were unable to cultivate themselves, and then encouraged to buy shares in the farms of smallholders, providing thereby the capital which the latter needed for improvements.[28]

Anxious to avoid misunderstanding, Fletcher was at some trouble to explain these draconian proposals. In general, he emphasised the need for 'the public authority' to take the initiative: there would be no overcoming bad custom otherwise. Specifically, he protested against the identification of domestic servitude with slavery, which was properly a political condition of subjection to despotism. What he had in mind was rather a return to the strictly domestic master–servant relation of pre-Christian antiquity. Under that system, he claimed, the poor had been provided for and every man made useful to the commonwealth, while the masters employed their wealth, not in conspicuous and competitive private consumption, but for the public good, embellishing their country with public works and monuments. Fletcher could think of no precedent for his agricultural reform; but his explanation of it reveals a concern very similar to that evident in the proposal of servitude. The husbandmen would have to be freed from all forms of dependence upon the great proprietors, and their land made allodial or freehold; nevertheless, they were still to be discouraged from seeking to rise above their station.[29]

If such explanations hardly mitigate the severity of the proposals of the *Two Discourses,* they should none the less be taken seriously: they indicate the principles which gave Fletcher's programme its visionary coherence. The principles, I suggest, are those of the civic tradition. More precisely, they are the principles which define the moral and material preconditions of political community: the placing of the public good before private interest, and the separation of the economic, servant classes of society from those who, without active economic interests of their own, are free to participate in public life. The first of these principles is evident in Fletcher's insistence that economic development be regarded as a public responsibility — meaning not only that its direction was a matter for the public authority, but, still more important, that its object, after the elimination of poverty, was the creation of public wealth in works and monuments. The second, interrelated principle can be seen in Fletcher's determination that economic development should not prejudice the maintenance of clear distinctions between the ranks of servants, freeholders and lords. Domestic servants were by definition excluded from political life, and it is made clear that freeholders should expect but a small part; only landed proprietors, engaging in a minimum of direct cultivation, would be free to devote themselves to public duties.

So to join these principles with a commitment to economic improvement was in itself, it should be recognised, an original departure within the civic tradition. Hitherto writers in the tradition had accommodated their principles, with greater or lesser facility, to the existence of wealth; but neither the Florentine humanists nor even Harrington had sought as Fletcher now did to make a civic social order the framework for the active pursuit of economic growth.[30] Applied to the case of Scotland, moreover, this conjunction of civic principles with a commitment to improvement yielded a peculiarly radical programme of reform. Sweeping away the remnants of Scotland's feudal social order, in which great lords had put the number of their dependents before the economic development of the nation, and the gentry had preferred service as soldiers of fortune to trade and husbandry, it would stabilise relations between ranks on a new basis of material welfare and respectful subordination, and stimulate the landed proprietors, as the nation's natural leaders, to a new sense of public responsibility and purpose.

Fletcher's intervention in the affairs of Scotland by no means ended with the *Two Discourses*. A few years later the national crisis took a political turn, and Fletcher responded with further proposals for constitutional change. The occasion of the crisis was provided by the English Act of Settlement in 1701, stipulating that in the event of Anne dying without heir, succession to the English throne was to pass to the Electress of Hanover and her issue. Infuriated as they had been by English obstruction of the Darien scheme, the Scots refused to follow suit without exacting concessions. Elected to the new parliament of Anne's reign in 1703, Fletcher immediately took the lead in denouncing the existing constitution of the Union of the Crowns, which he proposed to reform by adding to the Act of Security reserving the Scottish succession a series of 'Limitations' on the powers of any future monarch. His speeches, carefully prepared and explosively delivered, were published within the year as *Speeches by a Member of the Parliament which began at Edinburgh the 6th of May, 1703* (Edinburgh 1703).

As in 1698, Fletcher sought to make his fellow-countrymen recognise the underlying, structural causes of the crisis. And as before, he divided the blame. English exploitation and indifference were certainly part of the problem: Fletcher did not need to dwell upon Darien, but he reminded the Estates more than once of the burden imposed by the army and the danger it represented.[31] Fletcher's sharpest criticism, however, was reserved for Scots, and in particular for the Scottish ministers who allowed themselves to be bribed into subservience to English interests. As Fletcher well knew, these numbered, at one time or another, virtually all the great Scottish nobles. What is less to be expected, he asked, than that

> greedy, ambitious, and for the most part necessitous men, involved in great debts, burdened with great families, and having great titles to support, will lay down their places, rather than comply with an English interest in obedience to the prince's commands?

Under such leadership, Fletcher concluded, Scotland had in the last century been reduced to a condition 'more like a conquered province than a free independent people'.[32] The twelve Limitations by which he now proposed to recover Scotland's freedom and independence dealt with both the civil and the military institutions of the nation. In the case of the civil institutions, the relation between legislature, executive and judiciary was to be redefined. There would be annual parliaments, balloted rather than elected, and members would choose their own managing committee as well as the executive officers of state; the judiciary would be made independent of both legislature and executive. As for Scotland's military institutions, the maintenance of standing forces without consent of parliament was to be prohibited, and provision made for the immediate arming of all fencible men (those capable of bearing arms under old Scottish legislation).[33]

Fletcher presented the Limitations as if they were but a restoration of the form of government Scotland had enjoyed before the Union of the Crowns at the start of the seventeenth century. Until that Union subverted 'our ancient constitution', he claimed, no monarchy in Europe was more limited, no people more jealous of their freedom, than the Scottish: the Limitations simply renewed the most essential liberties of their ancestors.[34] Fletcher, however, was noticeably unspecific about the details of the ancient Scottish constitution: he was almost certainly aware that his argument threatened at this point to run into serious difficulty, if not positive contradiction. Given the manifest absence in Scotland of an inheritance of strong institutions, an absence with which Scottish political thinkers had wrestled since the sixteenth century, it is difficult to see what a return to the ancient constitution could mean other than a restoration of that gothic order of baronial power which Fletcher's social programme was designed to destroy. The most likely explanation for the apparent inconsistency is that Fletcher hoped to win the support of those — chiefly Presbyterians but also Jacobites — with whom ancient constitutional arguments were still popular. As William Ferguson has observed, there is a remarkable similarity between the Limitations and the legislation passed in the revolutionary, Covenanter parliament of 1641. But while Fletcher may well have wished to make his proposals as familiar as possible, it is another matter to suggest, as Ferguson goes on to do, that the Covenanting movement was the source of Fletcher's constitutional inspiration. Such an interpretation of Fletcher's thinking needs fuller elaboration if it is to be sustained: on the face of it, there are grounds for scepticism.[35] Even with the weight of Buchanan behind them, the constitutional principles of the Covenanters remained relatively weak: far more important to the movement were concepts of resistance and of the Covenant itself — concepts which were of no apparent concern to Fletcher. Moreover, Fletcher actually accompanied his invocation of the ancient constitution with an unequivocal dissociation from the Covenanting cause. It might, he told the Estates, have been the prelatical party which introduced the principles of tyranny with the Union of the Crowns; but 'the peevish, imprudent, and detestable conduct of the presbyterians' had only compounded the damage. There was no example in the 'ridiculous conduct of bigots of any sort'.[36]

A better indication of the nature of Fletcher's constitutionalism, I believe, is to be found in the last and perhaps most remarkable of all his writings, *An Account of a Conversation concerning a Right Regulation of Governments for the common Good of Mankind. In a Letter to the Marquiss of Montrose, the Earls of Rothes, Roxburg and Haddington, from London the first of December, 1703* (Edinburgh 1704). Addressed to the young nobles who had been Fletcher's closest supporters in the session of 1703, the pamphlet was presented as a report of a meeting in London between Fletcher, the Scottish unionist, the Earl of Cromarty, and two English Tories, Sir Christopher Musgrave and Sir Edward Seymour. Goaded by the congenitally anti-Scotch Seymour, Fletcher first defended the Limitations in much the same terms as he had used in the *Speeches*, and then proceeded to set them in the framework of a scheme for remodelling the government of Europe as a whole. Ideally, Fletcher envisaged Europe divided into ten natural geographical areas, each containing ten to twelve separate cities and their territories. The cities in each area would be united for common defence, preferably under a single prince, but would otherwise be 'distinct sovereignties', with their own justice, administration and military force. Such a division, Fletcher argued, would ensure a balance of power within Europe, checking the natural inclination of every society to exceed others. It would also ensure that individual governments were sufficiently small to encourage universal access to justice, virtuous conduct ·in political office, and the improvement of all arts and sciences. Bringing thereby universal peace, the scheme would, in short, create a citizenship of the world. Fletcher added that the islands of Britain might well form one union, and Scotland provide one or possibly two of the independent sovereignties within it.[37]

Fletcher professed to know of no previous political writer who had framed such a scheme for the general good of mankind; but he commended the ancient Greek Achaian League and its constituent city republics as an example of what he had in mind. This classical reference is, I suggest, as significant as that which supported his proposal of domestic servitude: it indicates that Fletcher's constitutional principles too were of civic derivation.[38] Re-examined, it will be seen that the Limitations prescribed what the civic tradition defined as the institutional conditions of political community — a balance and division of legislative, executive and judicial powers, and the fullest possible participation of citizens in government and defence. *An Account of a Conversation* then projected civic principles of balance and participation into a federal framework in which Scotland's provincial dependence on England could be seen as a particular case of the general problem of relations between the provinces of a large monarchy, the solution to which lay in preventing any one province from establishing a metropolitan predominance over others.[39]

Understood in these civic terms, the coherence of Fletcher's constitutional proposals can be vindicated. If under its 'ancient constitution'

Scotland had indeed once been 'free and independent', Fletcher's reforms would certainly restore it to that condition; but, by embodying the civic principles of regular, free government, they would do so on a new and much sounder institutional basis. Not only would Scotland possess, perhaps for the first time, a proper constitution of its own, its relative autonomy would be secured within a federal framework which did not deny its obvious geographical and military unity with England. Framed on civic principles, moreover, Fletcher's constitutional reforms emerge as quite compatible with his social programme, which, as we have seen, was designed to realise in Scotland the moral and material conditions of political community. In short, it was through a strikingly novel application of classical, civic ideals that Fletcher called upon the Scots at once to cast off their feudal inheritance in pursuit of improvement, and to reconstitute their independent institutions in a stable federal union with England.

If now *A Discourse of Government with relation to Militias* is considered afresh, it should be clear that the context provided by Fletcher's contemporary intervention in the affairs of Scotland is still more important than that of the pamphlet's immediate occasion, the Standing Army Controversy. For it is in Fletcher's response to Scotland's economic and political predicament at the end of the seventeenth century that the social and constitutional principles underlying his commitment to the militia are made manifest. The *Two Discourses* spell out the pattern of social division presupposed by the militia scheme: servants having been automatically excluded, the freeholders would form its rank and file, and landed proprietors its leadership. At the same time, the compatibility of a militia with the new economic order of modern society, suggested in passing in *A Discourse of Government*, is confirmed: in the *Two Discourses* the classic civic social prescriptions are combined with a commitment to economic development virtually unprecedented in the civic tradition. As long as the pattern of social division to be embodied in the militia was maintained, Fletcher appears to have believed that the danger of corruption posed by greater wealth could be kept at bay. Following the *Two Discourses*, the Limitations and the *Account of a Conversation* then clarify the militia scheme's constitutional framework: each with their own militia corps, Scotland and the regions of England would form independent political communities within a federal union of Britain. An independence which the Scots had formerly preserved by arms alone would thus be secured within a proper institutional framework, while a federal Britain, defended by militias, would provide both Scotland and England with a better security against the danger of a standing army than could be had under either separate mixed monarchies or one parliamentary sovereignty. It is, finally, in the Scottish context that Fletcher's concluding claim that his militia would be 'as great a school of virtue as of military discipline' gains its full force. A militia framed upon such social and political principles should effect a salutary transformation of values among a people for whom martial achievement had long been the touchstone of social precedence and national identity.

The ultimate significance of Scotland in Fletcher's argument, however, rises yet higher. In the singular historical perspective of *A Discourse of Government*, Scotland's predicament acquires a significance more remarkable than any that had been claimed for England. It was a predicament remarkable, in the first place, for its urgency. By remaining poor and backward, Scotland had not escaped the ill-effects of the alteration in the way of living elsewhere in Europe: on the contrary, as England's exaction of a standing army made all too clear, poor Scotland was only more vulnerable to corruption and arbitrary rule at the hands of richer neighbours. But the very urgency of Scotland's predicament also represented a remarkable opportunity. Still in a state of poverty, Scotland had not yet forfeited the chance to develop in a manner which would secure it against corruption and tyranny. If, as Fletcher proposed, the Scots could sweep away the remnants of feudalism and devote themselves to improvement within a social order framed upon civic principles of the public good and the separation of ranks; if, again on civic principles, they could institute regular free government in a federal relation with England; if, to confirm these changes, they could through a militia recast the social and political values bequeathed by their martial past — then not only would they thereby free themselves from dependence on England, but they would enjoy prosperity and liberty without corruption for many ages. So doing, finally, the Scots would transform their predicament into one of exemplary significance for the rest of the world. Thus Fletcher himself, in dialogue with Seymour, concluded *An Account of a Conversation*:

> I perceive now, said Sir Edward, the tendency of all this discourse. On my conscience he has contrived the whole scheme to no other end than to set his own country on an equal foot with England and the rest of the world.
> To tell you the truth, said I, the insuperable difficulty I found of making my country happy by any other way, led me insensibly to the discovery of these things, which, if I mistake not, have no other tendency than to render, not only my own country, but all mankind as happy as the imperfections of human nature will admit.[40]

Fletcher's reputation in Scottish historical memory rests chiefly on his intransigent opposition to the Treaty of Union in 1707; but until now his increasing political isolation as the Union approached has been taken to indicate that his impact on contemporaries was limited. After initial success in the stormy session of 1703, when a number of his demands were incorporated in the Acts of Security and of Peace and War, it is undeniable that Fletcher's influence in the Scottish Estates rapidly declined. The pressure of events in the next four years was too great for visionary schemes for the reform of that institution to have any prospect of success; and Fletcher, who acknowledged that the charge of visionary could be brought against him, virtually conceded that the significance of his proposals was exemplary rather than practical.[41] How therefore to combine institutional reform with the pursuit of economic improvement, as Fletcher urged, became increasingly difficult to conceive; and once the Treaty of Union had been negotiated, a clear majority in the Estates were prepared to sacrifice their independent institutions for the prospect of economic development. Yet for all the seeming finality of this decision, Fletcher's defeat was by no means as conclusive as may appear. Despite his increasing political isolation, the challenge of Fletcher's vision alone made his impact both profound and lasting. To a remarkable extent, the intense and often sophisticated debate which the Scots conducted on the economic, social and political condition of their country in the ten years preceding the Union may be interpreted as a series of responses to Fletcher's vision. As Phillipson has suggested before me, it is as much in these responses as in his own arguments that Fletcher's significance should be seen to lie; and, I shall now argue, central to these responses, as to Fletcher's arguments, was the problem of Scotland's martial heritage.[42]

The first stages of the debate on the predicament of Scotland naturally focused on the economic crisis of the 1690s, the subject of Fletcher's *Two Discourses on the Affairs of Scotland*. Not quite all Scots accepted that the crisis was structural, as Fletcher insisted: that worthy medical antiquary Sir Robert Sibbald supposed that the scarcity could be relieved by giving the poor the benefit of his knowledge of ancient and modern vegetables and meats.[43] But the overwhelming majority of commentators sought, like Fletcher, to diagnose the long-term roots of Scotland's poverty. Most looked no further than the neglect of Scottish trade. Immense expectations were attached to the Darien venture; and while its catastrophic collapse sobered, it did not inhibit the debate, which continued to consider schemes for the generation of credit and the protection of native manufacturers.[44] In their detail and technical economic elaboration such schemes went well beyond Fletcher's own limited proposals; but at least until the English offer of free trade was accepted, they commonly embodied two character-istic Fletcherian themes. There was widespread agreement on the need for public initiative: the most common proposal of all was for the establish-ment of a Council of Trade. Still more Fletcherian, there was a general recognition that economic recovery required a new sense of commitment to the public good from Scotland's leaders. There must be a re-orientation of values, even a transformation of the social order, to ensure that the improvement of the nation was put before particular, selfish interests. If need be, these changes should extend to the martial values and social relations bequeathed by Scotland's past. As the author of an *Essay upon Industry and Trade* (1706) put it, gentlemen must learn to regard it as more honourable 'to have the oversight of a hundred servants under due direction and management, as to be leading a hundred sentinels to the field to encounter the enemy'.[45]

The ill condition of Scottish agriculture, which Fletcher regarded as the original source of the country's poverty, received much less attention than trade. It was, however, noticed by one of the most interesting of Fletcher's contemporaries, whose range was nearly as wide as his own, William Seton of Pitmedden. In his *The Interest of Scotland in Three Essays* (1700), Seton observed that husbandmen were 'the most miserable of all the commons in Scotland', a condition which he blamed on the small size of farms and the prevalence of short leases. Seton's remedies were not nearly as bizarre and draconian as Fletcher's: but he too gave prominence to the Fletcherian themes of public initiative and public spirit. Seton pressed particularly for a radical change of outlook at the head of society. The nobility and gentry of Scotland, he argued, had always had 'the reputation of brave men and good scholars': it was imperative that they now add to this by devoting themselves to the improvement of their estates and the encouragement of trade and manufactures. So much depended on their leadership:

> It's their motion and example that influence all other people of a meaner character; so that it may be justly said, that all the advantages, or misfortunes which have befall'n this kingdom, are to be attribute to the conduct of its nobility and gentry. For had they always been of the same honest principles, designing nothing but the publick good, how happy had this nation been long e're now? And how much regarded by all Europe?[46]

Almost every contributor to the debate joined Fletcher in believing that the crisis was at least as much political as economic. Condemnation of the Union of the Crowns was universal: Fletcher's charge that it had reduced Scotland to a condition of provincial dependence was endlessly repeated. The long and varied list of grievances against England included some — notably the attempted subversion of the Kirk — which Fletcher had not cared to emphasise. But religion apart, the most commonly alleged defects of the Union of the Crowns were those identified by Fletcher. There was, in the first place, general agreement that the economic crisis had been exacerbated by that Union, and that as a result economic improvement would be impossible without a revision of relations with England. It was taken for granted that English sabotage was responsible for the Darien disaster. Less simply, it was also noticed, by Lord Belhaven, that even as the English government neglected and undermined Scottish trade, it did not hesitate to draw off Scottish soldiers to fight in England's wars.[47] As Fletcher had pointed out, Scotland's poverty only encouraged her exploitation. A second common Fletcherian conviction concerned the culpability of Scotland's political leaders, whose factious divisions merely facilitated English interference in Scottish affairs. Belhaven grew increasingly alarmed about this; but the menace was earliest and clearest apprehended by Seton of Pitmedden. Bitterly Seton denounced those of the Court Party who would betray Scotland's liberty for places and pensions; urgently he called on the nobility and gentry, this time in their capacity as members of parliament, to unite in pursuit of the national good. In the political no less than in the economic sphere, Scotland's future depended on their public spirit.[48]

Here, however, the Fletcherian consensus ended. There might be wide agreement on the causes of Scotland's poverty, on the dependence induced by the Union of the Crowns, and on the need for a radical change of values at the head of the social order. But there was no such agreement on the political framework which should replace the Union of the Crowns and encourage a new public spirit. On this vital point Fletcher's constitutional proposals provoked but did not persuade. Even when his influence was at its height, the full programme of Limitations was supported only by a few; and many who voted for the Acts of Security and of Peace and War did so for tactical reasons. As the English pressed insistently for a treaty of incorporating union, Fletcher's proposals simply fell by the wayside, and the debate polarised between the opponents and the supporters of such a union. Ranged in opposition was an unholy and always uneasy alliance of militant Presbyterians, committed Jacobites and independent patriots such as Belhaven. Support for the Union was more homogeneous, spokesmen such as Seton — convinced of the desirability of union as early as 1700 — being drawn from the main body of the Scottish elite. Thus arrayed, the two sides engaged in a debate the pattern of whose arguments was by no means as simple as the apparently straightforward issue of the Union would suggest — and whose relation to Fletcher's arguments was still more complex. Nevertheless, I shall now argue not only that there was a pattern to the debate, but that the pattern demonstrates the impact of Fletcher's challenge. It was a pattern shaped by a fundamental conflict of views over Scotland's historically martial identity — and by a search for alternatives to the strict civic principles on which Fletcher had proposed to re-model the Scottish political community.

In immediate political terms, of course, the opponents of the Union were Fletcher's allies, and their arguments necessarily share some common ground. To condemn the Union of the Crowns, but object to the proposed incorporating union, implied agreement at least in finding another way to strengthen Scotland's 'independence'. Beyond this, however, one critical difference was enough to cleave the ground beneath the feet of Fletcher and other anti-Unionists. Unlike Fletcher, the latter were unable to envisage Scotland's 'independence' without invoking the martial identity of the past.[49]

The fullest attempt to provide a constitutional framework for Scottish independence without renouncing the nation's martial identity was made by the Presbyterian journalist and historian George Ridpath. In *An Historical Account of the Ancient Rights and Power of the Parliament of Scotland* (1703), Ridpath sought to present an interpretation of the ancient Scottish constitution which would go considerably further than the Buchananite theory of resistance.[50] Ridpath was intelligent enough to recognise the difficulties facing a Scottish ancient constitutionalism. Not only was there a shortage of records, making it easy to question the antiquity of the constitution, but the constant importance of arms in Scottish history might make it seem doubtful whether there had ever been a regular constitution. Nevertheless, Ridpath believed that it should be possible both 'to vindicate the memory of our noble ancestors, who waded through seas of blood, and gloriously ventured their lives and estates in defence of their liberty, against domestic tyrants and foreign invaders', and simultaneously 'to set our ancient constitution in a true light'. History showed, he argued, that the Scots were 'men of counsel as well as courage', and that the prudence of the Estates had upheld the standing of the kingdom as much as the valour of the barons at war. Even so, Ridpath did not deny — indeed he was at pains to demonstrate — that the origins of the Estates' sovereign powers lay in the military independence of the old warlord nobility.[51] However ancient the constitution, however important its role, the martial basis of Scottish independence was still older, still more fundamental.

Ridpath declared that it was his purpose in giving an exposition of the ancient Scottish constitution to provide support for Fletcher's Limitations; and Fletcher's own references in his speeches to 'our ancient constitution' may well have encouraged Ridpath's enterprise. But by discussing the ancient constitution in such detail, and by insisting on its martial foundations, Ridpath in fact went much further than Fletcher. On Ridpath's argument, there was simply no need to strengthen the Scottish constitution with reforms based on new principles: all that was required was a restoration of the supposedly historic powers of the Estates, and a renewal of the martial values by which the Scots had earlier sustained their independence. That Fletcher believed those historic powers to be inadequate and those martial values to be dangerous, and therefore urged the radical reconstitution of the Scottish polity on civic principles, Ridpath either did not or would not understand.

At the other end of the spectrum of opposition to the Union, the Jacobite Patrick Abercromby had no qualms about raising martial achievement higher than any constitution as a means to independence. A skilful controversialist, Abercromby opened his tract *The Advantages of the Act of Security* (1706) by turning the 'Revolution Principles' of Daniel Defoe against an incorporating union. But this — though telling — was a debating point, for Abercromby set virtually no store by any constitutional safeguards for Scotland's independence, dismissing even Limitations. Instead Abercromby canvassed the possibility of leaving open the question of the succession and of renewing the old offensive and defensive alliance with France. Not caring to be explicit about the consequent restoration of the Stuarts, Abercromby stressed rather the renewed opportunity the alliance would give the Scots to export their 'most inexhaustible commodity' — soldiers.[53] Abercromby followed up this proposal by issuing a translation of a sixteenth-century French *History of the Campagnes of 1548 and 1549. Being an Exact Account of the Martial Expeditions perform'd in those Days by the Scots and French on the one side, and by the English and their Foreign Auxiliaries on the other* (1707). This was no mere antiquarian gesture. The Anglo-Scottish War of the late 1540s could not have been more appropriately chosen, following as it did the breakdown of the first attempt to achieve an agreed union between the two nations. As Abercromby admitted, the terms of that union 'could not fail of proselytising the most stubborn anti-unioner of our days'; and it was around that initiative that the project of an imperial union of Britain, subsequently pursued by Knox and James VI, had first been formulated. By demonstrating the manner in which the English had reneged even on that agreement, and had forced the Scots once more to rely on their own and French arms for their liberty, Abercromby pointed an unmistakable lesson for his contemporaries.[54]

Whatever the actual support for Jacobitism, there is no doubt that such unashamed pride in Scotland's martial independence before the Union of the Crowns struck a popular chord. A poetic variant, *A Pill for Pork-Eaters: or, A Scots Lancet for an English Swelling* (1705), rendered it thus:

Curs'd be the day (for then we were betray'd)
When first our King the *English* scepter sway'd;
Since when such fatal slav'ry we have bore,
As never state nor kingdom did before:
From neighbouring states we no assistance crav'd;
We scorn'd by foreign yokes to be enslav'd;
Had wealth at home, alliances abroad;
Yea, of our friendship *France* itself was proud;
Each *Scot* was brave, with noble courage fir'd;
Our Court polite, and every where admir'd.

As to the question whether Scots were born vassals of the English crown, the poet responded vehemently:

Forbid it Heaven! let's boldly claim our right;
Let *England* bully, but let *Scotland* fight:
And let another *Bannockburn* redress;
Too long endur'd affronts and grievances:
Our country, now oppress'd, shall then produce
Hero's, like DOUGLASS, WALLACE and the BRUCE,
Who *England's* insolencies dare chastize,
When *Scotland's liberties* shall be the prize.

And after all this, the conclusion was clear:

When our best troops are at the borders rang'd,
Then CALEDONIA's wrongs shall be reveng'd.[55]

In the debate as a whole, however, the most significant invocation of Scotland's martial heritage came from the outspoken peer, Lord Belhaven, who emerged to lead the opponents of the Union in the last Scottish parliament. Belhaven had early warmed to the martial theme. Even as he denounced English ministers in 1701 for sacrificing Scottish soldiers in England's wars, he found hope in the ancient Scots' struggles against the Picts and Britons for the inheritance of Caledonia. 'Let us then (he urged the Estates) imitate the *mavortia pectora* of our noble progenitors, and let us remember we have a warlike, valiant and noble king of the Fergusian blood.'[56] In the next few years, before the Treaty of Union was negotiated, Belhaven lent his support to the constitutional measures of the Acts of Security and of Peace and War. But in his speeches on these he was careful to distance himself from more radical demands for Limitations; and in general he made it clear that he put the preservation of unity among Scotland's leaders above constitutional reform. When united, he argued, their ancestors had always been able to defend their rights and liberties against the English; if such unity could only be recovered, it would in itself secure Scotland's independence.[57] In effect Belhaven seemed to be saying that independence was a matter of common moral purpose, rather than of institutions — and that the best expression of that purpose was to be found in the record of Scottish martial prowess.

Belhaven's crowning achievement, his 'Mother Caledonia' speech in the debate on the Treaty of Union in November 1706, confirmed his earlier line of argument, and carried it to a remarkable conclusion. As he contemplated the proposed Treaty, Belhaven informed fellow-members of the Estates, he could see, as in a vision, a kingdom which had forgotten that liberty was a matter of arms. Here, Belhaven lamented, was 'a free and independent kingdom delivering up that which all the world hath been fighting for since the days of Nimrod,...a power to manage their own affairs by themselves'. More particularly, he continued, he could see the noble and honourable peerage of Scotland, whose valiant predecessors had led her armies and conquered provinces, now divested of their followers and vassals, and obliged ever to lay aside their swords in the presence of the English. He could see too the barons, once bold assertors of the nation's rights and liberties, now cowed and silenced; the gallant Scottish soldiery broken and reduced to beggary; and Scottish mariners made underlings to the Royal English Navy. Not all that Belhaven thought he saw was of such a military nature. He also imagined the Kirk reduced to a level with Jews, Papists and Socinians, and the tradesman, ploughman and landowner labouring under insuperable economic difficulties. But when, at the climax of his vision, Belhaven saw Mother Caledonia struck down, like Caesar in the Senate, by her own sons, it was the martial theme that came again to the fore. 'Should not (he exclaimed) the consideration of these things vivify these dry bones of ours? Should not the memory of our noble predecessors' valour and constancy rouse up our drooping spirits?'

Unity of spirit, Belhaven went on, was now all. If only the Scots would be aroused by the memory of their ancestors to overcome their present self-destructive differences, God would be their deliverer, 'and that right early'. There would be a *Jehovah–Jireh*, and a ram would be found in a thicket for sacrifice instead of Mother Caledonia. In the meantime, while waiting for God and the ram, the Lord Commissioner of the Estates should organise an *agape*, or love-feast, that the members might have a day of united rejoicing and thankfulness. This curious proposal being received in silence, however, Belhaven had to end on a more melancholy note. Mournfully he conducted a roll call of Scotland's great families:

> Where are the names of the chief men, of the noble families of Stewarts, Hamiltons, Grahams, Campbells, Gordons, Johnstons, Homes, Murrays, Kers? Where are the two great officers of the crown, the Constable and the Marischal of Scotland? They have certainly all been extinguished, and now we are slaves for ever.

Faced in the Treaty with what seemed 'an entire surrender', Belhaven's heart filled with grief and indignation. He begged pardon to 'drop a tear as the prelude to so sad a story', and broke off.[58]

For all the absurd elevation of its rhetoric, this was a carefully crafted speech. At its centre lay a novel adaptation of Scotland's martial heritage. When Belhaven called on the Scots to remember their warlike ancestors, it was not to summon them anew to arms. Unlike the Jacobite Abercromby, Belhaven had no thought of actually fighting once again for Scotland's independence. Equally, Belhaven drew no connection between the memory of ancestral prowess and the existence of an ancient constitution, as Ridpath had sought to do. For Belhaven the significance of the martial past was purely moral and spiritual, without institutional association or application. By thus rendering the martial heritage a matter of the spirit alone, Belhaven obviously weakened its effectiveness as a counter to the Treaty of Union: it hardly offered an alternative to that institutional measure. But this, almost certainly, was just Belhaven's point. However much he might bewail its terms as 'an entire surrender', Belhaven could no longer hope for the Treaty's rejection. Instead, it seems clear that he had already begun to look beyond the Union, seeking a sphere in which Scottish independence could be preserved even within its framework. Through the recovery and remembrance of the martial past, he was suggesting, the Scots should be able to maintain their nationhood intact, whatever their constitutional relation with England.

Adapting the martial heritage in this way, Belhaven can be seen to have suggested a means of securing Scotland's independence that bypassed Fletcher's insistence on institutional guarantees. Instead of Fletcher's seemingly impossible programme of radical constitutional reform, Belhaven put his trust in the Scottish spirit: simply by keeping up the memory of ancestral valour, the Scots would remain free and independent at heart. In intellectual terms, Belhaven had substituted for Fletcher's strict civic principles the more flexible themes of humanist moralism. To the exaltation of arms which had long been a commonplace of Scottish humanist culture, he had added a specifically Stoic gloss, rendering the significance of martial virtue passive rather than active, a vehicle of resignation from rather than active participation in the given institutional framework. On these terms, the appeal of Belhaven's use of the martial past promised to be considerable. It appeared to enable the Scots to have a great deal of their cake and to eat it too, to accept the Union, and yet to retain a moral independence.

Even assuming that it did meet Fletcher's challenge that there could be no independence without institutions, however, Belhaven's argument did not quite give the Scots all the cake they wanted. For the values of the martial past, whatever their appeal as an expression of national identity, were not obviously the values required for the pursuit of economic improvement. Belhaven had earlier acknowledged the need for improvement, observing in his Speech of 1701 that trade had been responsible for the most universal revolution ever seen in the world, altering even the principle of war.[59] But before the end of the same speech such clear-sightedness had been clouded by the memory of ancestral '*mavortia pectora*'; and by 1706 economic decline was the least of the ailments Belhaven saw afflicting Mother Caledonia. By then, if not earlier, the preservation of an independent national identity was clearly being put before economic advance. Belhaven thus ran into the sort of difficulty that Andrew Fletcher, by his ingenious adaptation of civic social principles, had avoided. In the final analysis, it would seem that Belhaven was prepared, in a spirit of Stoic resignation, to countenance the sacrifice not only of Scotland's political institutions, but also of its prospects of economic development. As we shall now see, it was a vital strength of the case for the Union that it offered to secure, not to sacrifice, such development.

The supporters of the Union built their case on the rejection of two common propositions of its opponents. They denied any merit in Scotland's martial past; and they denied that Scotland could escape its present predicament without a new institutional framework. The Union's supporters, in other words, began by accepting just those central features of Andrew Fletcher's challenge that opponents of the Union, despite being his political allies, had found inadmissible or unnecessary. That there could thus be common ground between Fletcher and the supporters of the Union should not cause surprise. We have already seen the extent to which William Seton of Pitmedden endorsed Fletcher's diagnosis of Scotland's predicament. In his denunciations of the agrarian roots of the country's poverty, of the political dependence resulting from the Union of the Crowns, and of the complicity of Scottish political leaders in that dependence, Seton was almost more Fletcherian than Fletcher. The Earl of Cromarty was another prominent Unionist to feel the impact of Fletcher's challenge. *The Account of a Conversation* records him as one of those before whom Fletcher defended his Limitations and outlined his plan for European government: and although Cromarty reportedly remarked that Fletcher's proposals were better contrived for a 'Platonic Commonwealth', he is presented as far more comprehending than the intemperate Seymour. In return, it may well have been Fletcher whom Cromarty had in mind when, at the end of one of his pamphlets, he regretted his differences from several 'whose judgement in many things I prefer to my own', and from one in particular 'who I think is honest above bribes or fear'. But, Cromarty concluded, '*amicus Plato, sed magis, veritas*': however generously one might acknowledge the force of Fletcher's challenge, his solution must be discounted as visionary.[60] If Seton and Cromarty endorsed Fletcher's rejection of the martial past and his call for a new institutional framework, they did so in a cause — and, it will become clear, on principles — quite contrary to his.

From the outset the Union's supporters were open in their hostility to the martial past, not hesitating to condemn what Ridpath, Abercromby and Belhaven held so dear. Scotland might have been reduced to a state of provincial dependence by the Union of the Crowns, but the previous position of separation from England had had consequences still worse. Divided into separate governments, Seton argued in 1700, Britain had suffered so many 'bloody and fatal strugglings' that it had been simply 'a theatre of cruelty and barbarity'.[61] Cromarty took up the same theme in 1702. 'Lying always under a flux and reflux of invasions from and on England', with the consequent plundering and burning of the country and towns, and stopping of commerce, was, he pointed out, 'no desirable state'.[62] The Scots, he added in 1706, need only reflect upon

> the former horrid wars, rapines, robberies, invasions, incursions, murders, exiles, imprisonments, even of our sovereigns, of which our ancient histories, while we were in a separate state, give us many and sad examples,

to see that whatever the faults of the Union of the Crowns, 'the Egyptian flesh-pot of a divided lot' was no alternative.[63] Speaking in the debate on the Treaty in November 1706, Seton drove the point home. To seek separation again, he bluntly reminded the Estates, was simply to put Scotland 'in danger of returning to that Gothic constitution of government, wherein our forefathers were, which was frequently attended with feuds, murders, depradations and rebellions'. In such a state, it was obvious that the Scots would be quite unable to develop their trade.[64]

Rejecting separation and war as emphatically as provincial dependence, Seton and Cromarty concluded that Scottish society and its political life must be set in the new institutional framework that an incorporating union of parliaments would provide. Only within that framework, they argued, could the Scots hope to secure both economic improvement and their independence and liberty. With the latter claim, that the Union would secure independence and liberty, Seton and Cromarty were of course contesting ground which their opponents confidently supposed was theirs alone; and it is ground on which many historians have refused to take the Unionists seriously. Yet it is arguable that this was the most telling — and intellectually interesting — part of the case for the Union, fundamental to the more straightforward plea of economic advantage on which historians usually concentrate. Not only did the Unionists argue that independence, and therefore national identity, would survive the Union. But they made it clear that independence and economic improvement were alike dependent on the introduction, through the Union, of a new principle of liberty.[65]

Although the arguments for independence and liberty were presented by both, it was perhaps Cromarty who best put the case for Scotland's independence under the Union, and Seton who was clearest about the acquisition of liberty. In promising a renewed independence after the Union, Cromarty pursued two lines of argument. On the one hand, he held that the Union would not annihilate the Scottish people or nation. It might involve a change of names, from Scotland (and England) to the common name of Britain. But, according to Cromarty, Britain was anciently the 'mother name' of both Scotland and England: for the Scots to call themselves British — or, as it should strictly be, Britich — was accordingly to declare themselves the equal of the English, and remove all question of dependence.[66] Cromarty's other line of argument was to demonstrate the extent to which, within Britain, Scotland would remain self-governing. Sovereign power was indeed to pass from the Estates to one British parliament: but precisely because of this, Cromarty maintained, the Scots would have more scope to manage their own affairs. The distinct Scottish legal system would be preserved, and the authority of the Scottish judges enhanced.[67] Still more important, the end of the Scottish parliament, by removing the opportunity for political faction within Scotland, would also remove the reason for English interference. As no Scottish politician would have occasion to seek English support for his administration, 'Scotland will then and thereby be free of the fears and jealousies of English influence; and no Englishman or men will nourish a vain desire of having it'.[68]

Seton defined the liberty which Scotland would acquire by the Union in simple terms. Speaking to the Scottish parliament in 1706, he told the members that there are two 'fundamentals in nature, to wit, liberty and property', which constitute the indestructible rights of the subject.[69] These fundamentals or rights had not hitherto been secured in Scotland. Before the Union Treaty was negotiated, Seton had repeatedly urged the Scottish parliament to pass an Act of Habeas Corpus, 'for that is the true badge of a subject that pretends to liberty and property'.[70] But all along he had made it clear that only a union which resulted in one sovereign British parliament would render liberty and property as secure in Scotland as they already were in England. The English, he pointed out to Parliament, had made such liberty peculiarly their own. At all times 'noble assertors of the rights of the subject', it was for liberty and property that the English had in the past spent their 'blood and treasure'. If therefore the Scots (who had otherwise wasted their blood and treasure) would now obtain that liberty, they must, through the Union, put themselves in a position where a threat to the rights of the subject in any part of Great Britain would be treated as a threat to them everywhere.[71]

As Seton defined it, liberty was a precondition of the sort of independence envisaged by Cromarty: unless the rights of the subject were as secure in Scotland as in England, the possibility of greater Scottish self-government would be prejudiced. At the same time, the acquisition of such liberty was equally necessary for economic improvement. As Seton observed in a pamphlet of 1706, only once everyone could expect 'to reap the benefit of their labours' would a spirit of trade and industry flourish.[72] The much-advertised economic benefits of free trade with England would be set at naught if the Scots were unable also to enjoy the same form of liberty.

With these arguments, the supporters of the Union can be seen to have returned a remarkably direct answer to their opponents. They had exposed the martial past as a destructive state of war, and had upheld the Union as an institutional framework which would give substance and definition to Scotland's independence and liberty, as well as ensuring economic improvement. Simultaneously, the Unionists had matched the vision of Fletcher with an alternative that entailed far-reaching social and constitutional change. Through an incorporating rather than a federal union, they sought a transformation of Scottish society, politics and values little less radical than that advocated by Fletcher.

So arguing, moreover, the Unionists drew on intellectual resources distinct from those tapped by Belhaven or Fletcher. In part, and in particular in Cromarty's case, these appear to have been the resources of the earlier, late sixteenth and early seventeenth-century discussion of an imperial union of Britain. In maintaining that Scots and English must become British so that Scotland could enjoy the benefits of English institutions, Cromarty strikingly echoed the arguments of Knox and the circle of imperial unionists around James VI.[73] The dominant terms in the arguments of both Cromarty and Seton were, however, more novel in the Scottish context. From the central place they accorded the concepts of personal liberty and parliamentary sovereignty, it is clear that the Unionists were also drawing on the resources of the jurisprudential traditions of political thought. The Unionists' concept of liberty was the liberty of the individual and his property, the liberty of rights — in short, the distinctively jurisprudential liberty 'from' authority. In turn this concept of liberty was connected with a concept of sovereignty in the legislative power — a concept which, by the seventeenth century, was also an integral feature of the jurisprudential traditions. Taken together, these jurisprudential concepts of liberty and sovereignty were what gave the Unionist case its intellectual strength: they constituted a framework of principle as coherent and systematic in its chosen terms as Fletcher's own.[74]

It is precisely this framework of jurisprudential principle, however, which indicates how wide in the end was the gulf between the Unionists and Fletcher. For Fletcher's was a vision of Scotland which hinged on the civic concept of liberty as the liberty 'to' participate in public life. Without specifically Scottish political institutions (secured by a federal union) in which this liberty could be exercised, the Scots, Fletcher insisted, could have no true independence, and no control over their social and economic development. Adopting the jurisprudential concept of liberty, however, the Unionists committed themselves to a course which required the existence of no strictly political institutions within Scotland. The Scots might now freely pursue economic improvement; they might continue actively to practise their own system of law; and they might join in the common parliamentary politics of Britain. But there was to be no formal, institutional framework for participation in the direction of Scottish affairs. For all their agreement on the need to break with the martial past, therefore, the gulf between Fletcher and the Unionists on this ultimate point was greater even than that between the Unionists and their opponents. Seton, with his jurisprudential principles of liberty and sovereignty, and Belhaven, with his Stoic moralism, were agreed at least in this: that Scottish social and political life, Scottish liberty and independence, did not need the support of their own political institutions. Whether the Union was openly welcomed or tacitly accepted, whether the martial past was decried or revered, Scotland's liberty and independence could quite well be left to the public spirit, the virtue, of the landed and legal classes.[75]

What then of the institution which was to embody in itself both the social and the political changes for which Fletcher argued, and was thereby to transform the Scots' inheritance of martial values — the institution of the militia? Its fate was a paradigm of the fate of Fletcher's vision as a whole, and the clearest measure of his ultimate intellectual distance from his contemporaries.

At first there was general interest. Writing in 1700, Seton agreed that the size of the standing army maintained by the Scots was a major grievance; and he urged the Estates to set the militia on a proper footing. A similar call for the reduction of the army and the establishment of a 'constant country force' was made by James Hodges, subsequently an articulate opponent of the Union. Interestingly, Hodges combined this with another proposal for the institution of an Academy of War and Universal Learning. Though the noblest establishment of its kind, Hodges confidently averred, this would in no way exceed the capacity of Scotland to accomplish it.[77] The broad approval which the militia could command was reflected in the Act of Security passed by the Estates in 1703: while most of Fletcher's additional Limitations were rejected, the Act incorporated his demand for the immediate arming of fencible men.[78] This, however, was the extent of Fletcher's success: thereafter the issue fell swiftly out of contention. Among opponents of the Union there was considerable fear that the crisis might end in war: but almost all of them recoiled at the prospect, and there was no suggestion that the militia should be called out to defend Scotland in earnest.[79] The Union's supporters, on the other hand, made no attempt to discuss the future form of Scotland's defence, and the Treaty itself omitted any reference to it.[80] A Scottish militia bill was introduced in the first post-Union session of the Westminster parliament, to accompany the bill abolishing the Scottish Privy Council; but its failure, in what are still obscure circumstances, seems not to have antagonised Scottish opinion.[81]

After the Union, the fate of the militia was closely tied to the continuing threat from the Jacobites, and their resurrection of the martial heritage. The first Jacobite attempt to launch a revolt against the Union settlement was made immediately, in 1708; and while its dismal failure caused further action to be put off until after the death of Anne, Jacobite ideologists remained busy. None was busier than Patrick Abercromby, who now devoted himself to writing what may be regarded as the *summa* of the martial heritage. *The Martial Atchievements of the Scots Nation. Being an Account of the Lives, Characters and Memorable Actions of such Scotsmen as have signalis'd themselves by the Sword at Home and Abroad. And a Survey of the Military Transactions wherein Scotland or Scotsmen have been remarkably concern'd, from the first establishment of the Scots Monarchy to this present time* appeared in two folio volumes, with handsome lists of subscribers, in 1711 and 1715, the second volume during the 'Fifteen Rebellion'. Describing his purpose in a Preface, Abercromby admitted that he had felt unable to write an orthodox history. He had instead been obliged to adopt 'a method and way of writing quite new and unprecedented' in order to compass his design. This, he went on,

> was to give as distinct an account as was possible of all the important transactions of the Nation. For the martial ones, their causes and effects, especially when joined to the lives of so many warriors, must needs comprehend the whole.[82]

Abercromby was supported in his labours by another antiquary, Thomas Ruddiman, whose scrupulous edition of Buchanan's *Opera Omnia* (1715) may be seen as a further remarkable contribution to the Jacobite appropriation of Scotland's patriotic and martial past.[83]

Confronted with the Jacobite threat, it might be thought that the best response, both practical and ideological, would be the institution of a national militia on the lines Fletcher proposed. In the event, the reverse occurred: for as long as the Jacobite threat lasted, the cause of Fletcher's militia was to be frustrated. Even without new legislation, a Scottish militia could still be raised. Failing the 1708 bill, it was assumed that the

Restoration Militia Acts remained in force; and on this basis Lieutenants were named and some units of militia actually called out to meet the Jacobite rebellion in 1715. But the force proved to be of little military use, and made a minimal contribution to the suppression of the rebellion; the Lowland militia men, it was reported, took fright at the Highlanders.[84] In any case, there were serious legal difficulties in the way of raising the militia at all. With the abolition of the Scottish Privy Council in 1708, there was no longer anybody with a clear authority under the Restoration Acts to name Lieutenants and call out the men. These difficulties were partially overcome in 1715; but by the second Jacobite rising in 1745 legal doubts had quite gained the upper hand. Professing to know of no authority on which Lieutenants could have been named in 1715, the Scottish law officers prevented the weak Secretary of State for Scotland, the Marquis of Tweeddale, from issuing any commissions, except to the Duke of Argyll, who claimed a hereditary Lieutenancy. Other than Argyll's regiment of Campbell Fencibles and the Trained Bands of Edinburgh, there was thus no militia to assist the regular forces against the Young Pretender.[85]

Beneath their quibbling, it is obvious that the law officers were extremely reluctant to authorise any general arming in Scotland. In part this was no doubt due to fears of widespread Jacobitism. But there were almost certainly also ideological obstacles to the institution of a militia. In the face of the Jacobites' re-activation of the old Scottish martial identity, the Scottish Hanoverian establishment adhered to the priorities laid down by advocates of the Union before 1707. As we have seen, Cromarty and Seton began by insisting on a break with the martial past; and they went on to argue that the most important of all the gains to be brought by the Union would be a new concept of liberty, the liberty of person and property, established by parliamentary law. The other form of liberty, the liberty to participate and bear arms, had, however, found no place in their arguments. When therefore the law officers subsequently placed the rule of law, enforced if necessary by a British army, above the arming of Scots, even in self-defence, their position was quite consistent with original Unionist principles.

It is perhaps also worth observing — though as yet in parentheses — that one participant in the Union debate had pressed the juristic concept of liberty to a point at which it would directly undercut the principle of a militia. 'If I were to talk to the honest soldiery of Scotland', wrote the Englishman Daniel Defoe in one of his *Essays at Removing National Prejudicies against a Union* (1706)

> I could tell them, the Union will help them to such a thing in Britain, as they are unacquainted with in Scotland, I mean Liberty; and this liberty is such, as even a soldier cannot be listed but by his own consent....[86]

This argument was not repeated by any Scottish Unionist at the time; and it is unlikely that it was at the forefront of the law officers' minds when they subsequently frustrated the calling out of the militia against the Jacobites. It was a claim, moreover, of which actual recruiting methods in both England and Scotland were long to make a mockery, and which was deliberately overridden when the English militia was reconstituted in 1757. Nevertheless, the argument that a British subject possessed the liberty not to be conscripted was, in principle, a fundamental objection to the concept of a militia; and if Defoe was for the moment alone in expressing it, it was an argument that would soon be heard again.

While the Unionist outlook was unfavourable to a militia throughout the first half of the eighteenth century, there were no alternative sources of support. Non-Jacobite opponents of the Union showed no inclination to pursue the issue after 1707. Their leader Lord Belhaven, fresh from eulogising the values of the martial past in 1706, was — quite literally — mortified to discover in 1708 that those values could still be activated in earnest: arrested and dispatched to London on suspicion of involvement in the Jacobite revolt, he died of vexation. Andrew Fletcher, who was also arrested, was more philosophical, and lived until 1716. But he was now silent, publishing nothing after 1704. Although he gave his support to the Jacobite intellectual enterprise to the extent of lending Ruddiman books from his magnificent library, he was never a convert to that cause, and indeed regarded the politicians of all parties with contempt. At the last, on his deathbed, he could but seek the mercy of the Lord on 'my poor country that is so barbarously oppressed'.[87]

Yet the cause of the militia did not die with Fletcher. Forty years later, in the 1750s, interest in the issue suddenly revived, and it became the focus of Scottish political debate. Almost certainly the final destruction of the Jacobite movement in 1746 was necessary to make this possible. But the issue would never have had the significance it did without the simultaneous renewal of intellectual interest in the principles associated with the concept of a militia — the principles of the civic tradition. As we shall now see, this renewed intellectual interest followed two paths, as the strict civic principles articulated by Fletcher were combined in original ways with concepts drawn from the other intellectual discourses found in the Union debate. On the one hand David Hume sought to adapt civic concepts of free government and military organisation to meet the novel institutional requirements of commercial society, balancing the civic and the jurisprudential concepts of liberty. On the other hand the Moderate group of literati, led by Adam Ferguson, would attempt to combine a Fletcherian concept of a militia with the sort of moral perspective popularised by Belhaven. The resulting intellectual exchange, I shall argue, forms in its own right an important moment in early Scottish Enlightenment thought; it was also the prelude to the public agitation for a national militia which began in 1759.

NOTES

1. There is no satisfactory biography of Fletcher; and the details of his early career in particular are intriguingly obscure. The known facts are recounted in the *Dictionary of National Biography*; G. W. T. Omond, *Fletcher of Saltoun*, (Edinburgh 1897), a short sketch, includes illuminating contemporary anecdotes and judgements of the man.

2. [Andrew Fletcher,] *A Discourse concerning Militias and Standing Armies; with relation to the Past and Present Governments of Europe and of England in particular* (London 1697): the following four paragraphs summarise its argument.

3. This is the version of the pamphlet reprinted in the eighteenth-century collected editions of *The Political Works of Andrew Fletcher* (London 1732 and 1737, Glasgow 1749), and in the recent *Andrew Fletcher of Saltoun, Selected Political Writings and Speeches*, ed. D. Daiches (Edinburgh 1979). Despite the editorial deficiencies of the last selection, I have when possible given references to it, as the most readily available.

4. For this judgement on Queen Mary, Fletcher invoked 'the great historian', presumably George Buchanan.

5. *A Discourse of Government, Selected Writings*, pp. 8–10, 14–15, 17. In taking the example of Montrose, Fletcher compared his actions to Caesar's for their combination of military skill and bad tendency; but he did not comment further on the significance of his having raised his forces on a traditional kinship basis.

6. *A Discourse of Government, Selected Writings*, pp. 18–19.

7. *A Discourse of Government, Selected Writings*, p. 20.

8. *A Discourse of Government, Selected Writings*, pp. 20–24.

9. *A Discourse of Government, Selected Writings*, p. 25.

10. Schwoerer, *'No Standing Armies!'*, pp. 155–80. More generally on the radical Whigs: Caroline Robbins, *The Eighteenth Century Commonwealthman* (New York 1968), pp. 88–109; and on Toland and the possible existence of a distinct 'Calves Head' republicanism: A. B. Worden, Introduction to Edmund Ludlow, 'A Voyce from the Watch Tower', Part V 1660–1662, *Camden Fourth Series*, Vol. 21 (1978), pp. 17–55.

11. [John Trenchard,] *An Argument Shewing that a Standing Army is Inconsistent with a Free Government, and Absolutely Destructive to the Constitution of the British Monarchy* (London 1697), pp. 18–19; *A Short History of Standing Armies in England* (London 1698), pp. 43–4.

12. [John Toland,] *The Militia Reform'd: or, an Easy Scheme of Furnishing England with a Constant Land-Force, capable to prevent or to subdue Any Foreign Power; and to maintain perpetual Quiet at Home, without endangering the Public Liberty*, 2nd edition (London 1699).

13. [Trenchard,] *An Argument Shewing*, pp. 23–4.

14. [Daniel Defoe,] *An Argument Shewing that a Standing Army, with Consent of Parliament, is not Inconsistent with a Free Government* (London 1698), pp. 5–7; and *A Brief Reply to the History of Standing Armies in England. With Some Account of the Authors* (London 1698), pp. 10–14.

15. [John, Lord Somers,] *A Letter, Ballancing the Necessity of keeping a Land Force in Time of Peace: with the Dangers that may follow on it* (London 1697), pp. 10–13.

16. [Trenchard,] *An Argument Shewing*, pp. 2–17; *A Short History of Standing Armies*, passim.

17. [Somers,] *A Ballancing Letter*, pp. 3, 9–10.

18. [Defoe,] *An Argument Shewing*, pp. 2, 9–23; and *Some Reflections on a Pamphlet lately Publish'd, Entitled, An Argument Shewing that a Standing Army is Inconsistent with a Free Government*, 2nd edition (London 1697), p. 12.

19. [Trenchard,] *A Short History of Standing Armies*, p. 2; according to Robbins, *The Eighteenth Century Commonwealthman*, p. 181, Fletcher 'consorted with the club at the Grecian'.

20. *A Speech upon the State of the Nation: in April 1701.* Not reprinted in the *Selected Writings*, but in *The Political Works of Andrew Fletcher* (London 1732), p. 248.

21. Pocock's pioneering analysis of *A Discourse of Government* has been the starting point for all recent reconsideration of Fletcher's thought: 'Machiavelli, Harrington and English Political Ideologies in the Eighteenth Century', in *Politics, Language and Time*, pp. 138–40. Cf. now, more fully, in *The Machiavellian Moment*, pp. 427–35, where Fletcher is treated as the outstanding exponent of 'neo-Harringtonian' arguments, and the most serious challenge to Defoe. Yet this, I shall be arguing, still fails to do Fletcher justice: his European outlook rises above the anglocentricity of neo-Harringtonianism.

22. *Two Discourses Concerning the Affairs of Scotland; Written in the Year 1698* (Edinburgh 1698), 'The First Discourse', *Selected Writings*, pp. 31, 34–7.

23. T. C. Smout, *Scottish Trade on the Eve of the Union 1660–1707* (Edinburgh 1963), pp. 250–3; M. W. Flinn (ed.), *Scottish Population History from the Seventeenth Century to the 1930s* (Cambridge 1977), pp. 164–82.

24. 'First Discourse', *Selected Writings*, p. 31.

25. 'Second Discourse', *Selected Writings*, pp. 46–7.

26. 'Second Discourse', *Selected Writings*, pp. 58–9.

27. 'First Discourse', *Selected Writings*, p. 33.

28. 'Second Discourse', *Selected Writings*, pp. 56–7, 62–4.

29. 'Second Discourse', *Selected Writings*, pp. 61, 49–54, 64–5.

30. Skinner, *The Foundations of Modern Political Thought I: The Renaissance*, p. 74; Pocock, *The Machiavellian Moment*, pp. 390–1; Robertson, 'The Scottish Enlightenment at the Limits of the Civic Tradition', in Hont & Ignatieff (eds.), *Wealth and Virtue*, pp. 141–51.

31. *Speeches*, nos. v, vii, xiv, *Selected Writings*, pp. 81–4, 98.

32. *Speeches*, no. ii, *Selected Writings*, pp. 70–1.

33. *Speeches*, no. iii, *Selected Writings*, pp. 74–6.

34. *Speeches*, nos. iii, iv, *Selected Writings*, pp. 72–3, 79.

35. William Ferguson, *Scotland's Relations with England: a Survey to 1707* (Edinburgh 1977), pp. 190–2. A full interpretation of Fletcher's relation to Buchanan and Covenanting thought is presently being undertaken by Nicholas Phillipson for his study, *The Pursuit of Virtue*.

36. *Speeches*, no. iii, *Selected Writings*, p. 73.

37. *An Account of a Conversation*, *Selected Writings*, pp. 127–37. Fletcher named twelve possible capital cities in Britain and Ireland, including Stirling and Inverness (one Lowland and the other Highland) in Scotland. In the 'Second Discourse' he had pronounced Edinburgh most unsuited to be a capital: *Selected Writings*, p. 65.

38. Though it is the civic principles underlying the scheme of *An Account of a Conversation* that I want to emphasise here, their identification by no means

exhausts the analysis of that fascinating work. Despite Fletcher's profession of originality, the scheme is almost certainly of utopian inspiration, and needs to be examined in the context of early modern utopian writing. A further, connected intellectual setting is provided by the late seventeenth-century debate on the threat of universal monarchy and the possibilities of achieving a stable, plural balance between the states of Europe. In both this and the utopian settings, *An Account of a Conversation* needs to be related to the extraordinary *Discorso delle Cose di Spagna* ('Napoli' 1698), the only major work of Fletcher's not considered here. (It is reprinted in the *Political Works,* but not in the *Selected Writings.*)

Finally, though more distantly, it is not impossible that Fletcher's scheme for Europe owed something to the Scottish, but pre-Covenanting, apocalyptic vision of Napier of Merchiston. Despite the distance set between them by Fletcher's stringently secular cast of mind, their conceptions of Scotland's place in the European community of nations had much in common; and Napier was by no means a forgotten figure in the early eighteenth century. I intend shortly to pursue the interpretation of Fletcher's thought in these wider settings.

39. Despite his reference to the Greek republics, Fletcher was anxious to deny that the 'distinct sovereignties' he had in mind needed to be republican city states: *Account of a Conversation, Selected Writings,* pp. 131–2. His scheme may thus be interpreted as an attempt to transcend the common identification of the civic with the republican form of government, and to establish a framework in which monarchy too could be accommodated.

40. *Account of a Conversation, Selected Writings,* p. 136.

41. *Two Discourses on the Affairs of Scotland; An Account of a Conversation, Selected Works,* pp. 65, 110, 114, 127, 135.

42. Phillipson, 'Culture and Society in the Eighteenth Century Province', in Stone (ed.), *The University in Society,* II pp. 414–20, and 'The Scottish Enlightenment', in Porter and Teich (eds.), *The Enlightenment in National Context,* pp. 22–26. Though my interpretation of the debate is not always the same, I owe to Phillipson the original insight into its Fletcherian character.

43. R[obert] S[ibbald], *Provision for the Poor in Time of Dearth and Scarcity* (1699, 2nd edition, Edinburgh 1709).

44. Smout, *Scottish Trade,* pp. 261–70; J. M. Low, 'A Regional Example of the Mercantilist Theory of Economic Policy', *The Manchester School,* 21 (1953).

45. [David Black?,] *Essay upon Industry and Trade* (Edinburgh 1706), p. 20.

46. [William Seton of Pitmedden,] *The Interest of Scotland in Three Essays* (1700, 2nd edition, London 1702), pp. 73–80, 86–9.

47. *A Speech in Parliament on the 10th day of January 1701, by the Lord Belhaven, on the Affair of the Indian and African Company, and its Colony of Caledonia* (Edinburgh 1701), pp. 6–10.

48. [Seton,] *The Interest of Scotland,* pp. 89–104; *Memorial to the Members of Parliament of the Court Party* [1700].

49. Fletcher did once indulge in martial pride, in the splendid exchange of insults which he reported between himself and Seymour over the battles of Bannockburn and Musselburgh: *Account of a Conversation, Selected Works,* pp. 123–4. But otherwise the martial past is significant by its absence from his discussion of Scottish liberty and independence.

50. [George Ridpath,] *An Historical Account of the Ancient Rights and Power of the Parliament of Scotland* (1703, repr. Aberdeen 1823); the reprint is wrongly

ascribed to Andrew Fletcher. Ridpath frequently refers to Buchanan, and several of his arguments are similar to those found in Samuel Rutherford's *Lex, Rex* (1644), the classic statement of Covenanter political theory.

51. [Ridpath,] *An Historical Account*, pp. 2, 4, 8, 16, 105–37.

52. Conversely, the intellectual distance between Ridpath and Fletcher would seem to reinforce scepticism about Fletcher's debt to Covenanter political thought.

53. [Patrick Abercromby,] *The Advantages of the Act of Security, Compar'd with these of the Intended Union* (1706).

54. *The History of the Campagnes of 1548 and 1549..., Done in French, under the Title of, The Scots War &c by Mons. Beague* [i.e. Beaugué], *A French Gentleman* (Paris 1556); with an Introductory Preface by the Translator [P. Abercromby] (1707). Preface, p. xxxiii. On the ideological significance of the attempted union of 1547: A. H. Williamson, 'Scotland, Antichrist and the Invention of Great Britain', in Dwyer, Mason and Murdoch (eds.), *New Perspectives on Early Modern Scotland*.

55. *A Pill for Pork-Eaters: or, A Scots Lancet for An English Swelling* (Edinburgh 1705).

56. *A Speech in Parliament....by the Lord Belhaven* (1701), p. 11: '*mavortia pectora*' translates literally as 'manly courage'; and in the mythical royal genealogy propagated by Boece and Buchanan, Fergus I son of Ferchard was the first of the Scottish kings.

57. *A Speech in Parliament by the Lord Belhaven; Upon the Act for Security of the Kingdom in case of the Queen's Death* (Edinburgh 1703); *A Speech in Parliament touching Limitations* [1703?], attrib. to Belhaven; *The Lord Belhaven's speech in Parliament, the 17th of July 1705* (1705).

58. *The Lord Belhaven's Speech in Parliament the second day of November 1706. On the subject matter of an Union betwixt the two Kingdoms of Scotland and England* (1706), repr. in Daniel Defoe, *The History of the Union between England and Scotland* (London 1786), pp. 317–28.

59. *A Speech in Parliament....by the Lord Belhaven* (1701), p. 4.

60. *An Account of a Conversation, Selected Works*, p. 114; [Earl of Cromarty,] *A Letter from E. C. to E. W. Concerning the Union* [Edinburgh 1706], p. 16.

61. [Seton,] *The Interest of Scotland* (1700), p. 37.

62. [Earl of Cromarty,] *Parainesis Pacifica; or a perswasive to the Union of Britain* (London 1702), p. 19.

63. [Earl of Cromarty,] *A Letter to a Member of Parliament upon the 19th Article of the Treaty of Union between the Two Kingdoms of Scotland and England, 4 Dec. 1706*, p. 4; *A Letter from E. C. to E. W.*, p. 4.

64. *A Speech in Parliament the second day of November 1706. By William Seton of Pitmedden Junior, on the first article of the Treaty of Union* (Edinburgh 1706), repr. in Defoe, *The History of the Union*, p. 314.

65. The most obvious and common reason for disparaging the arguments of the Unionists is that they were so well rewarded by a grateful government. But to dismiss their writings as therefore mere 'propaganda' (as does P. W. J. Riley, *The Union of England and Scotland*, (Manchester 1978), Ch. VI, 'Trade and Propaganda') seems unduly simple-minded. Despite being recipients of government patronage, neither Seton nor Cromarty scrupled to denounce the corruption and dependence of Scottish political life. In any case, the absence of payment is not necessarily or universally a condition of intellectual merit.

66. [Cromarty,] *Parainesis Pacifica*, p. 4; *A Letter from E. C. to E. W.*, pp. 5–7.

E

67. [Cromarty,] *A Letter from E. C. to E. W.*, pp. 8–9; also *A Letter upon the 19th Article of the Treaty*, pp. 5–8.

68. [Earl of Cromarty,] *A Second Letter on the British Union*, (1706), p. 15.

69. Speech by William Seton of Pitmedden Junior, the 18th of November 1706, on the Third Article of the Union, repr. in Defoe, *The History of the Union*, p. 361.

70. [Seton,] *Memorial to the Court Party* (1700), p. 3; *The Interest of Scotland*, pp. 106–7.

71. Speech by Seton on the Third Article of the Union, in Defoe, *The History of the Union*, pp. 361–2.

72. [William Seton of Pitmedden,] *Scotland's Great Advantages by an Union with England* (1706), p. 5.

73. Cromarty's knowledge of that earlier debate is curiously displayed by his publication in 1708 of *Synopsis Apocalyptica: or, A Short Plain Explication and Application of Daniel's Prophecy and of St. John's Revelation, In Concert with and Consequential to it. By G. E. of C. Tracing in the steps of the admirable Lord Napier of Merchistoun* (Edinburgh 1708). Cromarty's interest in Napier makes one wonder the more about a possible relation between Fletcher and Napier.

74. The jurisprudential basis of Unionist argument deserves a fuller treatment. For all their desire that the Scots be associated with English institutions, it is more probable that Cromarty and Seton derived their concepts of liberty and sovereignty from the European Natural and Roman Law traditions. Seton spoke of the rights of liberty and property as 'fundamentals in nature', not in common law; and both he and, still more, Cromarty articulated a concept of parliamentary sovereignty far starker than anything yet advanced by English commentators, including Defoe. On Cromarty's concept of sovereignty, see in addition to the tracts cited: [Earl of Cromarty,] *A Friendly Return to a Letter Concerning Sir George Mackenzie's and Sir John Nisbet's Observation and Responce on the Matter of the Union* (22 Aug. 1706).

75. While this conclusion is broadly in line with that reached by Phillipson in his sketch of the Union debate in his 'The Scottish Enlightenment', there seem to be two differences of emphasis and one of substance between our accounts. Interpreting the case made by the Unionists, I have gone further than Phillipson in emphasising both their concern with 'liberty', taken in the juristic sense, and their consequent concern with realising a new institutional framework of British parliamentary sovereignty. These emphases, I believe, are necessary to distinguish the Unionists' arguments from the straightforward moralism indulged in by their opponents, and to explain their very different attitude to the martial past. But they do not alter the conclusion, common to Phillipson and myself, that supporters and opponents of the Union coincided in pointing the Scots away from the active political life.

The difference of substance between us concerns the interpretation of Andrew Fletcher. Phillipson suggests that by analysing Scotland's predicament in terms of 'dependence' on England, Fletcher himself initiated the shift of attention from the strictly political issue of 'liberty' to the broader question of 'independence' and its economic, social and moral conditions. Despite Fletcher's own conviction of the importance of political institutions, therefore, Phillipson believes him to have paved the intellectual way for their neglect in the subsequent debate. On my interpretation, however, Fletcher held political, participatory liberty to be an essential condition of independence: social and moral regeneration was to reinforce, not be a substitute for, such liberty. From this it follows that Fletcher's significance for the Union debate was provocative rather than indicative: he challenged other contributors to identify ways of securing liberty and independence that did not require the Scots to possess their own political institutions.

76. [Seton,] *The Interest of Scotland*, pp. 108–9.

77. James Hodges, *A Letter from Mr. Hodges at London, To a Member of the Parliament of Scotland* (Edinburgh 1703).

78. Ferguson, *Scotland's Relations with England*, p. 210.

79. [George Ridpath,] *The Reducing of Scotland by Arms, and Annexing it to England as a Province, Considered* (London, repr. Edinburgh 1705), [James Hodges,] *War Betwixt the Two British Kingdoms Considered* (1705).

80. The Articles of Union are printed in *A Source Book of Scottish History, III: 1567–1707*, eds. Dickinson & Donaldson, pp. 480–92.

81. According to P. W. J. Riley, *The English Ministers and Scotland 1707–27*, (London 1964), pp. 90–5, the Scottish militia bill was introduced by an opposition Whig, to offset the curbing of the executive power as a result of abolishing the Privy Council; but the Court too had apparently entered the session assuming that a militia was a necessity. The motive for Anne's use of the veto on the militia bill has not been identified: in the light of the attempted revolt that year, it may already have been fear of arming Jacobites.

82. Patrick Abercromby, *The Martial Atchievements of the Scots Nation*, Vol. I (Edinburgh 1711), Preface. The work was printed by the Jacobite publisher Robert Freebairn, who on the 1715 volume styled himself 'Printer to the King's Most Excellent Majesty', by whom he meant James the Old Pretender.

83. *Georgii Buchanani, Opera Omnia, curante Thoma Ruddimano* (Edinburgh 1715): also printed by Robert Freebairn as '*Typographum Regium*' — a nice irony at Buchanan's expense. On Ruddiman: Douglas Duncan, *Thomas Ruddiman. A Study of Scottish Scholarship in the Early Eighteenth Century* (Edinburgh 1965), Ch. 4, 'Patriotic Editing'.

84. William Ferguson, *Scotland 1689 to the Present* (Edinburgh 1978), p. 67; *Memoirs of the Life of Sir John Clerk of Pennicuik 1676–1755*, ed. J. M. Gray, *Scottish History Society*, XII (Edinburgh 1892), p. 89.

85. Rosalind Mitchison, 'The Government and the Highlands, 1707–1745', in N. T. Phillipson and R. Mitchison (eds.), *Scotland in the Age of Improvement* (Edinburgh 1970), pp. 38–43.

86. [Daniel Defoe,] *A Fourth Essay at Removing National Prejudices* (1706), p. 30. The first two of these *Essays* had been written to remove the prejudices of the English, the remaining four the prejudices of the Scots. Defoe had been sent to Edinburgh by Robert Harley to do his work on the spot.

87. The loan of books was fulsomely acknowledged by Ruddiman, who described Fletcher as '*Cato nostri seculi*': *Buchanani, Opera Omnia*, p. xxi. For Fletcher's views in his last years, and his final words: 'Letters of Andrew Fletcher of Saltoun and His Family 1715–16', Irene J. Murray (ed.), *Scottish History Society Miscellany X* (1965), pp. 164–5: Letter of Andrew to Henry Fletcher, 6 June 1716; and pp. 170–2: Letter of Andrew Fletcher (jun.) to his father Henry Fletcher.

3

David Hume and the
Moderate Literati

Together David Hume and the Moderate literati were responsible for the revival of interest in the militia issue in Scotland in the 1750s. Each, however, contributed in a different way, and requires a distinct approach to be understood. David Hume's contribution is to be found in the discussion of questions of military organisation that runs through his political and economic essays: for him the significance of the militia issue was primarily intellectual, being developed in the context of his theoretical enquiry into the progress of society. The approach proper in his case is therefore straightforwardly textual: I shall first survey the range of Hume's comments on military organisation, and then offer an interpretation of their purpose and significance. By contrast, the contribution of the Moderate literati to the revival of the militia issue was as much cultural and political as intellectual, being associated with a particular attitude to the Scottish past, and an active political commitment. Their case accordingly requires a broader approach, setting the development of their interest in an ideological and political context. This is not to say, however, that the Moderates' contribution was without intellectual significance. Faintly in the debates of the Select Society, and clearly in a pamphlet by one of their number, Adam Ferguson, there can be seen emerging a view of the militia in relation to the progress of society very different from the view suggested by Hume.

The subject of military organisation was not prominent in David Hume's early writings. There was perhaps little opportunity for its discussion in the *Treatise of Human Nature* (1739–40). Hume did, however, remark in the third volume, 'Of Morals', that the need for leadership in war was the common occasion of the first establishment of government (in its primitive monarchic form); and his general argument established the fundamental principle that government's provision of security through both defence and justice is the necessary condition of the progress of society.[1] More noticeable is the virtual omission of the subject from his first collection of essays, the *Essays Moral and Political*, published in Edinburgh in 1741–42. Here Hume limited himself to observing that the royal prerogative of command over military force was one of the reasons which might be advanced for supposing the British government to incline to an absolute monarchy.[2] Subsequently a curious footnote on the military organisation of China was added to the third edition of these *Essays* in 1748. Seeking to explain why China had achieved happiness, riches and good police despite being governed continually by a monarchy, Hume observed that the country's remoteness and the numbers of its people had obviated the need for an organised defence. As a result the standing forces of China were 'mere militia of the worst kind'; and the monarch, finding the sword in the hands of the people, had been obliged to set his ministers under the restraint of the law. Hume concluded: 'Perhaps a pure monarchy of this kind, were it fitted for defence against foreign enemies, would be the best of all governments, as having both the tranquility attending kingly power, and the moderation and liberty of popular assemblies'.[3] The significance of these remarks, thrown off in a footnote, was far from clear; but for the moment Hume offered no elaboration.

It was in the *Political Discourses,* written between 1749 and 1751 and published in Edinburgh in 1752, that military organisation emerged as a distinct and important theme in Hume's political thinking. The discussion was pitched at a high level of generality, and covered three aspects of the subject. First and foremost was the economic. In the opening essay of the collection, 'Of Commerce', Hume set himself to answer the question whether 'the greatness of a state, and the happiness of its subjects' are inseparable with regard to commerce. The prosperity of a society, he observed, is measured by the proportion of its inhabitants not directly employed in agriculture and the manufactures necessary to it. It is this surplus of labour which manufactures the arts commonly described as the arts of 'luxury', in whose possession lies the happiness of society's individual members. But might not the surplus be appropriated instead by the state, to support its greatness in the form of fleets and armies? Was there not powerful precedent for such a policy in the ancient republics of Sparta and Rome, states which, without commerce and luxury, had maintained larger armies than modern nations with three times the population?

Hume dismissed both the proposition and the precedent. The ancient policy, he proceeded to argue, had been 'violent, and contrary to the more natural and usual course of things'. The republic of Sparta was a 'prodigy', impossible, on all the other evidence of human nature, to repeat. Though the Roman republic had been somewhat more natural, still only 'an extraordinary concurrence of circumstances' — its small size, the degree of equality among its citizens, the consequent intensity of their public spirit — had enabled it to support such military burdens. In the 'natural' or 'common course of human affairs', Hume believed, those employed in agriculture produce a surplus in the expectation of exchanging it for luxury manufactures. If this expectation is frustrated, they will simply have no incentive to produce more than their own subsistence. Such, however, is precisely the effect of public appropriation of the surplus: it dries up the sources of its own support, so that its armies must eventually either make violent conquests or disband. If on the other hand individuals are given scope to pursue their natural interest in the production and exchange of luxuries, this will generate a store of resources on which the public may draw in emergencies. By raising a tax, the sovereign may oblige the people to retrench, and thus acquire the means and the manpower to raise an army for the duration of the danger.[4]

Having disposed of the general notion that the greatness of the sovereign may conflict with the happiness of society, Hume proceeded in subsequent essays of the *Political Discourses* to discuss several more technical features of the economics of defence. In 'Of Money', Hume pointed out the fallacy of identifying the power of a state with plenty of money. Generally, he argued, money is not wealth, but merely its representation: real wealth lies in labour and commodities, and an increase in the quantity of money in a nation, though initially a stimulus to industry, will in the end merely increase prices. There was only one circumstance in which a state might benefit from a greater plenty of money: this was if the money was withheld from circulation by hoarding, and then used to hire mercenary troops from poorer neighbours to fight on the state's behalf instead of its own population.[5] In this instance, Hume allowed, the ancients set an example, amassing remarkable hoards; the moderns, however, seemed determined to pursue a quite opposite policy, by the device of public credit.[6]

Hume devoted a separate essay, 'Of Public Credit', to exposing the danger. An expedient designed to mitigate the immediate economic impact of war, public credit, he argued, must result in severe long-term dislocation. It would artificially increase the wealth of the capital at the expense of the provinces, raise prices in the manner of paper credit, increase the burden of taxation on labour, render the nation tributary to foreign creditors, and make the situation of the idle rentier more attractive than that of the productive investor.[7] It is clear that, in thus criticising public credit, Hume did not expect modern states to return to the ancient practice of hoarding: his purpose was to reinforce his initial insistence on the need for the state to husband its resources for defence. Amplifying the prescriptions of the essay 'Of Commerce', he argued in 'Of Taxes' that the best taxes are those laid on consumption, especially on luxury articles. These taxes, he believed, are the least felt, and seem in some measure voluntary; the temporary retrenchment they require may even be a spur to industry.[8] At the same time, it is preferable to employ another nation's manpower as far as possible: it had been a distinct advantage of the Hanoverian connection in the last war that it had supplied Britain with a considerable number of brave and faithful auxiliaries.[9]

A second aspect of military organisation to be discussed in the *Political Discourses* was the moral. In the essay initially entitled 'Of Luxury', Hume followed up the analysis of the economic desirability of luxury by arguing that far from being a corrupting influence, as moralists complained, it positively enhanced the manners and values of a society. Here Hume had in mind not only private virtue and the polite arts; he was no less interested in the benefit to the public. It is only, he believed, by application to the vulgar arts of commerce and manufacture that laws and police are perfected; and knowledge of the arts of government in turn encourages moderation in its conduct. As in civil affairs, so, moreover, in military: the wars of commercial societies are less ferocious, but the marital spirit of men is rather improved. The sense of honour is given vigour by knowledge and education, while courage 'can neither have any duration, nor be of any use, when not accompanied with discipline and martial skill, which are seldom found among a barbarous people'. The schoolboy view that luxury had been the ruin of the Romans' virtue was, Hume went on, quite misplaced: their fall was really due to their ill-modelled government and unlimited conquests. The modern nation most defective in the arts of war as well as peace was Poland, where (apart from the regular sale of its crown) there was no commerce at all. Hume concluded by affirming that commerce and progress in the arts fostered not merely virtue but also liberty. Undermining the sharp division between landed proprietors and their vassals or tenants characteristic of rude societies, commerce enabled farmers and tradesmen to acquire a share of property, and thus drew authority and consideration to that 'middling rank of men' who, from their interest in equal laws, are 'the best and firmest basis of public liberty'.[10]

The theme of liberty was central to the third aspect of military organisation considered by Hume, the political. His arguments on this point, it should be noted, are particularly complex, the more so as there is no single essay to give them a clear framework, as has been the case with the economic and moral aspects of the subject. In places, it would seem that Hume regarded mercenary or standing armies as a grave threat to liberty: they are ever, he could remark, 'the beaten road' to arbitrary government.[11] But when considering particular examples, his views were less straightforward. In the case of the ancient republics, he accepted the conventional description of them as 'free states', and even attributed their citizens' intense public spirit to their liberty.[12] Yet it is clear that the maintenance of permanently armed citizens was attended with severe political as well as economic distortion. Implicit in 'Of Commerce', the point was elaborated in 'Of the Populousness of Ancient Nations' which included a remarkable discussion of social and political conditions in antiquity. For one thing, the liberty of citizens rested on the domestic slavery of many more — a denial of real liberty, Hume acidly observed, much greater than any under the most arbitrary government of modern Europe. For another, the artificial degree of equality maintained between citizens had made it impossible to establish a regular government: the republics' liberty had constantly been abused by the most violent faction.[13]

Although the evidence is much sparser, the case of the modern monarchies is another which suggests caution in taking Hume to have made a simple identification of standing armies with arbitrary government. He might remark that the mercenary armies with which the people had entrusted their princes after the decay of the Gothic militias had contributed to the decline of public liberty throughout the continent of Europe.[14] But he had already made it clear, in the earlier *Essays Moral and Political*, that he regarded the 'civilized monarchies' of modern Europe as free in so far as they ruled by law and guaranteed security to all their subjects and their property.[15] It is also worth observing that when in the *Political Discourses* he warned the Bourbons against persisting in the ambition of universal monarchy because it would end in military subversion, he identified the danger not in the French nobility, but in the foreign mercenaries who would have to be hired to defend the far-flung provinces.[16]

It is only in relation to Britain that Hume's judgement appears to have been unequivocal. Hitherto, he noted in 'Of the Protestant Succession', Britain's island situation had secured it without a standing army. But, he went on, the present disputed succession prevented the government from arming its subjects, although this was 'the only method of securing a people fully, both against domestic oppression and foreign conquest'.[17] And in the closing essay of the *Political Discourses*, the 'Idea of a perfect Commonwealth', he argued that in a limited monarchy where the sword was the prerogative of the king, there was always the danger that he would neglect the militia in order to have a pretence for keeping a standing army. Hume added:

> it is evident that this is a mortal distemper in the BRITISH government, of which it must at last inevitably perish. I must, however, confess that SWEDEN seems, in some measure, to have remedied this inconvenience, and to have a militia, with its limited monarchy, as well as a standing army, which is less dangerous than the BRITISH.[18]

In framing his own perfect commonwealth, Hume clearly stipulated that it be defended by a militia in imitation of the Swiss (adding only a provision for annual camps of twenty thousand men drawn out by rotation). For without a militia, he explained, 'it is vain to think that any free government will ever have security or stability.'[19]

Yet even in the case of Britain there is a complicating note. It was one of three 'remarkable customs' in government that in England, 'a country of the highest liberty', the king was tacitly permitted an irregular, illegal power of pressing seamen. Sailors were denied 'the rights and privileges, which the law grants, without distinction, to all ENGLISH subjects', because the danger to liberty always appeared greater from legalising the power than from allowing it as an exceptional usurpation.[20] Where, then, would liberty stand in relation to a universal, conscripted militia?

Bewildering alike in variety and brevity, Hume's economic, moral and political arguments on the subject of military organisation present considerable difficulties of interpretation. Given Hume's declared intention of contributing 'a lesson in moderation' to metropolitan political debate, that context would seem to provide the obvious starting point. Ever since the Standing Army Controversy of the 1690s the issue of military organisation had been a natural point of division between the Court and the Country; and once Walpole had consolidated the Whig monopoly of power in the 1720s, the army was one of the few issues on which the loose opposition alliance of Tories and radical or disaffected Whigs could combine. Within parliament the opposition forced a division over the army estimates every year between 1725 and 1742, except 1738.[21] Out of doors — outside parliament — the vigorous opposition press consistently denounced the government's preference for an army over a militia. In the 1720s the assault was led by *Cato's Letters*, the work of John Trenchard (of the 1697–98 controversy) and Thomas Gordon; and in the following decade it was renewed by Lord Bolingbroke and *The Craftsman*. Throughout, the opposition's case remained the same: a standing army threatened to subvert the constitution of a limited, mixed monarchy. Even so, the importance of the issue at this time should not be exaggerated: with Britain at peace, the army was not large enough or expensive enough for there to be any repetition of the successful opposition campaign of 1697–98. Ministers could afford to dismiss the divisions over army estimates as mere ritual gestures: and Walpole's press, quick to respond to the opposition on most issues, let that of the army lie by.[22]

Just as Hume began to publish, however, the outbreak of war brought the issue back into prominence. Opposition politicians and publicists renewed the attack with all the old arguments, though no new ones; government propagandists found themselves at last with something to answer for — and they did develop their defence of the army in two particular respects. First, the case for a standing army was openly linked with the case for public credit, and both were defended on the ground of parliamentary control of the revenue. Public credit, in the words of one prominent government apologist, had become 'the pulse of the nation'; and he went on:

> The support of the Government, the property of millions, and the continuance of our trade and manufactures depend upon this credit; and it is certain that any considerable reduction of our disciplin'd troops would immediately affect it.

Even if an army did increase the power of the crown, this was more than offset by the new extraordinary weight acquired by parliament in the constitution since 1688. The institution of the Civil List, and parliamentary appropriation of all other revenue, the writer argued, were effective guarantees of control of government expenditure.[23] The second development in the defence of the standing army concerned its subordination to parliamentary law. Responding to criticism of the arbitrariness of martial law, another government writer upheld the need for discipline while maintaining that the annual renewal of martial law would guarantee political control:

> A Standing Army, in time of peace, without consent of Parliament, is unconstitutional, and even with consent of Parliament may be dangerous. Regular military discipline is the only preventive of that danger; .... and while the chain by which military depends upon civil power remains entire, and without that rust which it must naturally gather without annual revisals, there can be no danger from military ambition.[24]

Complementing the case made for parliament's financial control, this elucidation of the relation between civil and military jurisdiction went some way to substantiate Daniel Defoe's earlier assertion of the compatibility of an army with parliamentary sovereignty.

If such was the spectrum of metropolitan debate on the army issue in the first half of the eighteenth century, where are Hume's arguments to be placed on it? The question has tended to puzzle commentators, particularly those, like Duncan Forbes, who take the metropolitan debate to be the main historical context of Hume's political thought, and who understand his principal intention to have been to provide the established Hanoverian regime with a proper intellectual foundation.[25] For not only was Hume slow to take up the issue in the 1740s; when he did, it is evident that many of his arguments sit oddly in the metropolitan context, while a number appear to be in direct conflict with government positions. Where a government writer could speak of public credit as 'the pulse of the nation', to Hume it was a potentially fatal cancer; where the standing army's defenders could contend that parliament's financial and disciplinary controls had made it consistent with free government, to Hume it still remained a 'mortal distemper' of the constitution. Faced with such contextual discordance, Forbes can only suppose that 'a stubborn preference for militias over standing armies' was one residue of 'vulgar whiggism' that Hume failed to purge from his otherwise admirably philosophical politics.[26]

But there is more to be made of Hume's arguments than this. Simply within the context of metropolitan debate, his contribution was by no means so slight and one-sided as Forbes suggests. Though Hume condemned a standing army, he did so with arguments very different from those conventional among anti-army writers; and at a number of points his arguments converged with, and even developed, propositions advanced by the army's defenders. Hume fully accepted that commerce had changed the nature of war, requiring — and, he would add, encouraging — greater discipline in its conduct. Courage was no longer a matter of simple moral virtue. As a corollary of this, Hume renewed and elaborated Lord Somers' claim that the military strength and zeal of the ancient republics had been quite unnatural, and offered no example to the present. If Hume continued to advocate reliance on a militia, it was therefore not from any simple moral concern or uncritical adherence to ancient models. In any case, it is clear that Hume's arguments did not prescribe either a complete or an immediate change in Britain's present military policy. He positively endorsed the strategy of paying subsidies to Hanoverians to fight on Britain's behalf on the continent (where it might be assumed that Britain did not have the imperial ambitions which could still be attributed to France). And even when at his most vehement on the potential dangers of public credit and standing armies, Hume was careful to indicate the length of his perspective. A series of explicitly stated suppositions prefaced his deduction of the probable fatal consequences of public credit;[27] and if his judgement of the standing army as a mortal distemper was more summary, still he noted that it was one of which the British government must 'at last' inevitably perish. Adoption of the Swedish compromise, in which a militia balanced the army, would avert the danger for at least a considerable time.

Further reason for interpreting Hume's contributions to metropolitan debate on the army issue as more than an expression of residual vulgar whiggism is provided by the subsequent adoption of very similar arguments by the Reverend Josiah Tucker. In 1755 Tucker deployed recognisably Humean economic principles in defence of a policy of subsidies and the maintenance of a small standing army. Tucker's starting point was a clear definition of the real wealth of a nation as the industry and domestic commerce of a people; like Hume, he insisted that real wealth was not to be equated with either money or foreign trade. On this basis, Tucker defended the payment of subsidies as enabling the nation to keep the people at work while others fought on their behalf: the people's industry would soon fetch back, with increase, the money paid out in subsidies. Insofar as some national defence was necessary, Tucker held that it was better to rely on a small standing army than a militia. There was no nation in history, he claimed, which was both famous for arts and manufactures and renowned for a militia. Ancient Rome and modern Switzerland, so often held up as examples, had traded only in war and soldiers, and had very few manufacturers. Even service in a part-time militia, Tucker argued, would render men unfit and unwilling for labour: it would therefore permanently diminish the productive capacity of the economy.[28] In implying an economic need for specialisation in military service, Tucker was certainly going further than Hume, who believed rather in the economic advantages of the militia's flexibility; but they were at one on the fundamental point of giving priority to the economic assessment of military organisation. Such common ground reinforces the other evidence of convergence between Hume's arguments and those of the army's defenders, and confirms that his support for a militia was the fruit of a perspective quite different from that of the English anti-army writers.[29]

Not only is it possible to vindicate the significance and originality of Hume's arguments in the metropolitan context: it is far from clear that interpretation should be tied to that one context. Hume's discussion of questions of military organisation can also be seen as part of a more general — and more important — theoretical enquiry into the relation between institutions and economic development in the progress of society. Specifically, Hume's observations on military organisation can be seen to illustrate two major problems which he identified in the relation between economy and government in a commercial society.[30]

The first problem concerns the distribution of resources between the economy and the institutions of government. When in the *Treatise* Hume defined government's provision of security through justice and defence as the necessary condition of the progress of society, it was on the explicit assumption that the interest of those in government would coincide with the interest of society as a whole.[31] This complementary relation between government and the progress of society corresponds with the 'natural course of things' described in 'Of Commerce'. Exemplified in the case of defence, it presupposes that government normally diverts only a minimum of resources to military ends: society is thereby given the greatest possible scope for the accumulation of wealth, contributing not only to the happiness of its members, but also to the store of resources on which government may draw in emergencies. However, such a natural identity of interests cannot be guaranteed: Hume's analysis of faction in the *Essays Moral and Political* obliged him to recognise that men acting together in parties may pursue a separate interest, and abuse the authority of government.[32] The apparent opportunity for using the surplus wealth of society for public aggrandisement instead of private luxury consumption offers the strongest temptation to such abuse — and, 'Of Commerce' proceeds to demonstrate, the clearest proof of its fatal consequences for society's future progress. Yet this was precisely the danger embodied in standing armies and public credit: as the institutions by which the power of the state had historically been enlarged at the expense of society, they provided the best illustration of the problem of government's misappropriation of resources.[33]

A second problem in the relation between government and economic development stems from the social and moral consequences of commerce. The problem is suggested by Hume's analysis in 'Of Luxury' of the improvement wrought by commerce upon society's system of ranks and moral values. According to this analysis, commerce will tend both to modify the clear class distinctions characteristic of primitive nations, creating a middling rank with a vested interest in the general security of property, and to enhance the public, military and political values of all society's members. Thereby commerce will foster a new and growing expectation of liberty, in two distinct forms. On the one hand, the interest of the middling rank in the security of property will lead them to seek the universal extension of the liberty which is given by the rule of law, liberty from government and one's neighbours. On the other, the gradual improvement of the moral capacities of an ever larger proportion of society will foster a growing demand for the liberty to participate in government. The problem created by these rising expectations of liberty is particularly acute in the case of military organisation. The proper form of defence in a commercial society would be one which ensures individual liberty and the rule of law, while yet matching the increasing capacity and desire for the freedom to take part in public life.

Though Hume did not explicitly present it as such, it is possible to identify a response covering both problems in the relation between government and economic development in another already-mentioned essay in the *Political Discourses*, the concluding 'Idea of a perfect Commonwealth'. Besides proposing defence by a militia, this essay outlined a model of government in which a certain number of provincial or 'county' assemblies would in turn elect a central senate, each level further appointing magistrates and councillors. By a careful division of legislative, executive and judicial powers, and, most important, their distribution between the centre and the localities, the model was designed to check the factious misuse of authority by those at the centre, and thus to prevent aggrandisement of the state at the expense of society; at the same time it would provide scope for the gradually increasing participation of citizens.[34] Although Hume did not similarly explain the proposal of the militia, it too could be set within the framework of these objectives. As a universal service, enabling as many or as few to be called out as the occasion required, it would obviate the need to keep a permanent establishment of any size, and thus forestall any attempt to misappropriate resources for an army. At the same time, it would harness the greater courage fostered by habits of industry in commercial society, and by putting arms in the hands of all, be the embodiment of the people's liberty.

So discussing military organisation in the framework of more general problems in the relation between government and economic development, Hume had far transcended the confines of metropolitan debate. He had set the subject instead at the centre of what was to be the principal intellectual project of the Scottish Enlightenment: the investigation of the conditions of the progress of society. Here indeed Hume was the pioneer: subsequent Scottish Enlightenment discussion of military organisation in the progress of society would start from, or respond to, his analysis. Original as his enterprise was, however, it was not without detectable Scottish roots. Both in the concerns which underlay his formulation of the problem of government and economic development and in his choice of concepts with which to discuss and respond to the problem, Hume can be seen to have retraced the steps of an earlier Scottish debate — that debate which Andrew Fletcher had initiated, and which opponents and supporters of the Union had continued.

The parallel between Hume's concerns and those of Andrew Fletcher and his contemporaries is striking. For Hume the abuse of society's economic resources by self-interested governments, exemplified in the maintenance of standing armies, constituted the first problem in the relation between government and economic development. For Fletcher and almost every other commentator on the predicament of Scotland around 1700 the English government's abuse of Scottish resources had been the major obstacle to the nation's economic improvement: and one of the clearest examples of such abuse had been the exploitation of Scotland's manpower to supply England's armies. As Hume presented it, the second problem of government and economic development turned on the need to adapt political and military institutions to the growing yet potentially divergent expectations of the members of commercial society for both individual security and political participation. As Fletcher and his contemporaries had debated it, the choice of Scotland's own political future had hinged on differing estimates of the expectations of an economically improving society — or whether the rule of law and individual security were compatible with the maintenance of an independent Scottish politics. And what had then made the problem especially acute was the historic identification of Scotland's liberty with martial independence, at the expense, it could be argued, of the maintenance of law and individual security. Hume's formulation of these problems was of course deliberately generalised: rather than focusing on Scotland, he illustrated his arguments from a wide range of experience, both ancient and modern. Even in generalising what had been specifically Scottish concerns, however, Hume's may still be seen as a Fletcherian enterprise. It had been Fletcher's last and most ambitious challenge to his fellow-countrymen that they recognise the potentially universal, exemplary significance of Scottish experience. Hume had accepted that challenge: in his work the investigation of Scotland's problems was transformed into the investigation of the problems of society in general.

The continuity between the earlier Scottish debate and Hume's theoretical enquiry is equally apparent at the level of concepts. The clearest evidence is provided by the essay identified as Hume's response to the problem of government and economic development, the 'Idea of a perfect Commonwealth'. In its strict division of power within a federal framework and insistence upon a citizens' militia, the perfect commonwealth reproduces the essential institutional principles of the civic tradition. Hume himself indicated that the civic tradition was his inspiration when he singled out Harrington's *Oceana* as 'the only valuable model of a commonwealth that has yet been offered to the public', and adopted it as his starting point.[35] Still more interesting, however, is the unacknowledged affinity between the perfect commonwealth and the scheme of government for Scotland and Europe outlined in Andrew Fletcher's Limitations and *Account of a Conversation*. This affinity is particularly striking in two respects. First, Hume, as Fletcher before him, deliberately modified civic concepts in an attempt to combine the vitality and freedom of small provincial political units with the advantages of scale found in large states. He insisted that the perfect commonwealth was applicable not only to republics such as Holland, or to the semi-republican mixed government of Britain, but also to a territorial monarchy such as France: it would be less easy to introduce in the latter, but more secure once established. Like Fletcher, it seems that Hume envisaged a political framework, both within Britain and across Europe, in which the demands of provincial independence and defensive unity would be harmonised.[36] The second respect in which Hume followed Fletcher was in consciously seeking to adapt the civic concepts of regular, free government to the pursuit of economic development: it was precisely Harrington's reluctance to do so, exemplified in an unworkable agrarian law, that Hume sought to improve upon.[37] Here, moreover, Hume may be seen to have pursued Fletcher's specific suggestion that a universal militia might actually be the most economic, because the most flexible, form of defence for a modern commercial society.

Significant as it is, however, the affinity between Hume's and Fletcher's models of government was far from complete. The common use of civic institutional principles notwithstanding, there were fundamental differences in their application: and when these differences are considered, it becomes clear that Hume was simultaneously drawing on the concepts of a quite separate intellectual tradition — a tradition, indeed, which had been deployed against Fletcher in the earlier Scottish debate. The divergence may be traced from the two points of particular affinity: where Fletcher had modified the civic concepts in a way which preserved traditional civic assumptions, Hume in each case can be seen to have transformed the concepts' implication.

In the first place, Hume's insistence on the applicability of the perfect commonwealth to a large, monarchical state rested on the conviction that the territorial monarchies were potentially the most progressive of modern governments. Far from branding these monarchies as 'despotisms' as Fletcher had continued to do, Hume distinguished clearly between the modern 'civilized' monarchy and its primitive, 'barbarous' ancestor. The latter had indeed been a despotism, but in some favoured circumstances primitive monarchies had given way to republics, which established the first regular, free government. Subsequently modern states, whether republican or monarchic in form, had improved upon the earliest ancient republics, whose government was still seriously flawed. And of all modern forms of government, Hume suggested, it was in the civilised monarchies that authority was most securely regulated by law, and the subject safeguarded against the abuse of power by faction. Not only, therefore, was the concept of regular free government no longer tied to the republican form of government: for Hume its best foundation was monarchical.[38]

Hume's second, still more critical departure from the assumptions of the civic tradition derived from his understanding of the causes and consequences of economic development. In sharing with Fletcher a commitment to combining economic development with the institutions of free government, Hume accepted neither Fletcher's civic definition of wealth as a public pursuit, nor his civic insistence upon a continuing distinction between the ranks of producers and citizens. On the contrary, Hume believed that development would only occur through the individual pursuit of personal and family interest, with the minimum necessary diversion of resources to public use. The consequences of development, moreover, would be to blur social distinctions and diffuse the moral qualities requisite for citizenship. Commerce, in other words, was simply incompatible with the traditional material and moral premises of political community to which Fletcher adhered. It was impossible, therefore, to identify free government exclusively with the liberty of a separate citizen class. In a commercial society, liberty must be extended to all.

It is here that Hume's debt to another tradition than the civic is evident. For when Hume spoke of liberty in commercial society, he had in mind not one but two concepts of liberty. The recognisably civic liberty to participate was indeed one of these; but the other was the liberty of person and property under the law, the liberty 'from' government and one's fellow men — the concept of liberty, in short, which derived from the jurisprudential tradition, and which had been articulated in the earlier Scottish debate by the Unionist William Seton. It was to this jurisprudential concept of liberty, moreover, that Hume gave priority. The securing of person and property with institutions of justice, he laid down in the *Treatise,* was (besides defence) the principal object of any government. Such liberty was the precondition of the free pursuit of individual interest on which economic development depended; and thereby it was the condition also of the individual's acquisition of the material and moral qualifications for citizenship. Only as individuals acquired these qualifications did the civic concept of participatory liberty become applicable, and Hume expect governments to provide for it. Participatory liberty could in turn strengthen personal: as participation extended, the interest of government would be bound more closely to society, and the possibility of government setting itself above the rule of law diminished. But this was in Hume's perspective a long-term prospect; meanwhile the diffusion of participatory liberty remained ever-dependent on the prior securing of a large measure of personal liberty.

It was through according such primacy to the jurisprudential concept of liberty that Hume transformed the civic institutional principles he shared with Fletcher. Because the civilised monarchies upheld personal liberty better than any other modern form of government, they could be said to provide the surest foundation for the gradual introduction of the participatory institutions of the perfect commonwealth. Because economic development requires security of person and property for all, the rigid distinction between freemen and servant must disappear, and all will eventually become capable of participation.

So transforming the traditional civic concept of free government, Hume, it may finally be suggested, also by implication transformed the traditional civic concept of a militia. In a commercial society in which there is no distinction between freemen and servants all will become capable of militia service: indeed, it is likely to be the first opportunity of involvement in public life extended on a universal basis. But in that case were not armies conscripted from among the people — armies such as those raised by China and now also by the modern monarchies — to be accounted militias?[39] On the other hand, conscription must render the liberty embodied in the carrying of arms distinctly ambiguous. Universal service may endow all with the liberty to participate; but conscription would also leave none free from service. And would not all then be in the position, hitherto accounted an extraordinary exception in Britain, of the pressed sailors?

However Scottish the roots of his theoretical enquiry into military organisation in the progress of society, Hume unfortunately did not bring his conclusions to bear on Scottish experience. On two occasions only in his published writings did he leave any indication of his views on the particular problems of military organisation in Scotland. The first of these was in a pamphlet entitled *A True Account of the Behaviour and Conduct of Archibald Stewart Esq., late Provost of Edinburgh, in a Letter to a Friend,* which Hume published anonymously in 1748. Stewart had been put on trial by the government for dereliction of duty as Provost during the 'Forty-Five rebellion: Hume wrote to vindicate his conduct by showing the weakness of Edinburgh's defences, and the incapacity of the forces then available. He commented first on the rebel Highland soldiers. They were certainly brave and warlike, fighting under their clan standards, but they had no discipline and poor weapons: for them to have advanced as far as they did was a clear indication of general military decay, in England as well as Scotland. As for the forces available to Stewart in Edinburgh, the hundred and twenty-six elderly Town Guards had been the best. The others, the Trained Bands, the seven-day-old Edinburgh Regiment and the four hundred Volunteers, had been virtually useless. The 'tatterdemallion' Trained Bands were wholly undisciplined and hence (for the two qualities, as Hume insisted, are inseparable) without courage. The Volunteers had likewise lacked spirit, and efforts to organise them had met with little response. A further two regiments of dragoons had simply fled. Edinburgh, Hume bluntly concluded, had better defended by its chamber pots than by such troops.[40]

Hume's second relevant comment occurs in the first volume of his *History of Great Britain* (1754). In a few paragraphs introducing an account of James I's Scottish policy, Hume sketched in the historically martial character of Scottish society. Scotland, he began by pointing out, had always possessed 'two kinds of inhabitants, very different in their language, manner, customs, habit, and whole train of life': the Lowlanders, of Saxon origin, and the Highlanders, of Celtic extraction. Whatever their differences, however, the two races had had this in common: both lived 'in a manner somewhat disorderly; governed by ancient customs more than by laws, and attached to their own families more than to their prince or country'. It was a vicious circle. Because the law was so weak, the inhabitants of Scotland sought security by a close adherence to their own tribe, which alone could protect them; but this attachment loosening their ties to their country, the authority of the laws was weakened still further. The problem was aggravated by the survival of the feudal law, especially in the Lowlands. 'Separate jurisdictions were maintained: Hereditary offices preserved: And an execution of justice took place, feeble, disorderly, partial and tumultuous.'

Caught between the contentions of powerful vassals — Hume went on — the authority of the Scottish king was necessarily uncertain and precarious. His best recourse against rebellion was to animate the clans traditionally hostile to the rebels; but the need to reward such supporters soon made them a threat which had to be reduced in the same way. Yet despite this 'destructive politics', the English had seldom been able to take advantage of the Scots' divisions. With no other enemy to consider, the national antipathy of the Scotch towards the English had risen to an extreme height: and by shedding 'an ocean of blood', the Scots had preserved the independence of their kingdom intact. If Hume then observed that that independence had been 'utterly lost' under the Union of the Crowns, there was no indication that this gave cause for regret. Like Seton and Cromarty before him, Hume was in no doubt that the rule of law was preferable to 'feudal anarchy'.[41]

If David Hume was the original intellectual pioneer of the Scottish Enlightenment, the Moderate literati — taken as a group — have a good claim to be seen as the leading representatives of enlightened Scotland.[42] Numbering William Robertson, Alexander Carlyle, Adam Ferguson, John Home and Hugh Blair, the group acquired its name, the 'Moderates', as an organised party within the Kirk. They were all initially ministers; and although Ferguson and Home resigned the cloth in 1754 and 1757 respectively, they remained involved with the others in ecclesiastical affairs. Born within five years of each other, between 1718 and 1723, they came from similar backgrounds: Robertson, Carlyle and Ferguson were themselves sons of the manse, Blair and Home were of bourgeois origin. Where not acquainted from childhood, they were brought together in the early 1740s while pursuing their education for the ministry at the universities of Edinburgh and Glasgow.[43] Thereafter they remained fast bound to one another both by personal friendship and by common commitments. Their first loyalty was naturally to a particular conception of the Kirk and its place in society; but this was combined with a clear view of the direction in which Scottish society at large should be moving, and with an unwavering adherence to liberal, enlightened cultural values. Two of the Moderate literati, William Robertson and Adam Ferguson, require to be considered also among the pioneers of the Scottish Enlightenment, Robertson specifically as an historian, Ferguson primarily as a moral philosopher. As we shall see, Ferguson was to make a major contribution to the Scottish Enlightenment's discussion of the militia issue in the context of the theory of the progress of society. But it is clear that Ferguson came to that intellectual discussion on the basis of a view of the significance of the militia developed within the ideological perspective of the Moderate group as a whole. For reasons I shall now explore, a commitment to martial values and to the idea of a militia was by the end of the 1750s central to the Moderates' cultural and political outlook.

The roots of that commitment may be traced back to two formative experiences in the 1740s, one academic, the other practical. The academic experience was provided by the courses of moral philosophy which the future Moderates were taught at their universities. As elaborated by its first professors, Scottish academic moral philosophy combined the study of human nature, covering man's mental faculties and moral sentiments, with a general theory of society and government, framed in the terms of natural jurisprudence. Drawing on Grotius and Pufendorf, Locke and Shaftesbury, the professors' enterprise had obvious roots in the seventeenth-century project to find an empirical basis for natural law.[44] But the Scottish professors gave their moral philosophy a distinctive character by their enthusiasm for drawing moral conclusions. Effectively they would reduce politics itself to a question of morals, to the neglect of problems of political institutions. Celebrating the life of virtue, they devoted their lectures to instilling in their students an active devotion to its pursuit.[45]

In this moralising perspective, questions of military organisation, when discussed, were treated very much as a matter of values. The approach is well illustrated in the work of the most distinguished of all the professors, Francis Hutcheson, whose lectures at Glasgow were remembered by Carlyle as explaining and enforcing the moral virtues with 'a fervent and persuasive eloquence which was irresistible'.[46] As presented in the posthumously published *System of Moral Philosophy* (1755), military organisation fell under the heading of Civil Laws. But Hutcheson made it clear straightaway that he understood the object of laws to be the positive inculcation of moral virtues:

> As the end of all laws should be the general good and happiness of a people, which chiefly depends on their virtue: it must be the business of legislators to promote, by all just and effectual methods, the principles of virtue, such as shall lead men to piety to God, and all just, peaceable, and kind dispositions

towards their fellows.... It is poor policy merely to punish crimes when they
are committed. The noble art is to contrive such previous education, instruction and discipline, as shall prevent vice....

Apart from piety, there were four virtues in particular which the legislator
should promote: sobriety, industry, justice and fortitude. Hutcheson was
keen that the last should be spread as universally as the others. 'It is
infamous to a country if men of the highest stations are not generally fitted
for the most honourable services, the defence of their country in times of
danger.' Thus Hutcheson urged that military service should not be the
constant profession of a few, but should be required of the whole people in
rotation. Reputable, virtuous citizens, many with a valuable stake in their
country, must possess greater courage and fidelity than lifelong mercenaries. Hutcheson acknowledged that the adoption of such a scheme would
be economically disruptive; but once established, its flexibility should
render it less of a burden than a force of mercenaries. The service would
teach habits of industry, and provide opportunities for practising it in
public works, to the benefit of men's bodies and minds.[47] This was the
most Hutcheson ever wrote — and, perhaps, said — on the subject of
military organisation. For all his early connections with the radical Whig
Commonwealthmen,[48] the militia issue was not central to his political
thinking. But the framework in which he approached the issue was
nonetheless significant: the same moral emphasis would be taken up and
developed by the Moderates.

A second formative experience shared by the Moderates in the 1740s
may have helped to direct their thoughts more specifically towards the
militia issue. In 1745 three members of the group — Robertson, Carlyle
and Home — found themselves caught in Edinburgh during the Jacobite
rebellion. Subsequently Home wrote a *History of the Rebellion in the Year
1745* (1802) which gave particular attention to the defence of Edinburgh,
while Carlyle recorded his personal recollections in his Memoirs. Eagerly,
it seems, the three friends had enlisted together in the College Company of
the Volunteers, and had sought to impress on their seniors the necessity,
and the possibility, of defending the city. As Home and Carlyle both
remembered it, however, their zeal was repeatedly frustrated. A proposal
to march out and assist the dragoons west of the city was defeated by the
reluctance of the other companies of the Volunteers to join them; and once
the Highlanders had come up and the dragoons had fled, the authorities
simply refused to authorise any action. Edinburgh falling, the valiant trio
made their way to Sir John Cope's camp east of Edinburgh, where they
offered their services as intelligence gatherers. John Home particularly
recalled how he had informed Cope of the numbers, equipment and
strength of the Highlanders, pointing out that if only they had been
clothed as Lowlanders, their inferiority to the King's troops would be
evident: the Highland garb favoured them by revealing their naked limbs.
Cope thanked him for 'such certain and accurate intelligence'. When it

came to battle, however, the three remained helpless spectators, though Carlyle busied himself as best he could giving assistance to the wounded.[49]

Quite how much significance should be attached to this experience is difficult to judge. It was evidently a vivid memory: both Carlyle and Home were able to give long and circumstantial accounts of the events over fifty years after they occurred, Carlyle to the extent of detailing the manner and amount of his sleep each night. It was, moreover, an experience about the interpretation of which the two had strong retrospective views. They differed from the account written at the time by David Hume in insisting that some at least of the volunteers had had the spirit to fight, and in accusing Provost Stewart of weakness and probable covert Jacobitism.[50] In longer perspective, Home argued in the introductory chapter of his *History* that the Highlanders' success could be traced back to the neglect of the Lowland militia after the Union of the Crowns. Before that, when all men between fifteen and sixty were trained to arms, the Lowlanders had been more than a match for the rude Highlanders.[51] This was of course a judgement of hindsight, and does not prove that the Moderates' later proposal to revive the national militia stemmed directly from their experience in the 'Forty-Five. Even the vividness of their memories may be misleading, for memory in old age is notoriously uneven; what is remembered best is not necessarily most significant. Yet when retrospective exaggeration is allowed for, it still seems plausible to suppose that the experience was an important one for the youthful Moderates. As we shall now see, the previously martial character of all Scottish society, Lowland as well as Highland, was to emerge in the 1750s as a major historical and literary interest of the group; and in their later advocacy of a Scottish militia, they constantly returned to the shame of the country's defenceless condition in 1745.[52]

One member of the Moderate group not in Edinburgh during the rebellion was Adam Ferguson: he was away serving as chaplain to the First Highland Regiment in the British Army. Nevertheless Ferguson also rallied to the Hanoverian cause, preaching his regiment a sermon in Gaelic on the duty to defend one's country, both in general and in the present circumstances. Whatever it sounded like in Gaelic, however, the published translation offered remarkably abstract fare, as Ferguson laboured to demonstrate that loyalty to one's country, as the society whose laws secure our persons and properties, religion and welfare, must take precedence over the (traditional clan) loyalties of place and family.[53] Just how much conviction went into this is uncertain: while Ferguson always insisted upon the importance of law, he was subsequently to take a very positive view of traditional martial values.

It was early in the 1750s that the Moderates first asserted their claim to leadership in the Kirk and in Edinburgh polite society. In 1751–2 a vigorous and well-orchestrated campaign under Robertson's direction persuaded the General Assembly to enforce the law of patronage in the appointment of new ministers. This tended to take the appointment of ministers out of the hands of congregations and presbyteries, and to transfer it instead to the landowning laity who possessed the rights of patronage. The Moderates nonetheless saw the measure as strengthening the independence of the Kirk from civil society, by enforcing within it society's standards of order and legality. Their victory gave the Moderates an initiative over their High-Flying or Popular Party opponents that was rarely lost over the next forty years, even though the Moderates were never numerically predominant within the ministry.[54] Their conception of the Kirk thus affirmed, the Moderates proceeded to display an equal enthusiasm for the defence and propagation of enlightened culture and enquiry. In 1754 they joined David Hume and others in directing the Select Society of Edinburgh as a forum for the debate of social and cultural questions. Among the most frequent recipients of Hume's suppers in his rooms, the Moderates made no secret of their close friendship with the notorious 'atheist'. They naturally rejected Hume's philosophical principles, but when in 1755 and 1756 Hume was denounced and threatened with excommunication by Presbyterian zealots, they rallied to the defence of his intellectual freedom, and successfully averted damnation. Nor was the Moderates' activity limited to the support and encouragement of others. They were by now actively engaged in literary endeavours of their own. In 1755–6 they brought out two numbers of an *Edinburgh Review*, and by the end of the decade the first of their individual works had been published.[55]

It was on the basis of this assumption of a prominent role in Kirk and enlightened society that the Moderates' commitment to the militia issue took explicit shape in the 1750s. Two contexts for this commitment may be identified, the first in their own literary work, the second in their political connections. From the outset the Moderates consciously thought of their literary activity in the perspective of the old humanist ideal of Scotland's particular distinction in arms and letters. As John Home announced in a letter of 1750, 'the Scotch genius tends altogether to arts and arms'.[56] For the moment the Moderates did not have occasion to seek arms for themselves; but they were particularly keen to explore the character of the Scottish martial past. The interest is displayed in both of the major works published by Moderate literati in the 1750s: William Robertson's *History of Scotland* (1759), and John Home's tragic drama, *Douglas* (1756).

As its title indicates, the focus of Robertson's *History of Scotland during the Reigns of Queen Mary and King James VI* was upon the period of the Scottish Reformation. But Robertson prefaced his main narrative with an introductory book surveying the course and character of Scottish history before the sixteenth century. The first ages of Scottish history Robertson found 'dark and fabulous', and he accordingly left them to the antiquaries.[57] After 1296, however, a more authentic and more interesting history became possible. It was clear that 'the feudal system of laws and policy, that stupendous and singular fabric', had by then prevailed in Scotland as it had almost throughout Europe. The character of that system Robertson defined as distinctively martial:

> A feudal kingdom was properly the encampment of a great army; military ideas predominated, military subordination was established, and the possession of land was the pay which soldiers received for their personal service.

Everywhere in Europe the consequence of this system was the same. Royal authority was weak, while the barons enjoyed considerable independence: 'the genius of the feudal government was purely aristrocratical'. But nowhere, Robertson maintained, had the barons enjoyed greater independence than in Scotland: even by feudal standards, theirs had been an 'exorbitant and uncommon power'.[58] There were several reasons for this. The geography of the country, mountainous and secluded, had provided the Scottish nobility with safe and easy retreats. The absence of large cities, on the other hand, meant that there was no social basis for the establishment of regular government and the rule of law. The small numbers of great nobility further encouraged them in maintaining a distinct identity, ever jealous of the crown. By means of the clan system, they could command from their followings a loyalty far stronger than mere money or political authority could secure, while the devices of leagues and bands enabled them to form less permanent alliances among themselves. Finally, the Scottish nobility had been favoured by political circumstances — by the long wars with England, which necessitated the devolution of considerable power on border lords, and by an unfortunate series of royal minorities.[59] If these were its causes, Robertson continued, nothing better illustrated the extent of the Scottish barons' power than the length of its duration. Long after the feudal system had been undermined by the monarchies of Europe, the Stuart kings of Scotland were still struggling to tame their nobility.[60] It was only with the Union of the Crowns that English wealth had at least had a subversive effect, providing the crown with the means to wield its authority and corrupt the nobility. Even then the nobility had clung on, exhausting their fortunes at the English Court and frustrating Scottish commerce and manufactures by their exactions. It was not until 1688 that the welfare of the people was recognised in Scotland as an object of government; and it required the Union of the Kingdoms to make its realisation possible by finally ending the nobles' power.[61]

Robertson's account of the 'feudal system' in Scotland merits examination as a major contribution to the Scottish Enlightenment's historical investigation of feudalism.[62] Here, however, my interest is limited to Robertson's characterisation of the Scottish martial past. It is clear that Robertson regretted the passing of the feudal regime no more than did Hume: his tone was judiciously hostile to the anarchic behaviour of the great nobility. Robertson did nevertheless introduce a qualification in the Conclusion to the *History*. The Scottish people, he believed, had been 'not altogether unhappy' under their feudal system, since the power of the nobility had depended to a considerable extent on the attachment of their inferiors. Aristocratic tyranny had thus been tempered with a mildness and equality foreign to its nature.[63] The Scots, Robertson seemed to be saying, were now well rid of their feudal system; but there might be something to be salvaged from the wreck, for harmony between ranks was a permanent value. As we shall observe, this was to be a judgement common to the Moderate literati as a group. Fierce critics of the feudal social system, and of aristocratic power, they yet found in the martial Scottish past values which they held worth preserving.

An attachment to the old martial values was openly avowed in John Home's *Douglas*. The staging of this play in 1756 was a further cultural triumph for the Moderate literati. Faced with Garrick's initial refusal to produce it in London, Home had been obliged to revise the script substantially. It had then been read, criticised and even acted by his fellow literati, and by a wide circle of their acquaintance, including David Hume. Emboldened by this support, the Moderates made arrangements to have it performed in Edinburgh. It was an immediate success, and was therefter able to transfer to London. The performance naturally caused still another furore in the Kirk, the brunt of which, since Home himself left the ministry, was this time borne by Carlyle. But the Moderates defended themselves with vigour; and when the fuss died, not only had the liberty of the stage been vindicated, but the play and its message had become widely known.[64]

The Prologue written for the Edinburgh production lost no time in announcing the theme of national prowess in letters and arms. First Caledonia was compared with ancient Athens for her combination of valour with the love of every literary art. Then the hero was announced:

> He comes, the hero of your native land!
> Douglas, a name throughout all the world renown'd,
> A name that rouses like the trumpet's sound!
> Oft have your fathers, prodigal of life,
> A Douglas followed through the bloody strife.[65]

The play itself unfolded a tragic tale of Douglas's noble identity hidden, revealed and finally betrayed, set against the background of an invasion of Scotland by the Danes. Over and over again the protagonists, the women in particular, praised the valour of the Scots, and the ties of kinship that bound all ranks together.[66] It is noteworthy, however, that it was the Danes, and not the English, against whom the Scots were exercising such values. To reinforce the point, Home had his tragic heroine, Lady Randolph, bewail the divisions which existed between the neighbour nations, and insist upon their natural union:

A river here, there an ideal line,
By fancy drawn, divides the sister kingdoms.
On each side dwells a people similar,
As twins are to each other; valiant both:
Both for their valour famous through the world.[67]

Celebration of the martial values of the Scottish past was evidently now subject to the qualification that anglophobia be denied.

Following the success of *Douglas*, Home was able to stage another play (which he had actually written first), the tragedy of *Agis*. This was set in ancient Sparta, not in historic Scotland: but it was equally concerned with martial themes, and as such it serves to introduce the second context for the growth of the Moderates' commitment to the militia. The Prologue again announced the moral. Sparta had been a country revered for virtue, admired by Greece and feared by Asia:

Then citizens and soldiers were the same;
And soldiers heroes; for their wealth was fame.[68]

But the play itself told of the subversion of the virtuous monarchy of Agis by factious traitors employing mercenary arms. In the 1750s, this was a contrast with clear political implications: it could only mean support for William Pitt and his causes, Patriotism in general and the militia in particular.

William Pitt was a novel phenomenon in the relatively quiescent world of mid eighteenth-century politics. Without a personal political connection among MPs, Pitt was distinguished for his reliance on 'popular' support, won by his convincing presentation of himself as an independent 'Patriot'. Recognising and exploiting the continuing decline in the significance of the old party distinctions, not only Whig and Tory, but even Court and Country, Pitt championed 'Patriotism' as a creed above party and corruption alike. It was a creed by no means original in content, being but a combination of well-worn Whig and Country slogans with imperialist bellicosity: yet precisely as such it was calculated to bring him widespread support both within and without doors.[69] Central to the Patriot creed, moreover, was a renewed commitment to the militia. Agitation for a new English Militia Act began early in the 1750s, and Pitt sedulously advertised his support for it; in 1757 he ensured the agitation's success by making the introduction of a militia bill the price of his joining the Duke of Newcastle's war-time 'broad-bottom' coalition government

The Patriot case for a militia in the 1750s had three strands, which together yielded a significant modification of the arguments inherited from the Standing Army Controversy of 1697–8. First, the strategic argument had changed to reflect new circumstances. It was increasingly recognised by 1750 that Britain's principal strategic interests were imperial, and that it was a diversion from these interests to commit troops on the European mainland. If the British war effort was to be concentrated in America, however, Britain itself must be far more directly exposed to invasion by its European enemies. As the Seven Years' War got under way, this was exactly what happened: from 1756 reports of invasion preparations in the French Channel ports were annual news. The advocates of a militia started from this obvious point. Unlike their predecessors in the 1690s, they did not dismiss the standing army as useless: they simply maintained that it was better employed in America, and that a militia would provide the most sizeable and the most economical defence for Britain itself. In the imperial perspective adopted by the Patriots, the militia and the army were complementary. This revision of the strategic case for a militia was accompanied by an equal readiness to dispense with the old shibboleths of the constitutional argument. No longer was it maintained that a militia was the only constitutional form of defence, while a standing army must be the harbinger of despotism. Rather the militia was presented, as in the title of the leading statement of the case, William Thornton's *The Counterpoise* (1752), as but a balance to the army. Reversing the traditional hostility of militia supporters to the crown and the monied interest, Thornton argued that a militia would be a positive support to these, offsetting the threat which an army might present to the wealth of the metropolis. Thornton even claimed that such a balance had been the laudable policy of William III.[70]

The third strand in the Patriot case for a militia exploited the vein of moralising lately so cultivated by Bolingbroke. The militia was held up as a salve for the corruption and degeneracy of the modern age. Thornton prefaced his tract with the claim that 'the depravity and selfishness of those in a higher class was never more remarkable than at present', and he went on to assert that a militia would revive the martial spirit of the nation, preventing it from sinking to the effeminacy of the Chinese.[71] The decade's most popular moraliser, John Brown, likewise lamented the decayed morals of the better sort in society, and the damage done to the spirit of national defence, while the most improbable, Edward Wortley Montagu, lent the weight of his support to the militia's cause.[72]

It is against this background that *Agis* should be — and was — seen: in its celebration of political virtue and the citizens' militia it echoed directly the themes of metropolitan Patriotism. That the Moderates were excited by Pitt, and still more by what he represented, is clear. As early as 1750 they had obtained Pitt's (curt and critical) opinion of the first version of *Agis*;[73] and subsequently Pitt interested himself in the London production of *Douglas* in 1757. At the end of the decade, when Pitt's stock temporarily faltered early in 1759 before the news of the year's great victories came in, Alexander Carlyle rose to the Patriot's defence with an anonymous pamphlet. Entitled, after the fashion for heavy irony, *Plain Reasons for Removing a Certain Great Man from His Majesty's Presence and Councils for Ever*, the pamphlet insisted upon Pitt's honesty, eloquence, encouragement of learning and indifference to luxury; and it singled out for notice his policies of supporting the navy, reforming the army, recruiting the Highlanders for service in America, and promoting the new militia.[74]

Possessed of such a strong sense of Scottish literary and martial identity, however, the Moderates could not be satisfied with this distant, impersonal connection with Pitt. To make their patriotism truly British, they must have Scottish connections too. The third Earl of Bute seemed ideally cast for their purposes. As the confidant of the young Prince of Wales, Bute was still waiting in the political wings, and was not yet an open rival of Pitt. But it was widely expected that Bute would before long succeed to Pitt's position as Patriot statesman; and it could be assumed that he would at the same time take over from the aging Duke of Argyll as the political manager of Scotland. With such apparent prospects, fellow Scots might well imagine that Bute would have a unique opportunity to realise in his own person the Patriot ideal of a national, non-party British government. Sharing this fancy, the Moderates were gratified to discover that Bute was a willing patron of their endeavours and persons. Like Pitt, but showing more enthusiasm, Bute was brought into the reading of John Home's plays. Following the success of *Douglas*, it was Bute who enabled Home to escape the Kirk by an appointment as Bute's private secretary and tutor to the Prince of Wales. Shortly afterwards, Home helped arrange for Bute to take Ferguson too under his wing, as tutor to his own son, Lord Mountstuart.[75] Bute's patronage was all the more welcome in that it seemed to involve a communion of ideas, Bute having both the leisure and the inclination for moralising correspondence. With Home in particular Bute sealed his connection by effusive professions of personal friendship and Patriot ideals; Home was apparently encouraged to reply in kind, making Bute the grateful recipient of a steady stream of elevated nonsense. The subject of arms roused Home to the highest flights. He longed, he informed Bute early in 1759, to attend the earl as his esquire or armour bearer on perilous expeditions. By August of the same year it was no expedition, but the defence of Scotland itself that was stirring him: 'no poet that ever foamed with inspiration can express the grief and indignation of those Scots that still love their country, to find themselves disarmed'.[76]

For all the high words, the clerical, bourgeois Moderates could not hope to be truly familiar with a London-domiciled aristocrat like Bute. Far more genuine was the intimacy they enjoyed with a circle of Scottish gentry politicians. James Oswald of Dunnikier, William Mure of Caldwell and Gilbert Elliot of Minto. Defying the reputation of Scottish MPs for slavish adherence to the Duke of Argyll and the government of the day, these three had seen in the drift from old-style Whiggery to broad-bottomed Patriotism the opportunity to shape for themselves a relatively independent political course. Entering parliament in the 1740s, both Oswald and Mure had early displayed opposition sympathies. Subsequently Oswald took government office, and remained there throughout the 1750s, largely because he preserved his independence from any major interest. Mure was meanwhile joined by Elliot, who was elected to parliament in 1753, in charting a course specifically towards Pitt and Bute. Mure became Bute's Scottish estate and election agent, and Elliot a correspondent and confidant of the Patriot earl still more extravagant — if possible — than John Home.[77] Pursuit of a political career in the metropolis did not, however, cut these gentry off from Scotland; generally they were able to spend several months of the year on their estates and in Edinburgh, and there the Moderates could enjoy their company on close and relatively equal terms. Relations with Elliot were closest of all, going back to the classes they attended together at Edinburgh University. As an elder in the General Assembly, Elliot was an active participant in the Moderates' initiatives on patronage in 1751–52, and he was again to the fore in the row over *Douglas* in 1757.[78]

On the basis of such acquaintance the Moderates gave the gentry every encouragement and exhortation in their political endeavours, corresponding freely on contemporary affairs.[79] And one point in particular which they urged on the gentry was the importance of martial values and a militia. It was in a letter to James Oswald that John Home made the remark, quoted earlier, about the Scottish genius tending to arts and arms: it occurred, however, in the context of a frank lament over Scotland's present unmartial state:

> The spirit of trade and manufactures runs high in this country. I wish that our political regulations kept pace with those that promote our wealth. We are in danger of becoming *populus mercatorum, sine armis et ingenio*. The Scotch genius tends altogether to arts and arms, and must be dragged by necessity (the necessity which luxury imposes) to commerce....[80]

Elliot received similar counsel from the same correspondent in 1756: congratulated on his adherence to Pitt, he was also advised that Pitt could do nothing without a militia.[81] Within just four years, the Moderates would again be urging Elliot to favour the cause of a militia — and then it would be one for Scotland.

While the approach of the Moderate literati to the militia issue in the 1750s was thus primarily cultural and political, David Hume's invitation to recognise the issue's potential intellectual significance was not ignored. One forum for the more general discussion of the issue in relation to the progress of society was provided by the Select Society, of which the Moderates were prominent members. Possibly on the basis of Select Society discussions, moreover, two pamphlets on the issue were written by Scotsmen in the 1750s, both of whom were prepared to set the subject in a theoretical framework. One of these, by Robert Wallace, was in a distinctively Humean vein; but the other, by the Moderate Adam Ferguson, can be seen to have pursued a fresh approach.

Perhaps the most famous institution of enlightened Scotland, the Select Society of Edinburgh was founded in 1754 by a small group of fifteen literati, apparently on the initiative of Allan Ramsay, David Hume and Adam Smith. Intended to be select, the Society was soon inundated with applications for membership from gentry and lawyers as well as literati: by 1759 the numbers had risen to some 135, despite the rejection of a significant proportion of applications. Recent studies have emphasised the remarkable homogeneity of the membership. Not only were many related to each other, but the great majority of landed members were heirs-apparent. Bringing together the literati and the young of the ruling élite as virtual equals, it was a body, in short, whose membership could confidently look forward to becoming the leaders of Scottish culture and society at large.[82]

The purpose of the Select Society was debate, which was to be conducted within strict formal rules: there was to be no interrupting of speakers, and no naming of anyone present. Members could propose any subject for debate, 'except such as regard Revealed Religion, or which may give occasion to vent any principles of Jacobitism'. In practice it would seem that the latter prohibition served to preclude almost any discussion of contemporary politics: none of the questions debated or accepted for debate relates to the political events, personalities or parties of the 1750s, or even, directly, to the creed of Patriotism. Comparatively specific issues might be set for discussion, but it is clear from the general tenor of the questions, which ranged over economics, politics, morals and culture, that the Society understood its concern to be with social progress in its broadest sense.[83] Regrettably there are no records of the actual debates, and there are obvious limits to the analysis which can be built on the evidence of the questions alone. Nevertheless, it has suggestively been argued that the outlook exemplified in both the questions discussed and the Society's constitution was characteristically practical, utilitarian — and Humean.[84] There can at least be no doubt that the debates took up very many of the subjects which Hume had explored in his *Essays* and *Discourses*; and they must also have provided the opportunity for the diffusion of the ideas circulating in Hume's informal circle of close friends. Whether or not Humean ideas were left unchallenged is another matter.

The general subject of national defence and military organisation was one to which the Society repeatedly returned, examining it from several different angles. On the first occasion, 2 April 1755, the question was quite specific: 'whether it is consistent with sound politics to allow British subjects to serve as mercenaries in foreign service?'[85] (A question, be it noted, in which 'British' very clearly means Scottish — and evincing a concern quite to the reverse of the English Patriot fixation with foreign mercenaries in British service.) Only three months later the central military and political question was posed directly: 'whether a standing army or a militia properly regulated be most advantageous for Great Britain?' Discussion of this took two sessions, on 23 July and 6 August.[86] Much the same pattern of debate recurred early in 1756. First, on 18 February , a particular aspect of the subject, whether soldiers or sailors should be engaged for life or for a fixed number of years, was considered.[87] A month later this was followed by a much more general question, discussion of which again took two sessions: 'whether a nation formed for war, or a nation formed for peace be most happy?'[88] At the end of 1756, in a move coinciding with the re-introduction of the English Militia Bill in the House of Commons and the public agitation in its favour, the Society chose to return to the question of the comparative advantages of a standing army and a militia, which it had first debated in the summer of the previous year. The same subject continued to be set for several meetings in January 1757, but the Minutes would indicate that this was because poor attendances prevented its proper discussion.[89] Thereafter the subject was in fact dropped altogether for two years. On 6 February 1759, however, an interesting new question was set, and debated over two sessions: 'Whether a commercial and military spirit can subsist together in the same nation?'[90] And in November of the same year a variant of the standing army-militia question was tried: 'Whether in the present state of Europe a nation might subsist without a standing army?' Two weeks were required for this also.[91] Finally, in July 1760, the Society returned to the more recent question of the compatibility of a commercial and military spirit in one nation.[92]

Even without reports of the actual debates, the catalogue of questions bearing on national defence does point to a number of conclusions. At the least it attests to the degree of interest which the subject held for Select Society members. It is clear from comparative examination of other questions that no subject, except perhaps the laws of entail and succession on landed property, occupied so much of the Society's time.[93] Hume's lesson that the problems of defence and military organisation were central to an understanding of social change would appear therefore to have been well learnt by the cultural and political leaders of Scottish improvement. At the same time, a shift of emphasis in the character of the questions may perhaps also be detected — from the institutional question of the comparative advantages of standing armies and militias, which preoccupied the Society in 1755 to 1757, to the moral problem of the compatibility of the commercial and military spirit, introduced in 1759–60. As other evidence, to which we shall now turn, makes plain, such a contrast in emphasis certainly did emerge in Scottish thinking on the militia question in the 1750s.

The evidence which survives to make possible a fuller account of the ways in which the Scots were now considering the militia issue comes from two pamphlets, both written by Edinburgh literati. One was by Robert Wallace, a friend and intellectual correspondent of Hume, and a clergyman of an older generation than the Moderates. His 'Scheme for a Militia in Brittain' was not actually published, but a copy was sent to the Lord

Advocate in London in 1756, and it very probably circulated in Edinburgh.[94] The other tract, *Reflections Previous to the Establishment of a Militia*, was published, anonymously, in London in 1756; it was by Adam Ferguson, the Moderate.[95] Although the two pamphlets were framed as contributions to the English — or, as the Scots saw it, British — Militia debate, they both ignored partisan political considerations, and concentrated deliberately on the general principles which they believed the issue to raise.

Carefully weighing the various alternative forms of national defence, Wallace's 'Scheme for a Militia' might have been framed precisely to answer the Select Society's question whether a standing army or a militia be most advantageous to Britain. Wallace began by acknowledging the pressing threat of French invasion. France already had a great standing army and militia; and even if naval inferiority made it unlikely that she could actually conquer Britain at the moment, twenty years of peace would enable her to augment her resources until she had a fleet which was Britain's equal or superior. Britain's security therefore depended on having either a numerous standing army or a well-regulated militia in addition to the navy. Since a militia could not be formed at once, the standing army must be maintained for the present. This, Wallace argued, involved no immediate danger: under existing regulations and the reigning royal family, there was little prospect of the army's subverting the constitution for perhaps a century. If a standing army must ultimately be considered dangerous, however, a militia should gradually be formed to replace it. What Wallace had in mind was a scheme for the universal military training of the population. He envisaged the compulsory training of youth in 'the mechanical part of fighting ... everything in short but downright killing', followed subsequently by a few days' mustering and exercising a year. The force would naturally be officered by the nobility and gentry, since these would likewise be educated to war. Wallace claimed three advantages for such a militia. It would be no more expensive than the present standing army. It would be no danger to the constitution as long as the crown appointed the officers and arms were held in safe-keeping. Above all, a universal militia would have the advantage of numbers over any invader. It need be supplemented only by a small regular force for garrison and guard duties, and in wartime by small continental expeditionary forces to ensure that some of the nation's soldiers had experience of actual fighting.

A further alternative which Wallace considered was a 'partial' militia of 100,000 men, taken wholly from their labour and dispersed around the country. Although this would be a strong defence, Wallace believed that it could not be as strong as a universal militia, and must be expensive. In any case the concept of a 'partial' militia was questionable. Either the period of service would be unlimited, in which case such a militia would be effectively a standing army. Alternatively, if there was a rotation of service, there would be universal military training, and hence no need to constitute a select militia. For, Wallace claimed, once the whole people are 'put upon a par' and trained to arms, '. . . . we are safe, absolutely safe, as far as human affairs will allow, without any militia at all'.[96]

Pedestrian and disorganised though the pamphlet is to read, Wallace's arguments do seem to embody a particular perspective, with recognisably Humean features. The 'Scheme for a Militia' does not of course restate Hume's analysis in its entirety: for both its moral and its economic dimensions are missing. (The choice of the most economic form of defence is of concern to Wallace, but there is no recapitulation of the economic principles elaborated in Hume's *Political Discourses.*) What is restated in Wallace's tract is specifically the Humean view of the significance of different forms of military organisation for the institutional structure of society. Like Hume, Wallace is concerned to identify the form of defence which will provide the greatest security whilst matching the institutional requirements of free government. Like Hume too, Wallace continues to find the solution to this problem in the concept of a militia, that is, the active participation of citizens in their nation's defence. Wallace's general perspective, in short, remains in line with that of the civic tradition, and, in its institutional emphasis, with the perspective of the civic tradition's distinctive Scottish exponent, Andrew Fletcher.[97]

But if Wallace thus reproduce's Hume's ultimate allegiance to the institutional concepts of the civic tradition, he does so with critical, Humean, modifications. First, there is a familiar scepticism to Wallace's projections: in the Humean manner he carefully distinguishes the short from the long term, and emphasises the importance of gradual change. Thus, in the face of apparently imminent invasion, it would be foolish to discard the standing army when it clearly presented no immediate constitutional danger. Equally it would be short-sighted to imagine that a 'partial' militia (of the type actually being proposed by English Patriots) would provide a real alternative. In the long run, universal military service was the only satisfactory solution, but its introduction must be gradual. Balancing such prescriptive scepticism, however, is the implicit social radicalism of a commitment to eventual universal military service. The traditional civic concept of a militia presupposed the limitation of citizenship and the permanent exclusion from service of subordinate social classes. This Hume had challenged: the militia envisaged in the 'Idea of a perfect Commonwealth' points towards what was in effect a system of general conscription. Wallace's scheme for a militia appears to be similar in design: he too, it seems, believed that it would be desirable gradually to extend to all society's members the opportunity and obligation to participate in the nation's defence.[98]

By contrast, the second substantial Scottish treatment of the militia question in the 1750s, Adam Ferguson's *Reflections Previous to the Establishment of a Militia,* points in quite another direction. For the focus of Ferguson's concern was very different. Where Wallace had seen the problem as one of deciding between alternative military institutions,

Ferguson would appear to have anticipated another preoccupation of the Select Society, whether a commercial and military spirit can subsist together in the same nation. Using almost exactly those terms, Ferguson defined the critical issue to be faced before establishing a militia as that of educating the nation 'to mix the military spirit with our civil and commercial policy'.[99]

Ferguson's starting point was a conviction that the military spirit was now far more difficult to preserve than in earlier ages of European history. In the past, arts and commerce had been insignificant, government was founded on military subordination, and society was like 'a great army in cantonments'. Under those circumstances, a militia was demonstrably superior to a standing army. But recently the manners of society had altered. The administration of justice had been civilised by the prohibition of private feuds. Britain's island situation had diminished fears of foreign enemies. Most significant of all had been the influence of commerce. Wealth had so become the measure of distinction and honour in society that traders mixed on the same level as the gentry. For all men, even the gentry, the choice of a career was determined by consideration of its profit. In consequence, 'the profession of arms, so becoming the birth and standing of a gentleman, is not courted, because its profits are trivial'.[100] Advances in government, commerce and manners were all, Ferguson emphasised, perfectly beneficial in themselves; and they were not necessarily unfavourable to a militia. Nevertheless, Ferguson argued,

> .... self defence is the business of all: and we have already gone too far in the opinion that trade and manufactures are the only requisites in our country. In pursuit of such an idea, we labour to acquire wealth; but neglect the means of defending it. We would turn this nation into a company of manufacturers, where each is confined to a particular branch, and sunk into the habits and peculiarities of his trade. In this we consult the success of manufacture, but slight the honours of human nature: we furnish good work, but educate men gross, sordid, void of sentiment and manners, who may be pillaged, insulted, trod upon by the enemies of their country.[101]

Ferguson did not consider that Britain had yet reached that extremity. But the change in manners was such that a militia would be much more difficult to establish than ever before: the distribution of a few arms and a little training would be quite insufficient. It was necessary that the people be re-accustomed to the use of arms throughout life. To this end restraints such as the Game Laws should be lifted, and there should be legislation instead to require 'every family possessing a certain number of acres' to be able to arm one man. Ferguson hoped thereby to arm 'that part of the nation which is the least corrupted, and the most to be trusted with its internal peace'. Later in the pamphlet he made it clear that he had in mind the class of 'freeholders', and meant to exclude cottagers, day-labourers, servants and criminals. As for the gentry, who Ferguson assumed would take command, they should not need a law to compel them to serve: 'the bias of their situation' should lead them to do so naturally. Ferguson expressed the hope, however, that their education would be better directed.[102]

Ferguson then dealt with possible objections to such an arming of 'the people', as he termed those eligible for service. It would not, he maintained, encourage political factions, but would enable the loyal majority to suppress them. In particular the cause of the Pretender, supported as it was by only 'a few banditti from the mountains', would become desperate. Likewise there was no reason to suppose that a knowledge of arms among the people would facilitate the rise of popular leaders on the model of Caesar and Pompey: in fact it was from a standing army that they had derived their strength. Lastly, Ferguson discounted the fear that arming would encourage simple popular disorder: the modern spirit was not one of 'savage ferocity'.[103]

Ferguson did believe, however, that 'a proper degree of authority and subordination' must be established by the militia. By this he meant a structure of command and discipline which reflected the hierarchy of subordination in society at large. Officers should be appointed by the crown, and eligibility for rank made dependent on existing social status. Conversely militia officers should be at least the equal of those in the standing army, and should enjoy precedence among the civil nobility. The ordinary militia men should enjoy privileges of jury service and voting. Ferguson also indicated that he would not have the militia subject to strict military law, but would reward service by marks of honour, and punish offenders by dishonour. By thus exciting the principle of honour among militiamen, Ferguson hoped above all to prevent the great evil of substitution, by which arms were devolved upon 'the meanest', the 'least reputable class of the people'. For men in that condition, Ferguson urged in his conclusion, were simply incapable of attaining the sentiments proper to those who would defend society.[104]

How does Ferguson's perspective on the militia question differ from that of Wallace — and Hume? Clearly, Ferguson's concern that the nation should learn to mix the military spirit with its civil and commercial policy has redirected attention from the institutions to the manners of society. More, however, has been involved than a simple shift of emphasis: Ferguson's response to the underlying question whether a commercial and military spirit can subsist together is not a straightforward one. Ferguson, it is evident, is not convinced that the influence of commerce on the manners of society is naturally beneficial: by implication he thus challenges Hume's confident argument that luxury refines and improves men's values, civil and military. Yet Ferguson is not simply claiming that commerce corrupts: his tract is not a fatalistic and indiscriminate jeremiad after the manner of English Patriot moralists. Rather Ferguson appears to be arguing that commerce and the military spirit can subsist together — if only they remain independent of each other. Thus the benefits brought by commerce in undermining the Gothic society of the past are to be welcomed, but they should not be allowed to alter men's continuing adherence to traditional martial values. By his conception of the militia, Ferguson further seems to suggest that the separation of commerce from the military spirit must be embodied in the material structure of society. The restriction of militia service to freeholders and exclusion of the meanest, labouring classes point to a clear division of functions within society, with one class permanently engaged in economic activity while the other remains free to cultivate its military spirit. Only on such a basis, it is implied, can a modern nation both enjoy its wealth and preserve the values necessary to defend it.

In marked contrast though it was with the Humean perspective, Ferguson's view of the militia's significance in the progress of society was not altogether novel. For Ferguson also may be seen to have resumed and developed an aspect of Andrew Fletcher's legacy. Instead of the concern with the institutions of the political community inherited by Hume and Wallace, Ferguson would appear to have returned to Fletcher's preoccupation with upholding the characteristic social and moral assumptions of the civic tradition. Like Fletcher's, Ferguson's militia was designed both to confirm a clear social hierarchy of gentry, freemen and (excluded) servants, and to inculcate the practice of moral virtue. Yet while continuing to insist on these civic principles, Ferguson may also be seen to have added a fresh emphasis on the moral, at the expense of the institutional, significance of the militia. For this divergence other sources of inspiration may be held responsible. One is the moral philosophy which Ferguson and the other Moderates had learnt from their professors. In insisting on the continuing importance of the military spirit in a commercial age, and in urging the encouragement of that spirit by means of rewards rather than punishments, Ferguson was recognisably arguing in the manner of Hutcheson. A Scottish inspiration may also be identified for Ferguson's conviction that the values, as distinct from the social order, of the martial past were well worth preserving. As we have seen, this was a recurrent theme in Moderate writing: it was a conclusion, albeit tentatively drawn, of Robertson's *History of Scotland*; and it was the moral, pointed with vigour, of Home's *Douglas*. Its inspiration, however, is almost certainly to be found earlier, in the Union debate. No argument of Fletcher's, such a moralising emphasis on the martial values of old had then been the particular contribution of Lord Belhaven.

It was to be Alexander Carlyle's retrospective judgement that in Ferguson's 'very superior militia pamphlet', 'all the genuine principles of that kind of national defence were clearly unfolded'.[105] Insofar as it ignored the alternative, Humean perspective, this was of course a decidedly partial assessment; but from Carlyle's point of view it had considerable justification. For, as we shall now see, it was to be Ferguson's perspective which inspired those, Carlyle at their head, who sought a militia for Scotland.

NOTES

1. David Hume, *A Treatise of Human Nature*, ed. L. A. Selby-Bigge, second edition, revised by P. H. Nidditch (Oxford 1978), Book III, 'Of Morals', Part ii, Chs. 2–8, particularly pp. 539–41.

2. 'Whether the British Government inclines to Absolute Monarchy, or to a Republic', repr. in *David Hume. The Philosophical Works*, eds. T. H. Green and T. H. Grose, Vol. III, *Essays Moral, Political and Literary* (London 1882, repr. Darmstadt 1964), p. 124. Hereafter cited as *Philosophical Works*, III.

3. 'Of the Rise and Progress of the Arts and Sciences', *Philosophical Works*, III, pp. 183–4n.

4. 'Of Commerce', *Philosophical Works*, III, pp. 288–95.

5. 'Of Money', *Philosophical Works*, III, pp. 309–13.

6. 'Of the Balance of Trade', *Philosophical Works*, III, pp. 341–3.

7. 'Of Public Credit', *Philosophical Works*, III, pp. 364–6.

8. 'Of Taxes', *Philosophical Works*, III, pp. 356–60.

9. 'Of the Protestant Succession', *Philosophical Works*, III, p. 478n: Hume removed the comment in 1770. Hume in fact was to make a number of revisions, additions and excisions in the essays discussed here; but in line with the chronological form of this study, I shall consider them later, in Chapter 7.

10. 'Of Luxury', renamed 'Of Refinement in the Arts' in 1760, and so titled in *Philosophical Works*, III, pp. 300–7.

11. 'Public Credit', *Philosophical Works*, III, pp. 372–3.

12. 'Commerce', *Philosophical Works*, III, pp. 291–2.

13. 'Of the Populousness of Ancient Nations', *Philosophical Works*, III, pp. 385–6, 402–10.

14. 'Protestant Succession', *Philosophical Works*, III, p. 472.

15. 'Of Civil Liberty' (originally entitled 'Of Liberty and Despotism'), 'Rise and Progress of the Arts and Sciences', *Philosophical Works*, III, pp. 161, 186–7.

16. 'Of the Balance of Power', *Philosophical Works*, III, pp. 355–6. This elaborated a note in Hume's 'Early Memoranda 1729–40', ed. E. C. Mossner, and printed in *Journal of the History of Ideas*, IX, (1948), pp. 517–18: note no. [258]. Another of these notes, not used in Hume's published work, runs: 'The Empress of Russia lately rais'd a Militia of 50,000 men at one in 105', p. 507, note [66].

17. 'Protestant Succession', *Philosophical Works*, III, pp. 472, 476.

18. 'Idea of a perfect Commonwealth', *Philosophical Works*, III, pp. 491–2.

19. 'Perfect Commonwealth', *Philosophical Works*, III, pp. 486, 490.

20. 'Of Some Remarkable Customs', *Philosophical Works*, III, pp. 379–81.

21. A. S. Foord, *His Majesty's Opposition 1715–1830* (Oxford 1964), p. 176.

22. [John Trenchard and Thomas Gordon,] *Cato's Letters*, 4 Vols. (London 1724), I, pp. 181–8, II, pp. 41–76, 106–20, IV, pp. 128–54. On Bolingbroke and Walpole: I. Kramnick, *Bolingbroke and his Circle: Politics and Nostalgia in the Age of Walpole* (Cambridge, Mass., and London 1958); Pocock, *The Machiavellian Moment*, pp. 480–6. Quentin Skinner, 'The Principles and Practice of Opposition: The Case of Bolingbroke versus Walpole', in ed. N. McKendrick, *Historical Perspectives. Studies in English Thought and Society* (London 1974), seems to me to exaggerate the importance of the army issue to Bolingbroke.

23. [Corbyn Morris,] *A Letter from a By-Stander to a Member of Parliament: Wherein is examined what Necessity there is for the Maintenance of a Large Regular*

Land-Force in this Island (London 1741, i.e. 1742 new style). Morris was later appointed Secretary of the Scottish Customs and became a friend of Hume's. *The Letters of David Hume*, I, p. 380.

24. Anon., *The Ancient and Present State of Military Law in Great Britain Considered* (London 1750); quotation on pp. 26–7. On the state of Martial Law: Sir William Holdsworth, *A History of English Law*, X, pp. 378–82.

25. Duncan Forbes, *Hume's Philosophical Politics* (Cambridge 1975), Preface, pp. vii, x.

26. Forbes, *Hume's Philosophical Politics*, pp. 126, 211–12.

27. 'Public Credit', *Philosophical Works*, III, pp. 371–4.

28. [Josiah Tucker,] *The Important Question Concerning Invasions, a Sea War, Raising the Militia, and Paying Subsidies for Foreign Troops* (London 1755), Parts III–IV. The tract was first published serially, in letters to the London *Evening Advertiser*; these were reprinted under the heading 'Subsidies or No Subsidies, That's the Question', in the *Edinburgh Evening Courant*, 27, 29 Nov., 2, 3, 11, 13 Dec. 1755.

29. This evidence of convergence in their approaches to the army issue is the more interesting in the light of the exchanges on matters of economic analysis which Tucker initiated with Hume in 1757. On these: I. Hont, 'The Rich Country — Poor Country Debate in Scottish Classical Political Economy', in Hont and Ignatieff (eds.), *Wealth and Virtue*. Though Tucker differed from Hume in using the argument of specialisation against the militia, it should be emphasised that he did not go on to make a positive case for the application of the concept of the division of labour to military organisation, as Adam Smith was to do.

30. The following analysis draws heavily on an interpretation of Hume developed and fully documented in my paper, 'The Scottish Enlightenment at the Limits of the Civic Tradition', in Hont and Ignatieff (eds.), *Wealth and Virtue*.

31. *Treatise of Human Nature*, Bk. III, Pt. ii, Ch. 7, pp. 534–9.

32. 'On the Independency of Parliament', 'Of Parties in General', *Philosophical Works*, III, pp. 118–19, 127–33.

33. For a broadly similar account of Hume's problem, cf. G. Giarrizzo, *David Hume Politico e Storico* (Turin 1962), pp. 24–5, 34–5.

34. 'Idea of a perfect Commonwealth', *Philosophical Works*, III, pp. 482–90; cf. for a pioneering analysis of the essay: Douglass Adair, '"That Politics may be reduced to a science". David Hume, James Madison and the *Tenth Federalist*', *The Huntingdon Library Quarterly*, XX (1956–7), pp. 349–52.

35. 'Perfect Commonwealth', *Philosophical Works*, III, p. 481. Significantly, Hume rejected the *Republic* of Plato and the *Utopia* of Thomas More as models because, in presupposing an extraordinary reformation of manners, they were 'plainly imaginary'. As in the case of Fletcher, there is more to be said about Hume's debt to and difference from utopian thinking.

36. 'Perfect Commonwealth', *Philosophical Works*, III, p. 492. Phillipson draws attention to this similarity between Fletcher's and Hume's models in 'Hume as Moralist: A Social Historian's Perspective', in S. C. Brown (ed.), *Philosophers of the Enlightenment* (Brighton 1979), pp. 150–1.

37. 'Perfect Commonwealth', *Philosophical Works*, III, p. 481. Cf. James Moore, 'Hume's Political Science and the Classical Republican Tradition', *Canadian Journal of Political Science*, X (1977), pp. 834–5.

38. 'Rise and Progress of the Arts and Sciences'; 'Civil Liberty', *Philosophical*

Works, III, pp. 177–86, 159–63. A range of comparative examples illustrated this general argument throughout the *Essays* and *Political Discourses*.

39. This may be the interpretation of Hume's cryptic note on the 'militia' raised by the Empress of Russia: see note 16 above.

40. [David Hume,] *A True Account of the Behaviour and Conduct of Archibald Stewart Esq., late Provost of Edinburgh, in a Letter to a Friend* (London 1748). On the circumstances of the pamphlet's production: E. C. Mossner, *The Life of David Hume* (Oxford 1970), pp. 182–6.

41. David Hume, *The History of Great Britain. The Reigns of James I and Charles I* (Edinburgh 1754), repr. ed. D. Forbes (Harmondsworth 1970), pp. 140–143.

42. For a major study of the Moderate literati as a group, covering their clerical careers, literary pursuits and ideology: R. B. Sher, *Church and University in the Scottish Enlightenment: The Moderate Literati of Edinburgh*. My understanding of the Moderates owes much to this and to correspondence with the author. The fundamental difference between us is that, through drawing a distinction between the Scottish Enlightenment and enlightened Scotland (above, p. 17), I take the Moderates as a group to belong in enlightened Scotland, and only individuals to have been members of the Scottish Enlightenment.

43. Alexander Carlyle, *Anecdotes and Characters of the Times*, ed. J. Kinsley (Oxford 1973), p. 29. These recollections were written in the last few years of Carlyle's life, before 1805, and were first edited for publication in 1860. Like any memoir written late in life, the *Anecdotes and Characters* has to be used with care. But as an account of the Moderate group, its outlook and development, the work is invaluable.

44. Duncan Forbes, 'Natural Law in the Scottish Enlightenment', in R. H. Campbell and A. S. Skinner (eds.), *The Origins and Nature of the Scottish Enlightenment* (Edinburgh 1982), pp. 189–90.

45. Peter Jones, 'The Scottish Professoriate and the Polite Academy 1720–1746', in Hont and Ignatieff (eds.), *Wealth and Virtue*. David Hume too of course designed in his 'Science of Man' to build a general, jurisprudential theory of society and politics on the foundation of an empirical theory of human nature. But the Humean conception of moral philosophy differed radically from that of the professors. Quite apart from removing God from the argument, Hume insisted on a distinction between 'moral anatomy' and 'moral painting' — between analysis and prescription; and, as we have seen, he continued to attach significance to the institutional dimension of politics. Just how incompatible Hume's approach to moral philosophy was with that prevailing in the universities was shown when virtually the entire academic establishment combined to block his appointment to the Chair of Moral Philosophy at Edinburgh in 1745.

46. Carlyle, *Anecdotes and Characters*, p. 36.

47. Francis Hutcheson *A System of Moral Philosophy*, 2 Vols. (Glasgow 1755), vol. II, Bk. III, Ch. ix, pp. 310, 317, 323–5.

48. Robbins, *The Eighteenth-Century Commonwealthman*, pp. 185–95.

49. John Home, *The History of the Rebellion in the Year 1745* (London 1802), pp. 65–122; Carlyle, *Anecdotes and Characters*, pp. 58–79.

50. Home, *History of the Rebellion*, pp. 97–8; Carlyle, *Anecdotes and Characters*, p. 59.

51. Home, *History of the Rebellion*, pp. 12–13.

52. Sher, *Church and University*, Ch. 1, insists on the importance of the experience. He has largely overcome my own previous scepticism on the point.

53. Adam Ferguson, *A Sermon Preached in the Ersh Language to His Majesty's First Highland Regiment of Foot, Commanded by Lord John Murray, the 18th day of December, 1745* (London 1746).

54. I. D. L. Clark, 'From Protest to Reaction: The Moderate Regime in the Church of Scotland 1752–1805', in Phillipson and Mitchison (eds.), *Scotland in the Age of Improvement;* Sher, *Church and University*, Ch. 2.

55. Mossner, *Life of Hume*, pp. 274–8, 336–69; Sher, *Church and University*, Ch. 3.

56. John Home to James Oswald, 1 Aug. 1750: in *Memorials of the Public Life and Character of the Right Hon. James Oswald of Dunnikier, contained in Correspondence* (Edinburgh 1825), pp. 110–11.

57. William Robertson, *The History of Scotland during the Reigns of Queen Mary and King James VI*, 2 Vols. (London 1759), Vol. I, pp. 1–6.

58. *History of Scotland*, I, pp. 12–21, 32.

59. *History of Scotland*, I, pp. 21–32.

60. *History of Scotland*, I, pp. 33–64.

61. *History of Scotland*, III, pp. 249–60.

62. Franco Venturi, 'Tra Scozia e Russia. Un dibattito settecentesco sul feudalesimo', in *Russia, Studi e Ricerche*, ed. Vittorio Strada (Turin 1974).

63. *History of Scotland*, III, p. 250.

64. Carlyle, *Anecdotes and Characters*, pp. 119, 152, 157–65.

65. John Home, *Douglas. A Tragedy*, repr. in *The Works of John Home*, 3 Vols. (Edinburgh 1822), Vol. I, pp. 291–2.

66. *Douglas, Works of Home*, I, p. 346.

67. *Douglas, Works of Home*, I, p. 301.

68. *Agis. A Tragedy. Works of Home*, I, p. 191.

69. John Brewer, *Party Ideology and Popular Politics at the Accession of George III* (Cambridge 1976), pp. 96–101. The terms Patriot and Patriotism are used hereafter with capitals but without inverted commas as indicating a specific political outlook, distinct from ordinary patriotism.

70. W[illiam] T[hornton], *The Counterpoise, being Thoughts on a Militia and a Standing Army* (London 1752). Thornton was an independent MP for York; he introduced a militia bill in 1752. For a fuller survey of the military and constitutional arguments for a militia in the mid-eighteenth century: Western, *The English Militia in the Eighteenth Century*, pp. 104–17. Western perhaps underestimates the changes in the case.

71. [Thornton,] *The Counterpoise*, Preface and pp. 24–5.

72. John Brown, *Estimate of the Manners and Principles of the Times* (London 1757), pp. 87–102; [Edward Wortley Montagu,] *Reflections on the Rise and Fall of the Ancient Republics, adapted to the Present State of Great Britain* (London 1759), pp. 378–83.

73. William Pitt to James Oswald, n.d. 1750, Oswald to John Home, 15 June 1750: *Oswald's Memorials*, pp. 97–106, 112–114.

74. Alexander Carlyle, *Plain Reasons for Removing a Certain Great Man from his Majesty's Presence and Councils for Ever*, by O. M. Haberdasher (London 1759). The title mimicked the motion to remove Walpole in 1741. The pamphlet was abstracted in the *Scots Magazine*, XXI (March 1759), pp. 165–6; and Carlyle himself remembered it as having 'a great run', *Anecdotes and Characters*, p. 195.

75. Home to Bute, 27 April 1755 and 7 August 1757. Bute Papers, Mount Stuart, 1755: no. 38 and 1757: no. 107.

76. Home to Bute, 3 Feb., 26 Aug. 1759, Bute Papers, Mount Stuart, 1759: nos. 14, 147. The character which encouraged such outpourings is nicely caught by Alexander Murdoch, '*The People Above*': *Politics and Administration in mid-Eighteenth Century Scotland* (Edinburgh 1980), pp. 85–6.

77. See their respective biographies in the volumes of *The History of Parliament*: R. Sedgewick (ed.), *The House of Commons 1715–54*, 2 Vols. (London 1970), II, pp. 282–3 (Mure), and 314–15 (Oswald); and L. Namier and J. Brooke (eds.), *The House of Commons 1754–90*, 3 Vols. (London 1964), II, pp. 390–4 (Elliot), III, pp. 181–82 (Mure) and pp. 237–40 (Oswald). For a specimen of Elliot's epistolary eloquence: letter to Bute [Aug.], 1755: Bute Papers, Mount Stuart, 1755: no. 47.

78. Carlyle, *Anecdotes and Characters*, pp. 22, 125–8, 161–2.

79. It should be noted that Oswald, Mure and Elliot were also close friends and correspondents of David Hume. But with him their correspondence was almost entirely literary and intellectual. As Forbes has commented, *Hume's Philosophical Politics*, pp. 127–34, Hume's letters before 1760 contain only fleeting references to contemporary political developments, and no trace of enthusiasm for Pitt, Bute or Patriot causes. After 1760, Hume was openly critical of all three.

80. Home to Oswald, 1 August 1750: *Oswald's Memorials*, pp. 110–11.

81. Home to Elliot, 5 November 1756: NLS Ms. 11008, ff. 16–17.

82. R. L. Emerson, 'The Social Composition of Enlightened Scotland: the Select Society of Edinburgh 1754–64', *Studies on Voltaire and the Eighteenth Century*, CXIV, pp. 291–329; Phillipson, 'Culture and Society in the Eighteenth-Century Province', in Stone (ed.), *The University in Society*, II, pp. 444–5.

83. 'Book of Rules and Minutes of the Select Society. With the Book of Questions, Lists of Members and Notes of Apology': NLS Advocates Ms. 23.1.1. The Minutes record the questions discussed, and the Preses of each meeting.

84. Phillipson, 'Culture and Society', pp. 445–6; and 'The Scottish Enlightenment', in Porter and Teich (eds.), *Enlightenment in National Context*, pp. 31–3.

85. 'Book of Rules and Minutes', pp. 55–6.

86. Ibid., pp. 60–3.

87. Ibid., pp. 83–4.

88. Ibid., pp. 86–7: debated on 17 and 24 March. On the first occasion attendance was low, and it was therefore decided to continue the debate in order to give absent members an opportunity of speaking on 'so curious a question'.

89. 'Book of Rules and Minutes', pp. 92–5. First set for 7 December, the discussion had to be continued through 14, 21, 28 December 1756, and 4, 11, 18 January 1757. On most of these days it seems unlikely that there was any debate at all. Such relative indifference at a time when the English Militia agitation was coming to a head underlines the non-political character of the Select Society. The situation required the establishment of a committee 'to revive the spirit of the society'.

90. Ibid., pp. 132–4.

91. Ibid., pp. 143–6: debated 27 November, 4 December, 1759.

92. Ibid., pp. 156–7.

93. Entails, primogeniture and the succession of females were all debated in 1755, and debt on landed property in 1756; entails were discussed again in 1757 and 1759, and female succession in 1758. Ibid., pp. 40–44, 67–9, 72–4, 80–83, 100–101, 111–13, 140–41.

94. Ms. Copy among Wallace's papers in EUL Ms. La.II.620[6].

95. This attribution is generally recognised. Carlyle mentions the pamphlet without giving its title in *Anecdotes and Characters*, p. 204, as does Hume in a letter to Elibank, 30 April 1757, in 'New Hume Letters to Lord Elibank 1748–1776', ed. E. C. Mossner, *Texas Studies in Literature and Language*, IV (1962), p. 441.

96. This exposition of 'A Scheme for a Militia' is a condensation and reorganisation of the whole, which is not clearly arranged. The quoted phrases occur on pp. 7, 16, 19.

97. 'That worthy Patriot and ingenious inquirer into political institutions', as Wallace himself elsewhere described Fletcher: *A Dissertation on the Numbers of Mankind in Ancient and Modern Times* (Edinburgh 1753), p. 88n.

98. Wallace did not, however, integrate his militia scheme into his own 'model of a perfect government' in his *Various Prospects of Mankind, Nature and Providence* (London 1761). This was in fact a utopia of the sort Hume had criticised and rejected in his essay, postulating a strict agrarian law and publicly enforced morals. In suggesting that Wallace adopted a Humean perspective on the militia question, therefore, I do not imply a more general harmony of views.

99. [Adam Ferguson,] *Reflections Previous to the Establishment of a Militia* (London 1756), p. 3.

100. *Reflections Previous*, pp. 4–9.

101. Ibid., p. 12.

102. Ibid., pp. 15–19, 50.

103. Ibid., pp. 21–30.

104. Ibid., pp. 30–53.

105. Carlyle, *Anecdotes and Characters*, p. 204.

4

The Scottish Militia Agitations
of the Seven Years' War

The Moderates' opportunity came at last in the winter of 1759–60. With a small French squadron threatening the Scottish coasts, the question of the country's defences became urgent. Rising eagerly to the occasion, Alexander Carlyle contributed a forceful pamphlet placing the militia issue in a broad political and social perspective. At the same time an agitation developed in the burghs and counties of Scotland, in support of a Scottish Militia Bill to be moved in Parliament by the Scottish MPs. That bill failed, but having once broken the ice, the Moderates and their allies lost no subsequent opportunity to press their case. There was a second chance early in 1762, just before the conclusion of the Seven Years' War; and the outbreak of the American War thirteen years later brought further opportunities. There was pressure for some form of additional defence in Scotland almost every year between 1775 and 1782; and Carlyle and his fellow Moderates renewed their propaganda efforts. This round of agitation lasted until the winter of 1782–83, when — even with peace in sight and a severe grain shortage at home — a final concerted effort by the militia's champions succeeded in eliciting a response in the localities as widespread and enthusiastic as ever.

My object in the present and the following chapters is to supply a narrative of these successive Scottish militia agitations of the Seven Years' and American Wars. In each case I shall combine exposition of the arguments presented by the militia's advocates, the Moderate literati in particular, with an account of the response to the demand in the localities and at Westminster. To avoid making the narrative unwieldly, however, I have not attempted in these chapters to analyse the response to the demand in relation to the arguments of the militia's advocates. The assessment of the extent to which the case for a militia struck a chord in Scottish political and social consciousness is reserved for the subsequent chapter on the achievement of the agitations.

The pamphlet with which Alexander Carlyle hailed the demand for a Scottish militia was entitled *The Question Relating to a Scots Militia Considered. In a Letter to the Lords and Gentlemen who have concerted a form of law for that establishment.* Ostensibly by 'A Freeholder' of Ayrshire, it was written by Carlyle at the prompting of Adam Ferguson and William Johnstone (a young advocate), and was read over by William Robertson; it appeared in mid-January 1760.[1]

The pamphlet opened by linking the case for a Scottish militia to the recent re-establishment of the militia in England. For almost half of the work Carlyle reflected on the circumstances in which the new English militia had been secured, and the traditional principles from which he believed it to derive. At the beginning of the present wars, Carlyle observed, Britain had relied only on the 'artificial' strength of the navy and standing army for defence. In consequence the whole country had been disgraced in 1745, when 'five thousand undisciplined militia from the most remote parts of the Kingdom' had spread terror to within a hundred miles of the capital, while the body of the people, who could have quelled the 'pitiful insurrection' within a week, were without the means of defence. At last, however, successive defeats had awakened 'the patriot spirit of England'. The Minister whose praises Carlyle had recently sung in *Plain Reasons for Removing a Certain Great Man from His Majesty's Councils* had restored England's 'natural' strength by trusting to the industry and bravery of its people. The re-establishment of the English militia under his aegis was enough, Carlyle believed, to obviate the need to look either to ancient times or abroad for examples to follow. Though 'engaged in commerce far beyond all the ideas of antiquity, and sunk in luxury that seemed to forebode a falling empire', England had shown that it was still possible for a free nation 'to mix the military spirit with our civil and commercial policy', and by means of a militia to secure itself equally against domestic tyranny and foreign invasion.[2]

England set such an example, Carlyle continued, because it had acted on the views of those 'speculative men, the friends of liberty', whose writings so abounded in proofs of the fatal effects of standing armies and of the superiority of free, armed peoples. In particular Carlyle quoted 'the renowned Fletcher of Saltoun' on the fundamental principle that possession of arms distinguishes the freeman from the slave. 'True distinction', Carlyle added,

> which will obtain while there are freemen and slaves. To be actually in bonds is not to be a slave, for that has happened to men of the noblest minds. But to be of a base, a dastardly and servile spirit, to want the desire and capacity of self-defence, that is to be a slave; for these vile qualities bring a man under the will and power of everyone who thinks it worthwhile to command him.

For all their clearness and certainty, such fundamental principles had indeed been almost forgotten since the Revolution. But necessity — the fear of invasion — had at last compelled their recognition. The 'spirit or force' which in every free government dictates salutary laws in cases of necessity had been activated; and men had only had to look back to 'the original principles of the constitution' to find a militia.[3]

Carlyle was quick, however, to qualify the argument from principle by emphasising that he did not seek a militia to replace the standing army. Rather he maintained that the militia would strengthen the army both through the extension of military training, at no expense in peacetime, and by stirring a spirit of emulation. As 'the manners of a nation have an irresistable influence over the mind', none would dare to be cowardly when all were supposed to be brave. Having thus made it clear that he was not anti-army, Carlyle then dealt with two important objections to a militia. One was the charge that a militia was contrary to the interest of a commercial nation. To this Carlyle replied that security was a necessary condition of trade, and that a militia removed less labour than a standing army. A militia, indeed, would foster industry: in the most industrious republic known to nature, the republic of the bees, every citizen is in arms, and the drones, who have no sting, are expelled as useless to society. The second objection was that a militia was inefficient, because it was not a man's sole profession. Against this, however, Carlyle pointed out that a militia was not as the Trained Bands of Edinburgh: it was truly 'an army of the people', equipped and trained as the regulars, and yet composed of 'sober and virtuous men', whose officers were 'gentlemen of the highest rank and greatest property in the country'. Fighting in defence of their fortunes, their families, their religion and their liberty, militiamen could not but excel hired soldiers in valour.[4]

Only after he had stated his general principles did Carlyle come to Scotland. Why, he now demanded, had the Scots been denied the benefit of the Union in this important article? The Scots had every right to share with the English 'the highest privilege of Britons'. It was not as if the ancient Scottish spirit was quite extinguished:

> The genius of the Scotch never shone with greater lustre than now: in war and in letters we have acquired our share of glory, and our generous fellow-subjects of England meet us half-way in every step we take towards the full completion of the Union.

Almost immediately, however, Carlyle struck another note. The Scots, he admitted, did not share 'that quick sense of liberty, which animates our countrymen beyond the Tweed'. National spirit was hardly yet diffused among the commons, who were accustomed to put implicit trust in their superiors; and those of rank and power in the country had taken no step to secure the most important right of freemen and Britons. Scotland might not be 'a province and a conquered Kingdom'. But, Carlyle would know, 'what avails it that we are free and independent, while we create to ourselves racks and bow strings in the fear of offending, and wear chains and fetters in servility of mind?'[5]

The tension between Scotland's entitlement to a militia under the Union and Carlyle's sense of the Scots' unwillingness to claim their due persisted through the remainder of the pamphlet. Had arms been explicitly excluded from the Fourth Article of the Union, communicating all the rights, privileges and advantages enjoyed by the subjects of each kingdom, it was not impossible, Carlyle conceded, that some in the Scottish parliament would have glossed the affront as a favour. They would have argued, Carlyle supposed, that the Scots had been too long addicted to arms, and needed to devote themselves to the arts of peace. Carlyle's response was to imagine the retort of 'the gallant Fletcher'. 'By arms (he supposed Fletcher would have said) and by arms alone, our ancestors sustained the reputation and power of this Kingdom.... It is by arms alone that we can preserve to ourselves a name among nations.' Manners and sentiments had of course greatly changed since the Union; but, Carlyle averred, no softness of manners should dispose men to brook the disgrace now lying on Scotland. For all his hearty approval of the Union, Carlyle felt obliged to conclude that if a Scottish militia bill did not pass, 'it had been good for Scotland, that there had been no Union'.[6]

It was above all the apathy of the county freeholders, as men of 'independent fortunes and good education', which Carlyle was anxious to overcome. If these could once be aroused on national points, Carlyle believed that there was no body of men in Great Britain capable of a more 'unconquerable integrity'. To spur them on Carlyle urged the calling of county meetings such as Ayrshire had recently held, and the sending of instructions to Scottish members of parliament. Elections, he pointed out, were due next year, and should be treated as were elections to the magistracy of ancient Rome — an opportunity to make an example of those who betrayed their country for pensions and places, and to reward those who served it well. But if the electors did not then put a mark of disgrace on any who dared to be cold or neutral on the militia question, then indeed it would be time to renounce the name of Scotchman, as equivalent to that of slave.[7]

Carlyle was hopeful that the application for a Scottish militia being made, it would be welcomed by English militia supporters and by an administration keen to prosecute the war. If doubts did persist in England, Carlyle would allay them by underlining the threat to Scotland from the French squadron still at sea; and he added that Scotland had even more need of a militia than England, since the latter, as the seat of wealth and empire, had the first call on the army. Carlyle was also at pains to deny that arming a militia in Scotland would lead to a repetition of the 'Forty-Five Rebellion. The friends of liberty and the government, who were overwhelmingly preponderant in the presbyterian Lowlands, had then been powerless to resist the clans; for their part, the Highlanders had since been reclaimed to loyalty. Here again, however, Carlyle struck a qualifying note. The Scots might be as loyal as any to the Hanoverians; but they were not all true to their own country. Scotland, Carlyle admitted, had always bred 'a race of fawning miscreants', who built their fortunes on the discredit of their country: these were now factiously spreading 'the odious and false imputations of Jacobitism' in order to obstruct the militia. Sternly Carlyle warned such 'parricides', who would 'stab their mother to the heart', to beware 'the just resentment of all her faithful sons.'[8]

Carlyle closed the pamphlet with one more appeal to the nobility and gentry of Scotland. They must follow the example of the nobility and gentry of 'our sister country':

> Let it not be said that you only rival their follies, but fall behind in a love of liberty and independence. The commons of Scotland, by nature a bold and hardy race, inspired by your example, and encouraged by your protection, will soon recover that manly spirit which becomes a free people, and members of the British community. To them your countenance is an honour; your smiles are rewards; these you can bestow upon all. Superior merit will deserve more substantial favours. Industry itself, it is hoped, may be improved by this new institution: for whatever brings the people under the immediate care and inspection of their superiors, puts them in a situation the most favourable for virtue and good morals.[9]

Carlyle later remembered the pamphlet as enjoying a 'great and unexpected success', hitting the tone of the country at the time.[10] It was reproduced, in whole or in part, in several Scottish newspapers and journals;[11] and in London it appears to have been reprinted in two separate editions, both with prefaces, one of which was said to be by General George Townshend (who had moved the 1757 English Militia Bill).[12] But the best measure of the pamphlet's success is that it established the platform for the agitation for a Scottish militia not only in 1760, but again in 1762 (when it was reprinted once more), and even in the later period of the American War (when Carlyle would return to and develop his original arguments). In anticipation of this, it may now be helpful to pause and look more closely at the character and inspiration of the pamphlet's leading themes.

Carlyle himself would seem to have been anxious to establish the continuity of his arguments with those of earlier champions of a militia, and with Andrew Fletcher's in particular. It was to Fletcher, as one of those 'speculative men' of an earlier generation, that Carlyle appealed for the general principles underlying a militia. Still more telling in the Scottish context, it was to Fletcher, as the unwavering defender of his country's interest at the time of the Union, that Carlyle appealed for an assertion of the peculiarly Scottish association of prowess in arms with national spirit. On closer inspection, however, it can be seen that Carlyle's arguments were at once simpler and less Fletcherian in inspiration than these invocations of the patriot's name would suggest.

To begin with, it is clear that Carlyle did not think of the institution of the militia in the same terms as Fletcher. Despite the reference to Fletcher and the radical Whigs of his time, Carlyle's introductory statement of general militia principles endorsed the recent revision of the strict anti-army position by English Patriot advocates of a militia in the 1750s. Carlyle's concept of the militia was not the antithesis of the standing army but its complement, at once an inexpensive strategic reserve and a constitutional balance. This adoption of the diluted Patriot case for a militia points in turn to another un-Fletcherian characteristic of Carlyle's pamphlet, its acceptance of the institutional framework of the parliamentary Union of 1707. Fletcher had not indeed been against union with England, a form of which he believed essential; but he was adamant in opposition to a union of legislatures. A Scottish militia must therefore be the offspring and support of an independent Scottish parliament. But Carlyle, for all the invocation of Fletcher's memory, was quite prepared to accept a Scottish militia direct from Westminster, in the form of a straightforward extension of English law. Whether this was Carlyle's preferred model of a Scottish militia is uncertain: later, as we shall see, he was to champion a more specifically Scottish form. At the least, however, it is clear that Carlyle had no fundamental objection to an English institution.

It is unlikely that Carlyle would have regarded these differences from Fletcher as critical. For the important terms in Carlyle's arguments for a militia were not institutional but moral. And here Carlyle evidently supposed that there was a direct descent from Fletcher's arguments to his own. Such a conviction is not implausible: Fletcher had planned his militia to be 'as great a school of virtue as of military discipline'. But it none the less overlooks the traditional civic conceptual structure in which Fletcher's proposal was set. For Fletcher the militia would be a school of virtue precisely because it was conceived as a political institution, the military arm of a free constitution: the virtue it taught would be the virtue of participation in public life, the active exercise of political liberty. For Carlyle, by contrast, the virtue to be inculcated by the militia is a more general moral condition, relatively indifferent to the constitutional framework, while liberty is but a state of mind. The difference between the two perspectives is clearly seen at the very moment when Carlyle quotes directly from Fletcher, on arms-bearing as the distinction between a freeman and a slave. In Fletcher's civic terms slavery is a political condition of subjection to despotic power. But on Carlyle's gloss, a slave becomes simply 'a dastardly and servile spirit', who lacks 'the desire and capacity of self-defence'.

Further examination of Carlyle's specifically national case for a Scottish militia not only confirms the gulf separating him from Fletcher: it points to the more likely inspiration of his arguments. Of the two themes historically embodied in Scotland's martial heritage, national identity and independence and social solidarity between nobility and people, Carlyle devoted most attention to the first. Untroubled by the prospect of adopting an English institution, he was repeatedly exasperated by what he saw as the Scots' own 'servility of mind', their backward 'national spirit' in this matter of arms. So arguing, it was not Fletcher whom Carlyle echoed, but, I suggest, the Earl of Belhaven. Though Carlyle put the words into Fletcher's mouth, the claim that it was by arms that our ancestors had hitherto sustained the kingdom's reputation, and by arms that the present generation must preserve its name, was far more characteristic of Belhaven. Equally Belhavenian — to the point of repeating the image of parricide — was Carlyle's denunciation of those who betrayed their country by factious disunity. Following Belhaven, in short, Carlyle discarded Fletcher's strict civic insistence on the necessary interrelation of political institutions and national values: the case for a Scottish militia that Carlyle now advanced was framed in the simpler Stoic moralist terms that Belhaven had popularised. Carlyle's acceptance of the framework of parliamentary union was of course open, where Belhaven's had been reluctant and tacit; indeed Carlyle was frank in wishing 'to complete the Union'. But the Union would only be completed on the terms that Belhaven had originally stipulated. The Scots must continue to assert their national freedom and independence in the realm of the spirit, by remembering and renewing their ancient commitment to arms.

In two respects Carlyle may be seen to have given this national case for a Scottish militia emphases not found in Belhaven, but foreshadowed in the more recent preoccupations of the Moderate literati in the 1740s and 1750s. Where Belhaven had fatally overlooked the Jacobites' readiness to take up and activate the martial heritage, Carlyle was haunted by the memory of their rebellion in 1745. He was plainly anxious lest the English continue to identify all Scots in arms with Jacobites; but he was still more anxious lest the Scots themselves fail to recognise the shame they had incurred in resigning their arms to the hitherto despised Highland clans. It was a major purpose of Carlyle's call for a national militia to lay to rest the bogey of disloyalty, and to break the identification of Scotland's ancient martial values with the cause of Jacobitism. A second emphasis reflects the Moderates' commitment to Scottish literature in the 1750s, and their revival of the humanist theme of national prowess in both arms and letters. For Carlyle it was the Scots' distinction in war and letters which had been their particular contribution to the completion of the Union. Though unmentioned in Carlyle's pamphlet, there is almost certainly also — as R. B. Sher has pointed out — a connection between the call for a Scottish militia and the discovery of Ossian. For it was just as Carlyle was writing that the Moderate literati started encouraging their protégé James Macpherson to concoct the epic celebrating the most wonderful of all Scottish martial heroes: Ossian's *Fingal* (1761).[13]

The second theme long embodied in Scotland's martial heritage, social solidarity, surfaces only in the interstices of Carlyle's discussion of national independence. This was a theme less easily developed than that of national independence, since the 'Gothic' social order of the martial past had been subjected to fierce and virtually unanswered criticism in the Union debate by both Fletcher and the Unionists. But just recently Home's *Douglas* and Robertson's *History of Scotland* had suggested that the most strenuous condemnation of the social power of the old nobility need not preclude recognition of a laudable degree of cohesion between ranks; and signs of the same argument can be found in Carlyle's pamphlet. More generally, Carlyle may also be seen to have drawn on the language of the Scottish academic moral philosophy which the Moderate literati learnt at college, and on the particular application of that language to the militia issue by Adam Ferguson. On this basis, Carlyle was able at least to outline a social case for a Scottish militia as the essential moral accompaniment to the country's economic improvement. Though as yet only fragmentary, this social case, as we shall see, was to assume increasing importance.

As a general premise, Carlyle assumed that as 'the manners of a nation have an irresistable influence over the mind', so it was the militia's purpose to uphold manners against the dangers of luxury and corruption. But Carlyle was also ready to acknowledge that manners had changed greatly since the time of the Union, and to adjust the case for the militia accordingly. It was now necessary — Carlyle repeated the exact formula Ferguson had used in his pamphlet — 'to mix the military spirit with our civil and commercial policy'. Martial virtue and the spirit of industry, Carlyle insisted, were not only both required in modern society: they went together — a point he neatly illustrated by referring to the subjects of Mandeville's allegory of commercial values, the bees. Applying this general perspective to Scottish society, Carlyle then suggested that the key to securing improvement without either reverting to the old Gothic order or plunging into corruption was to use the militia to renew traditional relations of solidarity between ranks. By crediting the people with the values of freemen, the militia, it is implied, will make any revival of aristocratic tyranny impossible. At the same time, by setting the higher ranks (including both nobility and gentry) in a position to give an example to the lower, the militia will equally foster public virtue in the former and a spirit of industry in the latter. While the nobility and gentry assert their 'liberty and independence', the people will be under the 'care and inspection of their superiors', the situation most favourable for 'virtue and good morals'.

Carlyle's pamphlet did not itself initiate the agitation for a Scottish militia: as its full title implies, it was written to reinforce and provide the platform for an agitation that had already begun.

The story begins in the summer of 1759, when a captured dispatch revealed to the British government an ambitious French invasion strategy. While the major French thrust would be an invasion on the south coast of England, there was also to be a sizeable division in the West of Scotland, and the privateer commander Thurot was to make a series of preliminary coastal raids with a small squadron.[14] The scale of the threat was sufficient to prompt the government to embody the English militia, and it was recognised at the same time that something would have to be done in Scotland to supplement the small establishment of regulars already there. The politicians, however, disagreed about the best measure to adopt. The Earl of Bute and Gilbert Elliot appear to have favoured the immediate establishment of a Scottish militia on the lines of that in England. But the Duke of Argyll, who carried more weight, persuaded Pitt and the Duke of Newcastle — who was instinctively suspicious of a Scottish militia — to authorise only the raising of a small number of auxiliary regiments from well-affected Highland counties, in accordance with the existing laws of Scotland on arming. Argyll had in mind the precedent of the regiment of Argyllshire Fencibles he himself had raised in 1745: he now proposed raising three such regiments, in Argyll, Sutherland and Perthshire.[15] The proposal was not executed without difficulty and modification. The idea of a Perthshire regiment had to be dropped because of rivalry between the Duke of Atholl and the Earl of Breadalbane for the Lieutenancy; and there were problems recruiting the other two regiments.[16] In the end, however, both the Argyll and the Sutherland fencibles were raised, and were considered sufficient for Scotland's needs: offers by other Scottish nobles to raise similar regiments were firmly refused.[17]

Within Scotland it took an English politician, Charles Townshend, to provide the spark to set passion for a militia alight. A political maverick with only a minor government post (despite being Newcastle's nephew), Townshend had acquired an excellent Scottish connection through his marriage in 1755 to the Countess of Dalkeith, niece of the Duke of Argyll and widowed mother of the third Duke of Buccleuch, whose guardian Townshend thus became. Paying his first and only visit to Scotland in July and August 1759, Townshend successfully dazzled the small social world of Edinburgh, and at the same time aroused large political expectations. There was talk of his standing for Edinburgh at the next election, and even of his succeeding Argyll as political manager of Scotland. Townshend set the seal on his popularity when, in a speech of thanks for the freedom of Edinburgh on 18 July, he made a forceful appeal for a Scottish militia.[18] Excitement ran particularly high among the Moderate literati and their associates: when Townshend departed Scotland, he was pursued by letters from Alexander Carlyle and William Robertson, and from Lord Elibank and John Dalrymple (advocate, and author of a *History of Feudal Property*, 1758), assuring him of their personal loyalty and their commitment to the cause of a militia.[19]

The cause received a further boost when news came of Thurot's escape from Dunkirk in the middle of October 1759. According to reports, Thurot's squadron was made up of five men o'war and two cutters, transporting 1,500 soldiers, 15,000 pairs of shoes, and a store of arms and guineas. The expedition's destination was widely believed to be Scotland,

and its target was variously conjectured as the Tay or Inverness.[20] A small British squadron was detailed to watch for the French on the east coast, but accurate intelligence was slow to reach Scotland, provoking anxious speculation. It was mid-November before it was known that Thurot had actually sailed to Gothenburg in Sweden; and only then did it also become clear, after Hawke had defeated Conflans off Brest on the 14th of the month, that the rest of the French invasion plan could not be carried out. Even so, Thurot's whereabouts continued to exercise the Scots, and the next definite news (of a visit to Bergen early in December) was not received until January 1760.[21]

The Moderates took early advantage of the threat within their own domain, the Kirk. In October and November three clerical bodies, the Presbytery of Edinburgh, the Synod of Lothian and Tweeddale and the Commission of the General Assembly, despatched addresses of congratulations to the crown and its ministers on the recent victories — adding appeals for the Scots to be given arms and assurances of the loyalty of the country.[22] At the same time Carlyle and Robertson wrote effusively to Townshend describing their actions; and John Home wrote no less effusively to Bute. Exploiting the incipient rivalry of the two grandees, Home urged that Argyll's scheme of raising a few regiments of fencibles was 'odious' to the people and 'ruinous' to the hope for a militia.[23]

There was scattered agitation too in the localities, though here opinion tended for the moment to favour an extension of Argyll's proposals. Two east coast burghs, Aberdeen and Montrose, had requested arms for their inhabitants in the summer of 1759; on the west coast Ayr and Irvine followed suit in October.[24] Among the counties, Ayrshire was the first to act (thus earning the honour accorded it in Carlyle's pamphlet). On 3rd October 1759 a public meeting of nobility, freeholders, J.P.s, Commissioners of Supply and clergy of the county voted on address of congratulations to the crown, including a request for arms. Although the request was deliberately framed in general terms, the meeting's preses, the judge Alexander Boswell, Lord Auchinleck, wrote a covering letter to the Earl of Holderness, Secretary of State for the Northern Department, which discussed the alternatives under the existing laws of North Britain: Auchinleck himself gave first preference to the older law relating to fencible men.[25] Carlyle reported to Townshend that it was he who had kindled 'Old Affleck's' enthusiasm, but it seems likely none the less that Auchinleck was acting in Argyll's interest.[26] The Argathelian interest is also implicit in the proceedings in Berwickshire. Thither Auchinleck had immediately posted news of the Ayrshire meeting, and only a few days later Berwickshire came up with a vigorous address which explicitly invoked the 'ancient laws of Scotland', and reminded the crown that commissions of lieutenancy had recently been issued under those laws.[27] The address was signed by the Earl of Marchmont, as preses of the meeting; but it is clear that it had actually been carried by the rival party of Lord Home, who had been commissioned Lord-Lieutenant in 1756. That commission, which was exceptional, had been the work of Argyll, simply on purpose to spite Marchmont, his longstanding (though relatively ineffectual) antagonist. Marchmont was naturally humiliated to find that Lord Home's commission might now be activated, and quickly made his displeasure known to Newcastle through his brother, Alexander Hume-Campbell, the MP for Berwickshire. But although Marchmont adopted a posture of principled opposition to old, obsolete laws from before the Revolution, Newcastle was unimpressed, immediately recognising it as a 'personal altercation'.[28]

Despite the persistent uncertainty over the proper form of additional defence for Scotland, supporters of a militia finally succeeded in launching a national campaign at the end of November. On the 30th a general meeting of some seventy gentlemen of property was held in Edinburgh to consider an application for a national militia. Lord Milton was placed in the chair; and although he was Argyll's Scottish agent, he was described as having exerted the spirit of his ancestor, Fletcher of Saltoun, in the cause. At the meeting a committee was appointed, consisting of four peers (Errol, Dunmore, Gray and Elibank), six law-lords (Milton, Strichen, Auchinleck, Nisbet, Coalston and Alemoor), four young advocates (James Burnett, David Dalrymple, George Dempster and Adam Fergusson), the Lord Provost of Edinburgh (George Drummond), another magistrate and a merchant. The committee was to draw up a bill for a Scottish militia, which was to be presented to parliament. It was evidently decided at the meeting to ask for the extension of the English Militia Act to Scotland, rather than the revival of any old Scottish laws.[29] Seized with enthusiasm for what he professed to regard as 'the most important event of my time', one committee member, Lord Elibank, informed Charles Townshend of the success of his endeavours of the previous summer: Scotland was at last to enjoy 'real liberty'.[30] But there were others in London whom the news would be less likely to please. Well aware of this, Milton immediately sounded Argyll and succeeded to the extent of obtaining the Duke's qualified approval to the extension of the English Act — 'that is to say, of something similar, and more suitable to the laws and customs of Scotland'.[31] When report of the agitation reached Newcastle and Hardwicke, however, the response was positively unenthusiastic: a Scottish militia, they were convinced, would undermine all the reforms they had pursued in that country since the last rebellion.[32]

The committee appointed on 30 November proved businesslike but too discreet. By 8 January 1760 its proposals, in the form of a draft bill, were ready for Lord Milton to send copies south for circulation among Scottish and sympathetic English MPs.[33] This was done without publicity: Milton was anxious to avoid obtaining addresses or instructions from the counties. 'Most part of the people of best sense', he wrote to one supporter in England, were already in Edinburgh; and the absence of any objection to the proceedings of the committee could be taken to imply general approval.[34] The Scottish MPs, however, proved reluctant to act without positive word from their constituents, and for more than a month nothing was done with the committee's proposals.[35]

It took the combined forces of Carlyle's pamphlet, published at this time, and a landing by Thurot to bring the militia agitation out into the open. Thurot appeared at last on about 20 February, off Islay on the west coast. First reports had it that the French had detained two gentlemen, plundered local vessels and shot many cattle. Although this impression was later corrected — it appeared that Thurot had paid generously for provisions, before sailing off to Ireland, where his squadron was soon caught and destroyed — the news from Islay was sufficient to create what Milton could describe as a 'clamour' on behalf of a militia.[36] A spate of activity followed. First Edinburgh Town Council voted on 20 February to ask their MP to support the introduction of a Scottish Militia Bill.[37] The next day, the Annual Committee of the Convention of Royal Burghs decided to request all its members to send similar instructions to their representatives.[38] For its part the 30 November committee, meeting again on 23 February, considered framing a public address; but several of the judges apparently objected, and it was decided instead that Lord Milton should write to six MPs, Elliot, Townshend, Oswald, Hume-Campbell, Henry Erskine and Andrew Fletcher, urging them to concert the introduction of the proposed militia bill in the House of Commons. Evidently, however, the committee was either unable or unwilling to organise a canvas of the counties, for this required the convening of a further general meeting of freeholders and other gentlemen in Edinburgh. Held on 4 March, with Lord Errol in the chair (although Elibank is said to have stood at his elbow to direct him), this assembly finally took the decision to procure meetings in the counties, in order to send instructions to MPs.[39]

Milton's letters to the six MPs reached London on 28 February, eliciting a favourable response from all except Hume-Campbell, who questioned the propriety of establishing a caucus among Scottish MPs.[40] But by then Sir Gilbert Elliot had already taken an initiative of his own, having announced to the Commons on the 26th that he would shortly move for a committee to examine the present state of the militia laws of Scotland. This motion he introduced on 4 March with what Newcastle sourly described as 'a most pompous flaming speech'.[41] Pompous or not, it is clear from Elliot's papers that this and subsequent speeches were prepared with considerable care. He acknowledged a debt to Carlyle, and obtained additional information on Scottish law and the condition of the Highlands from Lord Milton and from a pamphlet by George Dempster.[42]

He began his first speech by emphasising the obscurity of the existing Scottish militia laws: before 1660 there had been only feudal obligations, while the Restoration Militia law was 'slavish' and 'ineffectual'. The new English militia, by contrast, Elliot made the subject of a fulsome panegyric, stressing its consistency with the principles of free government. He was able to sharpen the contrast still further by comparing the confidence with which England had faced France the previous summer with the terror into which Thurot had recently thrown Scotland. Well aware of English concern on the subject, Elliot then went into considerable detail on the state of the Highlands. Listing the changes introduced in the previous fifteen years, he argued that these now made it safe to introduce a militia throughout the country. He concluded by affirming his wish to propose a militia as nearly as possible analogous to the English, since this would make the Union more complete.[43] Elliot did not dwell on the Scots need for liberty and independence, the values which so exercised Carlyle: though that was hardly an appropriate theme for an assembly dominated by Englishmen, Elliot does give the impression of a more positive commitment to legislative and institutional assimilation than can be found in Carlyle.

Elliot's motion for a committee was vigorously seconded by Oswald in similar terms (although he was obliged to correct Elliot's claim that the only arrangements for arming before the Restoration had been feudal). George and Charles Townshend also spoke in support; and with an amendment from Hume-Campbell that the committee's brief be extended to all laws relating to arming, the motion passed without dissent.[44] When the House went into committee on 12 March the debate was sharper, as several young supporters of the Whig Old Corps raised objections to a Scottish militia. However, they rashly attacked the utility of militias in general, thus bringing Pitt and English militia supporters actively behind the Scots. In a vote the Scots won a comfortable victory by 91–43: Elliot was given leave to introduce a bill, and a committee of 31, including 26 Scottish MPs, was appointed to prepare it.[45]

The bill which the parliamentary committee quickly produced must have differed little from that prepared in Scotland by Milton's committee, that draft in turn being modelled closely on the recent English Militia Act. (Neither the Scottish committee nor the MPs showed any interest in Argyll's alternative suggestion of a force based on old Scottish laws.)

The English Act had of course to be altered to meet the most obvious legal and constitutional differences between the two countries, but these seem to have been minimised. The numbers were of course different, but the figure of 6,000 for a Scottish militia was proposed as proportional to England's 32,000. To prevent division of the force into excessively small units, it was envisaged that six of the lesser Scottish counties would be paired with larger neighbours under a single Lieutenancy. There were to be five Deputy-Lieutenants per county or pair of counties, and the qualifications for these and other officers were fixed, in pounds Scots, at a level rather lower than their English equivalents, because of the acknowledged lesser value of Scottish estates. Alterations were also necessary in the times of training, the arrangements for storing arms and the method of paying allowances, the responsibility for the last being divided between the parish heritors and the kirk session, with reimbursement from the county stock. Finally there were special, though limited, provisions for the Scottish burghs. Only Edinburgh was regarded as a separate Lieutenancy, the others being included in their respective counties. Provision was made for townsmen to hold commissions, the qualifications of real or personal estate being fixed in sterling; but it is clear that appointments would not, except possibly in Edinburgh, be made by magistrates.[46] Changes to these proposals were at one point canvassed in a meeting of Scottish MPs: it was suggested that numbers be raised to 10 or 12,000, and Hume-Campbell wished to have the Lieutenancy put in commission (no doubt an expedient to salve his family pride).[47] But such ideas were not pursued in the official Commons' committee.

The second reading of the Scottish militia bill was fixed for 15 April 1760, by which time it could be expected that opinion in Scotland would have made itself clear. The burghs, circulated in the last week in February, were the first to declare themselves, early in March. Sixteen responded — Edinburgh, Glasgow, Aberdeen, Stirling, Haddington, Dunbar, North Berwick, Dunfermline, Perth, Dundee, Cupar, Montrose, Nairn, Renfrew, Ayr and New Galloway — and all approved the militia demand.[48] Though less than a quarter of the total of sixty-seven Scottish royal burghs, these were burghs whose opinions could be said to count. Either substantial inland centres or small coastal ports, they were most immediately threatened by any hostile landing, and were of most economic and political consequence. Even so, Glasgow did not make up its mind until it heard Argyll's opinion (or Milton's version of it). And both Stirling and Aberdeen protested against what they saw as the proposal's neglect of burgh interests, objecting particularly to the precedence given to country gentlemen in the distribution of commissions.[49]

Later in March and early in April ten counties (out of a total thirty-three) added their opinion. Five — Ayrshire, Midlothian, Stirling, Perth and Forfar — decided to petition the House of Commons for a militia, while another four — East Lothian, Peebles, Selkirk and Renfrew — sent instructions to their representatives.[50] Again this was a significant minority, including important central Lowlands and Borders counties, though none from either the south-west or (Perthshire apart) the Highlands. The five petitioning counties echoed the arguments used by Elliot: the example of the English militia, the rights of Scotland under the Union, the defenceless state of the Scottish coasts, the loyalty of the people and the eradication of disaffection were all cited as good reasons for the establishment of a militia in Scotland.[51] Nevertheless, there is evidence of misgiving in the counties as in the burghs. One county, Fife, was actually reported to have declared against a militia;[52] and a long account of the Midlothian meetings in the *Caledonian Mercury* alleged that support in that county was far from unanimous. The report claimed that the meetings were ill-attended, that a large proportion of those present were not freeholders, and that the vote for a petition had been narrow.[53] Even though the balance of opinion in the counties was greatly in favour of the militia bill, events were to prove that such well-publicised dissent was disproportionately damaging.

Meanwhile canvassing was also under way at Westminster. Gilbert Elliot and Andrew Fletcher were rallying their fellow Scots, and were reasonably optimistic of winning the vote in the Commons at least.[54] But they now faced determined opposition from the Duke of Newcastle, whose resolve, which wavered briefly after the setback in the Committee of the Whole, was stiffened by explicit instructions from the King — 'Pray, throw it out'. Newcastle was also encouraged by the knowledge that Pitt had doubts about the wisdom of extending the militia to the Highlands. Accordingly Newcastle 'went to work in the old way', as he later described it to his old Scottish confidant, Lord Kinnoul. The campaign was planned at a dinner of Whig leaders at Newcastle House on 20 March, and a full-scale canvas of MPs arranged. In all, 331 were to be approached, Newcastle himself being responsible for 110, including 13 Scots. Lord Mansfield was to lobby his Scottish relations; and the Lord Advocate, who was no supporter of a Scottish militia, was to see three others. In going to such lengths, it seems that Newcastle had decided to treat the Scottish militia as an issue of his own authority, a chance to prove to Pitt that the Whig Old Corps still commanded the big parliamentary battalions. But Newcastle clearly also regarded it as a matter of principle, believing, as he told Kinnoul, that a Scottish militia would be 'repugnant to the notions and practices of my Lord Somers, and those that formed and wished well to the Union'. Altogether, as he wrote to one English MP, it was an occasion on which 'all true whigs should attend'.[55]

Even so, when it came to the Second Reading debate on 15 April, ministerial supporters had to avoid the mistake which had brought the Scots their early success. The bill was now attacked from two distinct sides. English Whigs directed their opposition specifically against a militia for Scotland, emphasising its likely cost and the Jacobite danger. Probably just as damaging, however, was the contribution of the Lord Advocate of Scotland, Robert Dundas, who exposed the existence of opposition to the demand in his own country. Despite further strong speeches by Oswald and Elliot, the former urging the merits of militias in general and the latter condemning any attempt to draw a 'line' that would exclude the Highlands, the Scots were unable to retrieve the situation. The confusion which had successfully been sown in the minds of their potential English supporters was well expressed by Pitt, in a long, rambling speech which combined general support for the militia with opposition to the arming of the Highlanders.[56] The eventual vote, to reject the bill by 194–84, was conclusive, and greater indeed than Newcastle expected.[57] At least the majority of Scottish MPs did not crack under pressure. Only two, the Lord Advocate and Charles Hope-Weir, voted against the bill; and although there were probably several absentees and abstainers, it seems that over two-thirds may have voted in its favour.[58]

Retribution and recrimination followed hard on the bill's defeat. The victorious Newcastle did not attempt to penalize the recalcitrant Scottish MPs; but both he and Hardwicke were concerned about the equivocal part played in the agitation by the Scottish bench. They appear to have allowed Lord Milton to go uncensured, but found a perfect scapegoat in the unfortunate Lord Auchinleck, mover of the original Ayrshire resolution in October 1759. Newcastle evidently sent off an initial letter of rebuke early in March, while the agitation was still in progress. Mortified and perplexed, Auchinleck wrote back anxiously seeking to excuse and justify himself. But his carefully laboured apology succeeded only in provoking the ministers still further: the matter was not allowed to rest until Auchinleck had journeyed up to London and made oblation in person to Newcastle, offering profuse assurances of future good conduct.[59] No doubt aware of Auchinleck's embarrassment, several other Scottish judges made haste to express to ministers their disapproval of the militia demand once the bill had been defeated.[60] But perhaps the best guarantee of the bench's future behaviour lay in the appointment of Lord Advocate Dundas to the vacant Lord Presidency of the Court of Session. Although Dundas had for some time been the likeliest candidate for this post, his powerful opposition to the militia can only have confirmed his value in the eyes of Newcastle and Hardwicke.[61]

Among the militia's supporters, Elliot and his fellow MPs appear to have taken the setback relatively calmly, regarding it as defeat with honour. Elliot in particular enjoyed the consolation of being widely congratulated on his personal performance.[62] Within Scotland, however, the sense of disappointment and recrimination was much keener. The Moderate literati were especially aggrieved. William Robertson wrote to Elliot that 'it vexed me to see more done in one day to sower and alienate the minds of the people than the attention of many years will be able to counterbalance'.[63] In line with Carlyle's Belhavenian conviction that the militia was above all an issue of national spirit, the Moderates concluded that it was not so much English opposition but division among the Scots themselves which had brought defeat.

The sharpest expression of this belief was the anonymous allegory, *The History of the Proceedings in the Case of Margaret, commonly called Peg, only lawful sister John Bull Esq.*, published late in 1760 and most probably the work of Adam Ferguson.[64] Written in imitation of John Arbuthnot's *History of John Bull* (1712), and casting Scotland as Sister Peg to England's John Bull, the pamphlet traced the course of relations between the two countries from the Union, through the two Jacobite risings, up to the Seven Years' War and the refusal of a Scottish militia. Although hardly polite about the English ministers, the pamphlet was still sharper in the treatment of Scottish deference to 'the people above': the account of the

Commons' debate on the militia bill dramatised the supposed perfidy of Dundas in particular. The pamphlet did not attempt to restate in full the positive case for a Scottish militia: but sentiments characteristic of the Moderate militia men were put into the concluding speech by a parliamentary supporter (identifiable as Elliot). The speaker denounced the way in which individuals had been encouraged to put private industry before their obligations to their country:

> A little reflection will convince, that the soul of a man is of more value than his possessions, and that the happiness of individuals, as well as that of the families which they compose, depends more on the generosity, justice and fortitude of their spirit, than on the wrappings in which they are cloathed, or the quantity of merchandize they sell to their neighbour.[65]

Another pamphleteer to suggest that it was division among the Scots which was fatal, albeit in calmer tones, was one Andrew Henderson. Recognising the strength of concern over Scottish disaffection, Henderson made a further attempt to dispel fears on this score by undertaking a county by county survey of economic and social change in Scotland.[66] But it was the aggressive satire of *Sister Peg* which had most impact. The pamphlet was noticed as far afield as London and Aberdeen,[67] while in Edinburgh it provoked a vigorous defence of Dundas. Ridiculing the 'declamatory pamphlets' and 'satirical pasquinades' which were all that militia advocates seemed to produce, the writer of *The Public Catechised* questioned whether the Scottish gentry were really in favour of a militia. The true Scottish patriot, he claimed, gave priority to the nation's manufacturers, and looked for the preservation of its military glory in the Highland battalions.[68]

The recriminations after the militia bill's defeat were accompanied by a scatter of more constructive gestures. Robertson and his friends in the Kirk arranged for suitable addresses from the Synods of Moray and Perth (both disarmed counties);[69] and the annual address of the General Assembly in May 1760 included a passage testifying to the loyalty of the people, and their desire to bear arms in defence of the crown.[70] There were continuing murmurs too from both burghs and counties. In July a majority in the Annual Convention of Royal Burghs voted thanks to Elliot, Oswald and Erskine for their endeavours on a militia's behalf, a gesture which infuriated both the Duke of Argyll and Lord President Dundas.[71] Elliot also received the freedom of the burgh of Stirling.[72] Among the counties Roxburghshire, Selkirk and Kirkcudbright Stewarty instructed their MPs to continue to propose a Scots Militia Bill.[73] And in Linlithgowshire Charles Hope-Weir found that his negative vote in Parliament was immediately used as a 'handle' against him by his electoral opponents: even after appeals for ministerial support, he only scraped back by one vote at the eventual poll early in 1761.[74]

The frustration of Scottish militia supporters after the disappointment of

1760 was relatively short-lived, for within two years they were able to mount a fresh agitation. The English Militia Act of 1757 was due for renewal in the parliamentary session of 1761–2, and the Scots were thus presented with a second chance to press for its extension. The revival of agitation in the first months of 1762 was heralded by a strident paper war in the Edinburgh press.

Two extravagantly rhetorical anonymous letters in the *Edinburgh Courant* opened the hostilities. Continuing the recriminations of 1760–61, the letters railed at the Scottish judges, lawyers, clergy and landed gentry for their failure to act to secure a militia, although it was plain that they knew the way to government well enough when places, preferment and commissions were at stake. As the nation's leaders, they seemed unaware of the indignity it suffered: exclusion from the militia was a 'mortifying distinction' which made Scotland the 'dependent' of England. Not even 'the warm and fertile imagination of Fletcher' had ever conceived of such an injury to his country. In lurid tones the letters denounced the waste of the nation's reserves in continental wars, and depicted the moral and physical degeneration of a defenceless Scottish people.[75]

This initial barrage provoked a vigorous correspondence, which continued to dominate the columns of the *Edinburgh Courant* until March.[76] The sheer extravagance of the language of the two letters irritated some, one writer commenting that it was language more suited to the stage, and the mouth of an Agis or a Douglas, than to serious enquiry.[77] More than style was at issue in the correspondence, however, as for the first time the substantive merits of a Scottish militia were subjected to serious critical scrutiny.

On the one hand, there were strong objections to a militia on military and political grounds. Correspondents questioned the military necessity of such a force: the French, it was argued, were now unlikely to invade Scotland, and if they did there was so much inaccessible territory in the Highlands that no militia would be able to prevent them. No less damagingly, the example of the English militia could be turned against its Scottish supporters. Critics pointed out that in England the militia was widely resented as a burden: it had been the cause of disorder when raised, and was expensive to maintain.[78] The extension of so unpopular an institution to Scotland could hardly be desirable, and its refusal could not therefore be regarded as a national insult. One self-styled 'Country Gentleman' went so far as to contend that government and parliament should rather be thanked for not imposing the militia on Scotland. The Scots, he claimed, should be grateful that ministers had chosen instead to encourage the country's manufactures and fisheries — just as they had answered the recent rebellion of the 'Forty-Five not with repression but with social and political liberalisation through the abolition of hereditary jurisdictions. Even so, this critic was not convinced that all disaffection had disappeared: at least it was perfectly understandable that the English should remain suspicious of Jacobitism.[79]

It was not only the military and political case for a Scottish militia that came under fire in the paper war: its desirability on economic, social and even moral grounds was contested as well. The most often repeated objection of all was that a militia would exacerbate the present severe shortage of manpower in Scotland, and increase still further the cost of labour. The country had already been drained by levies for the regular army; and since it had taken off 'the idle, the profligate and the vagabond', the burden of the militia must fall on the industrious. 'The labourer must be taken from his plough, and the manufacturer from his loom.' In addition, it was feared that the cost of maintaining the families of men away on service would be greater than the land tax or the best minister's stipend. In the eyes of the critics, in short, the militia would be a hindrance to the growing spirit of improvement in Scotland's agriculture and manufactures. Concern was also expressed about a militia's possible social consequences. It was objected that habits of industry and application so laboriously acquired in recent years would be lost, and the martial spirit of old rekindled. Power would be restored to the lords, who would appoint their relations and dependents as subalterns, and be able to rule once more as petty tyrants in their neighbourhoods. Finally, the critics left not even the most sacred moral assumptions in the case for a militia unchallenged. The same 'Country Gentleman' professed it to be the first time he had heard it suggested that military courage was necessary to virtue. 'A hapless nation it is indeed, that is obliged to go to the school of the militia to learn ... to be good, honest and virtuous men.'[80]

Confronted with these objections, partisans of a Scottish militia responded in a style less histrionic than that of the two letters which had begun the war. They were quick to riposte in the *Edinburgh Courant,* and the counter-attack was strengthened by the re-issue, at the end of February, of Carlyle's *The Question Relating to a Scots Militia Considered,* with a new preface 'in which some late objections against the establishment of a militia are considered'.[81] While on the available evidence it is not certain that Carlyle himself was the author of this preface,[82] it is noteworthy that both there and in the press the main arguments advanced in favour of a Scottish militia followed closely the lines already laid down in Carlyle's original pamphlet.

On the political side, the demand for parity in principle with England was reiterated again and again. Beside this the actual institution of a militia was but a secondary consideration. Criticism that a militia was an inappropriate form of defence for a country such as Scotland received virtually no attention; and objections based on the supposed defects of the existing English militia were answered simply by pointing out that any such defects were being rectified by parliament in the new law which provided the occasion for the present Scottish demand.[83] As for the allegation of lingering Jacobitism, this was again angrily dismissed by militia supporters. Challenging those who would rely on civil measures such as the abolition of hereditary jurisdictions to reform the Highlands, one correspondent invoked Montesquieu's opinion that by making every office dependent on the crown, such change threatened merely to transform feudal monarchy into despotism.[84] The preface to Carlyle's pamphlet maintained that the militia itself would be the best answer to disaffection. By replacing the old dominion of the clan chiefs with the authority of Lords-Lieutenant appointed by the crown, a disciplined militia would 'disconnect' men from their former leaders, and attach them to king and country.[85] Ultimately, though, it was, as Carlyle had argued in 1760, the 'privilege' of a militia which mattered: if that could be secured, more than one correspondent was prepared to concede that the militia's actual institution might be deferred.[86]

Insistent as they were on the privilege, however, supporters of a militia in 1762 were by no means indifferent to considerations other than political. In particular, they were anxious to refute the charge that the new force would drain the nation of its manpower. On the contrary, they claimed, the militia would keep men in Scotland who would otherwise have been taken for service abroad; and they emphasised that the militia was being sought for the sake and benefit of the industrious.[87] The preface to Carlyle's pamphlet contained the further claim that the militia, unlike the regular army, would spread the burden of recruitment equally, instead of concentrating it on the largest towns; and the writer added that the expense of maintaining the families of men on service would be lessened by the relatively low cost of maintenance in Scotland. Besides, the preface argued, by establishing that 'band of union...between high and low' which Scotland had so long wanted, the militia would foster just those social conditions most favourable to population. It would define by law 'a regular subordination', in which the commons of Scotland, 'neither slaves like their forefathers, nor licentious like the present generation', would find paternal encouragement and protection from their superiors, and so enjoy at last 'true liberty'.[88] Secondary in Carlyle's original pamphlet, the theme of social solidarity was thus presented in the new preface as of equal importance with the national case for a Scottish militia.

There is almost no evidence identifying the participants in the paper war of 1762. But among those who wrote in favour of a militia, the hands of the Moderates and their associates may well be suspected. If Carlyle was not the author of the preface to his pamphlet, he was very probably a contributor to the press: as we shall see, he was later to make zestful and ingenious use of their columns.[89] As the correspondent who detected the language of an Agis or a Douglas may have meant to indicate, John Home is another likely to have been involved. Among associates of the Moderate circle, Patrick Ferguson, soldier cousin of Adam Ferguson, was later described by the latter as having contributed 'some of the ablest and most intelligent publications' to appear at that time.[90] The suspicion of Moderate involvement is the greater because of their known preference for discretion. The surviving anecdotes of the genesis of Carlyle's pamphlet and of *Sister Peg* indicate that the group was not keen to flaunt authorship of its productions, accepting that it would be neither politic nor socially proper for clergymen to be seen to take so public a part on a political issue.

The Moderates were none the less active in the cause in other ways. Once again the Kirk authorities were mobilised, and a clause expressing the desire of the Scots as a 'free and loyal people' to bear arms in their defence was inserted into an address of congratulation to the king on his marriage.[91]

It was at this time too that Carlyle and his friends took the initiative to found the Poker Club — so called, at Ferguson's suggestion, because it was to stir the flames of enthusiasm for a Scottish militia. The fifteen original members included Carlyle, Home, Ferguson, Lord Elibank and several other known militia supporters, along with David Hume. Although there was provision to blackball applicants, it is clear that the Poker Club was much less formal than the Select Society, and its membership probably extended rapidly. Carlyle recalled that:

> This club consisted of all the literati of Edinburgh and its neighbourhood, most of whom had been members of the Select Society, except very few indeed who adhered to the enemies of militia, together with a great many country gentlemen, who though not always resident in town yet were zealous friends to a Scotch Militia, and warm in their resentment in its being refused to us, and an invidious line drawn between Scotland and England.[92]

There is no evidence that the Poker Club was itself the organiser of the agitation for a militia in 1762. As in 1760, there was an *ad hoc* public committee for that purpose; and there is nothing to suggest that the Poker Club as such was clandestinely at work in the background. But the Poker Club must none the less have been a source of strength to the Moderate militia activists. It provided the literati with a social forum in which to cultivate acquaintance with the gentry over the dinner table, and hence to pass on the Moderates' values and aspirations. Continuing to meet, despite various vicissitudes, until the mid-1780s, the Club established a long-term basis for agitation on the militia issue, while fulfilling — as I shall argue at greater length below — a social function at least as important to the Moderates as the cause of the militia itself.[93]

The committee to organise the 1762 agitation was appointed on 26 January at a public meeting chaired by the Earl of Haddington. The committee was twenty-six strong, but its composition was not advertised.[94] To judge by the reports which William Mure sent to his old friend Elliot in London, the committee's members appear to have been youthful, and were probably of less political and social weight than their predecessors of 1759–60. They certainly did not have the benefit of the experience of the previous chairman, for Lord Milton now heeded word from above that judges were not supposed to meddle in such matters.[95] Nor, though Mure tried to help, did they enjoy close relations with Elliot and the Scottish MPs at Westminster. Their enthusiasm was such, however, that they showed none of the hesitation of their predecessors in organising a national canvass of burghs and counties to rally support for a new bill.[96]

The canvass revealed open division. The sixteen burghs which declared an opinion were split equally for and against a Scottish militia. Of the eight which reported their approval, however, none was a burgh of the first importance.[97] Those hostile to a militia, on the other hand, numbered Edinburgh, Stirling, Dundee, Dunfermline, Haddington, St. Andrews, Montrose and Fortrose.[98] Glasgow appears not to have declared itself at all. In the counties, which met between late February and early April, the balance of opinion was rather less even. Nine out of fourteen were prepared to support the demand for a militia — East Lothian, Fife, Perth, Peebles, Lanark, Ayr, Renfrew, Banff and (unofficially) Inverness.[99] Against them there was explicit opposition from Midlothian, Stirling, Clackmannan and Linlithgow, while in Aberdeenshire there was a tied vote.[100]

On both sides the decisions were justified in forceful terms. The burghs and counties in favour of the demand echoed the claim of militia propagandists that it was a matter of national pride: the refusal of a militia was variously described as making a 'hideous', 'mortifying', 'stigmatising' and 'disagreeable and dishonourable' distinction between England and Scotland.[101] Localities opposed to a militia, on the other hand, insisted that different considerations must now be put first. The county of Midlothian's blunt formula is representative of many: 'at this time, in the present situation of the country, it is absolutely improper'. One or two burghs were more emphatic still. Stirling declared that a militia would 'not only be improper, but highly prejudicial', while to Dunfermline it would 'in very many respects, both of a religious and civil nature, be most hurtful to the nation in general, and to the royal burrows in particular'.[102] But the sweeping terms of Dunfermline's condemnation were exceptional. It is clear that in declaring the militia improper in present circumstances the great majority of localities were referring to the shortage of labour in the economy. One burgh to elaborate this concern to any extent was St. Andrews, whose council framed a public letter to its new (strongly pro-militia) MP, George Dempster. Those who insisted on the point of honour, St. Andrews argued, forgot that England was far more likely to be invaded than Scotland. The real 'grandeur and happiness' of Scotland lay in its agriculture and manufactures — and the imposition of a militia would damage these by intensifying the loss of available manpower which had already resulted from recruiting by the regular army.[103]

The economic argument against a militia was put most forcibly of all, however, in a series of well-publicised unofficial meetings of farmers and tradesmen held in Mid and East Lothian and East Fife. Early in March 'a considerable number of farmers' met in Edinburgh to declare a militia 'very inexpedient' because of the difficulties it would create for agriculture:

> At present there is nothing more certain in the farming business than a very
> great scarcity of servants, as also their high and extravagant wages, which is
> daily experienced to the cost of all those that has any experience with them;
> and if this be the case at present, it is evident, if the militia takes place, that
> these evils will greatly increase, and be more and more hurtful, not only to the
> farmer, but to every other person concerned in trade and manufactures.[104]

These Midlothian farmers were effectively seconding the opinion already expressed by the county's gentry; by contrast, those of East Lothian and East Fife were ranging themselves against their social superiors. The farmers and manufacturers who met in Haddington on 19 March reiterated concern over the labour shortage, adding that since the regular army had already recruited the idle and profligate, the militia must remove the industrious and the husbandman.[105] A few days later the farmers of East Fife were quite explicit in contradicting their own gentry, declaring themselves astonished to find any gentleman·of property promoting such a pernicious object as a militia. The farmers feared that the most substantial and industrious of their number would be dragged off to serve, while their labourers would be hired as substitutes in place of those landed proprietors without valued rent sufficient to qualify as officers. In any case, at the end of a victorious war there was no need for a militia. Declaring it as an institution of 'perpetual legal slavery', the farmers concluded by addressing a simple question to their brethren elsewhere in Scotland: 'whether they chose to remain free, or to be inslaved?'[106]

While Scotland was dividing, the fate of the 1762 agitation was decided at Westminster in less than a fortnight in mid-March. The expediency of moving a Scottish militia bill during the current session was initially discussed at a meeting of Scottish MPs on 9 March. Despite pessimism about the chances of success, it was generally agreed to support Elliot when he declared that he would move a bill. Elliot sought to encourage his fellow MPs by claiming that some in administration were now favourable to a Scottish militia: although he avoided names, it must have been clear that he was referring principally to Bute.[107] Long the object of Scottish Patriot expectations, and now the new king's most trusted minister, surely Bute was in a position to obtain his countrymen's request. In fact Bute was distinctly unenthusiastic, and immediately rebuked Elliot when the latter suggested that he could command a bill's success. Bute was well aware of the divisions on the issue in Scotland; and in addition he was already subject to the pressure of mounting anti-Scottish opinion in London.[108] As those old antagonists of a Scottish militia, Newcastle and Hardwicke, lost no time in pointing out, Bute could ill afford to seem too partial to Scotsmen. Confident that they were in a position of political strength on the Scottish militia issue, the Whig ministers acted immediately on hearing of the intention to move a bill. Hardwicke's straightforward solution to the difficulty was to delay the conclusion of the English Militia Bill until the end of the session, and to advance the date of that, thus depriving the Scots of their opportunity. He and Newcastle then made certain of their success by exerting pressure on the new Lord Advocate and other MPs. With Mansfield's help they persuaded the Scots to hold another meeting, on 22 March, when it was agreed to defer an application for the session.[109]

Briskly and effectively Newcastle and Hardwicke thus laid to rest the agitation for a Scottish militia in their own lifetimes. The second failure at Westminster was followed by none of the recrimination heard in 1760: in Scotland the paper war and canvass of the localities simply petered out in April 1762. A meeting was convened in Edinburgh early in 1763 to renew the demand, but nothing appears to have come of it.[110] It would be thirteen years and another war before the issue of a Scots militia was agitated again.

The militia's supporters were not indeed idle throughout this interval. The Poker Club continued to meet for part of the period; and in 1767 Adam Ferguson published his *Essay on the History of Civil Society,* a work which may be read as an extended commentary on the themes he and Carlyle had articulated in their militia pamphlets. But these activities belong rather to the social 'achievement' and 'intellectual consequences' of the militia agitations than to the story of the agitations themselves: they are therefore reserved for separate discussion under those heads. Meanwhile I resume the narrative of the agitations in the following chapter on the outbreak of the American War.

NOTES

1. Carlyle, *Anecdotes and Characters,* pp. 203–4, recalls the writing of the pamphlet.

2. [Alexander Carlyle,] *The Question Relating to a Scots Militia Considered. By a Freeholder, Ayrshire* (Edinburgh 1760), pp. 4–11.

3. Ibid., pp. 11–15.

4. Ibid., pp. 15–23.

5. Ibid., pp. 24–26.

6. Ibid., pp. 27–32.

7. Ibid., pp. 33–34.

8. Ibid., pp. 35–43.

9. Ibid., pp. 44–45.

10. Carlyle, *Anecdotes and Characters,* pp. 203–4.

11. The pamphlet was reprinted entire in the *Edinburgh Chronicle,* 20, 23 Feb., 5, 10 March 1760, and in extracts, rather later, in the *Aberdeen Journal,* 5 May 1760. Extracts also appeared in the *Scots Magazine,* XXII (January 1760), pp. 53–6, and in the *Edinburgh Magazine* (February 1760).

12. Two several London editions are referred to in a preface to the later fourth edition of the pamphlet, published in Edinburgh in 1762. One of these London

editions was styled 'The Second Edition, to which is prefixed, a Preface by another hand' (London 1760). A different 'Preface by an Hon. Member of the House of Commons' was reproduced in the *Scots Magazine*, XXII (March 1760), pp. 167–8. Apparently both London editions claimed to be the second.

13. Sher, *Church and University*, Ch. 6, for a full discussion of the connection between the militia and Ossian, a discussion which it would be purposeless for me to repeat.

I do consider, however, that without an awareness of the Belhavenian character of Carlyle's arguments, Sher oversimplifies in his interpretation of the 'patriotism' involved in the Moderates' enthusiasm for a militia. Adopting the framework suggested by David Daiches (*The Paradox of Scottish Culture: the Eighteenth-Century Experience*, London 1964), Sher characterises the Moderates as suffering from 'cultural schizophrenia' in combining 'nationalism' over the militia with acceptance of the Union. But this overlooks the extent to which the Moderates were heirs to a particular view of Scotland's proper relation to England, a view which regarded the institutional relation as relatively indifferent, so long as the Scots preserved a moral independence. At least as old as Belhaven, this view was powerfully reinforced by Moderate moralism. If it is 'nationalism', it is clearly not so in the common nineteenth-century sense; at the same time it was not so unconscious and irrational as to merit the diagnosis of schizophrenia.

I myself owe to Nicholas Phillipson the original suggestion that Carlyle's arguments particularly echo Belhaven's; for a similar suggestion in relation to Ossian, Phillipson's 'The Scottish Enlightenment', in Porter and Teich (eds.), *Enlightenment in National Context*, p. 227 note 52.

14. Western. *The English Militia*, p. 156; P. Coquelle, 'Les Projets de Descente en Angleterre', *Revue d'Histoire Diplomatique*, XV (1901), pp. 591–624.

15. Newcastle Papers, B.L. Addit. Mss. 32893, ff. 189–93: Newcastle to the Earl of Hardwicke, 21 July 1759. Saltoun Papers, N.L.S. Ms. 16521, ff. 110–13: Andrew Fletcher (great nephew of the patriot, MP for Haddington Burghs and private secretary to the Duke of Argyll) to his father, Andrew Fletcher, Lord Milton (the Patriot's nephew, and Argyll's Scottish agent or 'sous-ministre'), 26 June and 14 July 1759.

16. Hardwicke Papers, B.L. Addit. Mss. 35450, ff. 261–4, 266–75: correspondence between Hardwicke and the Earl of Breadalbane, 30 June–11 Aug. 1759. Campbell of Stonefield Papers, S.R.O. Ms. GD 14 f. 145: Campbell of Stonefield to Argyll, 3 July 1759.

17. B.L. Addit. Mss. 32894, ff. 481–3: Newcastle's note of a conference with Hardwicke on the offers to raise regiments from Lords Marchmont, Lauderdale (who was particularly persistent), Eglinton and Breadalbane: 'No More Scotch Regiments', 27 Aug. 1759.

18. L. Namier and J. Brooke, *Charles Townshend* (London 1964), pp. 34–6, 57–9; Murdoch, '*The People Above*', pp. 87–9; Carlyle, *Anecdotes and Characters*, pp. 197–201.

19. Townshend Papers (William L. Clements Library, Michigan), S.R.O. Microfilm RH4/98/1: letters from Carlyle, 11 Sept., 6, 16 Oct., Robertson 25 Oct., Elibank 21 Dec., and Dalrymple, 29 Aug., 1 Sept., 20 Sept. etc., 1759.

20. N.L.S. Ms. 16708, ff. 93–4: Copy letter Cmmr. Boys to Lord Provost Drummond of Edinburgh, 20 Oct. 1759.

21. P.R.O. State Papers Scotland 54, vol. 45, ff. 331, 376: Lord George

Beauclerk (C.-in-C. Scotland) to the Earl of Holderness (Secretary of State for the Northern Department, covering Scotland), 13 Nov. 1759, 12 Jan. 1760. Thurot's progress was the subject of constant speculation in the papers of all three main Scottish burghs, the *Edinburgh Chronicle,* the *Glasgow Journal,* and the *Aberdeen Journal,* Oct.–Dec. 1759.

22. 'Minutes of the Presbytery of Edinburgh 1753–66', S.R.O. CH 2/121/17, pp. 337–38, 25 Oct. 1759: 'Minutes of the Synod of Lothian and Tweeddale 1747–61', S.R.O. CH 2/252/12, pp. 363–5, 13 Nov. 1759: 'Register of the Acts of the Commission of the General Assembly 1757–68', S.R.O. CH 1/3/27, pp. 101–13, 21 Nov. 1759.

23. S.R.O. RH 4/98/1: letters of Robertson, 25 Oct., and Carlyle, 15 Nov. 1759, to Townshend. Bute Papers, Mount Stuart, 1759, no. 184: Home to Bute, 8 Nov. 1759.

24. P.R.O. SP 54 vol. 45, ff. 244, 246–7, 254–5, 266, 282, 288: correspondence between Holderness and the Lord Provosts of Aberdeen and Montrose, along with the C.-in-C. Scotland and the Lord Justice Clerk. Leeds Papers, B.L. Egerton Mss. 3434, ff. 246–7: Alexander Boswell to Holderness, enclosing Ayr Burgh's Address, 12 Oct. 1759. Bute Papers, Mount Stuart, 1759, no. 174: Provost of Irvine to Bute, 23 Oct. 1759. See also Murdoch, *'The People Above',* p. 91, for political complications.

25. B.L. Egerton Mss. 3434, ff. 246–7: Boswell to Holderness, 12 Oct. 1759.

26. S.R.O. RH 4/98/1: Carlyle to Townshend, 16 Oct. 1759; Auchinleck, however, forwarded both the county and the burgh addresses from Ayr to Argyll, for transmission to Holderness: B.L. Egerton Mss. 3434, ff. 250–1: Argyll to Holderness, 23 Oct. 1759.

27. *Edinburgh Chronicle,* 15 Dec. 1759.

28. *Historical Manuscripts Commission 67, Polwarth Manuscripts,* Vol. V (London 1961), nos. 462 and 463, Marchmont to Auchinleck, 16 Oct., and Hume-Campbell to Marchmont, 20 Nov. 1759. Namier and Brooke, *The Commons 1754–90,* II, pp. 653–55: biography of Hume-Campbell.

29. *Scots Magazine,* XXI (1759), pp. 659–60.

30. S.R.O. RH 4/98/1: Elibank to Townshend, 21 Dec. 1759.

31. N.L.S. Ms. 16521, ff. 138–9: Andrew Fletcher to Milton, 8 Dec. 1759.

32. B.L. Addit. Mss. 329000, ff. 57–8, 88–9: correspondence between Hardwicke and Newcastle, 14, 15 Dec. 1759.

33. N.L.S. Ms. 16522, ff. 30–1: Andrew Fletcher to Milton, 17 Jan. 1760; Ms. 16714, ff. 119–22: Sir James Carnegie MP to Milton, 17 and 19 Jan. 1760.

34. N.L.S. Ms. 16717, f. 222: Milton to ? George Townshend, 8 Jan. 1760.

35. N.L.S. Ms. 16714, ff. 123–5: Carnegie to Milton, 26 Feb. 1760.

36. *Edinburgh Chronicle,* 23 Feb., corrected on 3 March 1760: the squadron which defeated Thurot was commanded by Gilbert Elliot's brother, John Elliot, a circumstance which enhanced Gilbert's political credit. N.L.S. Ms. 16713, ff. 147–8: Milton to Argyll, 23 Feb. 1760.

37. Ms. 'Council Records of the City of Edinburgh', Vol. 76, pp. 26–8.

38. *Extracts from the Records of the Convention of the Royal Burghs of Scotland 1759–79* (Edinburgh 1918), pp. 20–1.

39. N.L.S. Ms. 16713, ff. 147–8: Milton to Argyll, 23 Feb. 1760; Minto Papers, Ms. 11015, ff. 32–3, Milton to Elliot, 23 Feb. 1760; E.U.L. Ms. Gen. 1429/18/19: George Murray to James Murray, 29 May 1760 — a report of the part played by

the correspondents' father, Lord Elibank, in the agitation. *Edinburgh Courant*, 6 March 1760.

40. N.L.S. Ms. 16522, ff. 53–4: Andrew Fletcher to Milton; 16713, ff. 135–7: Hume-Campbell to Milton: 16715, ff. 1–2, 18–19: Elliot, Erskine to Milton, all dated 28 Feb. 1760.

41. B.L. Addit. Mss. 32903, ff. 81–3: Newcastle to Hardwicke, 4 March 1760.

42. Elliot's speech notes, along with a good deal of preparatory material, are in N.L.S. Ms. 11031: they include an abstract (ff. 26–7) and a complete ms copy (77–91), with corrections in a hand resembling Elliot's, of George Dempster, *Reasons for Extending the Militia Acts to the Disarm'd Countries of Scotland* (Edinburgh 1760). For correspondence with Milton, Ms. 16715, ff. 3–6: 6 and 25 March 1760; and the debt acknowledged to Carlyle, recalled in Carlyle's *Anecdotes and Characters*, p. 204.

43. B.L. Addit. Mss. 35878, ff. 106–10: Notes, probably by John Yorke, 'In the House, Thursday 4 March 1760', giving an extended report of Elliot's and other speeches.

44. B.L. Addit. Mss. 35878, ff. 106–10; *Commons Journal*, Vol. 28, p. 800.

45. N.L.S. Ms. 16522, ff. 64–65: Andrew Fletcher to Milton, 13 March 1760; *Commons Journal*, vol. 28, pp. 814–15.

46. There is a printed copy of the proposals produced by Milton's committee in the Hardwicke Papers: *Plan for raising a militia in that part of Great Britain called Scotland; Adapting the acts of Parliament lately made for regulating the Militia in England, to the Constitution and Laws of Scotland*. It is accompanied by an *Explanation of the particulars in which the plan.... varies from the Militia Laws now subsisting in England.* B.L. Addit. Mss. 35891, ff. 217–35. The plan adroitly emphasised its dependence on the English example by following the text of the 1757 Act as far as possible, and placing any necessary changes in italics. Milton explained the committee's procedure in a letter he drafted to ? Charles Townshend, enclosing a copy of the proposals: N.L.S. Ms. 16717, f. 225, 8 Jan. 1760. A full 'Abstract of the Plan of a Militia for Scotland' was later printed in the Edinburgh papers: *Edinburgh Chronicle*, 19 March 1760.

47. N.L.S. Ms. 16522, ff. 62–3: Andrew Fletcher to Milton, 11 March 1760.

48. *Edinburgh Chronicle*, 3, 8 March 1760; *Extracts from the Records of the Burgh of Glasgow*, ed. Robert Renwick (Glasgow 1912), Vol. VII, p. 6, 14 March 1760; S.R.O. Mss. B.18/13/5: 'Dunbar Council Minute Book 1754–62', 26 Feb. 1760; N.L.S. Ms. 11031, ff. 6–7: Lord Prov. of Aberdeen to Lord. Prov. ? of Edinburgh, 4 March 1760.

49. N.L.S. Ms. 16716, ff. 221–2: Provost Murdoch of Glasgow to Milton, 29 Feb., 14 March 1760. S.R.O. Ms. B66/21/11: 'Stirling Council Minute Book 1760–69', 25 Feb. 1760. N.L.S. Ms. 11031, ff. 6–7: Lord Prov. of Aberdeen to Lord Prov. ? of Edinburgh, 4 March 1760.

50. *Edinburgh Courant*, 20 March (Midlothian, on 19 March), 25 March (Stirling, 18 March), 5 April (Perth, 1 April), and 12 April 1760 (Selkirk, 2 April). *Edinburgh Chronicle*, 22 March 1760 (Ayr, 19 March), *Caledonian Mercury*, 14 April 1760 (Forfar, 1 April). *Glasgow Courant*, 24 March 1760 (Renfrew, 21 March). S.R.O. SC 40/68/1: Records of the Proceedings of the Freeholders Electors of the County of Haddingtonshire (East Lothian) 1743–75, pp. 83–4, 18 March 1760; and SC.42/40/1: Peebles Freeholders Sederunt Book, 25 March 1760.

51. The petitions were printed in the *Commons Journal*, Vol. 28, pp. 847 (Ayr),

852–3 (Midlothian), 856–7 (Stirling), 861 (Perth) and 862 (Forfar). Only the petitions of Midlothian and Stirling were identical.

52. So Lord Advocate Robert Dundas claimed in his Commons' speech on 15 April: B.L. Addit. Mss. 32904, f. 394, J. West to Newcastle, reporting the debate.

53. *Caledonian Mercury*, 22 March 1760: 'Detail of the Proceedings of Some Heritors of the Shire of Edinburgh, at two meetings held on 14 and 19 March 1760'.

54. N.L.S. Ms. 16715, ff. 5–6, 16522 ff. 70–1: Elliot, Andrew Fletcher to Milton, 25, 29 March 1760.

55. B.L. Addit. Mss. 32903, ff. 81–3, 296–9, 456–7: Newcastle to Hardwicke, 4, 15, 22 March 1760; 32998, ff. 418–19: Memo of dinner, 20 March 1760; 33034, ff. 351–72: canvass lists; 32904, ff. 184–5: Newcastle to Mr. White, 3 April 1760; 32907, ff. 16–23: Newcastle to Kinnoul, 1 June 1760 — a full retrospective account of Newcastle's motives.

56. B.L. Addit. Mss. 32904, ff. 392–4: J. West to Newcastle: Report on the speeches in the Scottish militia debate.

57. *Commons Journal*, Vol. 28, p. 872, 15 April 1760; B.L. Addit. Mss. 32907, ff. 16–17: Newcastle to Kinnoul, 1 June 1760.

58. Erskine-Murray Papers, N.L.S. Ms. 5081, ff. 46–7: John Swinton Jnr. to ? Charles Erskine (Lord Justice Clerk), 17 April 1760, believed that all Scots members except three were for the bill. But it is unlikely that all the Scottish members would have been present. The figure suggested by a hostile pamphleteer's references to 'the boasted thirty-three' seems quite probable: *The Public Catechised; or, A Few Cool Questions to the People*, n.d. [1761], pp. 3–4.

59. B.L. Addit. Mss. 32903, ff. 398–9: Auchinleck to Newcastle, 20 March 1760; 32905, ff. 244–5: Hardwicke to Newcastle, 2 May 1760; 32906 f. 102: 'Mem. for the King', 16 May 1760.

60. B.L. Addit. Mss. 35449, ff. 226, 232, 238: Lords Tinwald, Prestongrange and Ord to Hardwicke, 15, 24 May, 28 June 1760.

61. Namier and Brooke, *The Commons 1754–90*, Vol. II, pp. 361–3.

62. N.L.S. Ms. 11001, ff. 63–5: Elliot to Lord Minto (his father), 16 April 1760; *The Letters of David Hume*, Vol. I, p. 325: Hume to Lord Minto, 1 May 1760.

63. N.L.S. Ms. 11009, ff. 70–1: Robertson to Elliot, 30 April 1760.

64. There were two editions, both dated 1761. A new edition of the pamphlet has been produced by David Raynor, on the supposition that it was actually written by David Hume: *Sister Peg. A Pamphlet hitherto unknown by David Hume*, Cambridge Studies in the History and Theory of Politics (Cambridge 1982). While Hume's authorship is not impossible, Ferguson's still seems to me much more probable, for reasons I have given elsewhere: *English Historical Review* (Jan. 1985 pp. 191–2). See also the review of Raynor's edition by R. B. Sher, in *Philosophical Books*, 24 (1983), pp. 85–91. Carlyle's account of the pamphlet's composition is in *Anecdotes and Characters*, pp. 206–7.

65. *The History of Margaret*, p. 179; D. Raynor (ed.), *Sister Peg*, p. 100.

66. Andrew Henderson, *Considerations on the Question: Whether the Act of Parliament establishing a Militia through England ought to extend to Scotland in Time of War* (Westminster Hall 1760). Henderson was a London Scot, author of a *History of the Rebellion 1745 and 1746* (1748).

67. N.L.S. Ms. 16523, ff. 18–19: Andrew Fletcher to Milton, 17 Jan. 1761;

Aberdeen Magazine, Feb. 1761, p. 103 — 'a very unequal imitation of.... the admirable History of John Bull'.

68. *The Public Catechised; or, A Few Cool Questions to the People.* Another sought to defend Dundas by correcting distortions of his Commons' speech. *The Principal Heads of a speech in P--t, concerning the Scots Militia, By a Right Honourable M--r, from a certain County in N--h B--n* (1760).

69. S.R.O. CH 2/271/7: Minutes of the Synod of Moray, pp. 2–4, 22 April 1760; N.L.S. Ms. 11009, ff. 70–1: Robertson to Elliot, 30 April 1760.

70. S.R.O. CH 1/1/53: Register of the Acts of the General Assembly, pp. 416–19, 21 May 1760. But Dundas was glad to report that a more specific and forceful resolution had been avoided: B.L. Addit. Mss. 35449, ff. 234–5: Dundas to Hardwicke, 31 May 1760.

71. *Extracts from the Records of the Convention of Royal Burghs 1759–79,* pp. 40–1, 9 July 1760; B.L. Addit. Mss. 35449, ff. 250, 268–70: Argyll, Dundas to Hardwicke, 19 July, 16 Aug. 1760.

72. S.R.O. B66/21/11: Stirling Council Minute Book 1760–69, 9 May 1760.

73. *Edinburgh Courant,* 9 June (Roxburgh, 3 June), 6 Oct. (Selkirk), and 20 Dec. 1760 (Kirkcudbright, 10 Dec.).

74. B.L. Addit. Mss. 32906, f. 283: Hope-Weir to Newcastle, 26 May 1760; 35449, ff. 234–5: Dundas to Hardwicke, 31 May 1760. On the election: Namier and Brooke, *The Commons 1754–90,* Vol. II, p. 639.

75. *Edinburgh Courant,* 13 Jan. ('A Letter from the Country') and 20 Jan. 1762 ('To the Publisher').

76. Some of the letters were reprinted in the *Caledonian Mercury* and the *Scots Magazine,* XXIV, Jan.–Feb. 1762.

77. *Edinburgh Courant,* 22 Feb. 1762.

78. *Edinburgh Courant,* 30 Jan. 1762. Cf. Western, *The English Militia,* pp. 184–93, for contemporary complaints about the English force.

79. *Edinburgh Courant,* 10 Feb. 1762 ('Letter from a Country Gentleman to his Neighbour').

80. *Edinburgh Courant,* 30 Jan., 10 Feb., 3 March 1762 (the last being the same 'Country Gentleman').

81. 'The Fourth Edition' (Edinburgh 1762). It was advertised as published 'this day' in the *Edinburgh Courant,* 27 Feb. 1762.

82. In his *Anecdotes and Characters,* p. 204, Carlyle recollected that a Provost Ferguson of Ayr was responsible for publishing the pamphlet, with a preface, in Scotland; but he does not indicate which edition this was.

83. *The Question Relating to a Scots Militia Considered,* 4th edition, Preface, pp. 3–5.

84. *Edinburgh Courant,* 13 Feb. 1762. Montesquieu's general observation on the danger of making every office dependent on the crown occurs in *De L'Esprit des Lois* (1748), Bk. II, Ch. 4. Its particular relevance to the abolition of hereditary jurisdictions had already been remarked upon by several Scots. David Hume had pointed it out to Montesquieu himself, in a letter of 10 April 1749: *The Letters of David Hume,* I, p. 135. In print, John Dalrymple had commented on the subject in *An Essay Towards a General History of Feudal Property in Great Britain* (London 1758), p. 306; he argued, however, that the abolition of hereditary jurisdictions in a limited monarchy tended to strengthen law and liberty.

85. *The Questions Relating,* 4th edition, Preface, pp. 13–14.

86. *Edinburgh Courant,* 3, 15 Feb. 1762.

87. *Edinburgh Courant,* 25 Jan., 3, 13 Feb. 1762.

88. *The Question Relating,* 4th edition, Preface, pp. 8–13.

89. Among the 'Transcripts of Letters by Dr. C[arlyle] on the Militia, for the Press', in the Lee Papers, N.L.S. Ms. 3464, is one (ff. 71–9) which can be dated internally to 1762, although it does not appear to have been published. For others in the transcripts which were to be published between 1778 and 1782, see below, pp. 153 n. 27, 156 n. 83.

90. Adam Ferguson, *Biographical Sketch, or Memoir of Lieutenant-Colonel Patrick Ferguson: originally intended for the British Encyclopaedia* (Edinburgh 1817), p. 10.

91. S.R.O. CH 1/3/27: 'Acts of the Commission of the General Assembly', pp. 183–6, 4 March 1762; CH 1/1/53: 'Acts of the General Assembly', 22 and 26 May 1762.

92. Carlyle, *Anecdotes and Characters*, pp. 213–14. Cf. the similarly worded history of the club prefixed to its Minutes, 1774–84: EUL Ms. Dc.5. 126.

93. Below pp. 185–92 with a list of the known membership.

94. *Edinburgh Courant*, 20, 27 Jan. 1762.

95. Advice relayed to Milton by his son, Andrew Fletcher: N.L.S. Ms. 16523, ff. 83–4, 2 Jan. 1762.

96. N.L.S. Ms. 11016, ff. 4–5, 9–10, 20–21: Mure to Elliot, 7 Jan., 8 Feb., 25 March 1762; and f. 8: Lord Haddington to Elliot, 4 Feb. 1762.

97. The eight were Ayr, Kirkcudbright, Sanquhar, Stranraer, Dunbar, North Berwick, Bervie and Anstruther Easter. All are included in the list of returns up to 1 March 1762 in the *Edinburgh Courant*.

98. *Edinburgh Courant*, 1 March 1762, and later declarations by St. Andrews, 15 March and Fortrose, 22 March 1762.

99. *Edinburgh Courant*, 1 March 1762, with later returns from Inverness, 13 March; Banff, 10 April 1762; and from Lanark, reported in the *Glasgow Journal*, 8 April 1762.

100. *Edinburgh Courant*, 1 March 1762, with later returns from Linlithgow, 22 March, and Aberdeenshire, 29 March 1762.

101. *Edinburgh Courant*, 17 Feb. (Dunbar and E. Lothian), and 24 Feb. 1762 (Renfrewshire and Perthshire).

102. *Edinburgh Courant*, 24, 27, 17 Feb. 1762.

103. *Edinburgh Courant*, 15 March 1762; 'Letter from the Town Council of St. Andrews, to the Hon. George Dempster of Dinnichen, their representative'. The Council were supported by a 'Declaration of Burgesses, Guild-Brethren, Merchants, Tradesmen and others of St. Andrews', 20 March 1762.

104. *Edinburgh Courant*, 8 March 1762.

105. *Edinburgh Courant*, 27 March 1762.

106. *Edinburgh Courant*, 31 March 1762; similar language in the 'Declaration of Burgesses' of St. Andrews, 20 March 1762.

107. Bute Papers, Cardiff Central Library, Ms. 3.615, f. 2/138: Elliot to Bute [9 March 1762]; also f. 2/176: Henry Erskine to Bute, 8 Feb. 1762. N.L.S. Ms. 16523, ff. 111–12: Andrew Fletcher to Milton, 9 March 1762.

108. N.L.S. Ms. 11016, ff. 24–5, 30–1: Bute to Elliot, [9] March and [12 March] 1762.

109. B.L. Addit. Mss. 32935, ff. 312–13, 328–9, 331–2, 364–5, 368, 388–9, 392–5: correspondence between Newcastle and Hardwicke, 11–15 March 1762, with enclosures from the Duke of Devonshire and Lord Mansfield. N.L.S. Ms. 16523, ff. 115–16: Andrew Fletcher to Milton, 23 March 1762; Mackenzie of Delvine Papers, N.L.S. Ms. 1404, ff. 166–7: John Murray of Strowan MP to John Mackenzie, 23 March 1762.

110. *Edinburgh Courant*, 23 March 1763.

5

The Scottish Militia Agitations
of the American War

The War of the American Revolution began as a straightforward rebellion in the colonies in 1775; but as the revolt escalated and took hold, the war predictably acquired a European dimension. Seizing the opportunity to recover ground lost in the previous conflict, France allied itself with the rebels in 1778; and France in turn was joined by Spain in 1779 and Holland in 1781. The war placed Britain squarely on the defensive. Not only had sizeable expeditionary forces to be maintained in America, amidst a largely hostile population, but there were no longer allies on the continent of Europe to divert enemy energies. The hostile European powers were thus free to concentrate on breaking British naval supremacy — and on an invasion of the British mainland. The Franco–Spanish alliance of 1779 was specifically constructed on the basis of a grand invasion strategy, involving a joint attack on the British Channel Fleet followed by the seizure of the Isle of Wight and Portsmouth, and accompanied by a diversion in Ireland. Representing the most substantial invasion threat of the century, an enemy armada carrying thirty thousand men was at sea in the summer of 1779; and apparently only the refusal of the British fleet to engage in battle prevented the invaders from testing Britain's land defences.[1]

Scotland itself, it seems, was no longer a target of French invasion strategy, even for the purposes of a diversion. But it was not difficult to arouse Scots' fears, simply by sending privateers out of northern French ports to maraud along the Scottish coasts. Boldest of these privateers was the Scottish-born American rebel John Paul Jones, who began a series of raids in April 1778. Not content just to harass coastal shipping, Paul Jones also caused considerable alarm ashore. One of his first exploits was to land parties of men off the south-west of Scotland, at Whitehaven and St. Mary's Isle, where they burgled the Earl of Selkirk's house. In the autumn it was the turn of the east coast to feel threatened, although this time there was no actual landing. Alarm reached a climax in September of the following year, 1779: while the Franco–Spanish armada still hovered off England's south coast, Paul Jones sailed a small squadron up the Forth, and for a short time seemed set to attack Leith.[2] Other privateers subsequently imitated Paul Jones' example further afield. One Luke Ryan made a landing at Stornoway in the Outer Hebrides in 1780; and in 1781 Robert Fall raided Aberdeen harbour and bombarded the chimney pots of Arbroath.[3] But it was the activities of John Paul Jones which captured the public imagination, and helped rouse the Scots once again to look to their national defence.

Given such appearance of danger, there were several other circumstances which augured well for the success of a renewed militia demand. In England official suspicion of the militia had long been overcome. Ministers now valued the militia as a practical reserve force and as a useful indirect channel of recruitment into the regular army. In 1775 a bill was passed enabling the militia to be used in America; though never actually used there, it was embodied to meet possible invasion in 1778. Such was ministerial enthusiasm for the force that opposition parties now rather affected to fear the militia almost as much as the standing army. But the opposition did not deny the need for additional defence, and urged only other more local and voluntary forms of arming.[4]

As the government was now committed to the English militia, so the Scots were overwhelmingly committed to the government and the war it was fighting. Scottish MPs were regular government supporters almost to a man, the consistently independent George Dempster being a lonely exception. Erstwhile Patriot sympathisers such as Gilbert Elliot were by now thoroughly disillusioned with Pitt (since 1766 Earl of Chatham), and refused to follow him in his increasingly erratic opposition course.[5] Still firmer in his support for the government was the rising star of Scottish politics, Henry Dundas, who became Lord Advocate in 1775 and went on to establish himself as the country's effective political manager. At this early stage in his career Dundas was notably active in discouraging Scottish emigration to America and in encouraging the recruitment of Scots to fight here. Like Argyll before him, Dundas appreciated that the promotion of recruiting was the way above all to place ministers in his debt; and Scotland once again contributed twenty battalions to the British regular army.[6]

Scotland's political and manpower commitment to the American War was supported by a public opinion expressing far fewer misgivings than were voiced in England. The Scottish press expanded considerably during the war, exploiting the demand for information and comment.[7] Of those who articulated opinion, moreover, few were more bellicose than the previous champions of a national militia, the Moderate literati. Both Adam Ferguson and Alexander Carlyle contributed forceful pamphlets in favour of the war. In his *Remarks on a Pamphlet lately published by Dr. Price* (1776), Ferguson distinguished himself with a formidably reasoned answer to the leading English advocate of the American cause.[8] Less theoretical in quality was Carlyle's published sermon, *The Justice and Necessity of the War with our American Colonies Examined* (1777), which implicitly answered the rebels' most prominent Scottish champion, the Reverend John Erskine. Expressing unqualified admiration for the British constitution, Carlyle characteristically underlined the martial opportunity facing the British people:

> To be secure, we must be brave. All America is now in arms; shall we remain feeble and unwarlike? The plough and the loom must be left for a while, that we may not be obliged to abandon them for ever.[9]

With commitment such as this, what could now frustrate the demand for a Scottish militia?

In the event, no militia was established in Scotland during the American War; but perhaps the militia's supporters were able to express themselves in a manner, and to an effect, that gave them at least as much satisfaction. While they did seek to exploit the favourable circumstances of the war, they did so, as we shall see, in their own ways and for their own purposes. The story which follows is, unfortunately, more diffuse than the relatively straightforward tale of two agitations in the Seven Years' War. The American War stimulated a wider variety of initiatives, both central and local, on the militia issue; and the debate which accompanied them was less focused, in spite of renewed efforts by Alexander Carlyle. Unevenness notwithstanding, however, the agitations did reach a striking climax in 1782, confirming and highlighting the essential continuity of the case for a Scottish militia since 1760.

The new round of agitation opened on a low, comical note, in 1775, before the war had actually begun. Taking the opportunity provided by the government's precautionary bill to permit the use of the English militia against rebels anywhere in the king's dominions, the Viscount Mountstuart, son and heir of the Earl of Bute and MP for Bossiney, announced on 2 November 1775 his intention to move a militia bill for Scotland.[10] The initiative appears to have been Mountstuart's alone; there is very little evidence that the issue had yet been raised in Scotland itself.[11] Publicly Mountstuart's professed objective was to remove a stain on Scotland's honour. In private, however, Mountstuart confided other motives to his erstwhile companion on the Grand Tour, James Boswell. As Boswell recorded it, Mountstuart also saw an opportunity to restore the old Bute interest in Scotland, and check the rise of Henry Dundas and the Duke of Buccleuch.[12]

In the eager conviction that Mountstuart represented 'a noble Tory interest', Boswell was only too happy to abet the ambition of his patron and friend. The first active service Boswell undertook was to go down to Edinburgh in November, and do what he could to raise support there. At the Pantheon, a townspeople's debating society, he gave a 'vigorous harangue' in favour of a militia, in the course of which he eulogised Mountstuart as the 'tutelary patron' of his country. Boswell also thought of writing a pamphlet on the issue, but, doubting whether he had enough to say, does not appear to have done so.[13] Perhaps his example inspired the handful of letters which appeared in the *Edinburgh Advertiser* in December and January 1775–76.[14] But no organised agitation in support of Mountstuart's bill developed. The members of the Poker Club do not seem to have exerted themselves, although Mountstuart had written to William Mure early in November to ask for its support, and George Dempster was later to write to Carlyle, urging the Club to take up the pen.[15] The records of the Club do show that two or three meetings in November and December 1775 were well-attended. The Duke of Buc-cleuch was a visitor at one, and at another the Lord Advocate was proposed a member.[16] But Mountstuart himself had to wait until 1777 to be admitted to membership; and the Moderate literati, who formed the core of the Club, appear hardly to have stirred at all.[17]

If there is anything in Boswell's account of Mountstuart's motives, the Moderates would have had reason to be cautious. Through John Home and Adam Ferguson they had of course a long-standing association with the Bute interest — Ferguson indeed had been Mountstuart's tutor. But by the mid-1770s the Moderates had made up their previous quarrel with the Dundas family, and had come to count on Henry Dundas's support in the management of the Kirk. Buccleuch likewise was not one to offend, Carlyle from his neighbouring parish of Musselburgh being a frequent visitor to the Duke's house at Dalkeith.[18] The Moderates' active support of Mountstuart's bill would of course by no means have guaranteed its success, but they could at least have engendered a more forceful agitation than Boswell was able to raise on his own.

Some effort was made, however, to gather opinion in the localities. The Lord Provost of Edinburgh called a meeting of the Annual Committee of Royal Burghs in January 1776, and the delegates decided that a militia on a proper footing would be a great advantage to the country. They instructed their preses to circulate all member burghs, asking them to write to their MPs. The replies from the burghs were apparently favourable, although Glasgow called for an amendment to the bill, so as to give magistrates of towns which were counties in themselves the right to appoint officers.[19] Five counties also met to discuss Mountstuart's bill. Four — East Lothian, Kincardine, Aberdeen and Banff — declared in its favour, but Galloway was against it.[20] At least five other counties were summoned to meet, but either, as in the case of Midlothian, did not reach a decision, or made no subsequent announcement of their opinion.[21]

The relative lack of interest in the country left the London Scots to their own devices. Back up in the metropolis, Boswell busied himself anew on his patron's behalf, pertinaciously sounding Dr. Johnson and the Earl of Mansfield, in both cases without the least success. Later Boswell stayed up all night to copy Mountstuart's Commons' speech, thoughts of such an 'elegant connection' softening the 'dire labour'. For his part, however,

Mountstuart did virtually nothing, rather boasting to Boswell that he had not consulted his fellow Scottish MPs about alterations to the bill.[22] In fact several of them, including George Dempster, William Pulteney, Sir Adam Fergusson and, not least, Henry Dundas himself, were working hard to make the best of a bad job. Revision of the bill was certainly necessary, for its seems to have been drafted first by Englishmen, and to have reached the Scots full of anglicisms 'about as applicable to China as to Scotland'. After much labour, however, a bill was eventually produced which was very similar to Elliot's of 1760.[23]

The bill survived a Second Reading on 5 March 1776, and was sent into committee; but it was killed on 20 March, when the House considered the committee's report. The Scottish MPs, now joined by the ailing Elliot, argued as best they could on the bill's behalf, protesting that a Scottish militia should be seen not as a 'provincial' but as a 'national', British affair. This time the Scots also had formal government support, Lord North himself speaking in the debates. But the government's backing appears to have been conditional on the bill containing a clause expressly allowing the regular army to recruit from a Scottish militia, something quite unacceptable to the Scots. Meanwhile English opposition groups, the Rockinghamites and independents, were directly opposed to the bill. They claimed that the financial burden would fall largely on England, and, in a curious reversal of the Jacobite objection of 1760, voiced fears of the excessive loyalism displayed by the Scots during the present American war. The radical London MP Sawbridge went so far as to suggest that a Scots militia might well act as a standing army to impose despotism on England. These arguments carried the day, for the government made little attempt to rally its vote behind the bill. Defeat was by a margin of 112–93, on a motion to adjourn consideration of the committee's report on the bill for four months, well beyond the end of the session.[24]

The burial of the bill provoked Scottish opinion out of its previous indifference, and there was a noisy wake in the Edinburgh press in March and April 1776. Several letters protested at the 'gross affront' to Scotland, and at the insult perpetrated by Sawbridge in particular. Surely, a writer urged, the names of Knox, Buchanan and Fletcher proved the Scots' commitment to liberty. More than one correspondent professed to believe that continuation of the Union had become impossible; and a self-styled 'Vox Populi' argued that Scots should petition for a separate parliament like Ireland's, thus restoring their constitution to its ancient basis.[25] No action, however, followed these vapourings. As for the originators of the militia bill, Mountstuart and Boswell, they lost interest in the issue as suddenly as they had found it.

Following this Boswellian prologue, the cause of a Scottish militia lapsed until 1778. John Paul Jones then provided the excuse for a fresh agitation, Alexander Carlyle the necessary publicity. In January 1778 Carlyle completed his second full-length pamphlet on the issue, *A Letter to His Grace the Duke of Buccleugh on National Defence,* the first edition of which was published in London, and the second in Edinburgh in July.[26] A year later Carlyle followed up the pamphlet with further initiatives in the Scottish press: on this occasion there is positive evidence of his authorship of a series of pseudonymous letters in the *Caledonian Mercury* during the winter months of 1779–80.[27] Written specifically to exploit the anxiety created by Paul Jones, the newspaper contributions extended and applied the conclusions of the pamphlet *Letter on National Defence.* Together, in fact, the pamphlet and the letters to the *Caledonian Mercury* show Carlyle taking the opportunity for a major restatement of his case for a Scottish militia, in which he developed anew the political and social arguments he had first enunciated in 1760.

The general grounds on which Carlyle championed a militia remained those of the compromise English case of the 1750s. In line with principles of 'economy and preparation', a militia was conceived as a domestic reserve for an imperial regular army; it was by no means an alternative to that standing army.[28] On this basis the core of Carlyle's political argument for a specifically Scottish militia was likewise restated in terms almost identical with those he had used in his first pamphlet. Before all, it was still a matter of national pride and equality within the Union. It was humiliating that Scotland should lack adequate defence, and be exposed to the menaces of Paul Jones; exclusion from the militia was 'the badge of distinction between freemen and slaves'. The Scots had a claim of right to share 'the undoubted privilege of all Britons' to have arms for self-defence.[29]

While renewing the Scots' claim to share in this privilege, Carlyle's case had changed to the extent that he was now markedly less respectful towards the institution of the English militia. He might express regret over the failure of the 'Patriot Statesman' Mountstuart's English-style bill in 1776.[30] But he made it clear at the same time that the English model of a militia should not now command unquestioning acceptance. Betraying the intentions of its founders, ministers had so neglected the English militia as to reduce it to a condition in which the ignoble were able to obtain commissions and universal substitution was allowed in the ranks. In Carlyle's view examples more appropriate to Scotland were now to be found in America and Ireland. The rebel American colonists had in a few years become martial, and victorious, 'by the simple institution of a militia'.[31] No less pertinent in its way was the example of the (unauthorised) Irish Volunteer Associations. They provided the model for the 'private associations' which Carlyle wished to see formed in Scotland as a local defensive measure during the winter of 1779–80, while a national militia was being established by parliament.[32]

In forsaking the example of the English militia, and preferring that of the militias of the rebellious Americans and discontented Irish, Carlyle was far from countenancing disloyalty. On the contrary, being confident of Scottish commitment to the war, commitment to which he himself had given vigorous expression in his sermon *The Justice and Necessity of the War,* Carlyle had seen the opportunity to set his case for a Scottish militia in a new and larger imperial dimension. By the 1770s Scotland's own loyalty to the crown and constitution was no longer in doubt: Carlyle had no need to apologise for his countrymen's past Jacobitism. Instead he could point proudly to the most tangible evidence of Scotland's fidelity — the readiness of the common people, the gentry and not least the Highlanders to raise levies for His Majesty's service. In the present contest for America, indeed, it could plausibly be claimed that the Scots' record of loyalty was far better than that of the English themselves, misled as the latter were by 'popular demagogues'.[33] At the same time, Carlyle sought to show how the American War had given the concept of loyalty itself a new and extended significance. In the *Letter on National Defence* he went out of his way to insist on the unprecedented subversiveness of the present rebellion: where others could only have shifted the crown from one head to another, this one originated in 'republican principles of the most levelling kind', and attacked not only 'the person on the throne, but the throne itself; not only the royal power, but the supremacy of Parliament, the dignity and sovereignty of the State of Britain'.[34] In short, the American Rebellion had made it clear that it was the crown and parliament of the British Empire which now constituted the ultimate object of loyalty. As Carlyle then pointed out, this meant that the justification for a Scottish militia must transcend the simple relation between Scotland and England. Bound up with Scotland's national interest and honour were not only the interest and security of a united Britain, but the freedom, importance and dignity of the whole empire.[35] Though the association, if it was conscious, was unacknowledged, Carlyle had in effect placed the argument for a national militia within the most ambitious of Scottish unionist perspectives — the perspective of British imperial unionism that went back, through the Earl of Cromarty, to James VI and John Knox.

In its most fundamental respects, however, Carlyle's restatement of the case for a Scottish militia followed the lines laid down in 1760. On the one hand, it was still very much a matter of remedying the Scots' deficient 'national spirit'. Carlyle saw no reason to alter his early judgement that the Scots themselves were largely responsible for the neglect of their country's defences. In 1776 they had received the failure of Mountstuart's bill in 'silent submission'; and although support had indeed been greater for the previous bill of 1760, yet 'want of unanimity and zeal' had lost that too.[36] Even now the Scots appeared to be forgetting John Paul Jones almost as soon as he was off the horizon; and as for the disgrace of the 'Forty-Five, that had faded completely from memory.[37] Carlyle unhesitatingly singled out 'the gentlemen of Scotland' for condemnation. 'They, and they only, are to blame', he told readers of the *Caledonian Mercury* in 1779. He scoffed at the excuses offered. 'They were afraid of the expense; they disliked the trouble; they said it would draw too many hands from useful labour'. That the last in particular was a mere pretence was plain, Carlyle observed, from the gentry's subsequent zeal for new levies.[38] Once again, therefore, Carlyle exhorted the gentry not simply to look to Scotland's immediate defences, but 'to raise and preserve the warlike spirit in time coming'. By encouraging the military spirit, and making the military character more conspicuous and respectable, a militia would open new views to the nobility and gentry, and set before them at last worthy objects of their ambition.[39] The national case for a militia, in brief, was still presented in the essentially Stoic-moral terms which, I have suggested, Carlyle inherited from Belhaven. Cultivating anew the traditional martial values of the Scots, the militia was to preserve, within the framework of imperial union, the independent identity of the Scottish nation.

Continuity is likewise evident in a second fundamental feature of Carlyle's renewed argument for a Scottish militia. In terms very similar to those he had used in 1760, Carlyle insisted in the *Letter on National Defence* on the need 'to raise the military with our civil and commercial policy'. There should be no conflict between the two; but if there was, Carlyle was open in his conviction that 'it is surely better to be a little less rich and commercial, than by ceasing to be men, to endanger our existence as a nation'.[40] Again, too, Carlyle advocated the militia as an agent of social solidarity. As officers of the militia or leaders of the local defensive associations, the landowners would be placing themselves at the head of what Carlyle described in one of his letters as 'a superior order of men', the independent farmers, manufacturers and artisans of the country.[41] These were the themes of both Carlyle's and Ferguson's earlier militia pamphlets; and they reflected an attitude shared by the group of Moderate literati towards the Scottish past. Well rid though Scotland was of its Gothic barons, the social order still needed a martial framework to secure it against the corruptions and conflicts of the modern commercial age.

Carlyle's propaganda between 1778 and 1780 did not have all the success he might have hoped for: these years saw no coherent agitation for a militia to compare with the agitations of 1760 and 1762. Nevertheless the alarm over Paul Jones did prompt a number of other initiatives of a more local character to improve the country's defences, and to these Carlyle's contributions, along with those of several anonymous correspondents, offered timely encouragement.[42] All the more frustrating, therefore, that the Scots should find themselves faced with a government which had already made up its mind.

The authorities responsible for Scotland's defence — the Secretary of State for the Northern Department, the Lord Advocate, the War Office and the Commander-in-Chief in Scotland — had acted as soon as war in Europe became inevitable: their dispositions were agreed, if not yet put into effect, just as Paul Jones was making his first appearance. As a preliminary, they reviewed yet again the existing laws relating to a Scots militia; but by this time the law officers had no doubt that they were unworkable.[43] The concept of local defensive associations was similarly dismissed at an early stage: the Secretary of State was satisfied that they were illegal.[44] Rejecting these expedients, the government decided instead — as in 1759 — on the explicitly *ad hoc* solution of Fencible Regiments, embodied for the duration of the war only. Four such regiments were raised, of a thousand men each. Designated the Southern, Western, Sutherland and Northern Fencibles, their colonelcies were awarded respectively to the Duke of Buccleuch, Lord Frederick Campbell (brother of the fifth Duke of Argyll and MP for Glasgow Burghs), William Wemyss (cousin of the young Countess of Sutherland) and the Duke of Gordon. A commission was also issued to Earl of Eglinton, but was later withdrawn at Lord Frederick Campbell's insistence; other offers to raise regiments were reported, including one by the Duke of Queensberry, but must have been refused.[45] The Letters of Service expressly stipulated that the Fencibles were not to leave Scotland, except in the event of actual invasion of England, and that men should not be drafted from them into the regular army.[46]

Local anxieties, however, were by no means assuaged by the formation of the new regiments, and the government was soon pressed to permit more informal arming. In May 1778 the burghers of Aberdeen dusted off the weapons they had been sent in 1760 and began training; and despite explicit instructions from London, the Commander-in-Chief, General Oughton, felt unable to prevent them.[47] In September the re-appearance of Paul Jones persuaded Oughton to authorise the same thing at Ayr, and to issue arms to Dundee, Greenock and Campbeltown.[48] A year later it was the turn of the counties, the continued provocation of Paul Jones prompting East Lothian, Fife, Dumfries and Ross and Cromarty to draw up quite elaborate plans for local arming.[49] With the Fencibles now properly deployed, Oughton and ministers felt confident enough to refuse the proposals;[50] but the counties were far from satisfied. The gentry of East Lothian pursued the matter at a series of meetings in the winter months of 1779–80. A committee was established, the parishes were circulated, and on the basis of their reports Oughton was again requested to supply arms, the gentry accepting responsibility for their storage and distribution.[51] In December the Dumfries proposal was made the subject of a motion in the House of Commons, Lord George Gordon, seconded by George Dempster, requesting that ministers make arms available.[52] Later in the same month Ross and Cromarty renewed their request for arms through their original intermediary, the Lord Advocate Henry Dundas. Evidently swayed by the strength of public feeling on the issue, Dundas told the Secretary of State, Lord Stormont, that if something was not done he feared the Scots might take measures of self-defence without any authorisation at all. In reply Lord Stormont yielded to the extent of spelling out conditions on which the counties could be permitted to arm. Officers would have to be named and commissioned by the crown, and would not be regarded as holding permanent rank. There was to be no pay until the force was called out, and it would be liable to serve anywhere in Britain in the event of an invasion.[53] Such conditions, however, were not welcomed by East Lothian, whose spokesman, Lieutenant-Colonel John Fletcher-Campbell (Lord Milton's third son), protested that they had envisaged only a local force for coastal defence.[54] In one of his letters Carlyle publicly advised the gentry to ignore Stormont's conditions; and this they seem indeed to have done, continuing with the preparation of their own detailed contingency plan for future emergencies.[55]

At the same time as they requested permission to arm on a local scale, the gentry of East Lothian also attempted to interest other counties in a new demand for a national militia.[56] But although there was some response from Dumfries, Argyll and Berwickshire, the suggestion did not take hold.[57] Despite Carlyle's urging, the gentry do not seem generally to have regarded a militia as a natural extension of their own local initiatives; and as the Lord Advocate pointed out to Fletcher-Campbell, a proposal for a militia was idle unless the voice of the country was united. The experience of Mountstuart's bill had led Dundas himself to conclude that a militia was not generally acceptable among his countrymen.[58] The absence of a positive focus on the militia demand was underlined by the further diversion of its supporters' energies into the formation, early in 1780, of an 'Anti Gallican Society'. Of the sixteen reported present at the first meeting in Edinburgh, fourteen were Poker Club members. The list was headed by the Duke of Buccleuch, the Earls of Glencairn and Haddington and Colonel Fletcher-Campbell, and also included four literati, Carlyle, Ferguson, John Home and Adam Smith. The society's declared purpose was to contribute to national defence by offering prizes in marksmanship and cross-country hiking.[59] Its dignified membership, however, did not prevent it from becoming a target for some well-aimed ridicule in the newspapers, and it evidently achieved nothing.[60]

The entry of Holland into the war against Britain and the continuing attentions of privateers prompted one or two further local demands for arms in 1781. The Duke of Argyll requested a hundred stand of arms for Mull on the west highland coast; and in Aberdeen one John Ewen, a prominent merchant, renewed the proposal for a local defensive association.[61] In Edinburgh a volunteer 'Defensive Band' was actually formed, and paraded in uniform to musical accompaniment.[62] But not until 1782 were plans properly national in scale put forward again. And then the stimulus to do so seems to have been provided, not by any new military necessity, but rather by a change in political circumstances — the fall of Lord North and the advent of the Shelburne and Rockingham administration. It was the new government itself, in fact, which produced the first set of proposals, and these in turn triggered further initiatives from Scottish MPs, and, finally, from militia supporters in Scotland.

Shelburne and Rockingham came to power to make peace in the war which North had lost. None the less, one of their first acts in government was to attempt to strengthen the nation's defences along the lines they had suggested when in opposition. Early in May 1782 Shelburne announced proposals for additional defence that would tap hitherto neglected local and especially urban resources. Selected burghs were offered the opportunity to raise defensive corps from among their inhabitants, with officers named by the magistrates. Initially the scheme was to cover only major English towns. But following consultations between Shelburne, the Lord Advocate and the Lord Provosts of Edinburgh, Glasgow and Aberdeen, it was decided at the end of the month to extend the offer, in an altered form, to forty-five Scottish coastal burghs as well. From a comparison of the published English and Scottish versions of the proposals, it would appear that the latter diverged in two important respects. There was no provision in the Scottish version for appointing neighbouring gentlemen as officers in the burgh corps; and where the English proposals stated that a corps could be ordered to leave its own burgh in case of 'actual invasion or rebellion', the Scottish version contained the unprecedented stipulation that a corps could be so moved only with its own 'free will and consent'.[63] It would seem that the Lord Provosts were determined to assert their independence both of the Scottish gentry and of the metropolitan authorities.

In the minds of the Scottish burghs, however, fears over defence had already yielded precedence to other concerns: despite the consultations and alterations, Shelburne's plan was given a very mixed reception. The magistrates of Aberdeen approved of the scheme, but those of Edinburgh and Glasgow came out against it once they had consulted the trades' organisations in their cities. There was a strong feeling in Glasgow that Shelburne's proposals would make heavy demands on the labouring classes in particular, and thus disrupt the city's commerce and manufactures; in this regard, the magistrates believed, a proper militia, with ballot and substitution, would be greatly preferable.[64] A rather different reason for opposition was expressed by 'A. Burgess' of Pittenweem, writing in the *Caledonian Mercury*. The inhabitants of the East Fife burgh, he reported, had wished to take up arms, but they would not do so while a magistrate whom they had no vote in electing had the power to name their officers.[65] Later, in September, Shelburne's plan was supposedly followed in the formation of another Edinburgh defensive corps, styled 'The Caledonian Band'; but this was not organised by the burgh council.[66]

In spite of the indifferent response from the intended beneficiaries, Shelburne's proposals did stimulate fresh interest in a Scottish militia. First to stir were several young Scottish MPs. From John Sinclair, MP for Caithness and future statistician of Scotland, there came a portentous pamphlet, *Considerations on Militias and Standing Armies* (1782). Citing Machiavelli and Montesquieu, Robertson and Gibbon, Sinclair criticised

Shelburne's plan, and advocated instead both universal military training and the extension of the existing English model of a militia to Scotland.[67] More practical steps in this last direction were meanwhile being taken by another young Scottish MP, James, Marquess of Graham. Graham announced his intention to move a Scottish Militia bill on 10 May 1782, during the Commons debate on Shelburne's proposals; and he was promptly seconded by James, Lord Maitland.[68] Graham's motives appear to have been similar to Mountstuart's in 1776: the son of the second Duke of Montrose, he was then engaged in rebuilding his family's Scottish political interest.[69] Unlike Mountstuart, however, Graham did not seek to do so by challenging Henry Dundas, nor did he neglect to consult his fellow Scottish MPs about his bill. With Dundas's support, Graham proceeded almost immediately to convene a meeting at St. Alban's Tavern on 13 May, when he invited the forty-five Scottish MPs, the representative peers and some forty other noblemen and gentlemen in London to consider the best plan.

Unfortunately, Graham had reckoned without one wayward but still potent force in Scottish politics at the time — Lord George Gordon, the instigator of the No-Popery riots which had shaken London two years previously. As Graham rose to open his meeting, Dundas sitting at his right hand, he was sharply interrupted and called to order by Gordon. Gordon had three points to make. First, despite his manifold claims by birth, relation, wealth and independence, he, Lord George Gordon, had not been invited to the meeting. Second, Graham's taking of the chair was inadmissible: the most senior nobleman present at the meeting, the Duke of Hamilton, should have precedence. Third, and most important of all, Graham was in any case disqualified for want of the proper presbyterian credentials. None should be preses of such a meeting, Gordon explained, who had not subscribed to every one of the decrees, confessions and covenants which the Kirk had issued in Reformation, Civil War and Revolution — all of which Gordon then rehearsed for the benefit of those present. It was not to be expected, Gordon at last concluded, that 'in these rebellious times' so alarming an affair as changing the militia laws of Scotland could be allowed unless 'the true Church of Jehovah be guarded and defended, in the right stile, against all idolatry and profanation,... popery and prelacy, and foreign and domestic enemies'. At which imprecation the hapless Graham's meeting not unnaturally collapsed in uproar.[70]

Admirably undeterred, Graham pressed ahead with his bill, which appears to have been closely similar to the previous Scottish militia bills of Elliot and Mountstuart. But it did not last long in the Commons. It received a first reading on 27 May, and a second on the 31st, when Dempster spoke for it with much warmth. However, on 10 June, as the House prepared to go into committee on the bill, the Secretary at War, Henry Conway, successfully moved a clause to permit recruiting from the proposed militia. Both Graham and Dundas found the implicit distinction between England and Scotland on this point unacceptable, and Graham consequently had to withdraw the bill.[71]

With a Commons' career of just a month, Graham's bill had hardly had time to gather much support in Scotland itself: only one county, Dumfries, declared in its favour before it was withdrawn, and no burgh exerted itself.[72] A little more interest was shown once the bill had been lost. Kirkcudbright Stewartry and Linlithgowshire publicly voted thanks to Graham;[73] and as in 1776 there was a certain amount of recriminatory debate in the papers. On this occasion the press exchanges were sharpened by a new note of party politics, as contributors attacked or defended the Whig ministry's role in blocking the bill.[74] To one correspondent, however, this 'bawling for a militia' simply showed the Scots to be dupes of young men wishing to acquire popularity. Whilst 'foolishly clamorous for points of pride', they were neglecting much more important economic and political grievances, and forgetting indeed that

> .... so long as the people ... have no share in the administration of the country, or in the public purse, their interest will at all times be sacrificed to that of the great proprietors who choose their representatives in Parliament.[75]

As it happened, however, the season of foolish clamour had only just begun.

If neither Shelburne's plan nor Graham's bill could by themselves arouse more than limited enthusiasm in Scotland, they did suceed in provoking Scottish militia supporters at last to devise their own alternative model. Within three months of the loss of Shelburne's bill, a wholly new set of proposals had been produced, the so-called 'Sketch of a Bill for the Better Ordering the Fencible Men in that part of Great Britain called Scotland'; and in the autumn of 1782 a campaign to win national support for these new proposals was energetically set on foot.

The Sketch of a Bill ostensibly originated from a public meeting of 'noblemen and gentlemen from the different parts of Scotland', held under the chairmanship of the Earl of Glencairn at Fortune's Tavern in Edinburgh on 5 August 1782. Resolving unanimously that 'a proper distribution of arms and the establishment of a national defence is necessary to the safety and honour of this country', the meeting called for the formation of 'a constitutional, safe and useful militia, suited to the state of this part of the United Kingdom'. A committee was then appointed to prepare a bill in accordance with these resolutions. It was further agreed that, when ready, the bill would be submitted to the counties for their opinion: Sir John Dalrymple's warning from past experience that such consultation would only result in division was overborne. The committee was originally fifteen strong. Aside from its convenor, the Lord Provost of Edinburgh, and its secretary and treasurer, the Edinburgh bookseller William Creech, it consisted entirely of peers, gentry and lawyers. There were three earls, Glencairn, Moray and Haddington, and Haddington's eldest son Lord Binning, along with the Lord Advocate, Sir John Dalrymple, Sir John Halkett, Dewar of Vogrie, Col. John Fletcher-Campbell, Thomas Kennedy of Dunnure, Andrew Crosbie, Col. (probably Hugh) Montgomery and the Hon. William Elphinstone.[76] Subsequently, seven others were added to the committee — the Marquess of Graham, the Earls of Selkirk and Loudon, William McDowall of Garthland, Sir Alexander Don, John Shaw Stewart and Murray of Broughton. As the committee was enlarged, however, the actual drafting of the bill was delegated to a sub-committee, whose membership was not published. Its production thus expedited, the Sketch of a Bill was ready by late August.[77]

It would seem, however, that this new initiative in the campaign for a Scottish militia did not in fact begin with the 5 August meeting. For once the evidence points to a prior lead having been given by the Poker Club. At a regular meeting of the club at Fortune's on 19 July 1782, the four members who attended, Sir John Dalrymple, John Adam, Robert Chalmers and James Edgar, agreed to advertise a meeting 'on special business of the militia' in a fortnight's time. The proposed meeting was brought forward, and next Friday, 26 July, there was an unusually large attendance of seventeen at The Poker. At this special meeting the Marquess of Graham and Sir James Johnstone were elected members of the club, and Graham was thanked for his efforts on behalf of a militia in the last session. More significantly, the meeting also appointed a committee of nine to frame a bill for a Scotch militia. On this were placed Graham, Glencairn, the Lord Advocate, Sir John Halkett, Col. Fletcher-Campbell, Kennedy of Dunnure, James Edgar, Major Rutherford of Edgerton and Adam Ferguson — although five, including Graham, Glencairn and the Lord Advocate, were not actually present at the meeting.[78]

The overlap in the membership of the Poker and public committees was significant. Five of the Poker committee — Glencairn, the Lord Advocate, Halkett, Fletcher-Campbell and Kennedy — moved directly on to the public committee on 5 August, and they were shortly joined by a sixth in Lord Graham. In addition the full public committee contained another four members of the Poker Club, though not of its special committee — Haddington, Dalrymple (both of whom were present at the club meeting on 26 July), Binning and Crosbie.[79] Men of the Poker, therefore, eventually made up almost half of the total public committee of twenty-two. Furthermore, it would seem that one of their number, Colonel John Fletcher-Campbell, assumed the leadership of the vital drafting sub-committee. It was Fletcher-Campbell, on behalf of the public committee, who corresponded with Graham, then out of Edinburgh 'shooting in the hills', about the new proposals. Fletcher-Campbell was also in communication with one Atkinson in Dublin, who knew the Patriot leadership there, and reported on the role of the Volunteer Companies in the 'emancipation' of Ireland.[80] Most important, it appears to have been Fletcher-Campbell, with some help from Adam Ferguson (another member of the Poker committee), who wrote the Sketch of a Bill and the explanatory official 'Observations' which were appended to it.[81] As we shall now see, this collaboration between a Fletcher of Saltoun and the ablest Moderate militia theorist brought the demand for a Scottish militia to a remarkably radical climax.

The Sketch of a Bill was unashamedly ambitious.[82] Defining its object as 'the greatest safety at the least expense', the Sketch envisaged the training of 25,000 men annually in strict rotation, virtually without exemption or substitution, until all 'fencible' or arms-bearing men in Scotland were qualified for national defence. Although stated to be concerned primarily with providing instruction in the use of arms, rather than with settling the form of organisation in which the men would serve, the proposals suggested a clear structure of both administration and command. The units of organisation were to be the parish and the county: there was no mention of separate arrangements for burghs, and only Edinburgh was recognised as raising a quota of its own. Commissions of Lieutenancy were to be issued in each county, and Deputy Lieutenants appointed to organise balloting. The purpose of the balloting was simply to decide the order in which men did their service, but there would be separate ballots for field officers, subalterns and the ranks. The qualifications for field officers and subalterns were fixed at £300 and £100 worth of lands respectively, although it was said not to be the intention to exclude subalterns from promotion if a method consistent with the principle of qualification could be devised. Both classes of officers would serve for two years at a time. The ballot for the ranks would cover all fencible men of fixed abode between the ages of 16 and 56. The men were to serve for a year only, and thereafter were not to be balloted again until all other qualified men in the parish had taken their turn in training.

The ambitious scope of the Sketch of a Bill is equally evident in the arrangements it proposed for training such numbers. In the first place, it was stipulated that the arms, though provided at public expense, were to be kept by the men, on their swearing on oath not to use them to destroy game or assist 'tumultous assemblies'. This extraordinary proposal was justified in the 'Observations' on the bill with the argument that arms kept in depositories could be seized by the evil-minded, while a lawfully armed people was the best security against either faction or tyranny. The training itself was to be unusually intensive. The men would be exercised several times a week, outside the usual hours of labour, in their parishes; and twice a year, at Midsummer and Christmas, the whole force of the country was to be assembled. On these occasions emulation among the ranks was to be encouraged by premiums for marksmanship and exercise; and this appeal to the 'interest' of the men would be reinforced by the example and influence of the officers, in whom it was presumed that a regard for the public would be a sufficient motive for service. Lest such stimuli be still inadequate, however, the Sketch of a Bill envisaged a further source of inspiration in religion. Every Sunday the parish corps was to parade to Church; and the annual delivery of arms was to be solemnised by a prayer and homily from the parish minister. The 'Observations' emphasised that it was a particular object of the plan to connect the new force 'intimately . . . with the established religion of the country, one of whose happy effects is to form those opinions that are the basis of civil and military authority'. In this and other respects, the 'Observations' continued, the new plan closely resembled the celebrated military establishment of the free states of the Alps, to which they owed not only their security, but their excellent national character.

Finally, the Sketch of a Bill outlined a procedure for calling out the proposed force on active service. It was made clear that it could expect to be deployed against civil tumult as well as invasion; in the former case the force would be under the direction of the magistrates. The civil liberties of the men themselves, however, were to be respected: they were not to be subject to martial law, except when called out on pay. Even then the object and duration of their march were to be specified to them, and any subsequent change or prolongation was not to be made without the consent of the corps (although how this was to be obtained was not stated).

In addition to Fletcher-Campbell's official 'Observations', the Sketch of a Bill was glossed and supported by two other powerful contributions published in the Edinburgh papers. One of these, under the pseudonym 'Nestor' in the *Caledonian Mercury*, is definitely attributable to Alexander Carlyle.[83] Carlyle hailed the new proposals as proof that 'some remains of national spirit' still survived. The departure from the English model of a militia was especially welcome. While continuing to regard the rejection of the English-style Scottish bill in 1760 as 'a truly national affront', Carlyle confirmed his recent renunciation of that model by declaring roundly that the English militia had been 'depraved' into a standing army. Its great defects of substitution and lengthy embodiment were, however, avoided by the Sketch of a Bill, which ought, Carlyle calculated, to have all the fencible men in Scotland trained to arms within ten to twelve years.[84] Carlyle justified the break with the English model in terms both general and particular. As well as referring to the 'inherent right' of free men to a military education, he now also invoked the specific obligation of Scotsmen to bear arms under their ancient and feudal constitution. This obligation was documented in an appendix to the letter, in which Carlyle listed the relevant pre-Union statutes. Citing the opinion of the seventeenth-century Jacobite jurist Sir George Mackenzie, Carlyle claimed that 'the established constitution of Scotland with regard to arms' continued 'unaltered to this day'. By recurring to that ancient constitution, Carlyle was confident that the Sketch of a Bill would revive 'the general spirit and manhood of the people'.

The second unofficial gloss on the new plan, entitled 'Observations on the Intended Scots Militia Bill', provides a striking complement to Carlyle's contribution.[85] For the unknown writer of this piece it was the social implications of the Sketch of a Bill which needed emphasis; and he drew them out by means of a remarkable comparison between England and Scotland:

> As most of the tenantry in England are, by the laws of that country, entitled to vote at elections to Parliament, there is a mutual tie between landlord and tenant; for the landlord depends on the tenant for his vote, and the tenant on his landlord for a cheap rent; and, as the clergy preach only the simple beautiful truths of Christianity, they are respected both by the high and the low. But in Scotland there are no such fortunate types of human life. The tenant hates his landlord, because he thinks he takes too much rent; the landlord thinks he does not get enough. If the clergyman preach the simple truths of Christianity, the lower order of his hearers will turn Seceeders; and if he preach mysteries only, the gentry will not go to Church. Hence the ranks of men are estranged from each other in this country.

The Scots had indeed come, the writer concluded, to a virtually Hobbesian state of *'bellum omnium contra omnes'*. But the proposed new militia could yet retrieve them from this predicament. By uniting the higher and lower orders with the clergy in one common interest, honour and activity, it would bring Scotland to 'the noblest state of civil society, that in which there will be *amicitia omnium cum omnibus'*. Thus, declared the writer, the Sketch of a Bill, 'considered relatively to the circumstances of the country to which it is to apply, may be justly termed the completion of human wisdom'.

Expounded and glossed in such expansive terms, the Sketch of a Bill is a document of considerable potential significance. In several respects, it is true, the Sketch did merely build on recent initiatives. The possibilities of a more flexible, locally organised defensive force had already been indicated on several occasions during the American War. In particular the local distribution of arms and private training had both been canvassed by the Scottish counties; and the stipulation that a corps should not be moved out of its locality without its own consent had apparently been accepted in Shelburne's plan. Even admitting such precedents, however, the ambition of the Sketch of a Bill is remarkable. In scale and form it broke conclusively with the model of the English militia. Sacrificing numbers to the supposed requirements of military efficiency and the need to safeguard central executive authority, the English militia had effectively renounced any pretension to being a national service. The Sketch of a Bill, by contrast, would universalise military education by aligning its organisation and command directly with that of civil society in parish and county community. In the process it would annually re-institute a force of 25,000 permanently armed and minimally trained men, responsible first to their local communities, and only then to the central authorities. Not since

Andrew Fletcher's visionary scheme for a militia in 1698 had so ambitious a plan of national defence been prepared in Scotland — and not even that had actually been put to the Scottish counties and their representatives, as the Sketch of a Bill was now to be.

Why should the demand for a Scottish militia have culminated in a plan so far-reaching? The explanation, I suggest, lies in the aspirations to which the militia demand had all along given expression. From the previous writings of Alexander Carlyle, persistently the demand's leading publicist, I have already analysed these aspirations as twofold. The first was to renew the traditional martial spirit of the Scots, and hence to affirm the survival of an independent national identity within the Union. The second was to restore the cohesion of Scottish society in a reconstructed martial framework that would secure it alike against a return to the oppressions of the Gothic past and against a descent into the corruptions of the commercial future. The Sketch of a Bill, I would now argue, was designed to fulfil both aspirations to an extent impossible with the English model of a militia.

In the first place, the new plan unequivocally asserted Scotland's independent identity within the Union. Proposing a form of defence adapted to specifically Scottish circumstances, and in line with Scottish constitutional custom, the Sketch of a Bill signalled that partnership with England was not automatically to be interpreted as assimilation to English institutions. Carlyle's ancient constitutional gloss of the Sketch underlined the point quite explicitly — if also, given Carlyle's adoption just four years earlier of an imperial unionist perspective, somewhat inconsistently. But perhaps the end of a war in which half the empire had been lost was not the moment to insist on the imperial dimension; and while ancient constitutionalism was enjoying a certain vogue in Scotland at this time, it is most unlikely that Carlyle wished seriously to question the Union itself. Much more probably his resort to ancient constitutional rhetoric only reflected his confidence that the Scots need no longer slavishly follow English examples. In any case, the primary concern of Carlyle and, it would seem, of the author of the Sketch, was less with the militia as a military and political institution than with the restoration of martial and hence national spirit. Uppermost in Carlyle's mind all along, this was a concern whose full expression had hitherto been inhibited by the need to follow the English model of a militia: with the Sketch of a Bill it could be brought into the open. The new plan might well be supposed to offer a more effective physical defence of Scotland. But this was secondary, if not incidental, to its fundamental purpose: to enable every qualified member of the national community by the possession and practice of arms to cultivate the military virtues, and so to affirm the distinct national identity of Scotland within the Union.

The second, social aspiration articulated in the Scottish militia demand had in the past tended to receive less attention, even though its general principles had been clearly stated in Ferguson's pamphlet of 1756. In the Sketch of a Bill, however, the social aspiration is given at least as much emphasis as the national. Avowedly the Sketch sought to match the organisation of national defence as closely as possible to the existing structure of Scottish society. In fact the view of Scottish society which the Sketch projected was at best a simplified one, being framed in terms of two criteria only, landownership and residence within a parish community. By its explicit provisions, the Sketch of a Bill specified a social order of three levels of landownership: an upper rank of substantial (noble and gentle) landowners, qualified to be field officers; a middling rank of smaller landowners, qualified as subalterns; and a lower rank of householders, the main body of the force. At the same time the criterion of landownership also implicitly entailed exclusion and omission. Excluded from the provisions of the Sketch were those of no fixed abode; and omitted was any recognition that the town might constitute a social system distinct from that of the land. Both exclusion and omission were rendered plausible, however, by the second social criterion assumed in the Sketch, residence within the parish community. In effect the parish community was presumed to be the universal base unit of civil society, the key to its cohesion. On the one hand, therefore, residence within the parish community was an obvious prerequisite for full membership of civil society; while on the other, the universality of the parish community made it possible to integrate the town within a single, essentially territorial conception of the social order.

As glossed by the second, anonymous commentator, this vision of Scottish society presents something of a paradox. Where Carlyle commended the Sketch precisely because it followed Scottish rather than English precedents, it was the adoption of English in place of Scottish standards of social harmony which drew the anonymous commentator's praise. The paradox is nevertheless more apparent than real. The hollowness of Carlyle's ancient constitutionalism was here matched by the unreality of the comparison with English society. Clearly a simplification of existing Scottish society, the social assumptions of the Sketch were still more so of the increasingly developed and diversified society south of the border. The image of English social harmony which the Sketch supposedly projected was itself the product of a Scottish imagination; and what was being imagined was rather, it may be suggested, the martial cohesion held to exist in Scottish society of old. First displayed in the historical and dramatic works of the Moderate literati in the 1750s, this conviction of the traditional martial cohesiveness of Scottish society still seems to underlie the social case for a militia in 1782. In projecting this simple, traditional image of social harmony, moreover, the authors and exponents of the Sketch of a Bill can again be seen to have laid their emphasis on the moral rather than the institutional purposes of the militia. Instead of establishing a distinct institution, the Sketch sought as far as possible to merge the militia's organisation into the desired social order, making the bearing of arms into the symbol of each rank's allegiance to the values appropriate to its station. Promoting responsibility in the higher ranks, respect in the lower, and rational religion in all, the proposed new militia would provide the moral framework needed to ensure the continuing cohesion of Scottish society.

So it was, I suggest, in giving such full expression to the twin national and social aspirations of the Scottish militia demand that the Sketch of a Bill offered the most ambitious plan of a militia since Andrew Fletcher's scheme of 1698. Just because it merits such comparison, however, the Sketch of a Bill prompts one further observation. Fletcherian as it was in scope, it was yet far from Fletcherian in character. Rather the reverse: the Sketch confirms the extent to which the Moderate militia men had moved away from Fletcher's original vision. What distanced the Moderates from Fletcher was, above all, their devaluation of the institutional significance of the militia, and concentration instead on its moral implications. Where Fletcher had sought a Scottish militia as an institutional guarantee of national liberty and independence, the Moderates, following Belhaven, would rather put their faith in the preservation of independence by martial spirit alone. Where Fletcher had envisaged the militia as an institution to shape society and school men in virtue — by compulsion if necessary — the Moderates, after their teacher Hutcheson, would rather rely on the gradual diffusion of martial values of responsibility, respect and solidarity. Where Fletcher, in other words, conceived of the militia in strict civic terms as the institutional framework in which to affirm citizenship of the Scottish political community, the Moderates cast it rather in the Stoic–Ciceronian terms of moral commitment alone. In the final analysis, therefore, the ambition of the Moderate militia men, even in the Sketch of a Bill, fell far short of the genuine radicalism of Andrew Fletcher. Fletcher intended the militia to transform the nation's martial inheritance, reconstituting the Scottish political community and remodelling social relations. The militia of the Moderates, by contrast, would do no more than adapt that inheritance to the circumstances of the Union and of commercial society, the better to preserve its traditional, moral contribution to national identity and social solidarity.[86] For the heroic, transforming — but utopian — vision of Fletcher, the Moderate advocates of a militia had substituted aspirations altogether less radical — but perhaps also less impractical.

It remains now to see what response the Sketch of a Bill did in fact arouse in the Scottish political community.

In the event, the winter of 1782–83 was to see the final frustration of the Scottish militia demand during the American War. It was a winter which began early, and, succeeding as it did a wet summer and another hard winter, it saw Scotland suffer its most severe harvest shortage for forty years.[87] Yet if the militia eventually fell a casualty of this crisis, it did not do so without a spirited fight. For in the six months between October 1782 and March 1783, months corresponding with the height of the shortage, the issue of a Scottish militia aroused more public interest than ever before. What did most to frustrate the agitation, in fact, was not indifference but indecision: in their own enthusiasm, the county gentry could not be brought to concentrate their support behind any single plan.

A canvass of the counties had been agreed at the public meeting on 5 August; and subsequently, in October and November 1782, as many as twenty counties are recorded as having met to consider the issue. Before them they had both the Sketch of a Bill issued by the 5 August committee, and the Marquess of Graham's earlier, more conventional English-style bill. Unfortunately, however, the counties seem to have felt no compulsion to produce a clear answer: Sir John Dalrymple's fear that the canvass would merely result in division was to be justified. Only one county, Midlothian, actually declared against a militia altogether. At a thinly attended meeting Sheriff Archibald Cockburn scorned the demand at a time when Scotland was still far behind England in agriculture and manufactures, and recommended the gentry to devote themselves to the more urgent business of supplying the poor with meal at a moderate price.[88] But although such considerations did not divert the other counties, these were none the less unable to reach a definite decision. No more than six expressed a reasonably clear preference for either the Sketch or Graham's bill. Two of these, Dumfries and Inverness, declared for the Sketch,[89] while Berwick, Fife, Aberdeen and Linlithgow (the last two with reservations) were in favour of Graham's bill.[90] The remaining thirteen — Perth, Forfar, Dumbarton, Ayr, Lanark, Renfrew, Kirkcudbright, Wigton, Argyll, East Lothian, Stirling, Ross and Cromarty — expressed in various ways their conviction of the necessity of a militia, as a national defence and constitutional right, but felt that they could not approve of either plan proposed.[91]

The counties' reservations about each plan followed a common pattern. Of Graham's bill it was objected that it imitated the English model of a militia too closely: the force it proposed would be too much like a standing army.[92] In the case of the Sketch of a Bill, it was feared that a militia such as it envisaged would be inconveniently and expensively large.[93] It was also protested by a writer in the press and a pamphleteer that the Sketch was too 'republican', since by providing that men should only be mobilised with their own consent it placed an unprecedented limitation on the authority of the sovereign.[94] This constitutional objection, however, did not noticeably trouble the counties. To the contrary, the Kirkcudbright Stewartry meeting was confident that the Sketch of a Bill was at least 'more advantageous to liberty' than Graham's bill.[95]

The remarkably high level of interest — and of indecision — aroused by this militia agitation is reflected as well in the manner as in the scale of the counties' response. Almost all the county meetings appointed committees to pursue the matter in more detail, and to confer with representatives of other counties and the central Edinburgh committee. Some counties were quite ostentatiously diligent. Kirkcudbright appointed a Stewartry committee of thirty-two, and urged the gentry to meet in local sub-committees as well, so that 'the sense of many be collected in a manner becoming a free people'. In East Lothian the special committee speedily drew up a long list of detailed amendments to the Sketch, while the Stirlingshire committee apparently prepared an entirely new bill of its own.[96] The instigators of the agitation were active in these local proceedings: there were members of the 5 August Committee on at least seven county committees, and Poker Club members on as many as twelve.[97] The involvement of these at the centre of the agitation signally failed, however, to improve co-ordination at the local level: their participation indeed rather underlined the incorrigible diversity of the counties' responses. The Earl of Glencairn, preses of the public meeting on 5 August, was appointed to the committees of both Ayrshire and Renfrewshire; yet these counties were among the majority which had objections to both the Sketch and Graham's bill. In East Lothian Col. Fletcher-Campbell and Lord Binning were on the county committee which came up with a string of amendments to the bill which Fletcher-Campbell himself had originally drafted. The gentry, it seems, would suffer no dictation on a matter as interesting as the militia.

The counties having pronounced, the organisers of the agitation had to do what they could to impose order on the hundred flowers of the gentry's imagination. On 27 November 1782 a joint meeting of the 5 August Committee and the appointed delegates from the counties was convened at Fortune's Tavern in Edinburgh. The meeting was evidently something of a celebration, since at least eight toasts were reported, honouring among others the King, the Land of Cakes and its sister kingdoms, and the memory of the Marquess of Montrose and Andrew Fletcher of Saltoun. Duly fortified, the gathering re-affirmed the principle that 'an internal constitutional defence is necessary for the safety and dignity of... Scotland', and agreed on several modifications to the Sketch of a Bill. The number to be trained each year was halved, to 12,500, and the period of service was made two years instead of one. Although the ban on substitution was confirmed, some exceptions were now to be allowed. The meeting continued to insist, however, on the distribution of arms to the people, and demanded an explicit prohibition on recruiting from the force. To determine the details of the revised plan the meeting then appointed another sub-committee, headed by Fletcher-Campbell, and including also Islay Campbell, John Johnstone, William Nairne, Alexander Gordon and Andrew Crosbie. Of these six, Fletcher-Campbell and Crosbie were both on the original 5 August Committee, and they, Islay Campbell and Nairne were Poker members.[98] The new committee's draft, the so-called 'Heads of a Bill for the Better Ordering the Fencible Men in that Part of Great Britain called Scotland', was ready in mid-December. It was approved at a further general meeting on the 16th, published early in January 1783, and sent out to obtain again the opinion of the counties. Copies of the plan were also dispatched to Lord Graham, the Scottish MPs and English sympathisers, in the hope that it would be introduced as a parliamentary bill.[99]

Fourteen counties reconvened in the New Year to consider the Heads of a Bill. But even though the new plan contained modifications suggested and endorsed by their own delegates, the counties still could not give it their undivided support. Only three, Stirling, Dumbarton and Kirkcudbright, were prepared to accept the revised proposals.[100] Five others, Ayr, East Lothian, Inverness, Ross and Cromarty continued to demand changes; Berwick upheld its earlier preference for a militia on the English model; and Forfar reached no recorded decision.[101] Most damaging of all, four counties, Fife, Linlithgow, Lanark and Aberdeen, joined the original dissenter Midlothian in outright opposition to any militia (although Linlithgow would have settled for one on English lines if absolutely necessary). Briefly but emphatically, Lanark and Aberdeen declared that they found the proposals unnecessary and improper in present circumstances.[102]

Still stronger views were held by the burghs, which had hitherto been entirely omitted from this agitation. At the prompting of Glasgow and Paisley, these now voiced their resentment. A meeting of the Annual Committee of the Royal Burghs on 31 January 1783 sharply criticised the noblemen and gentlemen of Scotland for failing to consult the burghs, and recorded the conviction that the Heads of a Bill was 'eroneous in principle and hurtful and injurious to the commerce and manufactures of this country'. As with Shelburne's plan, the absence of provision for substitution aroused particular concern. The Committee of Royal Burghs accordingly declared its intention to oppose any attempt to have the draft bill passed into law.[103]

The agitation for a Scottish militia petered out in the fortunately mild spring of 1783. Since opinion, solicited and unsolicited, was so divided in the localities, there was little more that the activists in Edinburgh and London could do. In May Fletcher-Campbell travelled to London with letters from an Edinburgh committee, requesting Graham to introduce a bill;[104] but although Graham did raise the subject during a Commons' debate on army estimates in June, there was no bill.[105] As late as December Graham dutifully attended a meeting of Scottish MPs in London on the militia — to find that only' one other member appeared.[106] By then public interest in Scotland had long since died.

Little more than a decade later, in 1797, a Scottish Militia Act would pass through parliament virtually unopposed; and within another year the ten regiments of the six thousand strong force would be embodied. The story of the Scottish militia's formation during the Wars of the French Revolution has been told elsewhere, and is not my concern here.[107]

Nevertheless, by way of postscript, it is worth recapitulating briefly the circumstances in which a national militia was at last established in Scotland: they stand in salutary contrast with the history of the earlier, unsuccessful agitations for a Scottish militia during the Seven Years' and American Wars.

There was, in the first place, no agitation for a militia in the 1790s. The decision to institute one was taken and carried out by the government, and was the particular responsibility of Henry Dundas, now Secretary for War. Straightforwardly military considerations were uppermost in the decision: in the face of the unparalleled mobilisation achieved by revolutionary France, the government's traditional resort, regiments of Fencibles (raised in 1793), was no longer regarded as providing adequate defence. Even so, Dundas prepared the ground for a new militia with care: no doubt he was still mindful of the lack of unanimity on the subject which he had detected during the American War. The difficult but crucial political decision to appoint Lords Lieutenant was taken in 1794. To accustom the gentry to a military role, the Lieutenants and their Deputies were encouraged to raise volunteer companies for internal security, and to make preliminary arrangements for the compulsory militia ballot. If the gentry were thus well prepared for the institution of a militia, however, so too were those who would be obliged to serve in it, the common people of Scotland. First attempts to raise the regiments in August and September 1797 were met by a wave of rioting, spreading from Berwickshire and Galloway in the south, through the Lothians and central Scotland, and finally reaching the highlands of Perthshire and Aberdeenshire.[108] The protest was on a scale unmatched by any other popular action in Scotland in the eighteenth century, and in some places almost certainly had the benefit of radical political leadership. For a moment the authorities wavered; but convinced that Jacobin sedition was at the root of the trouble, Dundas and the Home Secretary insisted that the militia be enforced. Exhortation was backed up by coercion: the worst incident was at Tranent in East Lothian, where twelve were indiscriminately slaughtered by dragoons in the aftermath of a riot. In effect it needed the standing army to institute the militia in Scotland, English soldiers to impose military service on Scottish citizens.

NOTES

1. A. Temple Patterson, *The Other Armada. The Franco–Spanish Attempt to Invade Britain in 1779* (Manchester 1960).

2. *Aberdeen Journal*, 4 May 1778 (extracts of letters from Dumfries, 25 April), 17 Aug., 14 Sept. 1778; *Caledonian Mercury*, 20 Sept. 1779, *Glasgow Mercury*, 23 Sept. 1779.

3. *Glasgow Mercury*, 17 Aug. 1780; *Aberdeen Journal*, 28 May 1781.

4. Western, *The English Militia*, pp. 198, 205–15. Direct recruitment from the

militia into the regular army was forbidden under the 1757 Act, but numbers of militiamen did proceed to enlist in the army.

5. Namier and Brooke, *The Commons 1754–90*, II, pp. 390–4.

6. Murdoch, '*The People Above*', pp. 128–31; Duff, *Scotland's War Losses*, pp. 14–16.

7. D. I. Fagerstrom, 'Scottish Opinion and the American Revolution', *William and Mary Quarterly*, 3rd series, XI (1954); D. B. Swinfen, 'The American Revolution in the Scottish Press', in O. D. Edwards and G. Shepperson (eds.), *Scotland, Europe and the American Revolution* (Edinburgh 1976).

8. [Adam Ferguson,] *Remarks on a Pamphlet lately published by Dr. Price intitled: 'Observations on the Nature of Civil Liberty, the Principles of Government, and the Justice and Policy of the War with America', in a letter from a Gentleman in the Country to a Member of Parliament* (London 1776).

9. Alexander Carlyle, *The Justice and Necessity of the War with our American Colonies Examined. A Sermon, Preached at Inveresk, December 12, 1776* (Edinburgh 1777). Quotation on p. 23. It was a reply to Erskine insofar as it took the same Biblical text, Judges XX.28, as Erskine's *Shall I go to War with my American Brethren?* (1769, 2nd edition, Edinburgh 1776).

10. *Parliamentary Register, on History of the Proceedings and Debates of the Houses of Parliament, during the Fourteenth Parliament of Great Britain, 1774–80* (London 1802), II, p. 275.

11. The early evidence of prior interest in the issue comes from the Michaelmas Head Court meeting of Stirlingshire freeholders on 3 Oct. 1775, when a motion supporting the introduction of a Scottish militia bill was agreed. 'Minute Book 1774–90': S.R.O. SC 67/59/4, p. 107.

12. *Boswell: The Ominous Years 1774–1776*, C. Ryskamp and F. A. Pottle (eds.) (Yale 1963), pp. 130, 268.

13. *Boswell: The Ominous Years*, pp. 268, 186–7, 214.

14. *Edinburgh Advertiser*, 8 Dec. 1775, 2, 5 Jan. 1776.

15. *Caldwell Papers*, II, Part ii, pp. 264–5: Mountstuart to Mure, 1 Nov. 1775; E.U.L. Ms. Dc.4.41.90: Dempster to Carlyle, n.d. [late 1775 or early 1776].

16. 'Minutes of the Poker Club', E.U.L. Ms. Dc.5.126: meetings of 17 Nov., 8, 22 Dec. 1775. The Minutes give no indication that the Club took any other, positive steps to support the militia demand.

17. Ferguson wrote to John Home expressing hopes of the bill's success: Henry Mackenzie's Letters and Papers, N.L.S. Ms. 124, ff. 76–7, 27 Jan. 1776; but that is all.

18. Carlyle, *Anecdotes and Characters*, pp. 221, 254 (on Dundas), 250–1, 269 (on Buccleuch). In 1769 Carlyle had also taken the tenancy of a hundred-acre farm from Buccleuch.

19. *Records of the Convention of Royal Burghs 1759–79*, pp. 521–4 (12 Jan., 8 March 1776).

20. *Edinburgh Courant*, 13 Jan. (E. Lothian, Kincardine), 10 Feb. (Banff), 12 Feb. (Galloway), 6 March 1776 (Aberdeen).

21. *Caledonian Mercury*, 6 Jan. 1776 (Midlothian); *Edinburgh Courant*, 3 Jan. (Selkirk), 26 Feb. (Falkirk), 9 March (Berwick), 20 March (Linlithgow).

22. *Boswell: The Ominous Years*, pp. 267–69, 343. A note by Elliot confirms Mountstuart's boast: N.L.S. Ms. 11031, ff. 18–19.

23. E.U.L. Ms. Dc.4.41.90: Dempster to Carlyle, n.d. gives an account of the

bill's preparation. There is a copy of the bill, with amendments, in the Minto Papers: N.L.S. Ms. 11031, and an abstract was printed in the *Scots Magazine*, XXXVIII (1776), pp. 681–9.

William Pulteney had changed his name in 1767 from Johnstone as a result of his marriage. He had assisted Carlyle with his militia pamphlet in 1760, and was a founder member of the Poker Club; he now sat for the English constituency of Shrewsbury. Sir Adam Fergusson had been a member of the 30 Nov. 1759 organising committee; he was now MP for Ayrshire.

24. *The Parliamentary History of England, from the Earliest Period to the Year 1803*, printed by T. C. Hansard (London 1806–20), Vol. XVIII, cols. 1228–1237; *Commons Journal*, XXV, p. 670 (20 March 1776).

25. *Caledonian Mercury*, 27, 30 March (two letters signed 'Stuart'), 3, 13 April, 1 May (three letters signed by 'Vox Populi'), 6 April ('Anti-Junius'), 20 May 1776 ('A Scot'). The extravagance of these laments prompted burlesque: ibid., 10 April ('Hurlothrumbo') and *Edinburgh Advertiser*, 19 April 1776 ('Christopher Crabtree').

26. [Alexander Carlyle,] *A Letter to His Grace the Duke of Buccleugh on National Defence, with some Remarks on Dr. Smith's Chapter on that Subject in his Book entitled, 'An Inquiry into the Nature and Causes of the Wealth of Nations'* (London 1778, text dated 26 Jan.; 2nd edition, Edinburgh 1778). The significance of the second part of the full title will become clear later.

27. *Caledonian Mercury*, 3 Nov. 1779, 'A Freeholder'; 24 Jan. 1780, 'Lysander'; 31 Jan. 1780, 'Cimon'. The attribution is based on the close similarity or actual correspondence between these published letters and a set of manuscript 'Transcripts of Letters by Dr. C[arlyle] on the Militia, for the Press', in the Lee Papers, N.L.S. Ms. 3464. The letter signed 'A Freeholder' accords with letter 6 in the Transcripts (ff. 63–7). The first half of 'A Freeholder' is similar, the second verbatim. The Letter of 'Lysander' accords with the first part of letter [7] in the Transcripts (H.67–9). The second part of letter [7] (ff. 70–1) and letter [5] (ff. 61–2) in the Transcripts are printed as 'Cimon'. The confirmation of these ascriptions lies in the Carlyle–Bell Papers, to which I have not had access, in N.L.S. Two other letters probably written by Carlyle at this time are those signed 'Aratus', *Caledonian Mercury*, 29 Sept. 1779 and *Scots Magazine*, XLI (Oct. 1779), and 'Junius', *Edinburgh Advertiser*, 1 Sept. 1778, the latter jointly with John Logan, as a puff for Carlyle's *Letter on National Defence*.

28. *Letter on National Defence*, pp. 22–3.

29. *Letter on National Defence*, pp. 57–9; 'A Freeholder', *Caledonian Mercury*, 3 Nov. 1779.

30. *Letter on National Defence*, pp. 2–5; in a footnote, however, Carlyle also praised the efforts of the Lord Advocate. Cf. 'A Freeholder', *Caledonian Mercury*, 3 Nov. 1779.

31. *Letter on National Defence*, pp. 8–9.

32. 'A Freeholder', 'Lysander', 'Cimon', *Caledonian Mercury*, 3 Nov. 1779, 24, 31 Jan. 1780. The Irish Volunteer Companies were raised in 1778 on the initiative of the Irish parliament, and in anticipation of Westminster's approval. This was not forthcoming, but the British government was powerless to disband the Companies, which by August 1779 claimed to have enrolled tens of thousands. They visibly strengthened the hand of Irish leaders in their successful attempt to force the British government to alter discriminatory trading regulations. H. Butterfield, *George III, Lord North and the People 1779–80* (London 1949, reprinted New York 1968), Chs. 3–4.

33. *Letter on National Defence*, pp. 18, 57–64.

34. *Letter on National Defence*, p. 53.

35. *Letter on National Defence*, p. 59.

36. *Letter on National Defence*, pp. 4–5; 'A Freeholder', *Caledonian Mercury*, 3 Nov. 1779.

37. 'Lysander', *Caledonian Mercury*, 24 Jan. 1780.

38. 'A Freeholder', *Caledonian Mercury*, 3 Nov. 1779.

39. 'Cimon', *Caledonian Mercury*, 31 Jan. 1780; *Letter on National Defence*, p. 72.

40. *Letter on National Defence*, pp. 54, 46–7.

41. 'Cimon', *Caledonian Mercury*, 31 Jan. 1780.

42. Most of the correspondence was concentrated, like Carlyle's letters, in the months from September 1779 to January 1780, and was placed in the Edinburgh papers.

43. P.R.O. SP 54 Vol. 47, f. 104: Lord Marchmont to Lord Suffolk, Secretary of State for the Northern Department, 24 March 1778, suggesting the review; f. 106: Suffolk to the Attorney and the Solicitor General of England, and the Lord Advocate of Scotland, 28 March 1778; ff. 110–11: Lord Advocate to Suffolk, 1 April 1778; ff. 112–21: 'Scroll of an Opinion by the Attorney and Solicitor General, and Lord Advocate'.

44. P.R.O. SP 54 Vol. 47, ff. 137–8: Lord Weymouth to General Oughton, C.-in-C. Scotland, 23 May 1778. Weymouth, Secretary of State for the Southern Department, took on Suffolk's work as well while Suffolk was indisposed with gout.

45. *Edinburgh Courant*, 11 April 1778 (Buccleuch Fencibles and Queensberry's Offer of Service); David Stewart, *Sketches of the Character, Manners and Present State of the Highlanders of Scotland. With Details of the Military Service of the Highland Regiments*, 2 Vols. (Edinburgh 1882), II, pp. 345–50 (on the Western, Sutherland and Northern Fencibles, and Eglinton's withdrawn commission).

46. *Edinburgh Courant*, 25 April 1778: copy of Lord Barrington's Letter of Service to Lord Frederick Campbell.

47. P.R.O. SP 54 Vol. 47, ff. 137–8: Weymouth to Oughton, 23 May 1778; f. 149: Oughton to Weymouth, 28 May 1778; f. 153: Suffolk to Oughton, 15 June 1778; ff. 155–8: Oughton to Suffolk, 23 June 1778, enclosing Provost of Aberdeen to Oughton, 2 June 1778.

48. P.R.O. SP 54 Vol. 47, f. 187: Oughton to Suffolk, 7 Sept. 1778. Oughton's action was approved, even commended by Suffolk: f. 193: 18 Sept. 1778.

49. East Lothian: Haddingtonshire Freeholders Records, S.R.O. SC 40/68/2, pp. 126–8: meeting of 23 Sept. 1779; Fife: P.R.O. SP 54 Vol. 47, f. 340: Oughton to Suffolk, 24 Sept. 1779; Dumfries: *Scots Magazine*, XLI (Oct. 1779): report on the offer of the noblemen and gentlemen of Dumfries, under the Duke of Queensberry, to raise ten volunteer companies; Ross and Cromarty: P.R.O. SP 54 Vol. 47, ff. 306–7: Lord Advocate to Weymouth, 7 Aug. 1779, enclosing ff. 308–9: letters from the Sheriff-Depute of the County, 28 July and Sir John Gordon, preses of the County Meeting, 28 Aug. 1779, and a 'Memorial of the … Counties of Ross and Cromarty', offering to raise 600 men in ten companies.

50. P.R.O. SP 54 Vol. 47, f. 340: Oughton to Suffolk, 24 Sept. 1779; ff. 324, 328: Weymouth to Lord Advocate, 27 Aug., 11 Sept. 1779; *Caledonian Mercury*, 25 Sept. 1779.

51. Haddingtonshire Freeholders Records, S.R.O. SC 40/68/2, pp. 128–32, 145–

56: Committee and General Meetings on 24, 28 Sept., 26 Oct., 4, 8 Nov. 1779, 3 Jan. 1780.

52. *Parliamentary Register*, 1774–80, XV, pp. 79–86: 3 Dec. 1779.

53. P.R.O. SP 54 Vol. 45, ff. 771–2: Lord Advocate to Stormont, 21 Dec. 1779; SP 54 Vol. 47, ff. 378–9: Stormont to Lord Advocate, 28 Dec. 1779.

54. Haddingtonshire Freeholders Records, S.R.O. SC 40/68/2, pp. 159–60: 17 Jan. 1780; Melville Papers, S.R.O. G D 51/1/819, f. 7: Fletcher-Campbell to Lord Advocate, 'by order of the committee', 27 Jan. 1780.

55. 'Lysander', *Caledonian Mercury*, 24 Jan. 1780. Haddingtonshire Records, S.R.O. SC 40/68/2, pp. 161–70, 23 March 1780: Heritors Meeting, and Report of the Committee, with a Plan for County Defence.

56. Haddingtonshire Records, S.R.O. SC 40/68/2, pp. 146–54, 159–60: general and committee meetings, 4, 8 Nov. 1779, 17 Jan. 1780; *Caledonian Mercury*, 13 Nov. 1779; *Edinburgh Courant*, 19 Jan. 1780.

57. *Edinburgh Courant*, 25, 29 Dec. 1779 (Dumfries, Argyll), 1, 12 Jan. 1780 (Berwickshire, Dumfries).

58. S.R.O. GD 51/1/819, f. 9: Lord Advocate to Fletcher-Campbell, 29 Feb. 1780.

59. *Edinburgh Courant*, 9 Feb. 1780: notice of meeting on 31 Jan. Attendance list collated with Minutes of the Poker Club, List of Members 1776 and later elections, E.U.L. Ms. Dc.5.26.

60. *Caledonian Mercury*, 7 Feb., 1 March 1780: 'An Old Trojan'; 23 Feb. 1780: 'A Soldier'.

61. P.R.O. SP 54 Vol. 48, ff. 99, 103–7: General Alexander Mackay (Oughton's successor as C.-in-C. Scotland) to Stormont, 23, 27 Jan. 1781, the second enclosing letters from Lord Gardenstone and John Ewen.

62. *Edinburgh Courant*, 16 April ('Senex') and 22 Sept. 1781.

63. Western, *The English Militia*, p. 217. P.R.O. Home Office Papers Scotland, HO 103 Vol. 1, pp. 34–40: Circular Letter from Shelburne to 28 Scottish counties and 45 Scottish burghs, 'Heads of a Plan for raising Corps in the Several Principal Towns in Scotland', and Letter to the C.-in-C. North Britain. The English and Scottish proposals were both published in the *Scots Magazine*, XLIV, in May and July 1782 respectively.

64. *Caledonian Mercury*, 8 June 1782 (Aberdeen's approval); Edinburgh City Council Records, Vol. 102, pp. 281, 291–2: 5, 19 June 1782; *Extracts from the Records of the Burgh of Glasgow*, Vol. VIII, pp. 46–50: 12, 26 June 1782.

65. *Caledonian Mercury*, 15 July 1782.

66. *Edinburgh Courant*, 7 Sept. 1782; however, the magistrates did give the Caledonian Band a cautious blessing: Edinburgh City Records, Vol. 102, pp. 348–51: 14 Aug. 1782.

67. John Sinclair, *Considerations on Militias and Standing Armies. With some observations on the Plan of Defence suggested by the Earl of Shelburne, and some thoughts on the propriety of Military Exercises on Sunday, and on the Necessity of a Scotch Militia* (London 1782).

68. *Parliamentary History*, XXIII, Col. 6–7; Maitland was the future eighth Earl of Lauderdale, the political economist.

69. Namier and Brooke, *The Commons 1754–90*, II, pp. 526–7.

70. *Edinburgh Courant*, 29 May 1782: this extraordinary account of an extraordinary meeting was reprinted from the London papers, and said to have been written by Lord George Gordon himself.

71. *Commons Journal,* Vol. 38, pp. 1007, 1023, 1037, 1048; *Scots Magazine,* XLIV (Aug. 1782); *Parliamentary Register 1780–1803,* Vol. VII, pp. 221–2.

72. *Edinburgh Courant,* 12 June 1782: notice of Dumfries meeting on 7 June.

73. *Edinburgh Courant,* 26 June, 1 July 1782.

74. *Caledonian Mercury,* 29 June ('An Independent Highlander'), 1, 10 July ('L'), 3 July ('A.B.'), 8 July ('An Independent Burgher'), 17 July ('Civis Glasguensis').

75. *Edinburgh Advertiser,* 12 July 1782 ('Civis').

76. *Edinburgh Courant,* 7 August 1782: an unusually full report, not only of the resolutions, but also of the debate.

77. *Edinburgh Courant,* 14, 24 Aug. 1782.

78. E.U.L. Ms. Dc.5.126: 'Minutes of the Poker Club', 19, 26 July 1782. The special meeting was thrice advertised in the *Edinburgh Courant,* 20, 22, 24 July.

79. Crosbie was a founder-member of the Club, Dalrymple one from an early period, and Binning and his father had been elected in 1779 and 1780 respectively. The public committee also appears to have numbered one ex-member of the Poker in John Shaw Stewart, who features on the membership list of 1768, but not on that of the reconstituted club in 1776.

80. N.L.S. Ms. 16736, ff. 124–5: Graham to [Fletcher-Campbell], 25 Aug. 1782; ff. 126–7: J. Atkinson to Col. [Fletcher-]Campbell, Dublin 6 Sept. 1782.

81. N.L.S. Ms. 16737, f. 204: Adam Ferguson to Fletcher-Campbell, n.d. [Aug. 1782?]. Since there is no date on the letter, I quote Ferguson: 'I am exceedingly pleased with the Sketch and the Appendix. I have touched it with my pen where that appeared requisite but you will judge the propriety of keeping my corrections. I send it back with the least possible delay.'

82. *Edinburgh Courant,* 30 Sept. 1782: 'Sketch of a Bill for the Better Ordering the Fencible Men in ... Scotland'; 4, 7 Sept. 1782: 'Extract from the observations tending to explain the Sketch of the intended Bill for obtaining a constitutional, safe and useful defence for Scotland'. (In fact the paper would appear to have printed the whole of the 'observations', not merely an extract.) What follows is a composite summary of the Sketch itself and the Observations.

83. *Caledonian Mercury,* 14, 16 Sept. 1782: letter by 'Nestor' to the Printer, and 'A View of the Law of Scotland with regard to Fencible Men' by 'Nestor'. The attribution of this letter to Carlyle is made on the same basis as in the case of his previous letters to the *Caledonian Mercury* in 1779–80: it corresponds with a transcript in the Lee Papers: N.L.S. Ms. 3464, ff. 56–60, transcript [3]. Nestor's letter was subscribed Aberdeen, the place which had given a lead in forming a local defensive association: Carlyle had adopted the same conceit in his first militia pamphlet, styling himself a freeholder of Ayrshire.

84. Carlyle's calculation, presumably made also by those who drafted the Sketch of a Bill, may well have been based on Alexander Webster's contemporary population census, which had included an estimate of the 'Number of Fighting Men' in Scotland as some 253,000: *Scottish Populations Statistics, including Webster's Analysis of Population 1755,* J. G. Kyd (ed.), The Scottish History Society (Edinburgh 1975), pp. 8–9, 77. Though not published at the time, Webster's Census was generally known through several manuscript copies: that printed by Kyd is a relatively late, revised copy, but the figure for fighting men is unlikely to have been altered much since 1755. See Flinn (ed.), *Scottish Population History,* pp. 58–60, 250–1.

85. *Edinburgh Courant*, 11, 14 Sept. 1782.

86. Particular points of superficial similarity between Fletcher's arguments and those of the Moderates only underline the gulf between them. Both Fletcher and Carlyle were prepared for tactical reasons to invoke the rhetoric of Scottish ancient constitutionalism. But Fletcher's recourse to such rhetoric covered a vision of Scotland as an institutionally independent political community in a federal relation with England, in the context of a European system of similar provincial federations; Carlyle's ancient constitutional rhetoric, by contrast, must be set beside his previous fulsome adherence to the alternative vision of complete, imperial union with England. Again, Fletcher had supported his case for remodelling Scottish society with a vividly unfavourable but unrealistically simple comparison of Scottish with English social relations, just as did the anonymous commentator in 1782. But Fletcher had sought to reform Scottish society precisely in order to break with the hierarchy and values of the martial past; at least in part, the Sketch of a Bill sought to recover and perpetuate that hierarchy, those values.

87. Ramsay of Ochtertyre left a particularly graphic account of the weather and crop in 1782: *Scotland and Scotsmen in the Eighteenth Century*, edited from the Ochtertyre Manuscripts by A. Allardyce (Edinburgh and London 1888), II, pp. 256–8. An account confirmed, if tempered, in Flinn (ed.), *Scottish Population History*, pp. 233–7.

88. *Caledonian Mercury*, 18 Nov. 1782; the militia had earlier received no support at all at the Michaelmas Head Court meeting of the county, chaired by the Lord Advocate: *Edinburgh Courant*, 2 Oct. 1782.

89. *Edinburgh Courant*, 5, 12 Oct. 1782.

90. *Caledonian Mercury*, 7 Oct. 1782 (Berwick and Fife); *Aberdeen Journal* 14 Oct., 4 Nov. 1782 (Aberdeen); *Edinburgh Courant*, 23 Nov. 1782 (Linlithgow).

91. *Edinburgh Courant*, 5 Oct. (Perth, Forfar, Dumbarton, Ayr), 7 Oct. (Lanark), 12 Oct. (Renfrew), 21 Oct. (Kirkcudbright), 23 Oct. (Wigtown), 30 Oct. (Argyll), 6 Nov. (E. Lothian), 11 Nov. (Stirling) and 23 Nov. 1782 (Ross and Cromarty).

92. E.g. Perth, Kirkcudbright: *Edinburgh Courant*, 5, 21 Oct. 1782.

93. E.g. Perth, E. Lothian: *Edinburgh Courant*, 5 Oct., 6 Nov. 1782.

94. 'Amor Patriae', in *Edinburgh Courant*, 26 Oct. 1782; Anon., *Remarks on the Proposed Laws for establishing a Militia in Scotland. By a Country Gentleman* (Edinburgh 1782).

95. *Edinburgh Courant*, 21 Oct. 1782.

96. *Edinburgh Courant*, 21 Oct., 6, 11 Nov. 1782.

97. The existence and (with three exceptions) membership of the county committees was advertised in the press, under the references above. They can thus be collated with the published membership of the 5 August Committee and the list of members in the Poker Club Minutes.

Members of the 5 August Committee were appointed to the county committees of Dumbarton, Ayr, Berwick, Renfrew, Kirkcudbright, Wigtown and E. Lothian. Another 5 August Committee member, Dewar of Vogrie, tried but failed to have a committee appointed in Midlothian. Poker Club members sat on the above seven county committees, and also on those of Perth, Forfar, Lanark, Stirling and Ross and Cromarty. There were no members of either the 5 August Committee or the Poker Club on the committees of Inverness, Argyll and Linlithgow. The three counties which did not publish the membership of committees were Dumfries, Fife and Aberdeen, though Dumfries and Aberdeen were reported to have appointed them.

98. *Edinburgh Courant,* 27 Nov., 4 Dec. 1782.

99. *Edinburgh Courant,* 18 Dec. 1782, 4 Jan. 1783.

100. *Edinburgh Courant,* 4, 11, 22 Jan. 1783; Kirkcudbright at least 'unanimously and highly' approved of the bill, and resolved to give it 'the utmost support and encouragement'.

101. *Edinburgh Courant,* 11, 18, 20 Jan., 3 Feb. 1783; Haddingtonshire Records: S.R.O. SC 40/68/2, pp. 239–40, 9 Jan. 1783; *Caledonian Mercury,* 12 March, 1783.

102. *Edinburgh Courant,* 18, 22, 25 Jan. 1783; *Aberdeen Journal,* 20 Jan. 1783.

103. Mss. Records of the Convention of Royal Burghs (Edinburgh City Chambers), Vol. 14: Annual Committee meetings of 17, 31 Jan. 1783; *Glasgow Mercury,* 30 Jan. 1783.

104. N.L.S. Ms. 16736, ff. 196–7: 'Minute of the Committee appointed by the meeting of noblemen and gentlemen of Scotland to conduct an application to Parliament for the establishment of a militia. Present, the Earls of Glencairn, Moray and Haddington, Gen. Fletcher-Campbell, William Muirhead, 3 May 1783'; ff. 201–4: Glencairn to Adam Ferguson, 13 May, and Ferguson to Fletcher-Campbell, 15 May 1783.

105. *Caledonian Mercury,* 18 June 1783: House of Commons, 13 June.

106. N.L.S. Ms. 16736, ff. 259–60: John Spottiswood to Fletcher-Campbell, 1 Dec. 1783.

107. J. R. Western, 'The Formation of the Scottish Militia in 1797', *Scottish Historical Review,* XXXIV (1955).

108. K. J. Logue, *Popular Disturbances in Scotland 1780–1815* (Edinburgh 1979), Ch. 3.

6

The Achievement of the Agitations

Throughout the successive Seven Years' and American Wars the case for a Scottish militia was both consistent and wide-ranging. It was far from simply a matter of the defence of Scotland. At stake, the militia's supporters repeatedly claimed, were issues as large as the preservation of national independence after the Union and the continuance in a commercial age of the cohesion and harmony which were held to have been such a feature of Scottish social relations in the martial past. As it had been since mediaeval times, the question of the nation's military organisation was presented as inseparable from the questions of its political identity and social order.

For all the consistent ambition of this case, however, the successive militia agitations had persistently failed in their apparent object: no Scottish militia was established in either war. It was a failure the more marked when circumstances seemed so favourable. At the outset, it is true, there was still doubt over the Scots' loyalty, no more than ten years separating the start of the Seven Years' War from the Jacobite 'Forty-Five. But even then the Scots soon demonstrated their commitment to the war: there was widespread support for William Pitt, as war-leader and principal begetter of the English militia, while Scotland itself was threatened by French invasion plans. In the later American War the circumstances were, if anything, still more favourable to the militia demand. The Scots were overwhelmingly supporters of the war and the government, and the government was fully convinced of the value of the English militia. Yet the demand remained unfulfilled. In 1760 and again in 1762, in 1776 and once more in 1782, Scottish militia bills that were closely modelled on the 1757 English Militia Act failed to carry the Commons. Likewise frustrated were other, less formal initiatives of the Scottish burghs and counties in the late 1770s; and a last vigorous agitation during the winter of 1782–83, while stirring as much enthusiasm as ever, none the less petered out before a bill even reached Westminster.

To explain such persistent failure is one concern of this chapter. The agitations failed to secure a militia, I shall suggest, not primarily because of English opposition. What was decisive was rather the division and the hesitation of the Scots themselves over the issue. In turn, the reasons for this division and hesitation can be identified by examining the likely implications of the militia's actual establishment. With each of the military, national and social aspects of the case for a national militia, there were, I shall argue, good grounds for Scots to doubt whether the institution of a militia was in their interests.

This is not, however, to conclude that the partisans of a Scottish militia simply misread the interests and aspirations of their countrymen — that the consistent ambition of their case was no more than an inflexible refusal to face reality. For it is doubtful whether the failure to establish a militia is the proper measure of the agitations' achievement. Even if the demand remained unfulfilled, the agitations themselves aroused a broad and en-thusiastic response: the principal themes of the case for a militia would seem to have struck a resonant chord in Scottish consciousness. This was a response, moreover, with which the Moderate literati who championed the militia had their own reasons to be satisfied. To them, as I have sought to demonstrate, what mattered was not so much the institution of the militia as the national and social values it embodied: and such values, it can be argued, were as well — or better — displayed in the agitations as they were likely to be in any actual militia. To explanation of the failure to secure a militia, therefore, this chapter adds a second concern: de-monstration of the extent to which the agitations were none the less successful in appealing to national spirit and social responsibility.

The Military Case

The claim that a national militia was essential to the defence of Scotland may have been only the starting point of the case developed by its advocates; but it was clearly necessary, for agitations were mounted only in wartime. At least in the early stages of the two wars, moreover, public apprehension lent weight to the cause. In 1759 and again in the late 1770s, a number of coastal towns and shires were sufficiently anxious to anticipate the demand for a militia with their own requests for arms; and the threats from Thurot and John Paul Jones evidently gave impetus to the agitations for a militia proper. Equally clearly, however, the level of public apprehen-sion was never sufficient to make the military case for a militia overwhelm-ing, either to the authorities in London or to the Scots themselves. To understand why this was so, it is necessary to assess in more detail the extent of the threat to Scotland's defences, and the difference a militia might have been expected to make.

The threat to Scotland could not be dismissed out of hand. If in the event Thurot called only to trade, while John Paul Jones could perpetrate no more than common burglary when he landed in the south-west in 1778, both had the capacity to do worse. There was, too, some reason to fear that both were curtain-raisers for more serious attacks. Thurot's expedition was supposed to herald an invasion which would involve a major landing in the west of Scotland, while Paul Jones' privateering took place in the context of the massive Franco–Spanish armada of 1779.

On the other hand, those officially responsible for Scotland's defence, both the ministers in London and their civil and military subordinates in Edinburgh, were well placed to put the threat into perspective. Their intelligence was comparatively good. They had early warning of Choiseul's plan in 1759, and subsequent French invasion schemes in the 1760s and 1770 likewise regularly found their way into British hands: these showed the French to be less and less interested in Scotland.[1] Declining French interest, of course, mirrored the decline of Jacobitism, a fact of which the authorities were independently well informed (although they did not always care to admit it). In 1757, early in the Seven Years' War, there was rumour of Jacobite correspondence in the west Highlands; but the Commander-in-Chief in Scotland was confident that its purpose was to support the spirit rather than the reality of the rebellion — or at worst, as he remarked a year later, to obstruct recruiting.[2] When invasion loomed in 1759, a network of agents reporting to the law officers in Edinburgh could find almost no disaffection in the Highlands;[3] and while English ministers were still intensely suspicious, even they accepted that it was now unnecessary to take suspected chiefs into preventive custody.[4] By the 1770s, the Jacobite problem had disappeared completely; and there was little fear of any radical fifth column for republican America.[5]

So informed, the authorities could also reasonably argue that the existing provision for Scotland's defence was adequate. The navy provided a first line of defence. Successful, at the second attempt, in catching Thurot, its resources were however overstretched in the American War. The land forces were rather stronger: in the Seven Years' War the Scottish establishment was eight to ten regiments strong, and in the American War there were between two and six thousand men in arms in Scotland.[6] The core of these was formed of (mostly English) regulars, concentrated in camps around Edinburgh and Glasgow, with small garrisons at Inverness and Fort William. Little point was seen in attempting to deploy the regulars against minor coastal raids; and in the unlikely event of a large-scale invasion in the Highlands, the authorities were determined that their main force should not repeat Cope's mistake in 1745 of seeking the enemy there.[7] It was the role of the native Scottish auxiliaries, the so-called Fencibles, to protect coastal districts. Two such regiments, the Argyll and the Sutherland, were raised in 1759, and four, the Argyll or Western, the Sutherland, the Gordon or Nothern and the Buccleuch or Southern Fencibles in 1778. The government resorted to these auxiliaries with some reluctance. Their legality might be questioned; the distribution of commands involved political favours; and there was dislike of having to promise that service would be restricted to within Scotland. As many offers from Scotch noblemen to raise such regiments were refused as were accepted. Nevertheless, scattered from the south-west to the Shetlands, the Fencibles gave valuable reassurance to anxious localities, and helped to forestall or discourage local arming, which government liked even less.[8]

What difference would a national militia have made, had one been established? The answer is complicated by the putting forward of two quite distinct models, the select 'English' model of the successive parliamentary bills and the nearly universal model of the Sketch of a Bill. Simply in terms of numbers, the select militia of six thousand would have doubled the existing forces, the universal one of twenty-five thousand quintupled them. With both models, however, the apparent gain in point of numbers would have had to be set against problems of organisation. Raised on a county basis, the regimental units of a militia of six thousand would have been absurdly small. Even if six smaller counties had been paired with larger neighbours, as Elliot's bill proposed, the average complement would still have been less than two hundred and fifty men. More realistically, the militia of 1797 had ten regiments of six hundred men each, only Lanarkshire and Perthshire supporting regiments of their own.[9] In any case, the combining of counties created fresh problems of inter-county jealousy and exacerbated the difficulty of deciding between the competing claims of important families for the Lieutenancy. In a militia of twenty-five thousand, county regiments would on paper be more viable. But the central direction of a force whose units had the degree of autonomy envisaged in the Sketch of a Bill would have been — and was presumably intended to be — loose at best.

The difference which a national militia would have made in its recruitment is perhaps the most important, but also the most difficult, point to determine. Despite its economic, social and political implications, the whole subject of recruiting in eighteenth-century Scotland has yet to receive adequate attention, and comment on the hypothetical cases of the proposed militias must be especially tentative. At best one can extrapolate from the limited available evidence of recruitment to the regulars, the Fencibles and the English militia, and then speculate on the extent to which the Scottish militias would have diverged from the patterns they set.

The constant demand for regular commissions for the sons of the Scottish landed classes is well attested; but whether there would have been the same enthusiasm to officer a militia is more doubtful. Although the noblemen who offered to raise regiments for internal defence were confident that they could fill their lists, evidence of the recruiting of the Argyll Fencibles in 1759 suggests that the comparative inferiority of such service was felt.[10] There was little prospect of promotion and none of half-pay; and it is hard to believe that these disadvantages were outweighed by the attraction of remaining within Scotland, since conditions of service were so unappealing. Contingents of Fencibles were shuffled across the country between camps and quarters, the facilities for which, at least outside the two main cities, were still less satisfactory in Scotland than in England.[11] While a militia commission was formally no better than one in the Fencibles, there was perhaps more chance of the county contingents remaining in or near their localities, the more so if, as the Sketch of a Bill proposed, the consent of a contingent was required before it was moved. The gentry might then have enjoyed parading before their inferiors. But the example of the contemporary English militia is not encouraging: embodied for long periods in camps on the south coast, it became the resort of the impoverished and the incompetent, and manifestly the worse for it.[12]

With the men, the example of the English militia suggests a slightly better prospect. Almost all its recruits, indeed, were substitutes, and a large number were drawn from the same source as the regulars relied upon, the urban poor. Nevertheless, it would seem that a significant proportion of English militiamen came from rural areas which the regulars did not generally tap.[13] It must be doubted, however, whether this pattern would have been reproduced in Scotland. Impressionistic though it is, the available evidence suggests that the pattern evolving there was one of regular recruitment from particular rural areas and auxiliary recruitment in the towns. Increasingly the Highlands and Border uplands were regarded as the prime recruiting grounds for the regulars. Their value is indicated as early as 1757 by complaints of over-recruiting; and the government continued to rely on these areas throughout the Seven Years' and the American War.[14] Nominally the Fencibles were drawn from the same areas. In practice, however, they appear to have experienced difficulty in recruiting: there is evidence that in both wars they were obliged to make up their numbers from the Lowland urban centres.[15] From this it seems reasonable to infer that any militia permitting substitution would have fallen back on the same urban sources. At the least, it is clear that rural areas — Lowland quite as much as Highland — would have produced very few willing recruits. The hostility of east-coast farmers and tradesmen in 1762 could not have been franker: they wanted neither to be dragged off to serve themselves, nor to lose their labourers as substitutes. When service was actually required in 1797, it would encounter not merely verbal, but active and violent opposition from farmers and labourers alike. And if such was the response to a select militia of six thousand, what would have been the reaction to the virtually universal force of which the militia's champions dreamed?

In sum, there would have been little defensive gain from the establishment of a national militia; indeed, it would almost certainly have been more trouble than it was worth, whether to the authorities or to the Scottish people themselves. The threat of serious invasion was diminishing; the existing forces were sufficient for the purpose; the militia must have been cumbrous to direct, and was most unlikely to attract a better class of recruit. From a purely military point of view, at least, it would seem that for the moment the Scots could do without the institution: it was enough that by agitation they reminded the authorities to keep up the existing defences.

The National Case

The claim that Scotland's defences needed strengthening might be a necessary condition of a credible demand for a militia. But the aspect of the case to which the militia's advocates consistently gave most public weight was the national — the claim that a militia was required to ensure the continuing independence and identity of Scotland within the Union. On the evidence, moreover, it was this national case which aroused most enthusiasm for a militia in the Scottish political community at large. In agitation after agitation the public declarations of the burghs and counties warmed with disgust at the distinction drawn between Scotland and England, protesting at the denial of Scotland's just claim and asserting keenness to remove the indignity. To all appearances, Scottish public opinion saw the issue in straightforward national terms: refusal of a militia was a slight on Scotland by the English, which the Scots must redeem.

But was it a straightforward matter of English refusal? Ministerial suspicion and backbench Scotophobia were plain enough. The actual voting on the successive Scottish militia bills in the House of Commons indicates, however, that so conveniently simple an explanation will not do. In 1760 the bill passed its first division by 91 votes to 43; when it went down on the Second Reading, 194 were opposed but 84 still in its favour. In 1776 the first hurdle was cleared by 67 votes to 54; defeat came when the opposition rose to 112, although the number in favour was also up, to 93. There was only one division in 1782, when an amendment unacceptable to the Scots was carried by 41 to 37.[16] These figures point to a series of conclusions. In the first place, it can be seen that in both 1760 and 1776 the hard core of English opposition — those who opposed the bills from the first — was weaker than the hard core of support: those who voted for the bills until the end. Second, the assured support of the bills in 1760 and 1776 must have included up to 50 English MPs in addition to the Scots members themselves. (The Scots were generally loyal, none apart from the two in 1760 being reported as dissentients; but it is most unlikely that the full complement of 45 Scots MPs would have been present for the votes.) Third, what therefore defeated the bills was the hesitation and eventual opposition of English MPs, who were initially either supporters or neutrals — the Pittite County MPs in 1760, and government members in 1776 and 1782. In other words, it was not simply a matter of intransigent English hostility; the decisive English votes were those initially open to, but finally unconvinced of, the strength of the Scottish case. What fuelled and justified the doubts of these unconvinced English was, moreover, the absence of overwhelming and unambiguous support for the measure from within Scotland. The Scots might fall only a little short of unanimity; but it was enough to allow uncommitted Englishmen to conclude that the Scots were not really in earnest about their militia. Far therefore from its being the fault of the English, as the Scots' declarations claimed, the Scots themselves were ultimately to blame. Carlyle, it seems, was right: despite the widespread enthusiasm for the militia demand, the Scots' national spirit was still insufficient for the task.

The accusation of deficient national spirit was one that Carlyle the moralist almost relished levelling at his fellow-countrymen. It was, I shall now argue, none the less unjust, and even disingenuous. For if the implications of the militia demand for the political order of post-Union Scotland are examined more closely, a more complex assessment of the response to the national case for a militia becomes desirable. It can be seen that while the actual institution of a militia could have threatened the position of all sections of the political community, the agitations themselves provided an ideal vehicle for the expression of the national spirit which Carlyle so desired.

The political order which emerged in Scotland in consequence of the Union was remarkably close to that predicted at the time by the Earl of Cromarty.[17] Deprived of its sovereign legislature, the nation was at last laid open to the formal rule of law and regular, centrally directed civil government. The key to the transformation was the breaking of the vicious circle of magnate bullying and English bribery by which the country had been ruled in the late seventeenth century. Removed from the Estates which they had dominated and disrupted since the Restoration, the aristrocratic factions were faced with insignificance in the much larger metropolitan parliament; and if ministers continued to subsidise Whig interests, it was simply to counter the Jacobite threat. Active Jacobitism was the last, and after 1715 almost exclusively Highland, refuge of the old order of aristocratic-kinship politics; and the conclusive defeat of the 'Forty-Five was its end. For a short time after the rebellion Cumberland threatened to impose direct military rule, and for a few years more Newcastle and Hardwicke strove to maintain direct control over Scotland's civil administration. But with the clans broken, the English army of occupation could safely be reduced to a few strategic garrisons; and with faction dissolved, English ministers gradually lost interest.[18] Inside Scotland the new elites of Edinburgh lawyers and county gentry, along with the older-established urban oligarchies, were able to assert the rule of law and to assume powers of civil administration whose exercise had hitherto been severely restricted; and at Westminster the development of an unofficial Scottish 'ministry' ensured control of Scottish patronage and the effective representation of Scottish interests. Thus was constituted anew within the framework of the Union a distinct Scottish political community, one enjoying — just as Cromarty had forecast — more genuine, albeit informal, self-government, and hence far greater stability, than could ever be achieved under the old, independent magnate order. But it was precisely this self-governed stability within the Union that, I would argue, the institution of a militia could be seen to endanger.

Of those parts of the political community regularly involved in the militia agitations, the burghs were for the moment in the weakest position.

The burghs had a tradition of administrative, fiscal and electoral independence which reached back into the middle ages: the disappearance of the old magnate order after the Union was not therefore a condition of their political autonomy. Much of this independence survived in the more regular political conditions of the eighteenth century. The larger burghs at least preserved considerable autonomy in their internal affairs; and together the burghs possessed in their Annual Convention a collective agency well practised in defending their interests. But the Union had undermined rather than strengthened the burghs' position in relation to parliament. Ceasing to constitute a separate estate of parliament in Scotland, the burghs were now almost universally represented at Westminster by landowners. Edinburgh, which alone had an MP to itself (the other burghs, including Glasgow, were grouped for the purpose of parliamentary representation), did strive to sustain a measure of independence in its choice; but even there tactful management was enough to tie it to prevailing landed interests.[19]

From this weakened but still distinct position in the post-Union political order the burghs had less reason than most to welcome the institution of a militia. Their suspicions were never far below the surface. Indignant though they might sound over the injustice of refusing Scotland a militia, it is clear that the burgh oligarchies were also concerned that the militia might encroach yet further on their independence. Manifesting their concern at first simply in reservations added to their declarations of support, but later in outright opposition, the magistrates complained in particular of the failure to guarantee them a share in the command of the militia. Apart from Edinburgh, the burghs were not to raise separate regiments of their own, but to contribute men to the regiments of the counties in which they lay; even if qualifications for burgh officers were specified — and there was no mention of them in the 1782 Sketch — it was only to be expected that county Lords Lieutenant would favour their fellow-landowners with the commissions. At least under the old order the burgh oligarchies had often been able to stand aside from the nobility's factions and feuds: the proposed militia, however, offered only to set burghs wholly under the hegemony of the landed interest.

The legal profession — the judges and advocates based in Edinburgh (the solicitors or writers were of lesser consequence) — did not offer an independent, corporate response to the militia agitations; but their position in the post-Union political order was of sufficient importance for their attitude to warrant separate consideration. The lawyers had perhaps gained most of all in the aftermath of the Union. The passing of the feud and the statutory abolition of heritable jurisdictions in 1747 had made it possible to consolidate the rule of law on a regular, centralised basis. At the same time the choice of a legal career by growing numbers of sons of the landed classes had enhanced the status of the profession. With their landed origins, the lawyers would never be (or wish to be) quite free from the traditional obligations of kinship. But their corporate organisation in the Faculty of Advocates and concentration in Edinburgh secured for them an increasingly independent role at the centre of Scottish affairs. Interpreting and even making the law anew for what they believed to be the general good of society, the courts seem to have set themselves to reshape the framework of Scottish life, not least the old feudal basis of landownership. And by their appointment to many of the senior offices in Scotland's civil administration, the lawyers were able to assert a novel governmental authority over the localities.[20]

The extent of the lawyers' involvement in the militia agitations hardly indicates confidence that their new-found eminence would be enhanced by the demand's fulfilment. Early on, both bench and bar made a strong showing of support as individuals, six judges and four advocates sitting on the public committee appointed on 30 November 1759. Very quickly, however, the lawyers' support faded into indifference and even hostility; and those who remained adherents of the militia acted rather as land-owners than as members of the legal profession. One individual's silence is perhaps particularly telling. The judge Henry Home, Lord Kames, was not only familiar with the Edinburgh literati and indebted to the Moderates in particular, but one of his own works contained a radical new plan for a militia in Britain. Yet he played no part whatsoever in the militia agitations.[21]

The lawyers' reluctance to become involved is understandable. In 1760, at least, the most obvious and immediate reason for their defection was pressure from their ministerial masters, Lord Chancellor Hardwicke and the Duke of Newcastle. The exemplary humiliation meted out to the unfortunate Auchinleck made it quite clear that support for a Scottish militia would put career prospects in jeopardy. Pressure from above, however, cannot be a sufficient explanation for the lawyers' persistent lack of collective enthusiasm in later agitations, when government ministers did not show the same concern. Even in 1760, it may be suggested, the lawyers would have had their own reasons to agree with Newcastle that a Scotch militia would disrupt the basis of the Union. The form of any Scottish militia law presented one difficulty. As custodians of a national system of law, whose independence had been guaranteed by the Union, the lawyers could be expected to have reservations about the simple extension of the English Militia Act to Scotland. But there was not likely to be any greater enthusiasm for reviving the old Scottish laws of arming. The lawyers had already manifested intense suspicion of these during the 'Forty-Five, when they frustrated the efforts of the Secretary of State to appoint Lords Lieutenant and raise a loyalist militia. Perhaps still more inhibiting than doubts about the form of a militia law, however, was another consider-ation: the very rule of law in Scotland might be thought to be at stake. In the crisis of the 'Forty-Five, the lawyers had been no keener to arm the Lowland Whig nobility than the Jacobite clans: by implication, at least, any independent arming in Scotland, whatever its supposed political allegiance, was deemed a threat. A new militia might be legally constituted, but with its local organisation it raised the spectre of a restoration of that aristocratic military autonomy whose abolition had been the prerequisite of establishing the rule of law. The rule of law itself, of course, could not be sustained without some means of enforcement. But it was a further lesson of the 'Forty-Five that it was simpler and safer to call upon standing — and English — troops to do the work.

Much more involved in the militia agitations than either the burgh oligarchies or the legal profession were the landowners, who still made up by far the largest and weightiest part of the Scottish political community. Within the landed class, however, there had since the Union been significant changes in the location and nature of political authority. In an effort to keep their influence with English ministers, the great landowning nobility had had to move south to Westminster; and at that distance it proved impossible to maintain the ties of kinship, faction and force which had bound and divided the old order under the great nobility's hegemony. Instead patronage became ever more important as the lubricant of the Scottish political system, and of parliamentary elections in particular; and although great acres were a natural basis for the exercise of patronage, such acres were neither the monopoly of the nobility nor the only source of patronage. Increasingly the nobility had to compete for electoral influence with those, above all the law officers, who commanded government patronage, while learning at the same time to respect the political independence of their fellow non-noble landowners. What was true of elections was still truer of the machinery of government within Scotland. The authority of the lairds in the counties grew in conjunction with that of the lawyers in the centre, as the offices of Justice of the Peace and Commissioner of Supply at last acquired real responsibilities. In addition the semi-formal county meeting assumed in the second half of the century an increasing consequence as a forum for the discussion of administrative and political issues, both local and national. Such meetings commented freely on proposed legislation of Scottish interest at Westminster, and assumed the power to instruct the County's MP on his vote.

The changing pattern of political authority within the landed elite was directly reflected in the development of the unofficial Scottish 'ministry'. The new 'minister' was the successor to the old-style 'manager'. The role of the old 'manager', exemplified in the early years of the century by the Duke of Queensberry, had been little more than that of a faction leader, bribing and bullying friend and foe alike into submission. The new 'minister', by contrast, was much more a representative of the landed class as a whole. His patronage was not purely partisan (although there was always a strong personal element in the ministerial role), but served to secure the autonomy of the local elites in the administration of Scotland; and in addition the 'minister' was expected to press government and parliament for the satisfaction of a range of sectional and national interests. The pioneer of the new ministry was the third Duke of Argyll, in the years following the 'Forty-Five. The last of the magnates, Argyll, was none the less aware of the post-Union changes, and adapted to them with remarkable skill. Significantly, however, his effective successor was not the distant, dithering noble Earl of Bute, but the commoner Henry Dundas. At the start of his career not even a landowner in his own right, Dundas used legal office and government patronage as his power base, and won the confidence of the landed classes simply by his sedulous attention to their interests. Dundas even succeeded in securing the assistance of a great landowning peer, the Duke of Buccleuch, as his informal deputy — a subordination of great noble to commoner lawyer and politician that perhaps illustrates better than anything the extent of the transformation in the pattern of political authority in eighteenth-century Scotland.[22]

It was to this newly regrouped landowning elite that the advocates of a militia particularly appealed. On the face of it, the response was impressive. Not only did the counties produce some of the most ringing denunciations of the injustice of denying Scotland a militia. But the extent and depth of the response in the counties suggest that this was an issue with a specific appeal for landowners, both nobles and gentlemen. In simple numerical terms, over the whole period of the agitations as many as twenty-five out of the thirty-three Scottish counties met to declare their opinion.[23] Each individual agitation involved between a third and a half of the counties. Eleven declared themselves in 1760 and fourteen in 1762; in 1775–76, when there was no properly organised agitation, seven still met of their own accord; and finally in 1782–83 twenty responded to the agitation for a Sketch of a Bill.[24]

The impression of landowner interest in the militia issue is further strengthened by the geographical pattern of the counties' response. Interest was extensive from the start in the counties of the central Lowlands, and these remained involved throughout. Involvement was slower to develop in the west and south-west, but grew steadily in the second period of agitation, until every western and south-western county participated in the agitation of 1782. By contrast the eastern Borders' counties showed an early interest, but soon fell away, and played very little part in the later period. Least involved were the Highland counties, where interest was no more than scattered and occasional. Very broadly, this pattern may be related to the density of landownership in the different areas. The counties in which interest was greatest were those Lowland and increasingly also south-western counties where land was divided between numbers of landowners, both nobles and substantial and middling gentlemen. Conversely, interest was less in counties dominated by a few great (usually noble) landowning families, as in the eastern Borders and Highlands.[25] The denser the concentration of noble and gentlemen landowners, in short, the greater the apparent interest in the militia issue.

M

Such evidence of landowner interest in the militia issue may none the less be deceptive. An immediate question mark might be laid against the representativeness of the county meetings which declared on the issue. These meetings were not always restricted to qualified 'freeholders' on the electoral roll: peers, parish heritors, other gentlemen and even on one occasion (Ayrshire 1759) clergy were also reported as attending. But the relative openness of the meetings only increases the problem: for if attendance was in fact low, their claim to speak on behalf of the landowning community as a whole could be challenged. Unfortunately, evidence to settle this question is in short supply. Full attendance figures for meetings on militia business are available for only one county, East Lothian; these must be compared with the numbers reported in a handful of individual cases in which attendance was claimed to be insufficient.

To take the figures for the East Lothian meetings: in 1760 there was an attendance of eighteen, including twelve freeholders out of a possible total of fifty-five; in 1762 the numbers were fifteen, including nine freeholders out of a possible fifty-six; in 1776, twenty-seven, including twenty free-holders out of a possible seventy-six; in 1782, twenty-two, including ten freeholders out of a possible seventy-five; and in 1783, fifteen, including eleven freeholders out of a possible seventy-five.[26] By comparison, thirty-eight were reported present at the Midlothian meeting which decided to petition parliament in 1760; of these, the hostile reporter observed, twenty only were freeholders out of a possible seventy.[27] Two years later at Inverness an attendance of fifteen was held to be too low, at a time when the number of qualified freeholders was about thirty.[28] And at Perth, likewise in 1762, the reported attendance was a mere eight, when there were eighty freeholders on the roll.[29] Limited though such a comparison is, its implication seems, on the face of it, straightforward: the allegedly inadequate attendances in the three reported cases were barely worse than those regularly recorded in East Lothian, a county which participated in every militia agitation. It does look, therefore, as if the county meetings may have gathered only a minority of the landowning elite.

That minority, however, need not always have been unrepresentative. It can be argued that special considerations apply in the cases of Midlothian, Inverness and Perth, while there are good grounds for supposing that the East Lothian attendances were acceptable, and would have been regarded as such by most Lowland counties. In the case of Midlothian, a high attendance might be expected from the regular presence of many of the county's landowners, particularly the lawyers, in Edinburgh, where the county meetings were held. In Inverness and Perth, on the other hand, it is likely that the actual numbers in attendance were of lesser consequence: these were counties in which a few great landowners could still expect to determine the opinion of the whole. Significantly, the Inverness meeting recorded that those present, while in favour of the militia by a majority, were inhibited from making a formal declaration of their opinion by the absence of 'several noblemen and gentlemen with large property', who composed 'by far the greater part of the landed interest in the county'.[30] In East Lothian, by contrast, it is evident from the county records that militia meetings attracted as good an attendance as any on non-electoral business. Actual elections drew larger numbers; but whoever was then chosen as the county's representative subsequently showed no disinclination to act on instructions received from meetings at which attendance might not only be lower, but also diluted by the presence of non-freeholders. Successive East Lothian MPs accepted such meetings as the legitimate voice of county opinion — as indeed did the great majority of Scottish county MPs at Westminster. Other than in exceptional cases, accordingly, it seems that the representativeness of the county meeting can be vindicated.

A further, more serious question mark against the landowners' response to the militia agitations has still to be considered. In each agitation (except the smallest, in 1775–76), at least one important county registered outright dissent. In 1760 it was Fife, in 1762 Midlothian and Stirling; Midlothian again dissented in 1782, and was joined early in 1783 by Lanark, Fife and Aberdeen. Such opposition voices were always in a minority — yet they were of disproportionate consequence. Not only could they be taken by the English, as in 1760, to justify refusal of the demand. But they appear to have been accepted within Scotland itself as sufficient to thwart the great majority in the militia's favour. Does this indicate that behind even the majority's rhetoric there was a harder-headed hesitation over the militia's political desirability? Such hesitation was not openly avowed; and the dissenting counties themselves preferred to emphasise social and economic objections. Nevertheless, there are some — few but telling — indications that all landowners would have had reason to beware the political implications of establishing a militia.

A suggestive case is that of Berwickshire, at the very outset of the first militia agitation. In October 1759 a county meeting made a vigorous declaration in favour of the old militia laws of Scotland — only for the meeting's preses, the Earl of Marchmont, to make an immediate complaint to Newcastle, ostensibly because the declaration was contrary to Revolution principles, but in reality because it was in the interest of his rival the Earl of Home.[31] A similar incident occurred in Perthshire in 1760. Writing to Hardwicke some time after the meeting which had decided to petition for a militia, the County's MP, Lord John Murray, alleged that the vote had been taken in the interest of John Murray of Struan, supported by a large number of Jacobites and Non-Jurors. This too is most likely to have been a case of family rivalry: Struan, who was Lord John's nephew, had been chosen heir to the Duke of Atholl in preference to Lord John, and was moreover a challenger for the seat at the forthcoming election.[32] How far those attending the meetings did simply divide according to these family interests it is impossible to establish. Partisan alignment is quite probable at Berwick, where the meeting seems to have been called as part of a co-ordinated Argathelian initiative. But Lord John Murray's belated allegation against his nephew was all too obviously calculated to play upon Hardwicke's prejudices, and it is by no means certain that Lord John himself had been opposed to the militia.[33] Whatever the truth of the allegations, however, they do suggest that in counties where a few great families retained their pre-eminence, the agitation for a militia could easily become embroiled in their rivalries. And if the agitations could provoke such traditional behaviour, what might have been the consequences of the militia's establishment?

One county where family rivalries do not appear to have impinged upon militia meetings was East Lothian. There a well-documented and exceedingly bitter election dispute between Lord Milton and the sitting MP, Sir Hew Dalrymple, was just coming to a head as the militia was agitated in 1760. But even though Milton was the militia's champion, while Dalrymple was associated with Newcastle, there is no suggestion that the quarrel was allowed to spill over into the agitation.[34] Evidence as positive as this has not been uncovered elsewhere; but in counties like East Lothian, where landownership was spread across a number of nobles and substantial gentlemen, there is little to indicate that family interests played a decisive part in determining attitudes to the militia. Nevertheless, agitation was one thing, the actual institution of a militia another: at the prospect of the latter, even East Lothian drew back. As late as 1782 the committee appointed to consider the Sketch of a Bill was obliged to recognise the difficulty of allocating Lieutenancies among the county families, and the danger that those disappointed would thenceforth be hostile to the militia.[35] The traditional family hatchets might have been buried in these Lowland counties, but they were evidently still too close to the surface to risk exhumation.

The persistence of such fears is confirmed in the response to the militia agitations of the Scottish 'ministers', whose business it was to reflect and act upon the political interests of the landowners. With the temporary exception of Dundas in 1775–76, the 'ministers' were always less than enthusiastic. They might humour, even share, the sense of national resentment at the discrimination against Scotland. But the constant presence of division within the country imposed caution: and it was plain to the 'ministers' that raising a militia would create problems of patronage. For one thing, the appeal of militia commissions was, as we have seen, doubtful. On the other hand, there were grounds to fear that the Lieutenancies, which carried the authority to nominate officers, might be dangerously attractive to the greater nobility. The choice of a few noblemen to raise Fencible regiments in 1759 and 1778 was sufficient embarrassment; the responsibility of deciding on the Lieutenancies for a national militia amidst what Dundas called 'the jarring pretensions of contending noblemen not disposed to make concessions to each other' was still more unwanted.[36] It would simply re-open the family antagonisms which the stability of Scotland, and thus a successful Scottish ministry, depended on reconciling. When the necessities of war finally brought Dundas to establish a militia in 1797, it is noteworthy that he proceeded with great circumspection, appointing Lieutenants three years before the force was constituted.

In spite of the landowners' enthusiasm during the agitations, therefore, it would after all seem that the actual institution of a militia was hardly more in their interest than it was in the interests of the lawyers and burgh oligarchs. As likely to raise as to lay spectres of lawlessness and family division from a none-too-distant national past, the militia prospectively challenged the basis on which the landed and legal elites had together re-founded the Scottish political community in the wake of the Union and the 'Forty-Five.

Yet the enthusiasm shown in so many county meetings cannot simply be discounted. Whatever the doubts about the institution of a militia, the spread, the intensity and the persistence of landowner involvement in the militia agitations remain undeniable. The landowners' enthusiasm is underlined by comparison with the response to two other political issues agitated at this time, infringements of the freedom of the Scots peers to elect their sixteen representatives to the House of Lords, and the manufacture of fictitious votes in county elections. Both these grievances played on themes articulated also in the militia demand, insisting on the dignity and independence respectively of the Scots peerage and of the established county freeholders. With both issues, moreover, there was some overlap in leadership with the militia agitations. The peers who led the campaign to free their elections, Elibank, Haddington and Glencairn, along with the young Duke of Buccleuch, were all militia supporters; and Henry Dundas masterminded the campaign against fictitious votes in 1775–76 at the same time as he was assisting Mountstuart's militia bill. Despite the common themes and personal overlap, however, neither of the issues aroused a response to compare with that caused by the militia agitations. The peerage reform movement was a decorous, short-lived affair, while the campaign against fictitious votes lost its way, in 1776 and again in 1782–83, in disagreement over whether reform should extend beyond simple removal of the abuse.[37] A cause with a more straightforwardly national appeal, the militia held the attention of the landowners in the counties more often and more keenly than either of the other issues. Even if Scotland's rulers fought shy of the militia as an institution, they were satisfied that it was a cause well worth agitating for.

If so ambivalent a response still seems puzzling, it can perhaps best be explained in the terms of the choice with which Scotland's landed rulers were presented at the Union. On the one hand, the Earl of Cromarty had urged the Scots to accept the security and stability of the Union — in the expectation that it would bring them greater real independence and self-government. On the other, the Earl of Belhaven had called upon his countrymen, not so much to reject the Union, as to preserve and cultivate in spite of it the traditional, primarily martial, values which had for so long ensured Scotland's independence in spirit. In their response to the militia agitations, the landed nobility and gentry in their counties can be seen to have had the best of both Cromarty and Belhaven. Anxious not to endanger the post-Union political order, they held back from establishing a potentially disruptive institution, an institution which might have reversed the recent shift in the balance of political authority within Scotland, and undermined the independence of all but the greatest. Equally keen, however, to affirm their national spirit, the landowners seized on the agitations themselves as an opportunity to demonstrate their continuing adherence to the martial values of old. The militia agitations, in other words, epitomised the terms on which the Union 'succeeded' in the eighteenth century: freed from the responsibility for their own institutions, Scotland's landed rulers could concentrate on indulging the traditional values of national independence. It was an unfortunate — but unavoidable — irony that the agitations thereby also registered the landowners' complete repudiation of the vision of Andrew Fletcher, the original proponent of a Scottish militia.[38]

Despite Carlyle's righteous indignation at the gentry's failure to press the militia demand to a successful conclusion, there is little reason to doubt that he and his fellow Moderate literati would have been satisfied with the agitations. In pleading the national case for a militia, Carlyle and his associates had themselves placed the emphasis squarely on the values of national spirit, and had diminished the militia's institutional significance. They had more or less explicitly adopted the rhetoric and ideals of Belhaven, while alluding to the Unionist perspective of Cromarty; and in aligning their case with those predecessors they had tacitly rejected the radical alternative vision of Fletcher. Altogether, therefore, the literati were in no position to complain when the militia failed to materialise as an institution: what they sought, an enthusiastic demonstration of national spirit, had been amply achieved by the agitations alone.

The moderates' indifference to the institutional outcome of the agitations is confirmed by their attitude to political reform. For the repeated failure to realise the militia demand provoked no reconsideration of the political system which produced such frustration. On the contrary, the Moderate literati showed themselves hostile to every serious reform movement of their time. Both Carlyle and Ferguson, as we have seen, denounced the American rebels and their British supporters, eloquently eulogising the established constitution. So far as is known, they did not publicly criticise the various county and burgh reform initiatives launched in Scotland itself in the late 1770s and 1780s: but in private their hostility was vigorous. When Ferguson was respectfully approached by Wyvill, seeking Scottish allies for the Yorkshire Association for parliamentary reform, his reply barely concealed his distaste.[39] He was, he told a friend, thoroughly alarmed at the spectacle which the Yorkshire Association supplied of 'country gentlemen tasting of the importance they get in public assemblies by making speeches, tasting of party applause and receiving the infection of party enthusiasm'.[40] Evidently enthusiasm for national spirit was one thing, for reform quite another.

One of the Scottish militia's most consistent supporters, the MP George Dempster, did once urge the literati to extend their attention to political reform. Late in 1775 he closed a letter to Carlyle with the following suggestion:

> When the Poker has accomplished its favourite point of a militia may I beg they will turn their attention to the representation of Scotland and urge its extension so as to let the industrious farmer and manufacturer share at least in a privilege now engrossed by the great lord, the drunken laird and the drunkener baillie...The more this proposal is discussed the more its reasonableness and propriety will appear. And it becomes an enlightened society like the Poker to lead the way to changes for the better in our constitution.[41]

The Moderates gave Dempster their answer five years later. Over the summer months of 1780 Adam Ferguson, John Home and James 'Ossian' Macpherson were to be found exploiting every resource of the existing, corrupt Scottish electoral system to win the constituency of Perth Burghs for their friend John Fletcher-Campbell: his opponent, the incumbent member, was George Dempster.[42] Thus would the literati reward one who sought to dilute the pure milk of national spirit with the harder medicine of institutional reform.

The Social Case

As compared with the national, the social case for a militia aroused little public response. To the militia's advocates, the social case was indeed no less important than the national: preserving Scottish national spirit, they believed, was closely related to checking the potentially corrupting effects of economic improvement and maintaining the harmony between ranks characteristic of the martial society of the past. On the evidence of their public declarations, however, the Scottish elites paid much less attention to the social case for a militia than to the questions of defence and national identity. If any, it was opponents of a militia who publicly used economic and social arguments, objecting to the militia's expense, and worrying that the issue was diverting attention from more pressing social concerns. But these arguments were not an explicit response to the social case; and there is no direct evidence to show how far a wider public shared the literati's fear that unrestrained improvement would end in corruption, or their hope that a particular ideal of social harmony could be restored. Nevertheless, even without the starting point of a public response, it is still possible to assess the appeal of the social case for a militia within the general context of attitudes to economic improvement and the maintenance of social order. Here too, I shall argue, Scotland's rulers had reason to beware the institution of a militia — but reason also to endorse, through the agitations, the underlying principles of the militia advocates' case. Moreover, by turning finally to consider the implications of the militia for the social position of the Moderate literati themselves, in the Kirk and in the polite company of the Poker Club, it can be seen just how little the actual institution of a militia was necessary — or even desirable — for the literati's own purposes.

The economics of the militia would seem to have provoked some of the most clear-cut objections heard during the agitations. First, there was the militia's likely cost. This exercised English ministers and MPs every time the demand was put to them, and it was also an objection of the counties to the Sketch of a Bill in 1782. Second, there was its demand on manpower. This was a persistent concern of the burghs, which were anxious that there should be provision for substitution. Specifically in 1762, the militia also provoked opposition on this ground from several counties and a number of spontaneous and outspoken meetings of farmers and tradesmen.

The cost of the militia would not indeed have been small. In a memorandum drawn up by or on behalf of Hardwicke in 1760, it was calculated that a force of six thousand would cost £110,000 a year in service. When the further expense of allowances to serving militiamen's families was taken into account, the total cost would be greater than for an equivalent number of regulars.[43] Roughly the same calculation was made by an opponent of Mountstuart's bill in 1776; and he also estimated that even in peacetime the month's annual training of the force would cost £35,000.[44] The alternative militia proposed in the Sketch of a Bill, being four times as large, would have been still more expensive in service, although less formal organisation might have reduced its relative peacetime cost.[45] On these estimates, there is little doubt that the militia's cost would have exceeded the existing surplus on Scottish revenue. The Scottish land tax yielded but £48,000 annually.[46] The customs, excise and malt taxes, against which were chargeable the expenses of the Scottish administration and judiciary, as well as bounties, only began to yield any surplus in the 1750s, when returns rose during the war; and even then another of Hardwicke's memoranda calculated that the surplus was no more than £11,000 by the end of the decade.[47] By 1776 the surplus had risen — on what was said to be a generous estimate — to £47,000: but even when this was combined with the land tax, the total was still less than the cost of the proposed militia in service, and much of it was in any case already being spent on Scotland's defences.[48]

In sum, a Scottish militia would have had to be paid for either by additional Scottish taxation or by English subvention. The Scots themselves appear never to have contemplated any but the second option. Not even the most ardent Scottish militia advocate canvassed the possibility of an additional tax; and an English MP's proposal of a special levy was indignantly rejected as a national slight.[49] Yet the Scots could hardly accept English subvention without embarrassment: in refusing to pay for their own defence (let alone contribute to the support of the empire at large), the Scots were potentially placing themselves in a position no different from the rebel American colonists. Scottish face quite as much as English taxation would thus be saved if the militia was never actually established.

Whoever paid for the militia, its manpower must by definition have come from Scotland. A militia of six thousand represented 2–3% of the able-bodied male population, one of twenty-five thousand, 10%.[50] What counted, however, was the distribution of the burden among the labour force. If substitution was prohibited, and farmers and tradesmen were conscripted to serve as well as labourers, the potential economic disruption was greater than if the first two could purchase exemption. With substitution, on the other hand, it is, I have suggested, probable that the militia would have been recruited like the Fencibles primarily from among the casual, under-employed urban poor; and it is unlikely then to have placed a continuous strain on the nation's manpower resources.

In certain critical circumstances, however, the impact of the militia could have been positively damaging. This was clearly what was feared in 1762, when the militia demand provoked an outcry on the grounds that it would exacerbate an existing shortage of labour, and drive up already high wages. The labour shortage had developed towards the end of the Seven Years' War. By late 1760 meetings of farmers and landowners in Aberdeenshire, Stirling and Midlothian were complaining of 'extravagant' wage demands;[51] and it has been suggested that only a shortage of labour checked further war-time growth in the linen industry.[52] What was probably critical, however, was the coincidence of a sudden financial crisis in December 1761 and January–February 1762. A withdrawal of funds to the London Market in anticipation of peace threatened the fiduciary credit of the Scottish banks, and they responded by deflation, cutting cash–credit (overdraft) balances by a quarter in January.[53] Since wages were then fixed for the winter, and could not be adjusted until the spring hiring fairs, employers may well have been temporarily but sharply squeezed: under such pressure, the prospect of a militia would seem the last straw. Even though no subsequent militia agitation was so affected by adverse economic circumstances, and the objection to the loss of manpower was never so extensive again, the implication of the crisis was clear. In a growing economy liable to severe short-term fluctuations, the militia was one potentially disruptive institution which the employing classes could do without.

Just because the institution was likely to impede the pursuit of economic improvement, however, it does not follow that the self-appointed leaders of the improving movement, the landowners, disagreed with the militia advocates' contention that economic advance should remain subordinate to social priorities. At this perhaps more fundamental level of attitudes and values, a revealing comparison may be drawn with the landowners' response to the agitation in 1764 to abolish the Scottish law of entail. Dating only from 1685, the law of entail gave landowners extensive powers to determine the inheritance of their property, and to restrict their successors' ability to alienate, mortgage or lease. What inspired a committee of the Faculty of Advocates to draw up a bill in 1764 to abolish the law is still far from clear, but the case for doing so was lucidly argued by one of the committee's members, John Swinton, in *A Free Disquisition concerning the Law of Entails in Scotland* (1765). Entails, Swinton suggested, were a form of agrarian law, limiting men's natural right to acquire and improve land by industry; and he proceeded to argue that a free market in land was essential for continued economic development, and the extension of the credit system. Swinton also observed that the Statute of 1685 had been designed to make Scotland a military rather than a commercial country, reducing it to a nursery of soldiers, and thereby prejudicing public or political as well as economic liberty.[54]

These arguments, however, by no means commanded general acceptance. Opposition to the proposal to abolish entails was led by Sir John Dalrymple in *Considerations upon the Policy of Entails in Great Britain* (1764), and this apparently inspired Lord Elibank also to weigh in with *Queries Relating to the Proposed Plan for altering the Entails in Scotland* (1765). These challenged the economic case for abolition; but the burden of their own argument was on the need to preserve family as 'the single idea' which had made the Scots respectable in history, brave in war and courteous in peace, and which now carried them forward in arms, in the state, in professions, in letters and even — 'tho' slowly' — in trade. Dalrymple was most concerned that

> it is the fashion of the times, to allow mercantile considerations to enter too much into the scale of political deliberation; as if weavers and blacksmiths were the principal part of God's creation.[55]

Both Dalrymple and Elibank would allow some reform, to permit annuities, leases and exchanges, but they were anxious to preserve and even extend the essential principle of entail. Such was also, it would seem, the position of the majority of the Scottish landowning class. When the Faculty's proposal of abolition was put to the counties, only seven (including Midlothian) out of twenty-one respondents committed themselves to it; and the bill to implement the proposal made no progress at Westminster. Legislation was passed in 1770, however, removing the inconveniences acknowledged by Dalrymple and Elibank, but without prejudicing the principle of perpetuity.[56]

Both Dalrymple and Elibank were militia supporters; and the thematic similarity of their arguments and those of the Moderate advocates of a militia should not need pressing. That their defence of entails won the concurrence of most Scottish landowners suggests therefore that the social assumptions of the militia demand would also have met a favourable response. However progressive they may have been by comparison with the great majority of their continental counterparts, there were still, it may be inferred, definite limits to the Scottish landowners' zeal for improvement and commerce.[57] As we shall now see, moreover, the appeal of the social case for a militia to the Scottish gentry can be corroborated in a second context, the maintenance of social order — although in this context it once again becomes clear that there was also good reason to draw back from the militia's actual institution.

Given the pace and extent of social change in eighteenth-century Scotland, it is remarkable how small was the incidence of social breakdown. In the Highlands, of course, the death agonies of clanship contributed to the Jacobite convulsions in the first half of the century; but thereafter it was not until the 1790s that the sweeping economic changes imposed by Lowland improvers and non-resident chiefs provoked concerted dissent.[58] In the rural Lowlands there was one serious revolt early in the century, that of the Galloway Levellers against enclosing cattle-breeders in 1724. The high period of landowner-led improvement, from the 1740s to the 1780s, however, saw no repetition, even though the Scottish tenantry existed on sufferance, without legal or customary rights.[59] Only the burghs, in fact, show anything like a continuous record of disorder over the century. Glasgow suffered the Shawfield Malt Tax Riot in 1725, Edinburgh the Porteous Riot in 1736, and both were the scene of violent anti-catholic disturbances in 1779. Lesser riots occurred intermittently in smaller burghs, often though not always over grain supplies.[60] So far as is known, these disorders followed the pattern discernible elsewhere: participants were by no means rabble, and they had custom-defined objectives and methods. It has been suggested, however, that Scottish rioters were less interested in showing respect for superiors than counterparts elsewhere in Britain;[61] and it may be wondered, on the evidence of Porteous' lynching, whether they had as clear a notion of the limits of desirable action.

Relatively low though it appears, the incidence of disorder was sufficient to cause serious concern to those with the day-to-day responsibility for keeping the peace, the Lord Justice Clerk and the Commander-in-Chief Scotland. Particularly alarmed were the incumbents of these offices in the later 1770s, respectively Thomas Miller, Lord Glenlee, and General Sir James Adolphus Oughton. Threatened by an increase in ecclesiastical tensions, and by local grain shortages, they several times complained to their London masters of the inadequacy of the powers at their disposal. A particularly striking analysis of the problem was offered to the Secretary of

State by Glenlee in the aftermath of the anti-catholic riots early in 1779:

> Since the establishment of the standing army, the Magistrates naturally have resorted to the military for quelling mobs. This has gradually brought the legal establishment of peace officers, instituted for the support of magistracy, into disuse and insignificancy, upon such occasions. Justices of Peace will not act. The best men decline the active magistracys of our Cities and Burrows, where all mobs begin; and when the military are called, the Proclamation to disperse is read without effect, because the mob know that the magistrate, who commands the military, will not and dare not give the effective word of command.[62]

The problem was not limited to the weakness of the magistracy, however: the nature of the military forces available created further difficulties. The garrisons of the English regulars were unpopular, and themselves the cause of a certain amount of disorder.[63] The native Scottish Fencibles, on the other hand, were simply unreliable. The conduct of the Southern Fencibles in Edinburgh during the riots of 1779 aggrieved the magistrates.[64] And when the Western Fencibles mutinied in Edinburgh Castle later in the year, the exasperated Oughton demanded that the promise that they would remain in Scotland be broken, and that all the Fencible regiments be replaced with English.[65]

Theoretically, a citizens' militia might be thought to bridge the gap between the civil and military powers of which the Scottish officials complained. There is absolutely no sign, however, that the authorities ever saw the militia in this light. On the contrary, it is clear that they saw only a force potentially still more unreliable than the Fencibles — difficult to mobilise, and a probable source of disorder, if not insurrection, in its own right. The more 'civilian' the arming, indeed, the greater the danger: government officials had no liking at all for the informal defensive associations to which burghs and counties resorted in 1759 and again in 1779–81. Consistent with the Scottish lawyers' preference for the rule of law instead of force, what the Lord Justice Clerk really desired was the establishment in Scotland of the English system of civil policing by constables and bailiffs. Failing that, however, he had no alternative but to ask for more English regiments.[66]

The landowners in the counties evidently did not share official apprehensions of the militia — or worship quite the same image of English social order. If they had doubts about re-arming, the doubts were in relation to the aristocracy, not the people: the local plans made by East Lothian in 1779–80 and the general enthusiasm for the Sketch of a Bill show them perfectly happy to issue weapons to their inferiors, under the minimum of supervision. Not only were the landowners uncomprehending of the authorities' concern, however: their behaviour on two occasions when the militia demand was being agitated strongly suggests that they responded also to the positive vision of social harmony which its advocates projected.

In 1760, the militia agitation was almost exactly contemporary with a concerted agitation to abolish vails. These were tips given by visitors on departure to the servants of the house, under threat of future poor service for non or under-payment. The initiative to abolish them came from the county of Aberdeen late in 1759, and its lead was quickly followed by meetings of the Company of Hunters, the Select Society, the Faculty of Advocates, the Clerks to the Signet, the Masons, and more than twenty counties: generally they bound themselves neither to give nor to receive vails from a certain date. It was a remarkable collective decision, in which landowners were joined by lawyers and literati, and which apparently had no parallel in England, where vails disappeared much more gradually. The declarations of the participants make it clear that their motives were not principally economic; indeed there was considerable confusion about the economic implications. Rather the decision to abolish vails was taken in the name of politeness and a proper distinction of ranks: it was intended to replace a system of crude servility and (mutual) dependence with one maintaining a measured distance between master and servant. Such, however, was just the concept of social distinction being articulated in the co-incidental militia demand, which was predicated on the assumption that inferior ranks should be independent, but should also respectfully acknowledge their subordinate station. The campaign to abolish vails, therefore, may reasonably be taken to indicate approval for this essential social objective of the militia.[67]

The second occasion on which the landowners exerted themselves in a 'social' cause at the same time as agitating for a militia was in the winter of 1782–3: their concern now was the relief of dearth. The storm-swept year of 1782, contemporaries and historians have agreed, did not result in a famine. Nevertheless prices rose on average 60 to 80% over the winter; there was real starvation in the West Highlands; and in the Lowland cities of Edinburgh and Glasgow the crisis was aggravated by (unrelated) epidemics. The landowners' response was vigorous, firmly in line with their now established policy of voluntary, temporary subscription for relief rather than permanent compulsory assessment through the Kirk Sessions, and, at least in the Lowlands, not ineffective: serious mortality was averted, and there was very little disorder.[68] Ramsay of Ochtertyre no doubt exaggerated when he recalled that

> the lower classes of people behaved with more cheerfulness than could have been expected from their late giddiness. They were, indeed, sensible that the present calamity was not the work of man; and every precaution which human wisdom could suggest was taken by their superiors to procure a sufficient supply of provisions . . . The humanity of the rich never appeared with greater lustre than upon this occasion.[69]

But this picture of landed social responsibility was almost certainly what the landowners were pleased to imagine of themselves. It was also just what the advocates of a militia would have them imagine: the object of the militia was precisely to foster such a sense of paternal duty. Far from being a distraction from relief and the preservation of order, as Sherrif Cockburn of Midlothian feared,[70] the concurrent militia agitation may well therefore have reinforced the landowners' efforts. It was Cockburn, not the militia enthusiasts, who had misjudged the gentry: the bleak winter of 1782 was a perfect opportunity (just as the ill-year of 1698 had been for Andrew Fletcher) to set before the landed classes an ideal of responsible leadership.

In thus affirming the ideals of social distinction, respectful subordination and responsible leadership, by their initiatives over vails and poor relief, the Scottish landed class may also be seen to have bowed before the image of the English social order erected by the militia enthusiasts. That the image bore little relation to English reality does not diminish its significance: on the contrary, I would suggest, the difference between ideal and reality makes it possible to pinpoint one further characteristic of the Scottish landowners' social outlook, critical to an understanding of their response to the militia. Far from being a model of responsibility, the eighteenth-century English landed class, Edward Thompson has argued, was in fact peculiarly 'irresponsible': internally divided, arrogantly theatrical in its behaviour towards inferiors, and hence of necessity tolerant and even provocative of plebeian disorder.[71] By contrast, it seems clear that the eighteenth-century Scottish Lowland nobility and gentry were unusually class-cohesive, and attached the highest importance to not provoking their inferiors. The lessons of the Galloway rising in 1724 were learnt; and there is apparently no evidence in Scotland of the upper-class involvement in popular disorder so common in England.[72] Precisely such a fear of provocation, however, also provided the strongest of reasons for not proceeding to establish a militia.

For there is no doubt that the militia would have been a provocation. This was not, as the authorities supposed, because it would place arms in the hands of the people. Quite the opposite: the provocation lay in requiring people to arm at all. The danger was exemplified by the riots which occurred in England as soon as the Militia Act was passed in 1757; and Ramsay was to regard it as obvious that if a militia had been established in Scotland in 1760, there would have been similar 'mobbing and ferments'.[73] Ramsay was probably writing in the light of a much more recent experience — the nationwide movement of opposition to the raising of a Scottish militia in 1797, and its violent repression by English dragoons. But if that was indeed at the forefront of his mind, his inference back to the earlier militia agitation was almost certainly correct. Instead of realising an image of English social harmony, the institution of a militia would actually have entailed the forcible conscription of a reluctant Scottish people. The Scottish landowners, very properly, were therefore content with the image.

The landowners' conclusion cannot seriously have disappointed the authors of the social case for a militia, the Moderate literati. In stating the social (as the national) case, the literati had increasingly stressed the values enshrined in the militia rather than the institution itself; the landowners' response, suspecting that the institution would prove a hindrance to improvement and a provocation to disorder, but nonetheless welcoming the agitations in order to display their commitment to the values of family, hierarchy and social responsibility, had simply reflected the same bias. In this case, moreover, the Moderate literati had personal reasons to rest satisfied with agitations that stopped short of the institution. Their own social interests, both as leaders of the Kirk and as participants in the polite culture of Edinburgh, were directly involved in the militia issue.

The Moderates' articulation of the militia issue in relation to the Kirk was markedly different in the two periods of agitation. During the earlier period, the Moderates were active in securing the practical involvement of the Kirk. Ecclesiastical bodies were the first to make the demand for arms a national issue in 1759; and after the loss of Elliot's bill in 1760 two Synods and the General Assembly itself were mobilised to ensure that the cause did not die unlamented. Further declarations of ecclesiastical support followed when the cause was resurrected in 1762. Such direct intervention by the Kirk in a secular, political matter was unusual, and disliked by the government, but there is no evidence that the wider Scottish political community found it uncongenial.

Nevertheless, comparable ecclesiastical involvement was not forthcoming during the later agitations of the 1770s and 1780s.[74] Instead the proper place of the Kirk in Scottish society itself became an element in the case for a militia: the Sketch of a Bill took the parish as the base-unit of its militia plan, and expressly charged the parish minister with the moral guidance of the men. It was as if the Moderates were no longer sufficiently confident to take the position of the Kirk for granted, but must make it too depend on the remodelling of Scottish society by a militia.

The reason for this retreat from practical involvement to the mere projection of an image is almost certainly to be found in the Moderates' growing sense of the insecurity of their leadership within the Kirk. The early 1760s were in many respects the high point of their fortunes. Fresh from the ecclesiastical triumphs of the 1750s — the enforcement of the patronage laws and the successful defence of the three Homes — the Moderates had installed themselves in important Edinburgh parishes and university posts, and seemed set to command the General Assembly. They were very soon reminded of the fragility of their position. The first crisis came almost immediately after the opening round of militia agitations, in the uproar which accompanied the imposition of the Reverend John Drysdale at Lady Yester's, a plum Edinburgh parish, late in 1762. Encouraged by the difficulties the Moderates had suddenly got into, their opponents, the so-called Popular party, then maintained the pressure over the patronage issue throughout the 1760s and early 1770s.[75] Patronage was temporarily displaced in 1778 by the still more emotive issue of Popery — an issue on which the Moderates suffered a clear defeat. Their attempt to ensure the Kirk's support for a limited Catholic Relief Bill was overwhelmed by a countrywide campaign of petitioning; and the Moderates' humiliation was sealed by an outbreak of anti-Catholic rioting in Edinburgh and Glasgow early in 1779.[76] Having forced the withdrawal of the Relief Bill, the Popular party proceeded to re-open the issue of patronage. A further campaign of petitioning was launched in 1782–83, just at the time the Moderates' campaign for a militia was reaching its climax.

From the Moderates point of view, this Popular challenge must have seemed the more dangerous for its combination of old religious and new secular aspirations. Traditional presbyterian prejudices were of course to the fore in the opposition to Catholic Relief, and were one strand in the case against patronage. Another strand of anti-patronage argument, however, struck a newer note of political and social radicalism, drawing on the ideas of the rebel American colonists and their English sympathisers.[77] One bluntly outspoken application of such radical ideas to Scotland was provided by the Reverend Patrick Bannerman, presentee of the Fletcher family at Saltoun. In *An Address to the People of Scotland on Ecclesiastical and Civil Liberty,* he characterised the Kirk as a republic and patronage as the agent of its corruption, proceeding thence to denounce the 'despotic aristocracy' which had ruled Scotland since the Union, and to call upon the 'middle ranks of men' to vindicate both ecclesiastical and their civil liberty.[78]

To complete the Moderates' discomfiture, both the traditional and the radical wings of the Popular party sought to associate themselves with the demand for a militia. The anti-Catholic agitator Lord George Gordon spoke up for the counties which sought to arm in the winter of 1779, and then disrupted Graham's initiative in 1782 by his demented intervention in the meeting at St. Alban's Tavern. On the radical wing, Patrick Bannerman laced his anti-patronage pamphlet with a resounding call to the Scots to restore their martial spirit. 'Resume, Caledonians, resume your arms', Bannerman appealed, and he concluded in authentic Belhavenian tones:

> Prove to the conviction of the world, your title to the same extent of liberty with your brethren of England; and ascertain your relation to those free and warlike ancestors who atchieved the most heroic deeds of virtue.[79]

Neither the traditional nor the radical aspirations of the Moderates' opponents could be expected to find great favour with the ruling landed classes. Nevertheless, confronted with such an apparently mounting challenge to their position, it was natural for the Moderates to seek reassurance. Incorporating their conception of the Kirk's place in society into the Sketch of a Bill, they effectively appealed to the landowners for a show of support for their ecclesiastical leadership. The enthusiastic response which the Sketch of a Bill received may well have encouraged the Moderates accordingly. By 1784 they were once again in command within the Kirk, inflicting a heavy defeat on the Popular party on the issue of patronage. Even so, the emergence of the Popular challenge, and in particular its brazen appropriation of the militia issue, Belhavenian rhetoric and all, had also given the Moderates the strongest of reasons to be content with the image rather than the institution of a militia. Whatever its substance, the spectre of an armed, religiously enthusiastic and politically radicalised Scottish people was not one the Moderates would take the risk of seeing materialise.

The Moderate literati entered the militia agitations not merely as leaders of the Kirk, but as standard-bearers for polite, enlightened culture. This cultural role had been clearly established by the end of the 1750s, both by participation in the Select Society and by the Moderates' own literary productions. As we saw, moreover, the Moderates were especially keen to revive and to identify themselves with the traditional Scots association of prowess in arms with achievement in letters. It was very much as an extension of this cultural enterprise that the Moderates turned, at the end of the decade, to open agitation for a militia; and their continuing association of arms and culture was underlined in these agitations both in their militia propaganda and in their eager complicity in the fabrication of Ossian. Finally, just as the first period of agitation reached its climax early in 1762, the Moderates took steps to place the association of arms and polite culture on a regular footing through the founding of the Poker Club.

The Poker Club, it should be clear from the preceding narrative,[80] was not designed to take a leading organisational part in the militia agitations themselves. Despite the stirring intention announced in the first part of its name, there is no evidence that the Poker ever campaigned in its own right. It could of course have acted in secret: Carlyle and Moderate friends undoubtedly enjoyed a good conspiracy. Against this, however, there is no mention of any such conspiratorial role for the Poker in Carlyle's memoirs (written well after the need for discretion had passed); and in any case, then as now, few secrets could be kept in Edinburgh polite society. A partial exception proves the rule. In July 1782 the Poker clearly was used to launch a new agitation, an unusually well-attended meeting appointing a committee to frame a bill. But the meeting was no secret, being called by advertisement in the Edinburgh press 'on special business of the militia'.[81] Nor did the Poker continue to lead the agitation, instead yielding the initiative almost immediately to a public meeting and the committee it elected. Significantly too, while the literatus Adam Ferguson was placed on the Poker committee, he was not among the several Poker members who were appointed to its public successor; and although Ferguson continued to give advice informally to the public committee's effective leader, John Fletcher-Campbell, there is no suggestion that he did so on the Poker's behalf. Neither a public pressure group nor a secret society, the Poker was rather what its name's other half declared: a club.

The Poker's real purpose as a club is indicated plainly enough in Carlyle's brief history of the Club's early years prefixed to the Minutes for 1774–84, and reproduced in his memoirs. While the demand for a militia might be the occasion of its beginning, the key to the Club's subsequent development was the price of dinner. Meeting first at Thomas Nicholson's, where the dinner was no more than a shilling a head, and the wines only sherry and claret, the Club enjoyed six or seven years of frequent meetings and good company. An unfortunate quarrel with Nicholson, however, necessitated a move to Fortune's, the most fashionable tavern in the town, where dinner was three times as expensive. As a result many members, 'not the least conversible', were driven away, and new ones admitted whose views were not congenial to the old. Some of the latter went so far as to found a new club, the Tuesday at Somers Tavern; but after about two years they returned, the original Club having 'to a great extent dwindled away, in consequence of the death of some and the desertion of others'.[82]

Carlyle's chronology would appear to take the story of the Club no further than 1770, and the surviving minutes begin in 1774. But it is possible that the old members did not return until then, for the first minuted meeting, at Fortune's on 16 December 1774, was attended by seventeen, including a core of Moderates, and took a decision to elect new members because of a diminution of numbers. At all events the Club then appears to have flourished for three years (despite an apparent supplement on the price of dinner in 1776): attendance was often above ten, and the literati were strongly represented. From 1778, however, the frequency of meetings and level of attendances again fell away, literati in particular being almost absent for two years. Interest revived to some extent in the early 1780s, and there was a surge in attendance in the summer of 1782, when the Sketch of a Bill was launched. But thereafter the Club went into rapid and apparently terminal decline.[83]

Besides the evidence of Carlyle's history and the Minutes, additional light can be shed on the Poker by an analysis of its membership, on the basis of the list appended to this chapter. It is striking how small was the proportion of literati: out of a total known membership of one hundred and eleven, they account for some fourteen only.[84] The number of nobles and gentlemen, on the other hand, was more than seventy. There were ten peers and eldest sons of peers, and ten baronets; over sixty owned land, and thirty-two were advocates. Despite the disproportion of numbers, however, there were two circumstances in the literati's favour. First, there was a significant continuity of membership from the defunct Select Society. Eight of the literati had belonged to the Select, along with thirty other Poker members, making up over a third of the whole Club. Second, there was a significant homogeneity of age in the Poker, and most were of the same generation as had been members of the Select. The average age of the Select in 1754 was thirty-two;[85] in 1768 the average age of forty-six Poker members was forty-four, and in 1774, of thirty-one members, it was forty-nine. There was some infusion of young blood into the Poker, particularly in its later years; but throughout, the greater part of its membership was in middle or late middle age, with the literati slightly older than the average. When to these circumstances is added that of their usually assiduous attendance, it is clear that the Club gave a small group of literati an excellent basis on which to develop the relationship with the gentry already established in the Select Society.

The direction in which they proceeded to do so is the subject of two contrasting testimonials. One is Carlyle's own, at the end of his sketch of the characters of Blair and Robertson. Not only the literati, he recalled, but many noblemen and gentlemen of fortune and of the liberal professions

> mixed together with all the freedom of convivial meetings once a week during 6 months in the year; which contributed much to strengthen the bond of union among them. Altho' the great object of those meetings was national, of which they never lost sight, they had also happy effects on private character by forming and polishing the manners which are suitable to civilis'd society. For they banish'd pedantry from the conversation of scholars, and exalted the ideas and enlarg'd the views of the gentry: and created in the several orders a new interest in each other, which had not taken place before in this country.[86]

The second testimonial to the Poker Club's character is that recorded by James Boswell in his Journal after a meeting in London in 1763 with John Fordyce. Fordyce himself Boswell felt to be 'a sensible, clever, good-humoured man'. But — Boswell went on —

> I must find one fault with all the Poker Club, as they are called; that is to say, with all that set who associate with David Hume and Robertson. They are doing all that they can to destroy politeness. They would abolish all respect due to rank and external circumstances, and they would live like a kind of literary barbarians. For my own share I own I would rather want their instructive conversation than be hurt by their rudeness. However, they don't always show this. Therefore I like their company best when it is qualified by the presence of a stranger.[87]

In such matters of social taste one man's civilised polishing of manners between scholars and gentry may be another's barbarous rudeness between ranks (a general principle characteristically put in perspective by Boswell's very next sentence: 'This afternoon I had some low debauchery with girls who patrol the courts in the Temple.') But Carlyle and Boswell were at least agreed in identifying the informality of the relation between literati and gentlemen as the distinctive feature of the Poker.

In this respect, the Club had clearly moved some distance from its predecessor. The Select, it will be recalled, was a formal debating society, organised according to carefully prepared and well-observed rules. The tone of its proceedings was earnestly utilitarian; and the equality it established between men of letters and men of rank was self-consciously cultivated. In the Poker Club, however, organisation was informal and the proceedings convivial: the equality between the different types of member was familiar and almost spontaneous. By comparison with the Select, the Poker may thus be said to have given a new definition to politeness, identifying it fully with sociability. As such the Poker Club was certainly the most tangible, and very probably also for the literati the most desirable, achievement of the militia agitations. And by its very achievement, as a by-product of agitation alone, it underlined again the inconsequence of attaining the militia itself.

A final, summary balance sheet of the achievement of the Scottish militia agitations may now be drawn up. If the agitations failed to achieve the institution of a militia, it was evidently for the best of reasons. A militia would have done little to improve the nation's defences; it threatened the dominant interests in the post-Union Scottish political community; it could have disrupted the progress of economic improvement; it was likely to provoke the common people; and it might have encouraged the Popular challenge to the Moderates' leadership of the Kirk. But the failure to secure the militia's institution is only one side of the balance sheet of achievement. In projecting the militia as the touchstone of the nation's independent identity and the embodiment of an image of social harmony, the emphasis of its Moderate advocates was ever upon the values it would foster, rather than upon the institution itself. The militia was never meant to vindicate Scotland's independence by force, nor was it to impose a particular social order: it was simply to inspire and give expression to a renewal of Scotland's national spirit and traditional social values. And for this purpose the agitations themselves were almost certainly quite sufficient. They offered repeated opportunities to affirm Scotland's distinct national identity within the Union. They reinforced the efforts of landowners to regulate both the course of economic improvement and the pattern of social subordination. They reassured the Moderates of the landowners' support for their leadership of the Kirk. Above all, they created the opportunity for the literati to narrow still further the distance between themselves and the nobility and gentry in the polite, convivial company of the Poker Club. A great deal of national spirit and social harmony might thus be displayed without incurring any institutional responsibility beyond payment of the price of Poker Club dinners.

Appendix

Poker Club Membership

The following list is a composite of the two available lists of members, dated 1768 and 1774–84, with the addition of John Jardine, who died in 1766. The names are given in the order and in the style in which they occur in the two lists, beginning with those on the 1768 list.

In addition to the names, this composite list indicates, in order: (dates of birth and death); designation or profession; the list(s) on which recorded, indicated by date, or the date of election; and membership of or rejection by the Select Society.

John Wedderburn of Gosford Esq. (1720–93), landowner, soldier, 1768.

Dr. Alexander Carlyle (1722–1805), minister, founder, 1768, 1774, Select.

Dr. Adam Ferguson (1723–1816), professor, founder, 1768, 1774, Select.

John Fordyce of Ayton, Esq., landowner, merchant, Rec. Gen. Land Tax Scotland 1766–83, 1768, 1774, Select.

Mr. John Home (1722–1808), literatus, 1768, 1774, Select.

Mr. James Ferguson Jun. of Pitfour (1735–1820), landowner, advocate, 1768, 1774.

Lord Elibank, Patrick Murray, 5th Baron (1703–78), landowner, advocate, soldier, 1768, 1774, Select.

Baron Grant, John, of Elchies (–1775), landowner, advocate, and Baron of Exchequer, 1768, 1774, Select.

Dr. Francis Home (1719–1813), professor, 1768.

Dr. George Wishart (1712–95), minister, 1768, Select.

Mr. Andrew Crosbie (1736–85), advocate, founder, 1768, 1774, Select.

Mr. John Clerk [of] Eld[in] (1728–1812), merchant, landowner, author of *Essay on Naval Tactics* (1782), 1768, 1774.

Mr. Ilay Campbell (1734–1823), landowner, advocate, MP, 1768, 1774, Select.

Mr. William Nairne of Dunsinane (–1811), landowner, advocate, 1768, 1774, Select.

David Hume Esq. (1711–76), literatus, founder, 1768, 1774, Select.

Mr. W. Alexander, merchant, 1768.

Mr. James Russell (–1793), professor, 1768, 1774 (?), Select.

Mr. James Edgar, Commissioner of Customs, 1768, 1774, Select.

Mr. John Adam (–1792), landowner, architect, 1768, 1774, Select.

Dr. William Robertson (1721–93), minister, Principal of Edinburgh University, 1768, 1774, Select.

Mr. Andrew Stuart (1725–1801), writer, MP, 1768, 1774, Select.

William Pulteney Esq. (Johnstone) (1729–1805), landowner, advocate, MP, founder, 1768, 1774, Select.

Dr. Hugh Blair (1718–1800), minister, professor, 1768, 1774, Select.

Dr. Robert Dick (1722–82), minister, 1768, Select.

Dr. Robert Finlay (c. 1710–82), minister, professor, 1768.

William Graham of Gartmore, Esq. (c. 1732–75), landowner, advocate, 1768, 1774.

Sir Adam Fergusson, Bart. (1733–1813), landowner, advocate, MP, 1768, 1774, Select.

Mr. Alex Wight (–1793), advocate, 1768, Select.

Sir John Whitefoord, Bart. (c. 1730–1803), landowner, soldier, 1768, 1774, Select reject.

Dr. John Drysdale (1718–88), minister, 1768, Select reject.

Hon. Patrick Boyle (1717–98), 3rd son of 2nd Earl of Glasgow, chaplain, 1768.

Dr. William Wight (1730–82), professor, 1768.

Sir William Maxwell, of Monrieth, 3rd Bart. ? (1715–71), or, of Calderwood, 5th Bart. ? or, of Springkell, Bart. ?, landowner, 1768.

Patrick Heron of Heron, Esq., landowner, 1768.

Earl of Dunmore, John Murray, 4th Earl (1730–1809), landowner, soldier, 1768, Select.

John Stewart Shaw Esq. (1739–1812), landowner, MP, 1768, Select.

Sir Michael Stewart, Bart. (c. 1712–96), landowner, advocate, 1768.

James Dundas of Dundas, Esq. (1721–80), landowner, soldier, MP, 1768, 1774.

Dr. John Gregory (1724–73), professor, 1768.

Mr. Samuel Garbett, manufacturer, 1768.

Mr. William Hogg, minister (so designated in the list), 1768.

Mr. Andrew Grant, merchant, 1768, 1774.

Mr. Robert Stair Dalrymple, 1768.

Mr. Patrick Miller (1731–1815), merchant, 1768.

Mr. Robert Malcolm, merchant, 1768, Select.

Mr. John Macgowan, 1768, landowner?, Select?.

Sir John Dalrymple, Bart. (1726–1810), landowner, advocate, author of *History of Feudal Property* (1757), 1768, 1774, Select.

Mr. Houston Stuart Nicholson, 1768.

George Dempster Esq. (1732–1818), landowner, advocate, MP, 1768, 1774, Select.

Dr. Joseph Black (1728–99), professor, 1768, 1774.

Mr. Robert Chalmers, merchant, 1768, 1774, Select.

Col. Robert Murray (1730–95), landowner, soldier, MP, 1768, Select.

Mr. John Ross, landowner, 1768.

Col. James Stuart (–1793), soldier, 1768, Select (?).

Mr. Adam Smith (1723–90), literatus, 1768, 1774, Select.

Mr. Alex Home (–1770), advocate, 1768, 1774, Select reject.

Hon. Andrew Erskine (–1793), soldier, 1768.

Mr. Patrick Robertson, 1768.

Lord Elliock, James Veitch (1712–93), landowner, MP, judge, 1768, 1774, Select reject.

Mr. James Gordon, 1768.

Archibald Menzies of Culdares, Esq., landowner, Inspector-General of Annexed Estates, Commissioner of Customs, 1768.

Robert Keith Esq. (–1774), ambassador, 1768, 1774.

Matthew Henderson Esq., landowner, 1768.

Sir Robert Myrton, 2nd Bart. of Gogar (c. 1700–74), landowner, 1768.

Baron Mure, William, of Caldwell (1718–76), landowner, advocate, MP, Baron of Exchequer, 1768, 1774.

David Ross Esq. (1727–1805), landowner ?, advocate, judge (Lord Ankerville 1776), 1768, 1774, Select.

Archibald Cockburn of Cockpen, Esq. (1738–1820), landowner, Sheriff of Midlothian, 1768.

David Smyth of Methven, Esq. (1746–1806) ?, advocate, 1768.

Earl Marischal, George Keith, 10th Earl (1694–1778), landowner, soldier, 1768.

Mr. Henry Bethune, landowner, 1768.

Mr. Orr of Barrowfield (1745–1803) ?, advocate, 1768.

Mr. Robert Aberdeen (1744–1840), advocate, 1768.

Mr. W. Hamilton, landowner ?, merchant ?, 1768.

Mr. Gascoign, manufacturer, 1768.

Capt. Ross Lockhart, Sir John of Balnagowan, Bart. (1721–90), landowner, naval officer, MP, 1768.

Col. Mure Campbell (1726–86) ?, landowner, MP, 1768.
Col. Andrew Montgomery, 1768.
Hon. James Stuart (1747–1818) ?, soldier, MP, 1768.

Sir James Stewart (Steuart), of Coltness Bart. (1713–80), landowner, advocate, Jacobite, author of *Principles of Political Economy* (1767), 1774.
Lt. Col. John Fletcher (-Campbell), landowner, soldier, 1774, Select.
Mr. John Home of Ninewells (1709–85), landowner, 1774.
Col. Robert Campbell, Finab, landowner, Rec. Gen. Customs, 1774.
Mansfield Cardonnel, Commissioner Customs, 1774, Select.
Mr. Alexander Ferguson of Craigdarroch (1746–96), landowner, advocate, 1774.
Mr. Robert Cullen (1742–1810), advocate, 1774.
Mr. George Brown (of Ellieston), landowner, Commissioner Excise, 16/12/74, Select.
Professor Robison, John (1739–1805), professor, 16/12/74.
Mr. William Gordon (of Newhall) (–1778), landowner, advocate, 16/12/74.
George Home (of Branxon) (–1820), writer, 16/12/74.
Henry Dundas (1742–1812), advocate, MP, Lord Advocate, 26/1/76.
Capt. Elliot, John (1732–1808), naval officer, MP, 26/1/76.
Earl of Glasgow, John Boyle, 3rd Earl (1714–75), landowner, soldier, 1774, Select.
Baron Norton, 19/7/76.
Mr. George Ferguson (1743–1827), advocate (later a judge as Lord Hermand), 19/7/76.
Sir John Halkett of Pitferran, Bart. (–1792) ?, landowner, 24/1/77.
Duke of Buccleuch, Henry, 3rd Duke (1746–1812), landowner, soldier, 31/1/77.
Earl of Glencairn, James Cunningham, 14th Earl (1750–96), landowner, soldier, 31/1/77.
Mr. Fletcher of Saltoun, Andrew (1722–79), landowner, MP, 20/6/77.
Lord Mountstuart (1744–1814), heir to Earl of Bute, MP, 8/8/77.
Baron Gordon, Hon. Cosmo, of Cluny (–1800) ?, landowner, advocate, MP, 23/1/79, Select.
Mr. (later Sir) Thomas Dundas of Castlecary, Bart. (1741–1820), landowner, MP, 23/1/79.
Mr. Kennedy of Dunnure, Thomas (–1819), landowner, advocate, 23/1/79.
Lord Binning (1753–1828), heir to the Earl of Haddington, 23/1/79.
Mr. Mark Pringle (1754–1812), landowner, advocate, 23/1/79.
Mr. Rutherford of Edgerton, John (1748–1834), landowner, advocate, 14/1/80.
Earl of Haddington, Thomas, 7th Earl (1721–94), landowner, 21/1/80.
Mr. William Morehead, landowner, 9/2/81.
Mr. William Miller of Glenlee (1755–1846), landowner, advocate, MP, 25/1/82.
Marquis (Marquess) of Graham, James, from 1790 3rd Duke of Montrose (1755–1836), MP, 26/7/82.
Sir James Johnstone, 4th Bart. of Westerhall (1726–94), landowner, soldier, MP, 26/7/82.
Dr. John Jardine (1716–66), minister, Select.

Sources

(a) The Lists
'List of Members of the Poker Club 1768. From a Ms. in the Society of

Antiquaries of Scotland', *The Book of the Old Edinburgh Club,* III, pp. 152–3.
'Minutes of the Poker Club 1774–84', E.U.L. Ms. Dc.5.126.
D. D. McElroy, The Literary Clubs and Societies of Eighteenth-Century Scotland, Edinburgh University Ph.D. Thesis, 1952, App. K (includes both the above lists).
Alexander Carlyle, *Anecdotes and Characters,* p. 215 note: 'List of the Poker Club in 1774 and downwards to 1784'.

;(b) Identification

The Baronage of Scotland (Edinburgh 1798).
The Scots Peerage, ed. Sir James Balfour Paul, 9 vols. (Edinburgh 1904).
Complete Baronetage, 5 vols. (Exeter 1900).
Burke's Landed Gentry, 1st ed. (1846), 4th ed. (1862).
A Directory of Landownership in Scotland c. 1770, ed. L. R. Timperley, *Scottish Record Society,* New Series 5 (1976).
The Faculty of Advocates in Scotland 1532–1943, ed. Sir Francis Grant, *Scottish Record Society,* 74 (1944).
The Society of Writers to His Majesty's Signet, with a List of Members (Edinburgh 1936).
R. L. Emerson, 'The Social Composition of Enlightened Scotland, the Select Society of Edinburgh 1754–64', *Studies on Voltaire and the Eighteenth Century,* CXIV, pp. 323–9.
Dictionary of National Biography.

NOTES

1. P. Coquelle, 'Les Projets de Descente en Angleterre', *Revue d'Histoire Diplomatique,* XV, pp. 610–24, & XVI, pp. 134–57; Temple Patterson, *The Other Armada,* Ch. 1; M. Cotter-Morrison, 'The Duc de Choiseul and the Invasion of England 1768–70', *Transactions of the Royal Historical Society,* 3rd series, iv (1910).

2. Letter Book of Lord George Beauclerk (Commander-in-Chief Scotland), N.L.S. Ms. 13497, pp. 31–2, 154–5; letters to Lord Holderness, 27 Jan. 1757, 12 Sept. 1758.

3. Duncan MacVicar, Collector of Customs at Fort William, reported to the Lord Justice Clerk, Lord Tinwald: N.L.S. Ms. 5080, ff. 124–6, 136–7, 210–11, 219–20, 229–30, July–Nov. 1759; and also to Lord Milton: Ms. 16711, ff. 133–4, 9 Nov. 1759. Milton received further intelligence from various Campbells: Ms. 16708, ff. 231–2, 247: from Archibald and Duncan Campbell, Nov. 1759.

4. P.R.O. SP 54 Vol. 45, ff. 314–16, 377–8: Beauclerk to Holdernesse, 25 Oct. 1759, and Holderness's reply, 1 Nov. 1759.

5. P.R.O. SP 54 Vol. 47, ff. 208–9: Lord Justice Clerk Glenlee to Suffolk, 25 Jan. 1779.

6. For the Seven Years' War: Saltoun Papers N.L.S. Ms. 17506, ff. 61–4: 'List of Regiments Quartered in Scotland from year 1751 to 1763'; for the American War: P. Mackesy, *The War for America 1775–83* (London 1964), pp. 524–5: 'Appendix: Dispositions of Cavalry and Infantry, North Britain'.

7. P.R.O. SP 54 Vol. 45, ff. 314–16: Beauclerk to Holderness, 25 Oct. 1759.

8. For the disposition in 1779: *Glasgow Mercury,* 16 Dec. 1779; three companies of the Sutherland Fencibles were posted to the Shetlands in 1781: *Aberdeen*

Journal, 5 March 1781. The blatancy of the policy of appeasing local anxieties aroused comment: *Caledonian Mercury*, 25 Dec. 1779: 'Extract of a Letter from Aberdeen'.

9. Western. 'The Formation of the Scottish Militia in 1797', *Scottish Historical Review* XXXIV (1955).

10. S.R.O. GD 14, f. 145: Campbell of Stonefield to Argyll, 3 July 1759.

11. In one of his letters to the *Caledonian Mercury*, Carlyle complained bitterly of the uságe of the Fencibles: 'tossed North and South, East and West' within the space of a few months, their treatment, he feared, could only teach gentlemen to remain peaceably on their estates, and leave the profession of arms to the soldier of fortune. 'Cimon', 31 Jan. 1780.

12. Western. *The English Militia*, pp. 303–9.

13. Western, *The English Militia*, pp. 255–64, 271.

14. N.L.S. Ms. 13494, pp. 99–101, 104–5, 108–9: Beauclerk to Barrington, 13, 15, Oct., 1, 19 Nov. 1757; Duff, *Scotland's War Losses*, pp. 12–16; John Prebble, *Mutiny. Highland Regiments in Revolt 1743–1804* (Harmondsworth 1977), pp. 95–106.

15. Breadalbane's comment on the recruiting of the Argyll Fencibles in 1759: B.L. Addit. Ms. 35450, ff. 274–5, letter to Hardwicke, 11 Aug. 1759. General Oughton's comment on the slow raising of the Fencible regiments in 1778: P.R.O. SP 54 Vol. 47, f. 149, to Weymouth, 28 May 1778.

16. N.L.S. Ms. 16522, ff. 64–5: Andrew Fletcher to Milton, 13 March 1760; *Commons Journals*, Vol. 28, p. 872, 15 April 1760; Vol. 35, pp. 653–4, 14 March 1776 and p. 670, 20 March 1776; Vol. 38, p. 1048, 10 June 1782.

17. Above, p. 48.

18. On the decline of the magnates and their factions: P. W. J. Riley, 'The Structure of Scottish Politics and the Union of 1707', in T. I. Rae (ed.), *The Union of 1707: Its Impact of Scotland* (Glasgow 1974). On developments after 1745: Murdoch, *'The People Above'*, pp. 33–9.

19. Alexander Murdoch, 'The Importance of being Edinburgh. Management and Opposition in Edinburgh Politics 1746–1784', *Scottish Historical Review*, LXII, 173, (1983).

20. On the consolidation of the rule of law and the origins and status of the legal profession: N. T. Phillipson, 'Lawyers, Landowners and the Civic Leadership of Post-Union Scotland', *Juridical Review*, 21 N.S. (1976), pp. 97–107. On the development of the law and its making: *An Introduction to Scottish Legal History*, The Stair Society, Vol. 20 (Edinburgh 1958), Part i, Ch. 5; and Rosalind Mitchison, 'Patriotism and National Identity in Eighteenth-Century Scotland', in T. W. Moody (ed.), *Nationality and the Pursuit of National Independence* (Belfast 1978).

21. As evidence of Kames's indifference to the militia agitations: on 23 Feb. 1760, just as the news of Thurot's landing in the west was prompting a new series of pro-militia initiatives, Kames wrote to Charles Townshend, the English 'patron' of the cause. Kames's letter enclosed a plan for promoting the lace industry in Dalkeith, asked Townshend to read Kames's new book on Equity, and aired Kames's frustrated hopes of preferment, but there was no mention at all of the militia. On the same day William Robertson was writing to Townshend in quite ecstatic terms about the revival of the agitation. S.R.O. RH4/98/1: letters of Kames and Robertson to Townshend, 23 Feb. 1760.

There is no evidence that Kames was ever a member of the Poker Club, as Donald Winch claims in *Adam Smith's Politics* (Cambridge 1978), p. 104. Kames's militia plan is included in his *Sketches of the History of Man*, 2 Vols. (Edinburgh 1774), Vol. II, Bk . ii, Sketch 9: 'The Military Branch of Government'. See below, pp. 210–11.

22. The changing pattern of landowner politics and development of the Scottish ministry are central themes of Murdoch's '*The People Above*'; further on Dundas and Buccleuch: John Dwyer and Alexander Murdoch, 'Paradigms and Politics: Manners, Morals and the Rise of Henry Dundas 1770–1784', in Dwyer, Mason and Murdoch (eds.), *New Perspectives on Early Modern Scotland*.

I have referred to 'manager' and 'minister' in inverted commas to emphasise that these were not formal positions. For the sake of clarity I have also been anachronistic in associating the term 'manager' with the old political order and 'minister' with the new: contemporaries used the terms interchangeably.

23. The twenty-five counties which responded to the successive agitations of 1760, 1762, 1775–76, 1782 and 1783: East Lothian and Stirling (all 5 occasions); Ayr, Midlothian, Fife and Aberdeen (4); Berwick, Perth, Forfar, Renfrew, Lanark, Linlithgow, Inverness (3), Peebles, Dumbarton, Kirkcudbright, Wigton (Galloway), Banff, Ross and Cromarty (2); Selkirk, Dumfries, Clackmannan, Kincardine and Argyll (1). The remaining eight counties which apparently never considered the issue were Roxburgh, Kinross, Bute, Sutherland, Caithness, Moray, Nairn and Orkney and Shetland (counted as one).

24. Above, pp. 107–8, 111, 119, 131, 148, 150, 152 n. 11.

25. On the distribution of landownership: L. Timperley, 'The Pattern of Landholding in Eighteenth-Century Scotland', in Parry & Slater (eds.), *The Making of the Scottish Countryside*; and 'Land-ownership in Scotland in the Eighteenth Century', University of Edinburgh Ph.D. Thesis (1977), Ch. 5, 'The Distribution of Landed Estates' and App. 3, 'State of Landholding in the Counties 1770'.

26. S.R.O. SC 40/68/1: 'Records of the Proceedings of the Freeholders Electors of the County of Haddingtonshire 1743–75', pp. 83–5 (1760), 112–15 and 122–3 (1762); SC 40/68/2, 'Records of the County 1775–93', pp. 57–60 (1776), 233–8 (1782), and 239–43 (1783). The figures for 1760, 1762 and 1776 are a composite of two meetings.

The East Lothian records are exceptional not only in giving attendance lists, but in minuting all county meetings, on electoral and non-electoral business alike. The great majority of county records give details only of elections and the regular Michaelmas Head Court meeting in October when the freeholders' roll was revised: they are thus of very limited use in relation to the militia agitations, and it is necessary to rely instead on the generally cursory (and perhaps not comprehensive) reporting of meetings in the newspapers.

27. *Caledonian Mercury*, 22 March 1760: 'Detail of the Proceedings of some Heritors of the Shire of Edinburgh'.

28. *Edinburgh Courant*, 13 March 1762.

29. Dwyer and Murdoch, 'Manners, Morals and the Rise of Dundas', *New Perspectives on Early Modern Scotland,* p. 215.

30. *Edinburgh Courant*, 13 March 1762.

31. *HMC 67 Polwarth Manuscripts*, Vol. V, no. 463: Hume-Campbell to Marchmont, 20 Nov. 1759.

32. B.L. Addit. Mss. 35449, ff. 272–3: Lord John Murray to Hardwicke, 7 Sept. 1760. The militia meeting had been held on 1 April. On the background to the quarrel: Namier and Brooke, *The Commons 1754–90*, I, pp. 491–3.

33. In so far as it is separable from the family quarrel, Lord John's allegation of sizeable Jacobite and Non-Juror support for a militia in Perthshire is also impossible to test without further evidence, in particular the county freeholders' records. Although Perthshire is not specifically mentioned, some confirmation may perhaps be found in the general recollection, some thirty years after the event, of John Ramsay of Ochtertyre (an estate on the Stirling-Perthshire border). According to Ramsay, the Jacobites were 'exceedingly keen' for the measure in 1760, and 'a number of Non-Jurors' attended the county meetings: *Scotland and Scotsmen in the Eighteenth Century*, I, pp. 333–4. But Perthshire remains the only county for which there survives a specific allegation of Jacobite involvement. Since the Highland counties were anyway less interested in the militia agitations, there seems to have been little justification for the opinion, expressed by some, that a militia would revive Jacobite aspirations. Ramsay, it should be noted, wished to justify Lord Advocate Robert Dundas's opposition to the militia; and even then he acknowledged that the Jacobites had by now abandoned the abdicated family.

34. Milton's case is succinctly stated in a letter to Argyll, 28 June 1760: N.L.S. Ms. 16713, ff. 173–4. Dalrymple by contrast left a sheaf of self-justificatory 'Notes and Memoranda relative to E. Lothian politics, especially his difference with Lord Milton': S.R.O. Hamilton–Dalrymple of North Berwick Muniments, GD 110/1173. Dalrymple imagined many things of his enemies, even supposing that Milton suborned his former servant, William Alston, who had (according to a 'testimonial' concocted by Dalrymple) abandoned first his faith and then his wife, caught the pox from a strumpet, been circumcised as a cure, and now proposed himself for service under a Turkish conqueror. Never in his wildest fantasies, however, did Dalrymple suggest that Milton was using the militia against him.

35. *Edinburgh Courant*, 6 Nov. 1782. The committee accordingly suggested that there be no Lieutenancies, and that the JPs nominate officers.

36. P.R.O. HO 102 Vol. 1, ff. 3–4: Dundas to [Mr. Sec. Townshend?], 10 Oct. 1782.

37. On peerage election reform: M. W. McCahill, 'The Scottish Peerage and the House of Lords in the late Eighteenth Century', *Scottish Historical Review*, LI (1972); on fictitious votes in the counties: Dwyer and Murdoch, 'Manners, Morals and the Rise of Dundas', *New Perspectives on Early Modern Scotland*. Both studies refer comparatively to the militia issue, though Dwyer and Murdoch perhaps exaggerate the relative significance of the campaign against fictitious votes.

38. This analysis of the landowners' response to the national case for a militia suggests that the desire of eighteenth-century Scots to 'complete the Union' by assimilation with England may have been over-emphasised in recent studies. Rosalind Mitchison, in her essay on 'Patriotism and National Identity in Eighteenth-Century Scotland', in Moody (ed.), *Nationality and the Pursuit of National Independence*, pp. 90–1, straightforwardly identifies the patriotic rhetoric of the first, 1760 militia agitation with a desire to 'complete the Union'. More generally Nicholas Phillipson, in a study of the later eighteenth-century attitude to the Union, discerns a deeply rooted desire for assimilation with England, albeit on terms and at a pace determined by the Scots themselves: 'Scottish Public Opinion and the Union in the Age of Association', in Phillipson and Mitchison (eds).

Scotland in the Age of Improvement.

This assimilationist theme of 'completing the Union' was certainly present in the militia agitations. The Scots denounced their exclusion from the English militia as an obstacle to completing the Union: and, as we shall see, they were keen to assimilate to what they took to be the English pattern of social relations. But the ambivalent response to the militia agitations makes it clear that the Scots valued the Union for more than the rights and benefits it brought from England. Of still greater importance was the way the Union enabled the Scots to fulfill their own political and economic goals. Thus the wish to 'complete the Union' by rectifying Scotland's omission from the Militia Act yielded before the recognition that the actual institution of a militia would endanger the informal self-government which the Union had made possible; and in the agitations themselves the expression of patriotic resentment against the English was subsumed under the more general assertion of Scotland's independent national spirit. Scotland's rulers, in short, did not seek a militia simply because the English had one; they participated in the Scottish militia agitations for higher, national ends — ends to which the Union itself was little more than a means.

39. Rev. C. Wyvill, *Political Papers chiefly respecting the attempt . . . to effect a Reformation of the Parliament of Great Britain*, 6. Vols. (York 1794–1802), IV, pp. 215–16: Professor Ferguson to the Rev. C. Wyvill, 2 Dec. 1782. In reply to Wyvill's letter of 14 Nov., Ibid., p. 197.

40. E.U.L. Ms. Dc.1.77.18: Ferguson to Sir John Macpherson, 10 Jan. 1780. Generally on the political conservatism of the Moderates: Sher, *Church and University*, Ch. 7.

41. E.U.L. Ms. Dc.4.41, f. 90: Dempster to Carlyle, n.d. [Nov.–Dec. 1775].

42. N.L.S. Ms. 16736, ff. 10–11, 14–25, 27–34, 37–53: correspondence between James Macpherson, John Home, Adam Ferguson and Col. (Fletcher-) Campbell, 10 June–5 Sept. 1780. Carlyle at least seems not to have been involved in this despicable enterprise.

43. B.L. Addit. Mss. 35891, ff. 236–7: 'Memoire concerning the Proposal for raising 6000 men, as the militia for Scotland'.

44. *Parliamentary History*, XVIII, cols. 1231–2: speech by a 'Mr. Grenville', probably George, future second Earl Temple and first Marquess of Buckingham.

45. The Sketch itself estimated that £60,441. 13s. 4d. would be needed annually to defray expenses: *Edinburgh Courant*, 30 Sept. 1782 — though how such a precise calculation was arrived at was not indicated.

46. W. R. Ward, 'The Land Tax in Scotland 1707–1798', *Bulletin of the John Rylands Library*, 37 (1954–5).

47. R. H. Campbell, 'The Anglo-Scottish Union of 1707: the Economic Consequences', *Economic History Review*, 2nd series, 16 (1964); H. Hamilton, *An Economic. History of Scotland in the Eighteenth Century* (Oxford 1963), Appendix III, p. 402; B.L. Addit. Mss. 35891, ff. 238–9: 'Memoire Concerning the Proportion which the Public Revenues of England bear to those of Scotland with a view to the Present Proposal of a militia of 6000 men for Scotland'.

48. *Parliamentary History*, XVIII, Cols. 1231–2: speech by Grenville.

49. *Parliamentary History*, XVIII, Cols. 1233, 1235: speeches by Elliot, Fergusson, Mountstuart.

50. Calculated on the basis of Webster's estimate of the 'Number of Fighting Men': *Scottish Population Statistics*, ed. Kyd, p. 77. See above, p. 156, note 84.

51. *Aberdeen Journal*, 9 June 1760; *Caledonian Mercury*, 10 Sept. 1760; *Scots*

Magazine, XXII, Oct. 1760. Although they cannot be relied upon for precision, both Ramsay of Ochtertyre and the ministers who reported in Sinclair's *Statistical Account* in the 1790s recollected 1760 as a turning point in the movement of agricultural wages: *Scotland and Scotsmen*, II, pp. 210–11; Valerie Morgan, 'Agricultural Wage Rates in late Eighteenth-Century Scotland', *Economic History Review*, 2nd series, 24 (1971).

52. Hamilton, *Economic History of Scotland*, p. 307; but cf. A. Durie, 'The Scottish Linen Industry in the Eighteenth Century: Some Aspects of Expansion', in L. M. Cullen and T. C. Smout (eds.), *Comparative Aspects of Scottish and Irish Economic and Social History 1600–1900* (Edinburgh 1977), pp. 91–4.

53. H. Hamilton, 'Scotland's Balance of Payments Problem in 1762', *Economic History Review*, 2nd series, 5 (1952–3).

54. [John Swinton,] *A Free Disquisition Concerning the Law of Entails in Scotland. Occasioned by some late proposals for ammending that law* (Edinburgh 1765), pp. 61 ff.

55. John Dalrymple, *Considerations upon the Policy of Entails in Great Britain* (Edinburgh 1764), pp. 63–5; [Patrick Murray, Lord Elibank,] *Queries Relating to the Proposed Plan for altering the Entails in Scotland* (Edinburgh 1765), pp. 14–16.

56. For a first account and analysis of the entails debate in 1764: Phillipson, 'Lawyers, Landowners and the Civic Leadership of Post-Union Scotland', *Juridical Review* (1976), pp. 113–18. See also: *An Introduction to Scottish Legal History*, pp. 177–83. But the need for further work on Scottish entails is great.

57. Cf. R. H. Campbell, 'The Scottish Improvers and the Course of Agrarian Change in the Eighteenth Century', in Cullen and Smout (eds.), *Comparative Aspects of Scottish and Irish Economic and Social History*.

58. A. J. Youngson, *After the 'Forty-Five. The Economic Impact on the Scottish Highlands* (Edinburgh 1973); Logue, *Popular Disturbances in Scotland 1780–1815*, pp. 54–64.

59. T. C. Smout, *A History of the Scottish People* (London 1969), pp. 324–31; R. H. Campbell, *Scotland since 1707: the Rise of an Industrial Society* (Oxford 1965), pp. 24–7.

60. On the Shawfield and Porteous Riots: W. Ferguson, *Scotland 1689 to the Present*, pp. 141–2, 144–5. On grain riots: S. G. E. Lythe, 'The Tayside Meal Mobs 1772–3', *Scottish Historical Review*, XLVI (1967), and Logue, *Popular Disturbances*, pp. 23 ff. Other forms of minor disturbance were patronage and election riots.

61. Logue, *Popular Disturbances*, p. 206: although Logue's conclusions are based primarily on the period after that of the militia agitations, they appear no less applicable earlier in the century.

62. P.R.O. SP 54 Vol. 47, f. 230: Glenlee to Weymouth, 27 Feb. 1779.

63. One such incident in 1760 was bitterly guyed in *The Surprizing and Heroic Atchievement at Ravenshaugh Toll* [Edinburgh 1760]; on which now Alexander Murdoch, '"Beating the Lieges": The Military Riot at Ravenshaugh Toll on 5 October 1760', *Transactions of the East Lothian Antiquarian and Field Naturalists' Society*, 17 (1982). For another incident in 1777, between soldiers of a marching regiment and the Edinburgh Town Guard: Hugo Arnot, *The History of Edinburgh* (Edinburgh 1779), p. 506.

64. Anon., *A Narrative of the Late Riots at Edinburgh; and a Vindication of its*

Magistracy, against the charges advanced in the Memorial for the Papists in Scotland (London 1779). But if Oughton's commendation of the soldiers: P.R.O. SP 54 Vol. 47, f. 228: to Weymouth, 12 Feb. 1779.

65. P.R.O. SP 54 Vol. 47, f. 342: Oughton to Suffolk, 9 Oct. 1779.

66. P.R.O. HO 102.2, ff. 120–1: Glenlee to Lord Sydney, 19 July 1784.

67. The campaign was reported in the *Scots Magazine*, XXII, Feb., March, June 1760. For the situation in England: J. J. Hecht, *The Domestic Servant Class in Eighteenth-Century England* (London 1956), pp. 163–8. Mitchison, 'Patriotism and National Identity', in Moody (ed.), *Nationality and the Pursuit of National Independence*, pp. 90–1, comments on the coincidence of the militia and vails agitations, pointing a contrast between the 'patriotic' issue of the militia and the — for Mitchison, more fundamental — social concern evident in the case of vails. Once it is appreciated that the militia itself was no less a social than a national issue, however, the contrast becomes a deeper congruity.

68. Flinn (ed.), *Scottish Population History*, pp. 233–7.

69. Ramsay of Ochtertyre, *Scotland and Scotsmen*, II, pp. 259–60. Cf. the more tempered reflections of Thomas Somerville, a minister in the Borders: *My Own Life and Times 1741–1814* (Edinburgh 1861), pp. 383–4.

70. *Caledonian Mercury*, 18 Nov. 1782.

71. E. P. Thompson, 'Patrician Society, Plebeian Culture', *Journal of Social History*, 7 (1974).

72. Logue, *Popular Disturbances*, pp. 206–10; hence presumably the Scottish crowd's lack of respect.

73. Ramsay of Ochtertyre, *Scotland and Scotsmen*, I, p. 335.

74. Carlyle tried, but failed, to have support for Graham's militia bill included in the Address of the General Assembly in 1782: Watson Autographs, N.L.S. Ms. 588, ff. 46–7: Carlyle to Rev. Dr. McCormick, Moderator of the General Assembly [April 1782].

75. R. B. Sher, 'Moderates, Managers and Popular Politics in Mid-Eighteenth Century Edinburgh: the Drysdale "Bustle" of the 1760s', in Dwyer, Mason and Murdoch, *New Perspectives on Early Modern Scotland*; Richard Sher and Alexander Murdoch, 'Patronage and Party in the Church of Scotland 1750–1800', in Macdougall (ed.), *Church, Politics and Society: Scotland 1408–1929*, pp. 199–201.

76. E. C. Black, *The Association: British Extraparliamentary Political Organizations 1769–1793* (Cambridge Mass. 1963), Ch. IV; Sher, *Church and University*, Ch. 7.

77. For an analysis of the various strands of anti-patronage argument: Sher and Murdoch, 'Patronage and Party in the Church of Scotland', in Macdougall (ed.), *Church, Politics and Society*, pp. 205–11. Interestingly, besides the old presbyterian and new radical strands, Sher and Murdoch identify a third, which they characterise as 'Commonwealthman' and trace back through Francis Hutcheson to the radical Whig ideology of 1688–90. This line of anti-patronage argument had several themes in common with the Moderates' case for a militia, and might have been expected to appeal to the all-important landowners. But although Sher and Murdoch claim that the 'Commonwealthman' was the most important type of anti-patronage argument, they concede that it made almost no impact, and was dead by 1770. It was probably not, therefore, a type of argument troubling the Moderates in the early 1780s.

78. [Patrick Bannerman,] *An Address to the People of Scotland on Ecclesiastical and Civil Liberty* (Edinburgh 1782).

79. [Bannerman,] *An Address to the People of Scotland*, pp. 23–4.

80. Above, pp. 118, 131, 141–2.

81. *Edinburgh Courant*, 20, 22 July 1782.

82. E.U.L. Ms. Dc.5.126: 'Minutes of the Poker Club 1774–84'; Carlyle, *Anecdotes and Characters*, pp. 213–15. Corroboration of Carlyle's story can be obtained by comparing the two surviving lists of members, for 1768 and 1774–84. Of 78 names on the list of 1768, 44 do not recur on that for 1774–84. Since only a few had in fact died, most had presumably 'deserted'. One at least, Archibald Cockburn, would later show himself no friend of the militia; but several are to be found supporting the agitation of 1782 on county committees. It may also be noted, however, that a number on the 1768 list have proved particularly difficult to identify. For the sources of the two lists, and a composite of both, see the appendix to this chapter.

83. E.U.L. Ms. Dc.5.126: 'Minutes of the Poker 1774–84'. Use of the Minutes has been facilitated by the attendance analyses drawn up by Jeremy Cater.

84. Besides John Home, David Hume and Adam Smith, designated 'literatus' in the list, I have counted as literati Alexander Carlyle, William Robertson and all the professors — Adam Ferguson, Francis Home, James Russell, Hugh Blair, Robert Finlay, William Wight, John Gregory, Joseph Black and John Robison. Four of these — Francis Home, Finlay, Wight and Gregory — were not members in the later period; Robison only became a member in 1774. I have not counted as literati the five other ministers, the Moderates George Wishart, John Drysdale and John Jardine, the ex-Moderate turned Popular party leader Robert Dick, and the unidentified William Hogg. I have also excluded gentlemen-authors, such as Lord Elibank, John Clerk of Eldin, Sir John Dalrymple and Sir James Steuart. Although these might be thought to have a good claim to count, they were gentlemen first and literati second; moreover while Elibank and Dalrymple were connected with the Moderates, Clerk and Steuart, so far as is known, were not.

85. Emerson, 'The Social Composition of Enlightened Scotland: the Select Society of Edinburgh 1754–64', *Studies on Voltaire and the Eighteenth Century*, CXIV.

86. Carlyle, 'A Comparison of Two Eminent Characters Attempted after the Manner of Plutarch', *Anecdotes and Characters*, p. 282.

87. *Boswell's London Journal 1762–63*, ed. F. A. Pottle (London 1950), p. 300.

7

The Intellectual Consequences
of the Militia Issue

The eighteenth-century Scottish discussion of the militia issue was not confined to the case of Scotland: from the first, the issue had a wider intellectual dimension. When at the start of the century Andrew Fletcher introduced his fellow Scots to the idea of a militia, he had argued in terms which had no Scottish precedent. His concept of the militia, and the concepts of political community and social order he associated with it, were derived from the European civic tradition in political thought. Passionately though he then applied these concepts to the special predicament of Scotland, moreover, Fletcher's vision reached beyond his own country: for Fletcher Scotland was potentially an example to all of a society and polity transformed by the timely application of civic principles.

In the next generation David Hume scanned still wider intellectual horizons. Though he was well aware of the themes and concerns of Scottish debate, Hume's own work considered the case of Scotland only in passing. His concepts were drawn as much from English and European lines of the civic and jurisprudential traditions; and he addressed the subject of military organisation within the framework of a general historical and theoretical enquiry into 'the progress of society'. Hume's writing, in turn, may well have provided the stimulus for the recurrent debates on the militia and related issues in the Select Society, while these debates can themselves be regarded as the context for the militia pamphlets of Robert Wallace and Adam Ferguson. These debates and pamphlets were themselves of much lesser general significance than Hume's essays; but the implicit exchange over the militia issue was a fertile intellectual moment in the early Scottish Enlightenment.

This intellectual dimension of the militia issue did not disappear once the cause of a specifically Scottish militia began to be agitated in 1760. Rather, I believe, the agitations can be seen to have had positive 'intellectual consequences' for the political thought of the Scottish Enlightenment. These consequences are most manifest in two works in particular, Adam Ferguson's *Essay on the History of Civil Society* (1767) and Adam Smith's *Wealth of Nations* (1776). In the case of Ferguson's *Essay*, the intellectual consequences of the militia issue are almost explicit. For even if there is no definite evidence that the work was inspired by the preceding agitations of 1760 and 1762, the *Essay* clearly pursues and generalises the major themes of the Scottish demand. Such direct intellectual conse-quences of the issue are not to be found in the *Wealth of Nations*: still more than Hume's, Smith's discussion of military organisation was set within an investigation of the history and theory of society in general. But Smith's discussion did take up and develop many of the questions raised earlier by Hume; and it met the challenge of Ferguson at the point at which Ferguson might seem to have had the better of Hume. General though Smith's frame of reference was, moreover, contemporary partisans of the Scottish militia were far from happy with the implications of his discussion. If the arguments of the *Wealth of Nations* were not directly a consequence *of* the Scottish demand, they could yet, both Ferguson and Carlyle feared, have damaging consequences *for* it.

Focusing on the two works of Ferguson and Smith, this chapter follows a straightforward plan. The first part of the chapter examines Ferguson's *Essay*, the second the *Wealth of Nations* and the response its arguments provoked. In between the two parts, there are in addition brief discussions of Lord Kames's plan for a militia in his *Sketches of the History of Man* (1774), and of the handful of relevant revisions which David Hume made to his *Essays and Treatises* after 1760.

The circumstances in which Adam Ferguson composed *An Essay on the History of Civil Society,* and his purpose in writing it, present something of a puzzle. It is known that the *Essay* was preceded by another work, a manuscript 'Treatise on Refinement', which Ferguson appears to have begun in the 1750s, before he was appointed to the chair of Natural Philosophy at Edinburgh in 1759. The 'Treatise' was shown to Hume in 1759, and Hume liked it, writing to Adam Smith that 'with some amendments it will make an admirable book'.[1] It is by no means clear, however, that the 'Treatise' was an early draft of the *Essay*. For when Hume was shown the *Essay* in 1766, before its publication, he was severely disappointed. 'Neither on account of the style nor the reasoning; the form nor the matter' should the work be published, he wrote to Hugh Blair. A year later Hume reported with generous pleasure the warm response which the published book received in London; but this did not persuade him to alter his own critical judgement.[2] Unless Hume himself had simply reversed his earlier favourable opinion, it looks as if Ferguson had either radically altered the original 'Treatise' or written the *Essay* as a completely new work.

An explanation of the *Essay*'s origins may be found in Ferguson's transfer, in 1764, from the chair of Natural Philosophy to that of Moral Philosophy. The *Essay*, R. B. Sher has suggested, should be seen as a statement of the newly appointed Ferguson's commitment to the didactic and ideological purposes of Scottish academic moral philosophy — and as such as a response specifically to the sceptical philosophy of Hume, one-time candidate for the Moral Philosophy chair.[3] This suggestion is supported by the judgement of Ferguson's close friend Alexander Carlyle, who remembered (and excused) the *Essay* as 'a college exercise';[4] and it would explain the dismissive judgement of Hume, who had been reluctant to see Ferguson transferred from Natural Philosophy.[5] Nevertheless, the suggestion faces one obvious difficulty: the *Essay* was quite unlike the two other published works which were avowedly based on Ferguson's lectures, the *Institutes of Moral Philosophy* (1769) and the *Principles of Moral and Political Science* (1792). Where these works were didactic and academic, the *Essay* made strikingly ambitious use of the essay form to survey in a single connected volume the progress of society from the first stages of primitive rudeness to the ultimate corruption and collapse of refined, civilised nations.

If the *Essay* was not simply a product of Ferguson's academic commitments, another, or at least a further context for its writing can, I suggest, be sought in the militia agitations of 1760 and 1762, in which Ferguson played such an active part. Ferguson had of course laid the intellectual foundations of the case for a Scottish militia as early as 1756, in his *Reflections previous to the Establishment of a Militia;* but it is possible that the experience of actual agitation provided the necessary fresh stimulus for the *Essay*. This can be no more than a suggestion, for there is no direct evidence that the *Essay* as a whole was an 'intellectual consequence' of the militia issue. But there are two indications, one minor, the other substantial, in that direction. First, a simple intuition of style; the *Essay* is bold, uneven and loosely knit, rather rhetorical than deliberate in argument, and perhaps written at some speed. Second, and much more important, the issue of a militia can be seen to play an important part in the work's argument. This has struck more than one of Ferguson's modern commentators. For Duncan Forbes the militia question is the point at which all the leading themes of the *Essay* meet;[6] and David Kettler has concluded that participation in national defence is for Ferguson one of the few means by which members of a commercial society might act to sustain its progress.[7] Here I shall offer my own account of the place of the militia issue in the *Essay*, and indicate its relation both to the case for a militia developed earlier by Ferguson, and to the treatment of the issue by David Hume. I shall argue that the *Essay*'s development of the implications of the *Reflections* contains quite enough to account for Hume's irritation, while it confirms the centrality of the militia issue to an understanding of the work.

There is a great difference, Ferguson observed in the *Essay*, between the conduct of national defence in primitive or rude and in civilised society. Though he distinguished two different states of 'rudeness', the 'savage', in which men lived simply by hunting and fishing, and the 'barbarous', in which the economy was pastoral and there was some acquaintance with property, Ferguson recognised war to be 'the great business' of both.

Being generally divided into small parties, primitive mankind was engaged in almost perpetual hostilities.[8] With the progress of arts and policy, however, the warrior is separated from the pacific citizen, and the activity of war itself is devalued:

> The departments of civil government and of war being severed, and the pre-eminence being given to the statesman, the ambitious will naturally devolve the military service on those who are contented with a subordinate station. They who have the greatest share in the division of fortune, and the greatest interest in defending their country, having resigned the sword, must pay for what they have ceased to perform; and armies, not only at a distance from home, but in the very bosom of their country, are subsisted by pay. A discipline is invented to inure the soldiers to perform, from habit, and from the fear of punishment, those hazardous duties, which the love of the public, or a national spirit, no longer inspire.[9]

Ferguson readily acknowledged that 'the separation of arts and professions' was the key to society's material progress. It laid open the sources of wealth, and made it possible to produce goods ever more perfect in quality and abundant in quantity.[10] But Ferguson was most anxious that the moral cost of the separation of professions should be appreciated. He immediately emphasised its consequences for the 'subordination' of the labouring classes. Through the division of occupations, many mechanical arts now required no capacity in the labourer: indeed, Ferguson bluntly observed, manufactures 'proper most, where the mind is least consulted'. The lowest orders in modern society might no longer be slaves, but their values were more degraded than those of savages in their native environment. Nor could Ferguson see a remedy, least of all in education. Ignorance was the least of the labourer's failings; he was equally self-interested and servile. For such men there could be no participation in politics: a democratic form of government, Ferguson concluded, was impossible in an advanced commercial state.[11]

It was not only, however, in the lower ranks of society that the moral consequences of the separation of professions were to be feared. Its further extension to 'the higher departments of policy and war' might have apparent advantages in enabling the soldier and statesman to specialise, and thus to rely more on acquired experience and less on all-round capacity.[12] Nevertheless, Ferguson was in no doubt that

> . . . . to separate the arts which form the citizen and the statesman, the arts of policy and war, is an attempt to dismember the human character, and to destroy those very arts we mean to improve. By this separation, we in effect deprive a free people of what is necessary to their safety; or we prepare a defence against invasions from abroad, which gives a prospect of usurpation, and threatens the establishment of military government at home.[13]

To compound the danger, there was also the likelihood that the higher ranks of commercial society would tend to specialise in consumption, regarding wealth and its trappings — 'equipage' — as the basis of political standing.[14] From mistaken ideas of 'politeness' or — still worse — 'political order', these ranks might even be tempted to withdraw from politics altogether. Forfeiting the very justification for their existence, they must then, Ferguson feared, become 'the refuse of that society of which they were once the ornament; and from being the most respectable, and the most happy, of its members . . . become the most wretched and corrupt.'[15] And once corruption had taken hold, the nemesis of despotism was not far off.[16]

Unequivocal as these propositions appear, it is important to recognise that they embody critical distinctions. For one thing, Ferguson's focus upon the separation of arts and professions meant that he was not committed to a simple moraliser's equation of luxury and corruption. Luxury, he emphasised, is ever a relative concept: material prosperity is perfectly desirable in itself.[17] Furthermore, in assessing the impact of the separation of professions, Ferguson can be seen to have differentiated between the situations of the lower and higher ranks, treating them as distinct economic and political classes, and confining the incidence of corruption to the latter. The degradation of the lower orders is no doubt unfortunate; but it is irremediable, the price which must be paid for society's material benefit. In any case, it is not strictly what excludes them from political life. For the values of the middle ranks of merchants and traders have actually been improved by commerce: they have become 'punctual, liberal, faithful and enterprising'. Yet they too are disqualified from politics. With every virtue except the ability to defend their possessions, their sphere should remain the economic alone.[18] The higher ranks, on the other hand, being already in politics, need not incur the damaging effects of the separation of professions at all: requisite in economic activity, such separation is simply inappropriate in political. It is precisely because of this, however, that its encroachment is so dangerous. Dividing the civil and military functions of government, it draws citizens from their public responsibilities to pursue private interests: in other words, it corrupts them.[19]

The clearest example of the proper distinction between economic and political classes which Ferguson could think of was that provided by ancient Sparta. There all the material needs of society had been satisfied by slaves, whose exclusion from political life was obvious and automatic. Among the freemen, who were strictly 'strangers to lucrative arts', all further distinctions of wealth and status were prevented by a rigorous equality of property, while the form of government required their equal participation in political life. Educated and maintained collectively by the state, the citizens were wholly devoted to its service. They might be 'senators, magistrates, leaders of armies and ministers of state'; none were men of fortune. In short, the Spartans were the one people to make virtue truly an object of state.[20]

Ferguson did not pretend that the example of Sparta was directly applicable to modern commercial society. The simplicity of Spartan social structure was inimitable; not only was labour no longer servile, but distinctions of property could never again be levelled. As a result, Ferguson admitted, the first object of government must now be to secure the person and property of the subject, for liberty could not be made to depend on citizens' virtue alone.[21] Nevertheless, Ferguson was emphatic that distinctions remained. Slavery had been succeeded by a more complex pattern of 'casual subordination' according to the differences in men's talents and dispositions, the unequal distribution of property and the habits acquired by the practice of different arts.[22] It was still essential, accordingly, that the political be marked off from the economic, and that the integrity of citizenship as the single role of a political class be preserved. Otherwise, 'if the pretensions to equal justice and freedom should terminate in rendering every class equally servile and mercenary, we make a nation of helots, and have no free citizens'.[23]

Ferguson put no more faith in education to foster an active citizenry than to forestall the degradation of the labourer: even the example of the ancients was no substitute for activity.[24] Participation, therefore, would have to be compelled. One means to this was a permanent party system. Even if men did not act from a disinterested love of the public, Ferguson argued, their contests still served to check each other's errors, and to sustain political life. Party curiosity was far preferable to that 'pretended moderation' which the higher orders of society sometimes assumed, but which constituted 'the real corruption of national manners'.[25] The most important single context for the practice of citizenship, however, remained national defence: military training should continue to be required of all the propertied.[26] Referring now to 'the people', Ferguson would evidently extend this obligation beyond the higher ranks alone; but it is clear that the lowest orders are still to be excluded, while due subordination is to be preserved within the militia by placing the higher ranks in command:

> It is difficult to tell how long the decay of the states might be suspended by the cultivation of arts on which their real felicity and strength depend; by cultivating in the higher ranks those talents for the council and the field, which cannot, without great disadvantage, be separated; and in the body of a people, that zeal for their country, and that military character, which enable them to take a share in defending its rights.[27]

The *Essay*'s discussion of national defence can be seen to have started from the self-same proposition as had Ferguson's pamphlet of ten years before, the *Reflections previous to the Establishment of a Militia*. In both, what Ferguson identified as critical was the diversion of those traditionally responsible for bearing arms into the pursuit of wealth and civil power. Ferguson's response in the *Reflections* had been a plea to his countrymen to learn 'to mix the military spirit with our civil and commercial policy'. It was essential, he had argued, to maintain the profession of arms among the gentry and freeholders, the first commanding the second in a militia organised according to the due pattern of subordination in society at large. Without positively repudiating the benefits of commerce, Ferguson had implied that modern society should continue to uphold a clear distinction between those whose lives were devoted to labour and trade, and those who were free to cultivate the military spirit.[28] On these terms, as we have seen, the *Reflections* had provided the framework for the case for a specifically Scottish militia which Ferguson's Moderate associate Alexander Carlyle developed in pamphlets and letters from 1760 onwards. As Carlyle presented it, a national militia held the key to Scotland's continuing virtue in the post-Union, commercial world, giving expression to the values of both national spirit and social cohesion.[29]

From the same starting point, the modern devaluation of the military spirit, the *Essay* does not repeat the detailed case for a militia found in the *Reflections*. Instead the *Essay* develops and spells out the presuppositions on which Ferguson and Carlyle had rested their case. The previously implicit suggestion of a necessary distinction between the commercial and the political classes is in the *Essay* made explicit: the maintenance of such a distinction, on the model of ancient Sparta, is the touchstone of social and political well-being. Lest there be any confusion on the point, Ferguson further makes it clear in the *Essay* that this distinction does not simply reflect the separation of professions. Though far advanced in modern societies, the separation of professions is still only relevant in the commercial sphere: it should apply to labour and trade, but not to the higher arts of policy and war. To introduce the principle of separation into these arts is to confuse the proper distinction between political and commercial: it will corrupt the higher ranks, and plunge society into despotism. Against such a fate, the *Essay* affirms, the active pursuit of virtue by the higher ranks remains the only adequate protection: and military training, such as the *Reflections* had called for, is the most obvious and effective means to promote such virtue.

The *Essay* not only spells out the presuppositions of the case for a militia in the *Reflections*: it also confirms the intellectual character of the earlier argument. In its insistence on the need to uphold social distinctions and sustain the virtue of the higher ranks, the *Essay* may be thought still to rest on the civic social and moral principles found in Andrew Fletcher. Even more than in the *Reflections*, however, the emphasis on these principles is such that it effectively excludes other principles of equal or greater importance to a strict civic thinker such as Fletcher. The *Essay*'s concern with the social position and moral values of the higher ranks is not matched by any similar degree of concern with the institutional framework in which they were to act: even in urging the maintenance of martial spirit, Ferguson limited himself to broad references to military training, and made little of the actual institution of a militia. Such an emphasis in fact moves the *Essay* much closer to the outlook of Hutcheson and his professorial successors: though hardly just another 'college exercise', the *Essay* does show a similar dilution of civic principles with Stoic and Ciceronian moralism. Ferguson adds a concern with martial virtue far stronger than that shown by Hutcheson: but that again is less civic than in line with an older view of Scottish humanist moralism going back through Belhaven to the Renaissance.

Written in such moralist terms, the *Essay* confirms the impression of the *Reflections* in another respect: the intellectual target of Ferguson's discussion of national defence was David Hume. What really provoked Ferguson, it should now be clear, was the moral optimism underlying Hume's treatment of the issue. Hume sanguinely expected commerce to stabilise social relations and civilise moral values: in particular he was confident that courage would be strengthened, not undermined, by the greater military discipline developed in commercial societies. By contrast, Ferguson was convinced that commercial society lived under the mounting threat of a confusion of ranks and subversion of values: in abandoning arms and disowning the martial spirit, the higher ranks were hastening the onset of corruption. In the face of this danger, Ferguson was quite unable to share Hume's confidence that virtue — or at least a capacity for political participation — was being diffused more widely, among the middling and lower ranks of commercial society. Given the degradation of labourers by the separation of professions, there was no question of their ever being qualified for political or military service. As for the commercial middling ranks, whose contribution Hume thought so positive, there were still obvious dangers in according them a political role, since their values, however improved, remained single-mindedly economic. They may have been among the 'body of the people' whom Ferguson would require to undergo military training, but there must be no doubt of their continuing subordination. For Ferguson attention must continue to be concentrated upon the higher ranks and their moral welfare; and he defiantly asserted a principle of social distinction which Hume, in a major revision of civic presuppositions, had dismissed as characteristic of primitive societies alone. Untroubled by Hume's withering critique of its unnaturalness, Ferguson would affirm anew the relevance of the example of Sparta, even for modern commercial societies, and would reiterate the need for the particular cultivation of martial virtue by the higher ranks, setting themselves at the head of their free subordinates.

The moralist animus of Ferguson's challenge to Hume is highlighted by the *Essay*'s relative indifference to Hume's parallel concern, the relation between political institutions and social progress. Ferguson did devote a short section of the *Essay* to 'National Waste' as one of the causes of national ruin: under this head he counted great armies maintained without national object and public debts incurred at the expense of future generations.[30] But he gave no systematic consideration to the possibility that aggrandisement of government was an inherent and necessarily increasing problem for commercial societies: there is no suggestion that the militia is to be preferred to the standing army because it is more economical. On the whole Ferguson appears to have been confident that the requisite institutional development had occurred more or less in conjunction with increasing prosperity.[31] Most of Europe was now governed by 'mitigated despotisms' which at least fostered the commercial arts; and Britain in particular enjoyed a government which successfully mixed monarchy with republic, and ruled an extensive territory without military forces.[32] But in any case, Ferguson saw little point in deliberate initiative in relation to institutions. 'No constitution,' he pronounced, 'is formed by concert, no government is copied from a plan.'[33]

This indifference to the problem of institutions in commercial society sets Ferguson's moral emphasis firmly in perspective. On one side, it is clear that economic development was for Ferguson a subordinate social objective. His insistence that commerce prospers best when left to those who make it their sole profession may have the appearance of radical economic liberalism. But the confession that it was not a subject congenial to 'the views with which I write' indicates an attitude rather closer to the traditional civic one of uneasy tolerance:[34] there is none of the passionate commitment here to material improvement shown by both Hume and Andrew Fletcher. By the same token, it is also evident that Ferguson's conception of politics was more affirmative than constructive: the establishment of good institutions, to which Hume and Fletcher attached such importance, counted for little beside the moral commitment to activate them. A nation was not defended merely by numbers and resources, by the size of its armies, but by the courage and virtue of its citizens.[35] Laws were not observed from 'any magic power descending from shelves that are loaded with books'; they were effective when they represented 'the influence of men resolved to be free'.[36] And if enforcement of the law depended on the vigour of a people, Ferguson held it to be

> . . . . still more evident, that what we have called the political freedom, as the right of the individual to act in his station for himself and the public, cannot be made to rest on any other foundation. The estate may be saved, and the person released, by the forms of a civil procedure; but the rights of the mind cannot be sustained by any other force but its own.[37]

In such ringing affirmations of a purely moral commitment to liberty lay the core of Ferguson's politics.[38]

In confrontation with Hume, however, affirmations are not enough: Ferguson's lively eloquence cannot disguise the difficulties which the *Essay* left unresolved, even unrecognised. The difficulties came to a point precisely in Ferguson's treatment of liberty. For all his moral commitment to liberty, Ferguson never attempted to clarify the relation between the personal and the political forms of liberty involved in a continuing separation of the economic from the citizen classes. He might acknowledge that the first object of government must now be to secure the person and property of the subject — but this was not to form the basis for an equal liberty of citizenship. He would uphold political liberty as the highest expression of virtue — yet he would virtually compel its practice, through the imposition of military training.[39] Faced with such careless confusion over a principle as important as that of liberty, little wonder that Hume found the *Essay* so exasperating.

The militia issue, it should be emphasised, by no means exhausts the possibilities in interpreting the *Essay on the History of Civil Society*. Ferguson's concern in the *Essay*, as we have seen, was less with the militia itself than with its underlying social and moral premises; and these premises also underlay arguments concerned with other aspects of social progress. Nor was the book solely devoted to modern commercial society: much of the *Essay*'s originality lay in its opening discussion of savage and barbarian societies. A full interpretation of the *Essay* would thus have to go beyond the framework of the militia issue, to pursue themes — such as those of property, political authority and obligation, culture and civilisation — deriving from other lines of the Scottish Enlightenment's enquiry into 'the progress of society'. Nevertheless, it is clear that the militia issue, as Forbes and Kettler perceived, was the focus of several of the most important elements of Ferguson's account of social progress in the *Essay*. Above all, it may be suggested, it was through discussing arms and military spirit that Ferguson was brought to face the fundamental problem of corruption in commercial society. Without defence and martial virtue, corruption could not be held at bay; and Ferguson thence concluded that arms and martial spirit could only be maintained by permanently distinguishing between the ranks of commercial society, and dividing their moral responsibilities. Such, in Ferguson's *Essay*, were the 'intellectual consequences' of the militia issue.

The same significance cannot be claimed for the militia issue in Ferguson's later works, whether his college exercises in moral philosophy or his Roman history. The brief *Institutes of Moral Philosophy* and the much fuller *Principles of Moral and Political Science* were elaborations of his moral philosophy as a whole, complete from premises to conclusions: but martial virtue was conspicuous in both by its virtually complete absence.[40] *The History of the Progress and Termination of the Roman Republic* (1783) predictably gave Ferguson many opportunities to emphasise the fatal consequences of a loss of military virtue and of entrusting arms to mercenary soldiers — opportunities which Ferguson did not pass up.[41] Yet even here the military was no more than one of several themes pursued by Ferguson as he told the story of the Republic's corruption into the despotism of the Empire. Thus throwing into deeper relief the importance of the militia issue in the *Essay*, the comparison with Ferguson's other works only strengthens the possibility that it was the issue itself which actually inspired the writing of the *Essay*.

The discussion of 'The Military Branch of Government' in Lord Kames's *Sketches of the History of Man* (1774) may well have been another 'intellectual consequence' of the militia issue: but it was hardly so to the same extent as Ferguson's *Essay*, since, as we have seen, Kames was conspicuous by his absence from the Scottish militia agitations.[42] Kames had apparently written on the militia as early as the 1750s, for his correspondent Josiah Tucker kept promising to return the copy of the tract Kames had sent him.[43] But while this may have been the basis for his chapter in the *Sketches*, the latter was the first public indication of his interest in the issue. The significance of Kames's discussion lies in its clarification of the difficulties Ferguson had already run into in attempting to uphold the traditional concept of a militia in the circumstances of commercial society.

Kames's starting point was just that of Ferguson. 'Where arts, manufactures and commerce have arrived at perfection,' he affirmed, 'a pacific spirit prevails universally: not a spark is left of military ardour, nor will any man be a soldier.' Kames's formulation of the resulting problem then repeated Ferguson's almost word for word: it must be shown that the military and commercial spirits were not absolutely incompatible.[44] Kames, however, advanced the difficulty of the problem in two respects. First, he accepted the desirability of economic development. No economist himself (though a zealous practical improver), Kames was optimistic that 'patriotism' would flourish when a people was in a train of prosperity — even if he also believed that wealth would eventually engender corruption.[45] In the second place, Kames also accepted that commercial society could not simply continue with previous forms of defence, on the classical or feudal models. In language echoing Hume's, Kames declared that Rome's had been 'a forced constitution, contrary to nature'; and he discounted feudalism as 'a system that led to confusion and anarchy, as little fitted for war as for peace'.[46] Given the circumstances of commercial society, Kames was thus led to admit, the rationale of a standing army was undeniable. Nevertheless, Kames remained convinced that a standing army was both a militarily precarious defence, and a danger to liberty. 'At the hazard of being thought an idle projector', Kames would accordingly not shirk an attempt to devise a suitable plan of a new militia.[47]

Kames proposed that all men should be liable for service, by rotation, for a period of five to seven years; there would be no exemptions. As many as 60,000 men would be in regular service at a time. There would be two classes of officers, those with and those without pay: the latter could resign the service after seven years with honour, and would then be qualified to hold civil office and sit in parliament. Kames dwelt particularly on the benefit of the scheme for the education of young gentlemen. As for the private men, they should be led to combine the spirit of industry with that of service by being employed for nine months of the year on public works. Kames insisted on two particular features of the plan. Unlike the militia schemes of Harrington and Fletcher, it made effective provision for enforcing service; but it would not alienate the minds of the people from arts and manufactures. Kames concluded with this justification:

> My capital aim has been to obviate the objections that press hard against every military plan, hitherto embraced or proposed. A standing army in its present form is dangerous to liberty; and but a feeble bulwark against superior force. On the other hand, a nation in which every subject is a soldier must not indulge any hopes of becoming powerful by manufactures and commerce: it is indeed vigorously defended, but is scarce worthy of being defended. The golden mean of rotation and constant labour in a standing army, would discipline multitudes for peace as well as for war. And a nation so defended would be invincible.[48]

Kames's plan of a militia builds most obviously on Andrew Fletcher's. Like Fletcher, Kames envisaged universal service, while valuing above all those who served at their own expense, since the militia ought to be the educating of a gentleman. But Kames claimed that the plan went further than Fletcher's in insisting on the element of compulsion in the service, and on the need to make it compatible with the continuance of arts and manufactures. In these respects Kames may actually be thought to have advanced from Fletcher to Hume, since Hume had suggested that a militia would least disrupt economic activity, and had indicated that conscription was the necessary basis of the service. Despite the apparent convergence, however, Kames's thinking was not Hume's. For one thing, Kames proposed a sizeable permanent force, where Hume had suggested that the militia would be called out on service only when necessary for defence.[49] For another, despite his insistence on compulsion, Kames's plan was difficult to reconcile with his general distrust of legislative initiative: he was without Hume's commitment to constructive institutional change.[50] Finally, Kames remained oblivious to the problem of liberty involved in a compulsory militia: adamant that a militia was essential to political liberty, he quite failed to see that it must rest on a denial of individual liberty.

In the last analysis, therefore, Kames was no more able than Ferguson to overcome the difficulties facing their common project of reconciling the military and commercial spirits. He was still the moralist, convinced that commerce would undermine martial virtue unless positive steps were taken to sustain it, but unwilling or unable to recognise the economic and especially the political costs. At least, however, Kames did not actively visit his difficulties on his fellow Scots. Self-interested he may have been in not adding his weight to the agitation for a Scottish militia in 1760; but silence was an honest reflection — whether conscious or unconscious — of intellectual impasse.

David Hume's discussion of questions of defence and military organisation in his *Essays Moral and Political* (1741–42) and *Political Discourses* (1752) preceded the emergence of the militia demand in Scotland. But the essays were later subjected to a constant process of revision; and new editions of the collected *Essays and Treatises on Several Subjects* appeared in the 1760s and 1770s, after the first round of Scottish militia agitations. Hume had the opportunity, therefore, to modify his earlier arguments in consequence of the agitations.

One change in particular is of possible significance in relation to the militia issue. From 1770 the sentence in the 'Idea of a perfect Common-wealth' describing the army as a 'mortal distemper' in the British consti-tution was deleted.[51] On the other hand, there was a fresh pejorative reference to 'mercenary armies' in a passage added to 'Of Public Credit' in 1764: elaborating on the socially subversive consequences of the system of public credit, Hume remarked that it would leave mercenary armies as the only expedient for suppressing or preventing insurrection.[52] Such a remark was evidently rhetorical, but it does suggest caution in taking the deletion from the perfect commonwealth essay to mark a major change of position. What seems conclusive, however, is what Hume left unchanged.[53] Of the several relevant remarks in the perfect commonwealth essay in particular, it was only the description of the army as a 'mortal distemper' which was deleted. The immediately preceding sentence, which pronounced it one of the inconveniences of a limited monarchy that the sword is in the hands of a single person, who will neglect the militia to keep up a standing army, remained in place; and so did the proposal of a universal militia. There is thus very little reason to doubt that Hume persisted in his 'stubborn preference' for militias over standing armies. Having transformed the social and moral premises on which the concept of the militia rested, he continued to be faithful to the essentially civic institutional principle.

Adam Smith's *Inquiry into the Nature and Causes of the Wealth of Nations* (1776) was certainly not itself an intellectual consequence of the Scottish militia agitations. Like the earlier *Theory of Moral Sentiments* (1759), the *Wealth of Nations* was a development of material Smith had prepared for his college lectures on jurisprudence in the 1750s and early 1760s; and it is clear that both books were written as formal, philosophical treatises on the model of the works of Isaac Newton. That the *Wealth of Nations* was not a direct consequence of the Scottish agitations does little, however, to diminish its significance in relation to the militia issue. As we shall now see, the *Wealth of Nations* contained substantial discussions of defence and military organisation as they related to both the economic resources and the moral values of commercial society; and these discussions can be interpreted as a further, major contribution to the intellectual debate launched by Hume and Ferguson. Smith's contribution, moreover, was not purely intellectual. However general his own design, his treatment of the issue was immediately perceived by Ferguson and Carlyle as a threat to the principles on which they argued the case for a Scottish militia.

Smith discussed defence and military organisation in two separate passages in Chapter One of Book Five of the *Wealth of Nations*. The subject of Book Five as a whole was 'the Revenue of the Sovereign or Commonwealth', and Chapter One was devoted to 'the Expences of the Sovereign or Commonwealth'. The first of the two passages was the self-contained Part First of the Chapter, entitled 'of the Expence of Defence'. Smith immediately set this problem in historical perspective. The cost of preparing and employing a military force is very different, he showed, in the different 'states of society' of 'periods of improvement'. In the two most primitive states of society, the hunting and the pastoral, every man is naturally a warrior. A society of shepherds is indeed militarily more powerful than one of hunters, and is capable of fielding armies formidable enough to threaten even civilised neighbours: nevertheless the two forms of primitive society are alike in their ability to go to war *en masse,* without charge to the sovereign.[54] In the third, agricultural stage, a society can no longer go to war as a whole, at any time. For agriculture attaches a society to a particular territory, and limits the period during which men are free to fight to the summer months between seedtime and harvest. Even so, the normal occupations of a husbandman still fit him for the trade of a soldier, and the sovereign of such a society may command that military exercises be a part of public education at little cost to himself.[55] It is only in the final, most advanced, 'civilised' state of society that it becomes altogether impossible for those who fight to maintain themselves at their own expense.

Smith identified two causes of decisive change in the organisation of defence in civilised society: the progress of manufactures, and the improvement in the art of war. First, the progress of manufactures makes it impossible for men to give up their ordinary employments without suffering material loss. This applies to the husbandman no less than the artificer: the interest of each in improving their lot to the extent now possible leaves them without the leisure which those in earlier, poorer states of society devote to martial exercises. On Smith's analysis, civilised society thus faces an unprecedented dilemma: the wealth brought by agriculture and manufactures renders it the more vulnerable to attack by acquisitive neighbours, yet the natural habits of its people make them incapable of its defence.[56] Equally radical in implication are improvements in the art of war. As weapons and strategy become more complex, so wars last longer, and require greater skill and above all discipline in those who fight.[57] In effect, Smith argued, both the progress of manufactures and improvements in the art of war point in a single direction, the specialisation of the military function. To ensure that the art of war is at the same stage of perfection as the mechanical and other arts, 'it is necessary that it should become the sole or principal occupation of a particular class of citizens'. Smith emphasised, however, that the principle of the division of labour would not be introduced in the military art 'naturally . . . by the prudence of individuals': 'it is the wisdom of the state only which can render the trade of a soldier a particular trade separate and distinct from all others'.[58]

To provide for its defence, Smith believed, a modern civilised state can choose between two alternatives. One is a militia, consisting of all or a certain number of citizens, whom the state obliges to practise military exercises against 'the whole bent' of their interest and inclination. Such, in modern times, were the militias of Switzerland and England. The other possibility is to maintain a standing army, in which military exercises are the soldiers' sole profession.[59] As between the two, Smith was in no doubt which is to be preferred. 'A militia, in whatever manner it may be either disciplined or exercised, must always be much inferior to a well-disciplined and well-exercised standing army.'[60] It is true that with a standing army only a small proportion of the population can be employed as soldiers — perhaps not more than one in a hundred without ruin to the nation. But militiamen exercised only once a week or month, in small bodies, can never be so practised in arms or accustomed to obedience as regular soldiers trained every day, in large numbers.[61]

To emphasise his point, Smith readily pressed the logic of functional specialisation to its limit. A militia which served for successive campaigns would, he acknowledged, become in every respect as a standing army; he forecast that just one more campaign would make the American militia a match for the army of Britain.[62] By the same token, however, Smith could claim that regular soldiers who had never previously seen an enemy had often taken the field fit to face the most experienced veterans.[63] Once the distinction between a standing army and a militia was properly understood, indeed, Smith believed it would be found that 'the history of all ages' bore testimony to the 'irresistible superiority' of the one over the other. In particular, he instanced the decisive role of standing armies in each of the three great revolutions of the ancient world. It was the standing army of Philip of Macedon, perhaps the first such authenticated in history, which had vanquished 'the gallant and well-exercised militias' of the ancient Greek republics, and later conquered the great Persian empire. In the long struggle between Rome and Carthage it was only once the Roman militia had, by repeated campaigns, become a standing army fit to match Hannibal's that the tide turned against the latter. Finally, it could be seen that the Roman empire itself had lasted as long as it maintained standing armies: only when these were allowed to degenerate into undisciplined provincial militias had Rome fallen to the hardier, barbarian militias of the Germans and Scythians.[64]

For Smith a standing army is an essential feature of civilisation. It is, on the one hand, the only means by which the defence of civilisation can be assured: for as the fate of the Roman empire demonstrated, a militia of a civilised nation is inferior to that of a barbarous. On the other hand, it is only by the agency of a standing army that 'a barbarous country can be suddenly and tolerably civilised': with an army the law of the sovereign can be spread with 'an irresistible force' throughout the remotest provinces. All the improvements which Peter the Great had introduced into Russia could be resolved, Smith asserted, into the establishment of a well-regulated standing army.[65] But if an army is thus a strong support of authority, Smith was equally insistent that it is not always necessarily dangerous to liberty, as 'men of republican principles' had supposed. In the hands of a Caesar or a Cromwell, it could indeed be a threat. But, Smith believed,

> where the sovereign is himself the general, and the principal nobility and gentry of the country the chief officers of the army; where the military force is placed under the command of those who have the greatest interest in the support of the civil authority, because they themselves have the greatest share of that authority, a standing army can never be dangerous to liberty.

An army will rather be favourable to liberty, in so far as it enables magistrates to tolerate a greater degree of popular discontent without either showing that 'troublesome jealousy' characteristic of some modern republics, or needing a discretionary power. Supported by the 'natural aristocracy' of the country and a well-regulated standing army, the sovereign's consciousness of his own authority will enable him to pardon or neglect the most licentious remonstrances.[66]

The second passage discussing defence and military organisation occurs in Chapter One, Part Three, 'of the Expence of publick Works and publick Institutions', in a subsection devoted to 'the Expence of the Institutions for the Education of Youth'. Here Smith advanced a strong argument for the education of the common people at public expense, since, unlike people of 'some rank and fortune', the poor have neither the means nor the inclination to obtain education for themselves.[67] In famous words, Smith elaborated on this lack of inclination among the common people with a graphic account of the debilitating effects of the division of labour, prominent among which he believed to be the decay of martial spirit. In general, Smith wrote, the man whose work is reduced to a few simple operations has no occasion to exert his understanding or invention, and so 'becomes as stupid and ignorant as it is possible for a human creature to become'. Incapable of any just judgement in many even of the ordinary duties of private life, he is altogether unable to judge the great interests of his country, or to defend it in war. 'His dexterity at his own particular trade seems...to be acquired at the expense of his intellectual, social and martial virtues.'[68] A few paragraphs later Smith spelt out more particularly the implications of the decline in martial spirit, which he found evident throughout modern Europe. Even though martial spirit in itself might now be an insufficient defence, it still remained any society's ultimate source of security. Moreover, if every citizen had the spirit of a soldier, a smaller standing army would surely be required, and the dangers to liberty, 'real or imaginary', that are commonly apprehended from such an army would be diminished.[69]

To offset the decline of martial spirit, therefore, Smith would have military exercises made a compulsory part of public education. He readily acknowledged that such exercises could no longer equip the people for war as they had in ancient Greece and Rome: the regulations of a modern militia (other, perhaps, than in Switzerland) were too complex for more than a few to learn. Yet, Smith argued:

> Even though the martial spirit of the people were of no use towards the defence of the society, yet to prevent that sort of mental mutilation, deformity and wretchedness, which cowardice necessarily involves in it, from spreading themselves through the great body of the people, would still deserve the most serious attention of government; in the same manner as it would deserve its most serious attention to prevent a leprosy or any other loathsome and offensive disease....[70]

In turn Smith set the proposal of compulsory military exercises in the context of a recommendation of universal elementary parish education, teaching the common people reading, writing and accounting.[71] The purpose of this education was similarly to remedy the intellectual and moral mutilation of the people; at the same time, Smith emphasised that it would bring positive advantages to the state. An 'instructed and intelligent people', he wrote, would be 'decent and orderly' in their political conduct. Feeling themselves individually more respectable, they would be more likely to earn the respect of their lawful superiors, and thus to respect their superiors in turn. Vulnerable neither to the delusions of enthusiasm and superstition, nor to the interested complaints of faction and sedition, they would be less apt to be misled into unnecessary and wanton opposition to the measures of government. And, as Smith concluded,

> In free countries, where the safety of government depends very much upon the favourable judgement which the people may form of its conduct, it must surely be of the highest importance that they should not be disposed to judge rashly or capriciously concerning it.[72]

Framed in such general terms, Smith's discussions of defence and military organisation immediately invite interpretation in the context of the Scottish Enlightenment's investigation of the progress of society. More specifically, the very organisation of Smith's treatment of the issue, divided between economic and moral dimensions, suggests that he had chosen the same perspective as Hume, viewing the issue within the general problem of the relation between economy and government in commercial society. For Hume this problem had two aspects: on the one hand, the distribution of resources between the economy and the institutions of government; and on the other, the implications for government of the impact of commerce on morals and social structure. Smith, I shall now argue, tackled the problem under these same two heads, but developed his own distinctive responses.[73] His solution to the economic and institutional aspect of the problem departed significantly from Hume's in its choice of constitutional principle

— but it did so by developing an alternative political vision that was no less Scottish in inspiration, and it offered resounding confirmation of Hume's conviction, which Ferguson had so devalued, that institutions mattered to the progress of society. Smith's treatment of the moral and social aspect of the problem, on the other hand, began by accepting that commerce had the corrupting effects which Ferguson had insisted on — only to seek ways of renewing Hume's prospect of universal citizenship.

Considering the first aspect of the problem, government and economic resources, Smith's starting point was the same as Hume's. Like Hume, Smith identified the individual's desire to acquire goods as the motor of progress; and he took the same, characteristically jurisprudential view that the need for security of individual property was the origin of government, and that the provision of justice and defence were government's two primary functions.[74] At the same time, Smith followed Hume in recognising that the interest of those in government may diverge from the interest of society as a whole. But this was not simply the consequence of the general phenomenon of party or faction: Smith went beyond Hume in ascribing a distinct interest to each of the three great economic orders in commercial society — the landowners, the stockholders or capitalists, and the wage-earners. The interests of the first and last of these were, Smith believed, naturally aligned with the general interest of society. But the interest of the stockholders or capitalists was, as a result of the tendency for the rate of profit to decline as the wealth of society grew, antagonistic to society's: and this class was all too likely to apply its wit to take advantage of the indolence and lack of foresight of the landowners to impose its 'wretched spirit of monopoly'. The mercantile interest, as Smith proceeded exhaustively to demonstrate, was always pressing government to sanction its restrictive practices, thereby interfering with the free market and distorting the natural distribution of economic resources. And if the resulting 'mercantile system' was challenged by rivals without or rebels within, the stockholding interest would press government to divert yet more resources into the system's military defence.[75]

Taking the formulation of the problem of the misappropriation of resources further than Hume, Smith also broke new ground in framing a more explicit and systematic solution to it in Book Five of the *Wealth of Nations*. The solution was in two stages. First, Smith would apply economic standards of performance directly to political institutions: the organisation of defence, the administration of justice and the raising of public revenue should be rationalised in line with suitable commercial principles. The chapter on the expense of defence, summarised above, exemplifies Smith's argument. Extending the principle of the division of labour to military organisation, he advocated defence by a standing army rather than a militia because the former would cause less disruption of productive economic activity, while facilitating acquisition of the complex skills of modern warfare. A similar application of commercial principles could be made to the administration of justice. The judiciary, Smith believed, ought to be a separate, specialist profession, judges being rewarded on the basis of the number of suits they decided, with some measure of competition between their courts.[76] As for public revenue, it was best raised by taxation, not borrowing. A system of public credit, Smith agreed with Hume, must necessarily damage the long-term economic development of a nation by removing the incentive to invest productively. Taxation, on the other hand, could be economically levied, and allowed the possibility of a check on government: in particular it provided an incentive to end a war as soon as there was no longer 'a real or solid interest' to fight for.[77]

The second, less developed, stage of Smith's solution to the problem of the misappropriation of resources was political. Economical government, he believed, would also be 'free government'. Thus Smith argued that a standing army would not only cause less economic disruption: as long as it was commanded by those with the greatest interest in the support of civil authority, it would also enable a government to tolerate a much larger degree of popular liberty, and would obviate the need for a discretionary power. In the same way, Smith affirmed that the creation of a professional judiciary distinct from the executive was the essential condition of the impartial administration of justice, on which in turn depended '. . . the liberty of every individual, the sense which he has of his own security'.[78] Finally, it would seem to have been Smith's view that taxation on the scale required by modern governments could only be levied equitably and economically if it had the consent of at least a substantial body of the people; and such consent was most freely obtained when those taxed enjoyed some say in government, whether by direct participation, or, in a larger state, by representation in an assembly.[79] A free government so constituted, Smith's arguments imply, would then provide sufficient institutional safeguards against subversion by the mercantile interest. Assured of, but not overawed by, its military strength, impartially administering justice, and open, through the need to secure consent for taxation, to the influence of a wide body of the people, a free government would be better placed than any other to resist mercantile special pleading and prevent the misdirection of resources.

Not only was Smith fuller and more explicit than Hume in analysing the problem of economic resources and government, but Smith's response differed markedly from Hume's in the constitutional principles it embodied. For a concept of free government consistent with a standing army was quite incompatible with the civic idea of free government to which Hume — to this extent following Fletcher — still adhered. Smith showed himself well aware of this distance from civic thinking when he defended standing armies against 'men of republican principles' — among whom he would certainly have accounted Fletcher, and perhaps even Hume. On the face of it, those with whom Smith had most in common in his choice of institutional concepts were rather English than Scottish: the metropolitan Court Whigs. In claiming the historical superiority of standing armies over militias, for instance, Smith was elaborating an observation first made by Lord Somers in his *Ballancing Letter* of 1698. More generally, Smith's conviction that an army commanded by men of substance in society and subject to military discipline and parliamentary consent would rather strengthen than undermine free government can be seen to resume the arguments of a succession of Court Whig writers from Daniel Defoe to Josiah Tucker.[80] Beside the standing army, the other constituents of Smith's concept of free government, an independent judiciary and taxation by consent, were not so conspicuously anti-civic. Nevertheless, they were more consistent with Court Whig principles than with those of the civic tradition, even in Hume's revised version of them. In Hume's perfect commonwealth it was the division of the judicial function between different bodies which was important, rather than the independence of the judiciary; and it is arguable that where Hume apparently made little of the difference between delegation and representation, Smith favoured a concept of representation (an idea, he pointed out, 'unknown in ancient times') which was deliberately distinct from the civic idea of participatory delegation.[81] Together, in fact, the three pillars of Smith's concept of free government matched constitutional principles which by the last quarter of the eighteenth century were generally associated with the Whig doctrine of parliamentary sovereignty. In advocating a standing army, along with an independent judiciary and taxation by representative consent, as the institutions most appropriate to the government of commercial society, therefore, Smith would seem most likely to have drawn upon this, clearly non-civic, body of constitutional doctrine.[82]

Yet Smith's institutional principles should not be reduced simply to the anglocentric, self-congratulatory perspective of metropolitan Court Whiggism. Just as Hume's continuing preference for militias over standing armies was by no means due to an unthinking acceptance of the 'vulgar whig' shibboleths of the Country opposition, so Smith was no mere Court Whig. Smith transcended the English Court Whig perspective on two fronts. For one thing, as Forbes has emphasised, Smith shared Hume's respect for the modern European monarchies, particularly that of France. Like Hume's, Smith's respect was based on the way in which these monarchies ensured personal liberty. In Smith's view this was explained by the emergence in the monarchies of a professional judiciary separate from the executive, supported, as he also observed, referring particularly to the example of Russia, by the prevalence of standing armies.[83] These monarchies were not indeed without grave flaws: Smith was especially critical of the French debt and taxation system.[84] But his final assessment was that if still belonging to a 'gradation of despotism', France was certainly the great empire in Europe which, after that of Great Britain, enjoyed 'the mildest and most indulgent government'.[85] It was a judgement which testified to Smith's continuing allegiance to the main European (rather than simply English) tradition of jurisprudential thought, with its emphasis on the primacy of personal liberty.

The empire of Great Britain was the second, perhaps even more important front on which Smith transcended the limitations of the English Court Whig perspective. Writing the *Wealth of Nations* in the late 1760s and early 1770s, Smith was obviously aware of the challenge to the existing British empire from the rebel American colonists; and while for the purposes of his economic argument he devoted most attention to the issues of mercantile regulation, he recognised that the crucial problems were those of taxation and the ultimate sovereignty of the Westminster parliament. Smith, however, broke with the English Court Whig position by accepting neither the principle of 'virtual representation' in taxation nor the necessity of Westminster's sovereignty. Instead he insisted that representation should be directly proportional to taxation, and proposed that the colonists should be given representation in a new imperial parliament, which, if it would initially continue to sit at Westminster, might well eventually move to North America.[86] Smith was under no illusions about the practicality of this proposal of imperial parliamentary union, which he himself described as a 'new Utopia'; and he concluded the *Wealth of Nations* with a final paragraph exhorting Britain's rulers to recognise 'the real mediocrity' of their circumstances by abandoning the colonies.[87] But he evidently attached considerable importance to the proposal none the less, for he retained it in the third edition of the work, published in 1784 after the colonies had won their independence and all possibility of the proposal's implementation had passed. From this it would seem that the primary object of the proposal had all along been exemplary rather than practical. Smith, that is, would offer the 'new Utopia' of Anglo-American parliamentary union as a paradigm of free government for commercial society. Perfecting the military, judicial and parliamentary institutions of Britain's existing form of free government, the new imperial constitution would be cast on a scale to match the economic relations between Britain and America: it would thus be ideally fitted to secure individual liberty and to check vested mercantile interests on either side of the Atlantic.[88]

Such intellectual and political imagination was beyond English Whigs. Smith's proposal was still indeed grounded on indigenous constitutional doctrine: no abstract 'perfect commonwealth' like Hume's, Anglo-American parliamentary union was presented by Smith as simply the completion and perfection of the existing British constitution.[89] But the imperial ambition in Smith's thinking suggests that his ultimate inspiration lay outwith the English Whig perspective, in an older, distinctively Scottish vision. Smith himself supplied the clue, when in the antepenultimate paragraph of the *Wealth of Nations* he pointed to the advantages Scotland had derived from the Union. Placed at a distance from the capital, the Scots had become indifferent and impartial spectators of 'the great scramble of faction and ambition' which centred there. If Ireland and the American colonies (and even, eventually, on the relocation of parliament, England itself) would accept the same provincial status within an imperial union, all, Smith believed, 'would probably soon enjoy a degree of concord and unanimity at present unknown in any part of the British empire'.[90] Geographically enlarged and intellectually elaborated, such thinking is still recognisably akin to the imperial British vision that the Earl of Cromarty had held out to the Scots at the Union, and even, though the apocalyptic framework had gone, to the vision of an imperial monarchy offered at the Reformation by John Knox. Projected onto an Atlantic plane, Smith's union may be seen as the secular apotheosis of Knox's imperial British millenium; but more directly, it should be understood as the oceanic extension of Cromarty's still insular vision of a united 'Britich' empire under a single sovereign parliament.[91]

By restoring and enlarging the imperial vision of Knox and Cromarty, Smith did not of course narrow the distance between himself and Hume and Fletcher. These had combined their civic constitutional principles with an alternative Scottish vision of anti-imperial federalism. Nevertheless, the adoption of the imperial vision ensured that Smith had joined Fletcher and Hume in taking as his ultimate vantage point Scottish, not metropolitan, ground. Like Fletcher and Hume before him, Smith had recognised the potentially universal significance of Scotland's experience.

The importance of keeping Smith's difference from Hume in perspective is confirmed by another feature of Smith's response to the problem of government and resources: the renewed, characteristically Humean insistence on the need for constructive institutional change. Smith brought this out by applying to the problem of institutions the historical model of society's development through four 'stages', the hunting, the pastoral, the agricultural and the commercial.[92] Through the application of this stadial model, above all to developments in military organisation, Smith reached two complementary conclusions about the relation between government and economy in commercial society.

First, he showed that where in primitive societies the relation need be only loosely articulated, in a commercial society it must be one of close interdependence. In both the hunting and the pastoral stages of development, every man is naturally a warrior, and defence costs the sovereign nothing. Even in the early agricultural stage men are free to serve in summer, and such as it is, the cost of war can be paid out of hoards. In a commercial society, by contrast, men are disinclined to leave productive employments for military service, and the costs of war are heavy, while the very wealth of society attracts acquisitive neighbours. The means of defence, in short, become less readily available, just as the need for them increases. The same is true of justice, whose administration becomes more extensive and costly as the demand for its services grows. If commerce thereby requires a much more precise balance between the needs of government and of society than hitherto, it also, however, indicates the method of attaining it. Simply by the application of the principle of the division of labour, commercial societies can provide for defence at the least possible cost, and at the same time assure themselves of military superiority over their primitive neighbours. Likewise no more speedy, inexpensive and accountable system of justice can be envisaged than one which adopts commercial standards of specialisation and competitiveness. The complexity of commercial society may give the problem of institutions an unprecedented urgency, but it also, Smith's model suggests, makes possible its definitive solution.

The second conclusion demonstrated by the stadial model, however, is the dependence of that solution on human initiative. In primitive societies with crude and rudimentary institutions, economic, civil and military needs were harmonised virtually as a matter of course. In a complex commercial society, by comparison, the process of adaptation is by no means automatic. As Smith pointed out, the operation of the division of labour in the organisation of defence does not occur in the natural course of economic development: it must be introduced by 'the wisdom of the state'. The proposals for the economical administration of justice implicitly required similar deliberate implementation in order to have the desired effect. Through Smith's application of the stadial model, therefore, it is clear that the introduction of economical, free institutions of government is a matter of conscious choice. Far from being guaranteed by any 'invisible hand', the harmonisation of economy and institutions in commercial society is, Smith believed, the task of the legislator.[93] The argument, as Smith's treatment of the problem of government and resources generally, was fuller than Hume's had been: but the conclusion was the same. On the importance of institutions to commercial society, and hence, still more, on the importance of adapting them to meet the changing demands of economic development, Smith and Hume were completely at one.

Smith's second passage on defence and military organisation in the *Wealth of Nations*, where he advocated compulsory military training as an antidote to the 'mental mutilation' of the common people, can be interpreted as addressed to the other aspect of the general problem of commerce and government, that concerned with changes in values and social structure. The effect of commerce on the moral virtue and political capacity of the various ranks of society was, moreover, a subject which had exercised Ferguson as well as Hume: in considering the problem afresh, therefore, Smith was entering the lists of an already polarised debate. If anything, Smith's account of the degradation of the common people by the division of labour would appear still more damning — more precise and more conclusive — than Ferguson's. Not only is the labourer rendered stupid and ignorant; he becomes incapable of just judgement even of the ordinary duties of private life, and quite unable either to judge the interests of his country or to defend it in war. Nevertheless, closer examination leaves no doubt that a fundamental difference of perspective separates Smith from Ferguson: for Smith started from Hume's proposition that commerce has created the conditions for generalised moral improvement, and the consequent extension of political capacity.

It is clear from Smith's other major work, the *Theory of Moral Sentiments*, that the full range of moral values, including the sociable sentiments of justice and benevolence, can only be exercised in commercial society. The emergence of property and the development of a system of ranks are what foster a sense of justice and a desire for order; and the widest distribution of property and most extensive differentiation of ranks are to be found in commercial society. It is there, accordingly, that the sentiment of justice is keenest, and the same is evidently also true of benevolence.[94] Smith never suggests that the labouring classes are necessarily excluded from this diffusion of moral values. On the contrary, his analysis of the material condition of the common people under commerce indicates that they satisfy the essential requirements of the moral life. As producers they have free and independent property of their own labour, while the advent of 'universal opulence' allows them to acquire an increasingly wide range of goods.[95] For the first time in history, therefore, the common people can be both independent and self-sufficient, and as such they will have the opportunity to make a positive contribution to the moral as well as material welfare of society.

It is this opportunity of moral fulfilment which the mental mutilation of the division of labour threatens to abort: and it is accordingly the purpose of Smith's proposals for education and military exercises to ensure its survival. The proposals were thus not narrowly remedial, but had positive political implications, on which Smith laid stress. Martial spirit, he argued, enhances the solidarity of a nation. Even if the military exercises were not up to the standard required by the complex regulations of a modern militia, they would at least diminish fears of the standing army, and would enable the people to support the army against an invader. Furthermore, Smith believed, when such exercises are combined with an elementary education, they can help fit the people to play a constructive part in the directly political life of society. With the self-respect that comes from possession of an education and the assurance of martial spirit, the people would be far more likely to have the public spirit to resist the blandishments of faction and vested interests, and to support the proper exercise of government authority.[96]

Smith's reflection on the moral consequences of commerce was by no means limited to the common people. He was not less concerned with the values of the middle and higher ranks, and encountered persistent difficulties in his attempt to delineate the material and moral character of the political leadership required by commercial society. Faced with the capitalists' 'wretched spirit of monopoly' and the landowners' ignorance and gullibility, Smith struggled to elaborate a concept of a 'natural aristocracy', of a moral elite of the wise and virtuous, which would be fit to exercise the offices of ruler and legislator.[97] It is surely significant, however, that martial spirit and military training play no part in this quest for a solution to the problem of leadership. While private secondary and higher education may have an important role in preparing gentlemen for the business of the world,[98] there is no suggestion that their position depends on the cultivation of the military virtues: compulsory training in arms is advocated in relation to the common people alone.

In urging the claims of the common people to military exercises, and more generally to a measure of political participation, Smith shows himself still thinking within the conceptual framework of the civic tradition. His commitment to a non-civic concept of free government which makes the individual's liberty its priority, which is defended by a standing army, and which is governed by a parliament representative rather than delegated, does not, it emerges, altogether preclude a further commitment to the civic ideals of citizenship, participation and political liberty. But it is also clear that insofar as Smith invokes the civic concepts, he does so on the same terms as Hume. There is no question of a strict dividing line, such as Fletcher and Ferguson had insisted on, between the citizens and the servile or subordinate, still less of that moralising concentration of Ferguson's on the values of the upper ranks. Instead Smith has confirmed and reinforced Hume's reversal of the traditional civic social and moral order of things. Smith has done so, moreover, in what for the civic tradition was the most important sphere of all: arms-bearing. For Ferguson as for Fletcher, and indeed for almost the entire civic canon, arms had been the most potent symbol of a citizenship which excluded those engaged in labour. For Smith, by contrast, arms are to be the symbol of labour's passage into the political community. They are to be the school of universal citizenship.

In the end, therefore, the differences between Smith and Hume pale beside the extent of their agreement. In the Scottish Enlightenment's debate over economic development, government and the progress of commercial society, a debate in which the issue of military organisation had a central place, Smith can be ranged with Hume on one side, while Ferguson, along with Kames, stands on another. To begin with, Smith and Hume were in fundamental agreement on the dimensions of the problem: it must be considered as both institutional and moral. On the institutional side, Smith agreed with Hume on the conditions if not on the concepts of the problem's solution. Whether its constitutional principles are those of the civic tradition or of parliamentary sovereignty, the model of free government for a commercial society must be set in the universal perspective offered by Scottish traditions of thinking about provinces and their interrelations; and there must be constructive legislative initiative to ensure that the institutions of free government are continually adapted to the needs of commercial society. With economic development and the progress of society at stake, there could be no question of leaving institutions to

adjust for themselves, as Ferguson supposed. There was still more harmony of response to the moral dimension of the problem. Smith might
share Ferguson's concern with the debilitating effects of the division of
labour, but his starting point was a Humean confidence in the moral
potential of commerce. Complicating hitherto simple and rigid social
distinctions, and making possible a general diffusion of moral values,
commerce, Smith and Hume believed, will gradually extend political
capacity through society, bringing all within the pale of the political
community. To meet this challenge, therefore, the traditional civic concept
of armed citizenship must be universalised, and the militia, or at least
military training, become the labourer's education in political life.

So arguing, Smith, like Hume, was finally brought to confront the
problem of liberty in commercial society. For both the priority was
individual liberty — liberty, that is, of person and property under the law,
the juristic concept of liberty 'from' arbitrary interference, the concept
whose benefits Seton of Pitmedden had set such store by at the time of the
Union. Without this form of liberty there could be no economic development; if it was ever lost, the progress of society would certainly cease. At
the same time, Smith shared with Hume the recognition that the generalising of individual liberty in commercial society is likely to create the
conditions and foster the expectation of more extensive political freedom.
This other form of liberty — the freedom 'to' participate in political life,
the traditional civic concept of freedom which Fletcher had so passionately
affirmed — was by no means devalued by Smith any more than it was by
Hume: both looked favourably on its extension to the lower ranks of the
political community. The problem, however, is that while the two forms of
liberty may each be desirable, and may develop together, they are not
necessarily compatible. As the issue of defence and military organisation
makes clear, universal participation can be indistinguishable from compulsion. A nation must conscript its militia, or compel military training: and
in so doing — as Fletcher, Ferguson and even Kames had failed to grasp,
but as Defoe had pointed out — it would enforce political liberty only at
the expense of infringing upon personal. In commercial society, therefore,
the lofty moral ideal of absolute political liberty proclaimed by Ferguson is
an illusion: for Smith as for Hume, the two liberties of person and
participation are necessarily, by their universality, a compromise.

Universal as Smith's discussion of defence and military organisation was
in its scope, and free from the slightest reference to the specific issue of a
Scottish militia, the partisans of a Scottish militia immediately recognised
the *Wealth of Nations* as an unwelcome intervention. In April 1776, very
shortly after the work's publication, Adam Ferguson wrote to congratulate
Smith on his achievement — but added that he objected to Smith's
'provoking' the militia. Ferguson was happy to follow Smith in his
provocation of the church, the universities and the merchants; but in the

case of the militia Ferguson felt strongly that '...the gentlemen and peasants of this country do not need the authority of philosophers to make them supine and negligent of every resource they might have in themselves'.[99] It was Alexander Carlyle, however, who two years later undertook public and substantive criticism of Smith's arguments, in his *Letter to the Duke of Buccleugh on National Defence*. The criticism was set alongside Carlyle's own positive statement of the case for a Scottish militia, discussed earlier,[100] but was none the less sharply focused: Carlyle even gave notice of his polemical intent in the *Letter's* subtitle: *With Some Remarks on Dr. Smith's Chapter on that Subject, in his book entitled An Inquiry into the Nature and Causes of the Wealth of Nations.*

Carlyle freely acknowledged that 'Dr. Smith' was 'a very formidable antagonist', whose system as a whole commanded belief. But in Carlyle's view Smith had not confined himself within his system, and his 'excursions' into the field of general politics were open to criticism. The chapter on the expense of defence Carlyle regarded as one such 'excursion': however plausible in speculation, Smith's arguments there simply did not display his 'usual accuracy' in matters of fact.[101]

Carlyle's first objection on a matter of fact was to Smith's direct contrast between a militia and a standing army. This, Carlyle held, was to dispute without an opponent, since no friend of a militia in recent years had considered that it should altogether replace a standing army. In any case, Carlyle continued, the facts also contradicted the main ground of Smith's argument — the proposition that the division of labour makes it necessary for soldiering to be a separate trade. It was not true, as Carlyle believed Smith to maintain, that in an improved age the manufacturer or husbandman is unable to bear arms: modern armies are recruited from just such men. Nor was it the case that modern warfare is more difficult or more terrifying than ancient. Soldiers were now trained in a few months, where the Greeks and Romans trained from their earliest youth. Why then — Carlyle asked — should it be thought so difficult for men to add an art thus easily learnt to their ordinary trade? Would military exercise render men less perfect weavers or smiths any more than playing cricket or football or golf on holidays?[102]

In fact, Carlyle claimed, Smith had answered himself with his arguments that a militia which serves several campaigns becomes a standing army, and that even a newly raised standing army can fight with the courage of veterans. To Carlyle such arguments only proved that a militia was almost equivalent to a standing army, while showing that 'the Doctor has such a predilection for a standing army, that he ascribes bravery to the magic of that name'. Smith's historical examples relied on a similar alteration of names, so that successful forces were standing armies and the defeated militias. If Smith had only accepted 'the ordinary distinction' between a militia and a standing army, he would have seen that the Romans were most successful in the period of the Commonwealth, when all citizens took arms in turn, and the difference between citizen and soldier was unknown. As Carlyle interpreted them, therefore, Smith's arguments proved after all the usefulness of a militia on what Carlyle believed to be the essential grounds of 'economy and preparation'. Without replacing the standing army, the militia could provide a cheap and inexhaustible reserve of easily trained men that would ensure that the nation was always prepared for war, and much less damaged when it broke out.[103]

Having, as he thought, turned Smith's argument for the superiority of a standing army against itself, Carlyle naturally seized on the later passage in the *Wealth of Nations* where Smith urged the need for compulsory military training. Professing to approach Smith's work in the same way as Scripture, by a comparison of passages, Carlyle believed himself faced with a plain contradiction: he could explain Smith's previous criticism of militias only as an attempt to apologise for the 'weak conduct' of both administration and his own countrymen in 1776. Exultantly, Carlyle proceeded to insert in his pamphlet two lengthy extracts from Smith's second passage. The first of these extracts was Smith's statement of the advantages of maintaining the martial spirit of the common people: that a smaller standing army would be needed, and fears of the threat to liberty would be allayed. The other extract was Smith's depiction of the mental mutilation associated with cowardice, and his call for action by government to prevent it. Closing his critique of Smith with this second extract, Carlyle simply asked, 'has any other author ever used a stronger argument for military education...?'[104]

Carlyle was a fluent, plausible pamphleteer, but in this exchange of arguments with Smith he was hardly matching like against like. In his remarks on the chapter on defence Carlyle made no attempt to confront the theoretical logic of the argument from the division of labour; as a result his 'facts' were largely beside the point. Smith did not argue that manufacturers and husbandmen in commercial society were incapable of becoming soldiers, or of undertaking some military exercises in their spare time: Carlyle's empirical observations to the contrary were no answer to Smith's actual point that the division of labour now made it impossible in principle for one man fully to master two professions. A similar disparity of argument is evident in Carlyle's failure to consider Smith's subsequent reasons for believing military training to be particularly necessary and valuable for the common people, as opposed to those of rank and fortune. Carlyle simply assumed that a proposal of military exercises for the people was in line with his own conception of a militia: he was unable — or perhaps unwilling — to recognise that Smith had in mind a social order rather different from the one Carlyle was seeking to sustain, where the emphasis was on the people's continuing subordination rather than (as for Smith) their increasing participation. Fundamentally, Carlyle had missed Smith's point by taking the discussion of national defence in the *Wealth of Nations* to be merely an 'excursion'. It was precisely because Smith treated the issue as analytically central to the general problem of the relation between the economy and government in commercial society that he had raised his discussion to a level so much more theoretical and universal than Carlyle supposed to be appropriate.[105]

Yet whatever the intellectual shortcomings of his criticism, Carlyle's disquiet was justified. The *Wealth of Nations* did have adverse consequences *for* the Scottish militia. Wittingly or not, Smith's arguments would, at the last, provide the basis for a serious challenge to Carlyle's cause. The challenge was the anonymous pamphlet, *Reasons Against a Militia for Scotland.*

NOTES

1. R. Klibansky and E. C. Mossner (eds.), *New Letters of David Hume* (Oxford 1954), p. 52: 12 April 1759.

2. *Letters of Hume,* II, pp. 11–12, 133: to Hugh Blair, 11 Feb. 1766 and 1 April 1767.

3. R. B. Sher, 'The Road to Adam Ferguson: Ideology, Incentive and the Edinburgh Chair of Moral Philosophy', typescript paper.

4. Carlyle, *Anecdotes and Characters,* p. 144 note.

5. *Letters of Hume,* I, p. 438: to Hugh Blair, 26 April 1764.

6. Adam Ferguson, *An Essay on the History of Civil Society* (1767), ed. Duncan Forbes (Edinburgh 1966), Introduction, p. xxxvi. Hereafter cited as *Essay.*

7. David Kettler, *The Social and Political Thought of Adam Ferguson* (Ohio 1965), pp. 258–67.

8. *Essay,* Part II, Sections ii and iii and p. 147.

9. *Essay,* p. 151.

10. *Essay,* pp. 180–1.

11. *Essay,* pp. 182–3.

12. *Essay,* pp. 181–2.

13. *Essay,* p. 230.

14. *Essay,* pp. 250–3; David Kettler, 'History and Theory in Ferguson's *Essay on the History of Civil Society. A Reconsideration',* *Political Theory,* 5, 4 (1977).

15. *Essay,* pp. 256, 268, 259–60.

16. *Essay,* pp. 272–9.

17. *Essay,* pp. 244–8.

18. *Essay,* pp. 143–4.

19. The differentiation of the degradation of the lower orders from the corruption of the higher ranks lies in the structure rather than in the exact wording of the *Essay.* The situation of the labourer is dealt with in Part IV, 'of the Consequences that result from the Advancement of the Civil and Commercial Arts', under the sub-heading 'subordination'. The predicament of the higher ranks is left until Parts V and VI, 'of the Decline of Nations' and 'of Corruption and Political Slavery'. Ferguson does speak of the 'corruption and baseness' of the lower orders (p. 186), but I take this to be rhetorical rather than systematic usage.

20. *Essay,* pp. 158–61. In thus eulogising Sparta, Ferguson was defensive but unrepentant. 'After all, we are, perhaps, not sufficiently instructed in the nature of

Spartan laws and institutions, to understand in what manner all the ends of this singular State were obtained, but the admiration paid to its people, and the constant reference of contemporary historians to their avowed superiority, will not allow us to question the facts': p. 159.

21. *Essay*, pp. 161–2.

22. *Essay*, p. 184, cf. p. 133; Kettler, 'History and Theory in Ferguson's *Essay*', *Political Theory* (1977).

23. *Essay*, p. 186.

24. *Essay*, p. 30.

25. *Essay*, pp. 258–9.

26. Despite the separation of arts and professions, Ferguson believed that a novice could readily learn the use of modern arms: *Essay*, p. 232.

27. *Essay*, p. 227. The vagueness of the distinction between the 'higher ranks' and the 'body of the people' reflects Ferguson's persistent silence in the *Essay* on the socio-economic basis of citizenship: one may, perhaps, assume that by the two categories he had in mind landowners and freeholders respectively, but this is never made explicit. The absence of indication obviously facilitates the insistence upon a distinction of principle between economic and citizen classes, but leaves the application of the principle decidedly uncertain.

28. Above, pp. 87–91.

29. Above, pp. 100–5, 133–5, 143–7.

30. *Essay*, Part V, section v, pp. 234–5.

31. *Essay*, p. 261.

32. *Essay*, pp. 130–2.

33. *Essay*, pp. 122–3. Ferguson discounted the idea of the founding legislator.

34. *Essay*, pp. 144–5; see above, pp. 33–4.

35. *Essay*, pp. 61, 225.

36. *Essay*, pp. 263–4.

37. *Essay*, p. 167.

38. Cf. Kettler, *Social and Political Thought of Ferguson*, pp. 258–67, and 'History and Theory in Ferguson's *Essay*', *Political Theory* (1977), for what I take to be a broadly similar, if less critically phrased conclusion.

39. In the *Essay*, p. 148, Ferguson acknowledged and defended a distinction between martial and civil law, affirming the necessity to resign in the field that personal freedom which should be maintained in political deliberations. But military training is treated as an expression of freedom; and it may be noted that in his *Reflections* of 1756, Ferguson had not wished the militia to be subjected to military law.

40. Even when discussing 'the Characteristics of Fortitude' in the *Principles*, Ferguson made no reference to specifically martial virtue: *Principles of Moral and Political Science: being chiefly a retrospect of lectures delivered in the College of Edinburgh*, 2 Vols. (Edinburgh 1792), II, Ch. V, Section 6, pp. 391–9.

41. Adam Ferguson, *The History of the Progress and Termination of the Roman Republic*, 3 Vols. (London 1783). E.g. Vol. I, p. 350: on the soldiers raised by Marius; (cf. the altered wording of the same passage in the five-volume edition of 1799, Vol. II, p. 59). Vol. III, pp. 158, 380: on the military government of the Empire.

42. Above, pp. 167, 193.

43. A. F. Tytler, *Memoirs of the Life and Writings of the Honourable Henry Home*

of Kames, 2 Vols. (Edinburgh 1807), Vol. II, Appendix i: 'Letters from the Rev. Dr. Josiah Tucker to Lord Kames', pp. 6, 11, 13–14: letters of 6 July 1758, 10, 26 Dec. 1763.

44. Henry Home, Lord Kames, *Sketches of the History of Man*. 2 Vols. (Edinburgh 1774), Vol. II, pp. 4–5. Hereafter *Sketches*.

45. *Sketches*, Vol. I, p. 444.

46. *Sketches*, II, pp. 6–7.

47. *Sketches*, II, pp. 7–14.

48. *Sketches*, II, pp. 14–35: quotation on p. 35.

49. Kames's militia would, in peace, have spent three-quarters of its time on public works; but this conflicted with Hume's general commitment to the free market in labour.

50. On Kames's hostility to legislative activity (other than by judges): David Lieberman, 'The legal needs of a commercial society: the jurisprudence of Lord Kames', in Hont and Ignatieff (eds.), *Wealth and Virtue*, pp. 218–23.

51. 'Idea of a perfect Commonwealth', *Philosophical Works*, III, pp. 491–2. Forbes, *Hume's Philosophical Politics*, pp. 211–12, notes in addition the passage introduced into the last edition of the *History*, where Hume acknowledged 'a melancholy truth' that a magistrate must now either enjoy discretionary powers to execute the law, or possess 'a large revenue and a military force': *The History of England*, 8 Vols. (London 1778), Vol. VI, p. 163. But it is not clear that Hume thought a military force preferable to discretionary powers.

52. 'Public Credit', *Philosophical Works*, III, p. 368. One may assume that the dropping of the reference to Hanover as a source of auxiliaries from 'Of the Protestant Succession', Ibid., p. 478, was simply because the comment had become, for the moment, out of date.

53. As Forbes has emphasised, when Hume took such pains over the revision of the *Essays*, he must be presumed to have adhered to what he left standing: *Hume's Philosophical Politics*, p. 135.

54. Adam Smith, *An Inquiry into the Nature and Causes of the Wealth of Nations*, 2 Vols., eds. R. H. Campbell, A. S. Skinner and W. B. Todd (Oxford 1976), Bk. V, Ch. i, Part First, paras. 1–5. In accordance with the method of the Glasgow Edition of Smith's Works, I shall hereafter abbreviate references on the following model: *Wealth of Nations*, V.i.a. 1–5.

55. *Wealth of Nations*, V.i.a. 6–7, 12–13.

56. Ibid., V.i.a. 8–15.

57. Ibid., V.i.a. 10, 14, 22.

58. Ibid., V.i.a. 14.

59. Ibid., V.i.a. 16–20.

60. Ibid., V.i.a. 23.

61. Ibid., V.i.a. 11, 22, 24–5.

62. Ibid., V.i.a. 27.

63. Ibid., V.i.a. 38.

64. Ibid., V.i.a. 28–37.

65. Ibid., V.i.a. 37–40.

66. Ibid., V.i.a. 41.

67. Ibid., V.i.f. 48–9, 52–3.

68. Ibid., V.i.f. 50.

69. Ibid., V.i.f. 59.

70. Ibid., V.i.f. 60.
71. Ibid., V.i.f. 54–5.
72. Ibid., V.i.f. 61.
73. I have made a separate general study of Smith's treatment of the problem of government and economic development in: 'Scottish Political Economy beyond the Civic Tradition: Government and Economic Development in the *Wealth of Nations*', *History of Political Thought*, IV, 3 (1983).
74. *Wealth of Nations*, V.i.b. 1–3; V.i.a. 1.
75. Ibid., I.x. p. 1–10; IV. ii. 21; and IV. i–viii passim.
76. Ibid., V.i.b. 20–22.
77. Ibid., V.ii.b. 2–7; iii. 47–56.
78. Ibid., V.i.b. 25.
79. Ibid., V.ii.k. 80; IV.vii.b.51.
80. See above, pp. 27–9, 65–7.
81. Hume's dismissal of the controversy over instructions to MPs as 'very frivolous' suggests that he was not fundamentally concerned whether they were representatives or delegates: 'Of the First Principles of Government', *Philosophical Works*, III, pp. 112–13. Smith, on the other hand, explained the troublesomeness of the colonial assemblies as due to their being 'more republican' in form than the House of Commons — more equally representative and closer to the influence of their constituents: his remedy to the colonial crisis, an imperial parliament, would set a proper distance between the colony representatives and their constituents: *Wealth of Nations* IV. vii, b. 51; c. 75, 77.
82. See further my 'Scottish Political Economy beyond the Civic Tradition', pp. 478–80.
83. *Wealth of Nations*, V.i.b. 20, i.a. 40; Forbes, 'Sceptical Whiggism, Commerce and Liberty', in A. Skinner and T. Wilson (eds.), *Essays on Adam Smith* (Oxford 1976), pp. 188–91. But it is not clear why Forbes supposes that the standing army of France must have been as that of Caesar or Cromwell, and not commanded by those with an interest in the support of the civil authority.
84. *Wealth of Nations*, V.iii. 35–6, ii.j. 7 and k. 77.
85. Ibid., V.i.g. 19, ii.k. 78.
86. Ibid., IV. vii.c. 75–9.
87. Ibid., V. ii. 68, 92.
88. Also, my 'Scottish Political Economy beyond the Civic Tradition', pp. 476–7.
89. *Wealth of Nations*, IV. vii. c. 77.
90. Ibid., V. iii. 90.
91. On the British imperial unionism of Knox and Cromarty see above, pp. 4, 48–9. The analysis of Smith's proposal of imperial union in the tradition of Knox and Cromarty goes beyond that previously offered in my 'Scottish Political Economy beyond the Civic Tradition', where I focused attention on the proposal's incorporation of the principles of parliamentary sovereignty. The Scottish tradition of imperial unionism, however, by no means exhausts the interpretative context in which Smith's proposal should be placed: like Fletcher's plan in the *Account of a Conversation*, it should also be examined in relation to the European debate on universal monarchy. See above, Ch. 2, n. 38, p. 56. I propose to pursue these possibilities elsewhere.
92. On Smith's use of the Four Stages Theory: R. L. Meek, *Social Science and*

the Ignoble Savage (Cambridge 1976), pp. 116–26; A. S. Skinner, 'A Scottish Contribution to Marxist Sociology?', in I. Bradley and M. Howard (eds.), *Classical and Marxian Political Economy. Essays in Honour of R. L. Meek* (London 1982); and K. Haakonssen, *The Science of a Legislator. The Natural Jurisprudence of David Hume and Adam Smith* (Cambridge 1981), Chs. 7–8.

93. On Smith's concept of the legislator: Winch, *Adam Smith's Politics*, pp. 130–3; Haakonssen, *Science of a Legislator*, pp. 97–8, 188–9; and my 'Scottish Political Economy beyond the Civic Tradition', pp. 471–2 and notes. But there is more yet to be said on the subject.

94. Adam Smith, *The Theory of Moral Sentiments*, eds. D. D. Raphael and A. L. Macfie (Oxford 1976), II.ii; T. D. Campbell, *Adam Smith's Science of Morals* (London 1971), pp. 185, 199; N. T. Phillipson, 'Adam Smith as Civic Moralist', in eds. Hont and Ignatieff, *Wealth and Virtue*, p. 182 — though, as Phillipson goes on to point out (pp. 189–90), the level at which the sentiments of justice and benevolence will commonly be recognised in commercial society is the level of 'propriety', and not of true virtue.

95. *Wealth of Nations*, I.i.10–11. The emergence of free labour was not an inevitable consequence of commercial development, but it had been largely achieved in modern Europe (cf. III. iii. 15), and it was a necessary condition of a fully commercial order.

96. On the significance of military exercises, cf. Winch, *Adam Smith's Politics*, pp. 113–20.

97. J. Cropsey, *Polity and Economy. An Interpretation of the Principles of Adam Smith* (The Hague 1957), pp. 68–70; Phillipson, 'Adam Smith as Civic Moralist', *Wealth and Virtue*, p. 197.

98. *Wealth of Nations*, V.i.f. 45–6.

99. *The Correspondence of Adam Smith*, eds. E. C. Mossner and I. S. Ross (Oxford 1977), pp. 193–4: Ferguson to Smith, 18 April 1776.

100. Above, pp. 133–5.

101. [Carlyle,] *Letter on National Defence, with Some Remarks*, pp. 23, 29.

102. Ibid., pp. 23–77.

103. Ibid., pp. 22–3, 37–47.

104. Ibid., pp. 47–51; the extracts are from *Wealth of Nations*, V.i.f. 59 and 60.

105. Carlyle's failure to grasp the point of Smith's discussion of national defence is comparable to the failure of another Moderate clergyman and professor, Hugh Blair, to see the significance of the proposal of British–American Union. Blair thought this 'a publication for the present moment', and wanted it removed from subsequent editions: *Correspondence of Adam Smith*, p. 188: Hugh Blair to Smith, 3 April 1776.

8

Conclusion: *Reasons Against a Militia for Scotland*

Reasons Against a Militia for Scotland was a short, nineteen-page pamphlet published at Edinburgh early in 1783.[1] It was anonymous, and no evidence for an ascription of authorship has emerged. Unequivocally titled, the pamphlet's immediate target was the militia scheme drawn up in December 1782 and known as the Heads of a Bill, this in turn being a diminished version of the more ambitious Sketch of a Bill of the previous summer. Appearing just as public interest in the demand for a Scottish militia finally ebbed away on a tide of indecision in the early months of 1783, *Reasons Against a Militia for Scotland* effectively had the last word in the national debate. The pamphlet's significance, however, lies in more than the simple fact of its timing. For this last word was also the first pamphlet-length statement of the case against a Scottish militia; as such, moreover, it was explicitly founded on general principles, whose identity there is no mistaking. Thus, I shall now argue, *Reasons Against a Militia for Scotland* provides a telling conclusion not simply to the story of the militia issue and the Scottish Enlightenment, but also to the interpretation put upon the story here.

The pamphlet opened with an acknowledgement that the idea of a Scots militia had in the past been supported by persons distinguished for their abilities and patriotism. The writer accepted too that the intention of those who now revived the idea was good; and he observed that the militia they proposed was to be different from the English, which, he admitted, was 'almost indistinguishable' from a standing army. But the renewal of the demand for a Scottish militia was none the less devoid of 'policy or prudence'. It was the writer's wish, therefore, to draw his countrymen 'from sound to sense, from theory to practice', and to have them take a lesson from experience.[2]

First the pamphlet stated objections to the present militia proposal. On the one hand, the militia would do material hurt to Scotland's agriculture, trade and manufactures. Some men would be loath to leave the shuttle or the plough; others would be unwilling to return to them after service. The force would also be costly, and no indication had been given of the source of the funds which would be required to pay the expenses of the men when on service or duty. On the other hand, the proposed militia would simply not answer the purposes for which it was to be raised: suppressing rebellion and repelling invasion. The arming of artificers and labourers would be more likely to create than to suppress popular commotion. The advocates of the Scottish scheme wished indeed that their militia should be less rigid than that of England; but, this writer believed, the less a militia resembled a standing army, the more undisciplined and dangerous it would be. Recent experience of the 'No Popery' and 'No Patronage' agitations demonstrated plainly enough that 'fanaticism' was still prevalent among the lower ranks of the people in Scotland. It was but too probable that if the proposed militia was established, the public would find that 'bodies of armed men, not subject to daily habits of subordination, are many-headed monsters, let loose upon society to burn, ravage and destroy'. As for the second purpose of the proposed militia, repelling invasion, it was equally unlikely that this would be fulfilled. No more than any other force could such a militia prevent landings by small raiding parties; and against a full scale invasion, which was now most unlikely in Scotland, it would put up a very feeble opposition.[3]

Having set out his objections to the immediate Scottish militia proposal, the anonymous pamphleteer proceeded to consider the 'plain and general principles' which, in his view, ought to determine the proper form of defence for the country. To make a soldier, he argued, requires time and attention: constant exercise and unquestioning obedience are necessary if a man is to be a proper part of that 'great machine', an army:

> Is it, therefore, rational to suppose that the same person can at the same time be a labourer or a handicraftsman and also a soldier? The different professions are incompatible, and must necessarily interfere.

Unless impelled by necessity, a state should not permit the trade of a soldier to be mixed with any other. The Swiss, certainly, were under such a necessity — but no two states were more different in situation than Switzerland and Great Britain. Surrounded by ocean, Britain's natural defence was its navy; and in such a happy situation the British should give their attention to the encouragement of agriculture, trade and manufactures. Accordingly, the writer continued:

> Let such of our countrymen as chuse to be labourers or artificers not be compelled to be also soldiers. The more simple and less complex is any man's employment, the more perfect and dextrous he will be in it. Of such who chuse to be only soldiers, enough will always be found.

Such volunteer soldiers, the writer immediately added, need be no threat to liberty. On the contrary,

> . . . . though under the name of a standing army, as long as they are controlled by officers who do have an interest in the state, they will be less dangerous to the liberty and constitution of this country, than any militia or internal

defence whatever. Subject to discipline, regularity and good order, they will defend that liberty and that constitution as well from the encroachment of popular tumult as from the attacks of our enemies.

By contrast, militiamen were only too likely to join in a popular tumult. As for the military superiority of a standing army over a militia, the writer believed that this was proved by many examples in history, and he refused to accept the American War as an instance to the contrary. Though at first a militia, the American troops became a standing army, and besides they had avoided pitched battles. Lest any doubt about the relevance of his principles should remain, however, the writer emphasised again the extent to which they applied in a country such as Britain, in which agriculture, trade and manufactures were daily advancing.

> For the greater the improvements are, which the husbandmen and artisans make, and consequently the more they are thriving in their respective employments, the greater will be their attachment to them, and the more they will grudge at being interrupted amidst such favourite occupations.

At the same time, the regular troops of a country thus flourishing and cultivated will be excellent for the same reasons as are the husbandmen and artisans: having but one object in view, they can bestow on it all the time and attention necessary to bring it to the highest point of perfection.[4]

Judged by the writer's principles, then, the militia proposed was inappropriate to the country's existing, advanced level of economic improvement. It was also, he believed, particularly imprudent at the present time. With a long, destructive and exhausting war coming to an end, and the country drained of men, every expedient should be devised to turn the industry of its remaining inhabitants to the best account. At such a moment it seemed unaccountable that patriots should still be arguing for a militia in terms of the 'safety', 'dignity' and 'birthright' of Scotland: what had to be considered was rather a militia's 'fitness, prudence and propriety'. The anonymous pamphleteer refused, however, to answer more than one of the numerous and evident absurdities which he found in other publications on the issue. He selected only the proposal, in a scheme whose life and soul was said to be a regard for liberty and the constitution, that a man should be forced from his business, family and home to defend his freedom. This, according to the writer, was to annihilate freedom in one of its most essential forms under the pretext of protecting it:

> I lay it down as a principle, that no country can, with propriety, be called free, in which a man, however unwilling, is compelled to carry arms. Pressing seamen, though a necessary exception, has always been reckoned contrary to the spirit of the British Constitution.[5]

Without one reference to the *Wealth of Nations*, *Reasons Against a Militia for Scotland* vindicated the apprehensions of Ferguson and Carlyle. The Moderates might have been mistaken to suppose that Adam Smith's discussion of defence and military organisation was an 'excursion' from his general system; but they had certainly been right to fear that it could be turned against a Scottish militia. For those 'plain and general principles', those standards of 'fitness, prudence and propriety' to which the pamphlet appealed were unmistakeably Smithian. The first and fundamental principle was clearly that of the division of labour. In a society advancing in agriculture and manufactures, the profession of a soldier should be distinct from that of a husbandman or artisan. This is both economically less burdensome, since the labourer or artisan would otherwise have to be dragged reluctantly from his employment, and militarily advantageous, for the soldier's proficiency depends on his giving his whole time and attention to the service. A further Smithian principle — repeated almost word for word from the *Wealth of Nations* — was that a standing army commanded by those with an interest in the state would be a support rather than a danger to liberty. Itself subject to regular discipline, the army will be a defence against popular tumult as well as against foreign enemies.

Not all the arguments of *Reasons Against* can be so closely matched with those of the *Wealth of Nations*. In particular, the pamphlet's suggestion that a militia would actually encourage popular tumult struck a more aggressive note than any to be heard in Smith's discussion. Though Smith certainly feared a people imbued with fanaticism, he regarded the militia, or at least military exercises, as a helpful corrective to such delusions, and even as a positive education in responsible citizenship. Smith had, however, recommended military exercises with his eyes open to the point of principle to which the pamphlet finally brought its case: the infringement of personal liberty that compulsory military service would entail. Here, moreover, it was not only Smith's lead that the pamphlet was following. That the pressing of seamen was regarded as an exceptional denial of liberty was the very point previously made by Hume, with the similar implication that compulsory military service would transform the exception into the rule. In fact *Reasons Against a Militia for Scotland* was remarkable for urging the principle of personal liberty with greater frankness of emphasis than either Hume or Smith. But the point was the one on which the two thinkers had ultimately converged: in drawing it out, the pamphlet confirmed the extent to which their principles had provided the basis for a coherent case against the Scottish militia.

Thus building upon the principles of Hume and Smith, *Reasons Against a Militia for Scotland* does more than simply vindicate the fears of Ferguson and Carlyle. It also leads back to the larger question of the significance of the militia issue for the relation between the Scottish Enlightenment and Scottish experience. In the previous chapter, it was argued that Adam Ferguson's *Essay on the History of Civil Society* displayed the intellectual consequences of the Scottish militia agitation; *Reasons Against* has now shown just how Smith's *Wealth of Nations,* though written almost entirely within the framework of Enlightenment intellectual debate, could none the less have consequences for the militia demand. What remains to be seen, however, is the extent to which Hume and Smith themselves recognised such consequences of their work. In the intellectual debate, I have already suggested, Hume and Smith were ranged against Ferguson: were they likewise divided over Scotland and the Scottish militia?

Positive evidence of Hume's and Smith's attitudes to the Scottish militia agitations is unfortunately scarce, and confined to their correspondence. Such as it is, however, this evidence appears to show that they supported the demand. There are three references to the subject in Hume's correspondence. In 1760 he wrote a fulsome letter of congratulation to Lord Minto on his son Gilbert Elliot's speeches on the Scottish Militia Bill. It seems to be agreed, Hume reported, that 'such an exertion of eloquence, reason and magnanimity... probably never was surpassed by any one member'.[6] A year later, in what was almost certainly a joking attempt to discover the secret of Ferguson's authorship of the satirical *Sister Peg*, Hume wrote to Carlyle to claim it for himself.[7] Third and most curiously, in a letter to his London publisher, William Strahan, in 1769, Hume suddenly exclaimed: 'Woud to God we had a Scotch militia at present. This country is unanimous' — even though there appears to have been no agitation at all in Scotland that year.[8] Besides this correspondence, there is also the evidence of Hume's membership of the Poker Club. He was a founder and by all accounts a loyal member of the Club; the surviving Minutes, covering the 1770s, show him to have been a regular attender until his last illness. Hume also gave the Club one of its best testimonials, which nicely balances between those of Carlyle and Boswell, when he wrote to Ferguson from Paris that he wished often for 'the plain roughness of the Poker' to correct and qualify the 'lusciousness' of French polite society.[9]

The evidence for Smith's attitude to the Scottish militia is even thinner. His one explicit reference to the demand is also in a letter to Strahan, in 1760: Smith wrote of his fear that the publication of Hooke's *Memoirs* (of the Jacobite plots of 1707–8) came 'at an unlucky time', and might 'throw a damp upon our militia'.[10] Later, though without mentioning the demand for a Scottish militia in particular, Smith reacted sharply to 'the pamphlet concerning national defense' which accused him of being hostile to militias. The anonymous author of the pamphlet, he complained to a Danish correspondent, Andreas Holt, had not read his work to the end:

> He fancies that because I insist that a militia is in all cases inferior to a well regulated and well disciplined standing army, that I disapprove of militias altogether. With regard to that subject, he and I happened to be precisely of the same opinion.

Smith supposed the pamphlet to have been the work of one Douglas, an acquaintance of his, and expressed himself accordingly 'a little surprized at his attack upon me, and still more at the mode of it'.[11] If, as seems very probable, the pamphlet was in fact Carlyle's *Letter to the Duke of Buccleugh on National Defence,* the expression of surprise at the behaviour of an acquaintance would still have been appropriate. Finally, it can be observed that Smith, like Hume, was a loyal member of the Poker. If not a founder, Smith is likely to have joined at an early stage, and in the Minutes he appears as an occasional but persistent attender until the Club's end (although he was absent when the Sketch of a Bill was launched in 1782).

On the available evidence, then, it does not seem that Hume and Smith translated their intellectual difference with Ferguson into opposition to the Scottish militia. Hume's preference for a militia over a standing army, and Smith's liking at least for military exercises, appear to have been sufficient for them simply to support the Moderates' cause. Nevertheless, it can be argued that this evidence of their attitudes is not conclusive, and does not go far enough to offset the contrary indication of the consequences of their general principles given by the pamphlet *Reasons Against a Militia for Scotland.*

On the one hand, Hume's and Smith's expressions of support for a Scottish militia fell some way short of real commitment. Not only were they confined to private correspondence; but what their comments displayed was no more than the sort of instinctive patriotism that led Hume into initial enthusiasm for Ossian. Nor was much commitment entailed by membership of the Poker. As we have seen, this was not a campaigning organisation, but a dining club for literati and gentry: Hume and Smith could have enjoyed the company without joining in more than the odd convivial toast to the cause. (Perhaps it was a particularly convivial evening at the Poker which prompted Hume's exclamation to Strahan in 1769.) Altogether, in fact, the support Hume and Smith offered the militia was no more than was consistent with a natural sense of friendship and solidarity with fellow literati. Hume in particular was a close personal friend of the Moderate literati, and was obliged to them for their public defence of his integrity when the zealots threatened him with excommunication in the 1750s. In addition Hume had a clear view of the rules of literary controversy, which precluded personal attacks; and he was most reluctant to undermine the exposed position of the literati in Scottish society by open division.[12] The more reserved Smith was less friendly with and owed fewer obligations to the Moderates; but his reaction to criticism of his treatment of the militia in the *Wealth of Nations* indicates that he shared Hume's distaste for controversy between acquaintances. If Hume and Smith did have second thoughts after their first, instinctively patriotic response to the militia demand, therefore, they were unlikely to have publicised them.

For their part, on the other hand, the Moderate partisans of a Scottish militia clearly felt that they could not count on Hume's and Smith's support. In Smith's case, as we have seen, both Ferguson and Carlyle were open in their suspicions, Ferguson writing directly to Smith, Carlyle rebuking him publicly in a pamphlet.[13] With Hume the Moderates' suspicions were less acute; but evidence of an awareness of their differences is to be found in the anecdote recorded by John Home during the journey on which he and Ferguson accompanied the ailing Hume to Bath in the spring of 1776. Hume had told them how we would manage his kingdom if his two companions had been the princes of the adjacent states:

'He knew very well', he said (having often disputed the point with us,) 'the great opinion we had of military virtues as essential to every state; that from these sentiments rooted in us, he was certain he would be attacked and interrupted in his projects of cultivating, improving and civilizing mankind by the arts of peace; that he comforted himself with reflecting, that from our want of economy and order in our affairs, we should be continually in want of money; whilst he would have his finances in excellent condition, his magazines well filled, and naval stores in abundance; but that his final stroke of policy, upon which he depended, was to give one of us a large subsidy to fall upon the other, which would infallibly secure to him peace and quiet, and after a long war would probably terminate in his being master of all three kingdoms.'[14]

An admirably succinct summary of Hume's view of the economics and organisation of national defence, the passage suggests a disagreement that remained perfectly good-humoured, but was none the less recognised on both sides to be fundamental.

It is the scope of Hume's and Smith's disagreement with the Moderates on the militia issue that, I suggest, *Reasons Against a Militia for Scotland* can help to illuminate. For the pamphlet drew from the general principles of Hume and Smith a set of specific conclusions for Scotland. These conclusions covered both the priorities which the Scots ought to be pursuing in their present circumstances, and the perspective in which those priorities should be viewed. As the first and fundamental principle adopted by the pamphlet was that of the division of labour, so the first priority it emphasised was economic improvement. Rather than making an issue of the militia, the Scots should be concentrating their scarce resources of labour on agriculture and manufactures. The principles of liberty then suggested a second priority: the choice of institutions that would secure rather than undermine the rule of law and the freedom that followed from it. If a militia would simply give fresh opportunities for the tumultuous fanaticism to which the Scottish people were so prone, and would weaken respect for the law by its infringement of personal liberty, it was not at present an institution to be welcomed. Ultimately, the pamphlet made clear, it was a matter of perspective. Partisans of a militia protested about Scotland's 'dignity' and 'birthright', when it was the 'fitness, prudence and propriety' of the measure which ought to be considered. The Scots should view the issue in the light of general principles, not give way to simple national indignation.

Whether the conclusions of *Reasons Against a Militia for Scotland* matched Hume's and Smith's own thoughts on the Scottish militia issue cannot be positively determined. But even if the identification is speculative, the pamphlet's choice of priorities and perspective can be shown to be consistent with what is known of Hume's and Smith's views of Scotland's economic and institutional development. Faced with the very different priorities and parochial perspective of the Moderates, I therefore propose to argue, it is most unlikely that Hume's response to their agitation was guided simply by his standing preference for militias, or Smith's by his approval of military exercises. After their initial patriotic response, other priorities would, I suggest, have asserted themselves, and they would have viewed the issue in a consciously universal perspective.

Seeking the most general application for their political economy, neither Hume nor Smith commented more than occasionally on the economic condition of Scotland. But there can be little doubt that they shared the conviction of *Reasons Against* that economic improvement was Scotland's first priority. It is clear that Hume's persistent and optimistic reflection upon a poor country's prospects of catching up with richer neighbours reflected a close interest in Scotland's economic relation to England; and Smith, if less sanguine than Hume about the poor country's prospects of actually catching up, was none the less confident that Scotland's economy was now on a course of development. In these circumstances, any unnecessary diversion of resources, and in particular any interference with labour that threatened to reduce Scotland's low wage advantage, was to be avoided.[15] Moreover Smith indicated — and Hume's general principles leave no doubt that he would have agreed — that the initiative for improvement must be expected to come from particular classes. It would not come from the great aristocracy, jealous of their entails and negligent of their lands, but from the 'middling and inferior ranks' whom the Union had given a complete deliverance from aristocratic power.[16] Among the middling ranks Smith counted the gentry, although both he and Hume had reservations about how far a gentleman would carry improvement; but it was above all to the merchants and tenant farmers that Smith looked.[17] If these were only encouraged to pursue their economic interest, Scotland's improvement would be assured.

It was, however, precisely these classes, the gentry and their subordinates, to whom the Moderates appealed in their agitation for a Scottish militia, urging them to pursue other, contrary priorities. The Moderates professed, indeed, to support improvement, and claimed that a militia would do nothing to impede it. But their own priority, as we have seen again and again in following the course of the agitations, was not improvement: it was social harmony — the social harmony, moreover, that had supposedly prevailed in the unimproved, martial society of earlier centuries. As Ferguson and Carlyle never tired of emphasising, the wealth now being acquired by improvement was rapidly undermining what remained of the martial cohesion of old: in these circumstances, Scottish society's most urgent need was for a renewed assertion of martial values. This did not mean restoring the old 'Gothic' aristocracy, on whom the Moderates were as hard as Hume and Smith. But it did mean the assumption by the new landed elite, the gentry, of the aristocracy's traditional role of moral and social leadership, and the renunciation of newly acquired economic interests. Among the inferior ranks, tenants and small holders might be left largely to economic activity, but militia service would make them realise that theirs was a subordinate station, and their values dependent on those of their social superiors. As for the commercial interest of merchants and manufacturers, their enterprise was tolerable only if they accepted a landed social order that denied them recognition as a separate interest. Although the Moderates expressed admiration for the model of social harmony which they imagined to exist in prosperous England, their view of the desirable social order for Scotland was still effectively that proclaimed by the Earl of Belhaven at the Union, when he put the values of the martial past before the prospect of future wealth. This was an order of priorities quite the reverse of Hume's and Smith's: that the Scottish gentry showed every sign of warming to the Moderates' theme would only have underlined the danger. On reflection, therefore, Hume and Smith would almost certainly have concluded that the demand for a militia imperilled improvement.

The institutional condition of Scotland evoked even less explicit comment from Hume and Smith than the economic. From scattered observations in Hume's *History* and the *Wealth of Nations,* as well as from their general principles, however, it is clear that they would have endorsed the insistence of *Reasons Against* on the priority of the rule of law and personal freedom. They believed that regular government according to law had only too recently been achieved in Scotland, and was in great measure due to the Union's curtailment of aristocratic power. It was, moreover, precisely because the nobility had been so willing to resort to arms to defend their interests, and had been able to impose military obligations upon a compliant people, that the rule of law had been for so long frustrated.[18]

The institutions of personal liberty once properly secured, Hume and Smith would presumably have had the Scots think also of their political liberty. Though this is to speculate even beyond the scope of the conclusions reached by *Reasons Against a Militia for Scotland,* there is no reason to suppose that the Scots would be exempt from the responsibility of matching their institutions to the gradual enlargement of the capacity for political participation in commercial society. What is certain, moreover, is that Hume and Smith would have insisted on the need to develop Scotland's political institutions in the framework provided by the relation with England. They not only believed that the Union had contributed significantly to securing the rule of law; both also clearly valued it as a setting in which Scotland could exploit its advantages as a province distanced from metropolitan centres of power.[19] Hume, whose wider orientation was European, devised in the 'Idea of a perfect Common-wealth' a model of government on civic principles which had much in common with Fletcher's: it pointed Britain and other large European states in the direction of a federal system that would ensure their provinces a significant measure of autonomy. Smith, by contrast, shared with the Scottish Unionist, the Earl of Cromarty, a commitment to unitary parlia-mentary sovereignty within a British empire. But through the extension of representation in line with taxation, Smith envisaged such an imperial system of government as strengthening the independent contribution of provinces like Scotland. For Smith as for Hume, in other words, Scotland's political liberty depended on maintaining and developing insti-tutions which secured both its relations with others and its provincial independence. The benefits of the latter could not be enjoyed without a firm framework for the former, and both required a constant process of institutional adjustment.

Here too, however, the Moderates' agitation for a Scottish militia confronted Hume and Smith with quite different priorities. As with economic improvement, the Moderates professed regard for the rule of law and individual freedom. But, keeping silent on the infringement of individual freedom involved in militia service, their true priority was another ideal of liberty, expressed simply in the possession of arms by Scotland's rulers. This ideal of liberty did not involve the exercise of arms in earnest: with each successive round of agitation, in fact, it became clearer that neither the Moderate literati nor the Scottish gentry had a real interest in the actual institution of a militia. Rather the liberty that arms-bearing was to express was a thing of the spirit, above any institutional embodiment. Again the inspiration was Belhaven, who, on the passing of the Union, had pleaded with his countrymen to preserve their political independence in the realm of values, making a virtue out of their freedom from institutional encumbrances. On occasion, it is true, Carlyle reinforced the Belhavenian ideal by invoking Scotland's ancient constitution, while at another opportune moment he seemed willing to associate the Scottish militia with the imperial vision of Cromarty. But these contradictory invocations evidently implied no serious institutional commitment: as long as the Scots maintained their old martial spirit, the institutional framework of their liberty could be left to look after itself. Granted the right to a Scottish militia, the Scots could regard the Union as complete, even perfect, and could identify unquestioningly with the existing, unreformed system of imperial government. Such a purely moral and martial concept of liberty, combined with such an uncritical indifference to its institutional framework, was far indeed from the priorities of Hume and Smith. Instead of supporting the Moderates' militia agitation, therefore, they are much more likely to have regarded it as endangering the Scots' hard-won personal liberty, while merely trivialising their political liberty.

In the end, what divided Hume and Smith most radically from the Moderate militia men was the difference of their perspective. It was the constant lesson of Hume's and Smith's writings, and also, so far as one can tell, of their contribution to the Select Society, that Scotland's problems should be understood in a broad, comparative perspective. Absorbing and extending Andrew Fletcher's original lesson that Scotland's predicament was potentially exemplary, and its solution a model of the progress of society for all the world, Hume and Smith urged their fellow-Scots to rise above parochialism, to recognise the general, even universal nature of their experience. Yet the Moderates spoke only of Scotland's birthright and Scotland's dignity, and sought only to restore Scottish society to its own past. Turning their backs on Fletcher, the Moderates revived instead the pure nationalism of Belhaven, emphasising and embellishing anew his celebration of the culture and values associated with martial achievement. Collaborators in Ossian as well as enthusiasts for the militia, the Moderates well deserve to be counted with the earliest inventors of the modern, kilt-ridden tradition of Scottishness;[20] and their causes should be numbered among the first of the pathetic cultural substitutes which have kept and still keep the Scots from the institutional responsibilities and wider horizons to which Fletcher called them. To Hume and Smith, I therefore conclude, the Moderates' perspective must have seemed the most wilful parochialism. By their agitation for a militia, Ferguson, Carlyle and their associates were trifling not only with improvement, not only with liberty: they were trifling with Scotland itself.

NOTES

1. I have come across only one copy of the pamphlet, in Goldsmith's Library in the University of London.

2. *Reasons Against a Militia for Scotland* (Edinburgh 1783), pp. 1–3.

3. Ibid., pp. 4–9, 18.

4. Ibid., pp. 10–13.

5. Ibid., pp. 14–17.

6. *Letters of Hume*, I, p. 325: 1 May 1760.

7. *Letters of Hume*, I, pp. 341–2: 3 Feb. 1761. See also above, p. 125 (Ch. 4, n.64).

8. *Letters of Hume*, II, p. 212: 14 Nov. 1769.

9. *Letters of Hume*, I, pp. 410–11: 9 Nov. 1763. It was in connection with Hume's membership of the Poker Club that Henry Mackenzie reported, 'I see among these careless scraps of his earlier writings, which Mr. Hume had preserved, the beginning of a warm paper addressed to the landed gentlemen of Scotland, on the subject of the militia, ascribing to the want of it the early misfortunes of the Seven Years War, to which the subsequent successes, unparalleled in British history, afforded a sufficient answer'. Henry Mackenzie 'Account of the Life of John Home', published as the Preface to *The Works of John Home* (Edinburgh 1822), Vol. I, p. 27. Whatever it was, the paper has not come to light.

10. *Correspondence of Adam Smith*, p. 68: 4 April 1760. Hooke's *Memoirs* had just the effect Smith feared: four days later the Duke of Newcastle wrote to the

Duke of Devonshire that any English supporters of the Scottish militia bill 'must not have read Hook's account of the Scots invasion in 1708. The very methods *then* used, are such, as I own I fear, may one day arise from this Bill. *Arm the Country* was then the first point, *Arm them against England* was the next, and get all parties, Presbyterians and co. to join in it, was the consequence of these premises. It seems by that book to have been almost the Universal Principle of the whole Nation.' B.L. Addit. Mss. 32904, ff. 259–60: 8 April 1760.

11. *Correspondence of Adam Smith*, p. 251: 26 October 1780; the letter described the response to the first edition of the *Wealth of Nations*.

12. Hume's view of the rules of literary controversy is spelt out in his delightful, masterful letter of 24 February 1763 to the impertinent Boswell: *New Letters of Hume*, pp. 68–9. His practice is exemplified in the case of Ossian: though severely disillusioned, he forbore to publish his contemptuous exposure of the poems' implausibility. 'Of the Authenticity of Ossian's Poems' is included in Vol. IV of the *Philosophical Works*, pp. 415–24.

13. Compare with Carlyle's no less critical retrospective evaluation of the *Wealth of Nations* and Smith's political views in the *Anecdotes and Characters*, p. 142: 'His Wealth of Nations, from which he was judg'd to be an inventive genius of the first order, is tedious and full of repetition. His separate essays in the 2nd Vol. have the air of being occasional pamphlets, without much force or determination. On political subjects his opinions were not very sound'.

14. 'John Home's Journal of the Journey with David Hume to Bath 1776', printed in an appendix to Mackenzie's 'Account of the Life of John Home', *Works of John Home*, I, pp. 181–2.

15. Istvan Hont, 'The Rich Country — Poor Country Debate in Scottish Classical Political Economy', in Hont and Ignatieff (eds.), *Wealth and Virtue*, pp. 271–94 (Hume), 298–305 (Smith). Also: *Wealth of Nations*, I.xi.8 and I.xi.e.35 for comments on Scotland's development and lower wages.

16. *Wealth of Nations*, III.ii.6–7 (on the Scottish aristocracy; Smith was still sharper in a letter to Lord Shelburne, *Correspondence of Adam Smith*, p. 32: 4 April 1759); V.iii.89 (on the deliverance of the middling and inferior ranks).

17. *Wealth of Nations*, III.iv.3 (almost certainly a reference to Glasgow merchants); IV.ii.21 (a general commendation of country gentlemen and farmers as improvers); V.ii.c.15 (an expression of doubt about the extent of gentlemen's commitment to improvement). Also Hont, 'The Rich Country — Poor Country Debate', *Wealth and Virtue*, pp. 277–8, for Hume's reservations about the Scottish gentry.

18. For Hume's observations in Vol. I of the *History of Great Britain*, see above, pp. 73–4; for Smith's, *Wealth of Nations*, III.iv.8 and V.iii.89.

19. For previous, stimulating remarks on Hume's and Smith's sense of the importance of Scotland's 'provincial' status, see Phillipson, 'Hume as Moralist', in Brown (ed.), *Philosophers of the Enlightenment*, pp. 149–52, and 'Adam Smith as Civic Moralist', in Hont and Ignatieff (eds.), *Wealth and Virtue*, pp. 195–6. Consistent with the difference of my interpretation throughout this book, however, my focus on Hume's and Smith's concern with the institutional framework of provincial liberty challenges Phillipson's thesis that it was the province's cultural independence that was valued.

20. On which tradition: H. R. Trevor-Roper, 'The Invention of Tradition: The Highland Tradition of Scotland', in E. J. Hobsbawm and T. Ranger, *The Invention of Tradition* (Cambridge 1983); and Tom Nairn, *The Break-up of Britain. Crisis and Neo-Nationalism* (London 1977), pp. 155 ff.

Bibliography

Manuscript Sources

National Library of Scotland

Saltoun Papers

16502–03	: Family Correspondence 1651–1717
16521–23	: Family Correspondence 1759–62
16708–26	: General Correspondence 1759–62
16735–37	: General Correspondence 1766–83
17506	: Militia and Army Papers

Minto Papers

11001	: Letters of Sir Gilbert Elliot to his father, Lord Minto 1744–62
11009	: Letters to Sir Gilbert Elliot from various correspondents
11014–16	: Sir Gilbert Elliot: General Correspondence 1755–63
11031	: Correspondence and Papers Concerning the Militia c.1760
11036	: Miscellaneous Political Papers

Mure of Caldwell Papers

4941–42	: Correspondence 1643–1763
4946	: Correspondence 1773–1781
5006	: Public Affairs

Erskine-Murray Papers

5080–81	: Correspondence of Charles Erskine, Lord Tinwald, Lord Justice Clerk, 1758–61

Lee Papers

3464	: Transcripts of Letters by Dr. C[arlyle] on the Militia, for the Press
3458	: Copy of the Minutes of the Poker Club 1774–84 (original in Edinburgh University Library)

Letter Book of Lord George Beauclerk

13497	: Letterbook of Lord George Beauclerk, Commander-in-Chief in Scotland, 1756–60

Mackenzie of Delvine Papers

1404	: Correspondence with John Murray, future third Duke of Athol

Henry Mackenzie's Letters and Papers

124	: Letters to or regarding John Home

Watson Autographs

588	: Divines and Judges

Select Society

Advocates Manuscripts 23.1.1: Book of Rules and Minutes, with the Book of Questions, Lists of Members, and Notes of Apology

Scottish Record Office

Melville Papers (Henry Dundas)
GD 51/1/196   : Documents relating to the Bill for Altering Freeholders Qualifications 1775–76
GD 51/1/818–20   : The Defence of Scotland 1778–80

Hamilton-Dalrymple of North Berwick Muniments
GD 110/1173   : 'Notes and Memoranda of Sir Hew Dalrymple relative to East Lothian politics, especially his difference with Lord Milton'

Campbell of Stonefield Papers
GD 14/144–6   : Correspondence between the Duke of Argyll and Archibald Campbell of Stonefield on raising Argyllshire Militia 1759

Sherrif Court Records
SC 40/68/1–2   : Record of the Proceedings of the Freeholders Electors of Haddingtonshire (East Lothian) 1743–93
SC 42/40/1–2   : Sederunt Books, Freeholders of Peebles 1756–1820
SC 67/59/3–4   : Minute Books of the Freeholders of Stirlingshire 1754–90

Church of Scotland
CH 1/1/53   : Register of the Acts of the General Assembly 1756–62
CH 1/1/66, 67, 68 : Register of the Acts of the General Assembly 1776–78, 1779–81, 1782–84
CH 1/3/27   : Register of the Acts of the Commission of the General Assembly 1757–68
CH 2/121/17   : Minutes of the Presbytery of Edinburgh 1753–66
CH 2/252/12   : Minutes of the Synod of Lothian and Tweeddale 1747–61
CH 2/271/7   : Minutes of the Synod of Moray 1760–75

British Library

Newcastle Papers
Addit. Mss.   : 32893–32907: Correspondence July 1759–June 1760
32935: Correspondence March 1762
32998–99: Memoranda Vols. vi–vii
33034: Proceedings in Parliament, ii
33049: Political and other papers connected with Scotland

Hardwicke Papers
Addit. Mss.   : 35449: Correspondence on Scotch Affairs 1756–63
35450: Correspondence with Earl of Breadalbane 1740–61
35878: Parliamentary Papers 1758–63
35891: Papers relating to Scotland 1753–60

Leeds Papers (Earl of Holderness)
Egerton Ms. 3434

Public Record Office

State Papers Scotland
SP 54 Vols. 45–48 (1756–83)

Home Office Papers Scotland
HO 102 Vols. 1–2: 1782–85
HO 103 Vol. 1: Entry Book 1763–95

Edinburgh University Library

Ms. Laing II 620⁶: Robert Wallace, 'Copy of a Scheme for a Militia in Brittain'
Ms. Gen. 1429/18/19: Letter of George Murray (sixth Lord Elibank) to James
  Murray (his brother) 29 May 1760
Ms. Dc. 1.77: Letters of Adam Ferguson to Sir John Macpherson 1773–1808
Ms. Dc. 4.41: Letters to Alexander Carlyle
Ms. Dc. 5.126: Minutes of the Poker Club 1774–84

Edinburgh City Chambers

Records of the Convention of Royal Burghs, Vol. xiv, 1776–90

Council Records of the City of Edinburgh
  Vols. 76(1759–61), 77(1761–2), 93(1775–76), 102(1781–82)

Mount Stuart, Isle of Bute

Bute Papers
  Correspondence of the third Earl of Bute 1755–60

Loudon Papers
  Green Deed Box 1759–63: 1760, Bundle 1

Cardiff Central Library

Bute Correspondence 1752–90
  Ms. 3.615

William L. Clements Library, Ann Arbor, Michigan

Townshend Papers
  Letters of Alexander Carlyle, Lord Milton, William Robertson, Lord Elibank,
  Lord Kames and John Dalrymple to Charles Townshend, 1759–60 (Microfilms
  held at Scottish Record Office: RH4/98/1, 3)

Historical Manuscripts Commission

67: *Report on the Manuscripts of the Right Honourable Lord Polwarth, Vol. V 1725–
  80,* ed. Rev. Henry Paton (London 1961)

Newspapers and Journals

Aberdeen Journal 1758–62, 1775–76, 1778–84
Aberdeen Magazine 1761
Caledonian Mercury 1756–63, 1775–6, 1778–83
Edinburgh Advertiser 1775–76, 1778–83
Edinburgh Chronicle 1759–60
Edinburgh Evening Courant 1755–63, 1775–76, 1778–83
Edinburgh Magazine 1758–62
Edinburgh Magazine and Review 1773–76
Glasgow Courant 1759–60
Glasgow Journal 1759–62, 1781
Glasgow Mercury 1778–84
Scots Magazine 1756–82

Primary Printed Sources

Listed alphabetically by author; works that are anonymous and cannot be ascribed to an author are listed by the first word of the title (excluding the article).

I have indicated, using the standard abbreviations, the libraries in which the Scottish militia pamphlets are to be found.

[Abercromby, Patrick], *The Advantages of the Act of Security, Compar'd with these of the intended Union,* (1706)

Abercromby, Patrick, *The Martial Atchievements of the Scots Nation. Being an Account of the Lives, Characters and Memorable Actions of Such Scotsmen as have signaliz'd themselves by the Sword at home and abroad,* Two vols., (Edinburgh 1711 and 1715)

[Abercromby, Patrick, trans.], *The History of the Campagnes 1548 and 1549, Being an Exact Account of the Martial Expeditions perform'd in those Days by the Scots and French on the one Side, and by the English and their foreign Auxiliaries on the other.* Done in French, under the title of, 'The Scots War', by Mons. Beaugué, A French Gentleman. Printed at Paris in the year 1556 with an Introductory Preface by the Translator, Printed in the year 1707

The Ancient and Present State of Military Law in Great Britain Considered: with a Review of the Debates of the Army and Navy Bills. In Four Letters to a Friend in the Country, 2nd edn., (London 1750)

Arnot, Hugo, *The History of Edinburgh,* (Edinburgh 1779)

[Bannerman, Rev. Patrick], *An Address to the People of Scotland on Ecclesiastical and Civil Liberty,* (Edinburgh 1782)

Belhaven, John Hamilton, Lord Belhaven, *A Speech in Parliament on the 10th day of January 1701, by the Lord Belhaven, on the Affair of the Indian and African Company, and its Colony of Caledonia* (Edinburgh 1701)

———, *A Speech in Parliament by the Lord Belhaven; upon the Act for Security of the Kingdom, in case of the Queen's death,* (Edinburgh 1703)

[———?], *A Speech in Parliament touching Limitations,* (Edinburgh 1703)

———, *The Lord Belhaven's Speech in Parliament, the 17th of July 1705,* (Edinburgh 1705)

———, *The Lord Belhaven's Speech in Parliament the second day of November 1706. On the subject matter of an union betwixt the two Kingdoms of Scotland and England,* (n.p., 1706)

[Black, David?], *Essay upon Industry and Trade, Shewing the Necessity of the One, the Conveniency and Usefulness of the Other, and the Advantages of Both,* (Edinburgh 1706)

Bolingbroke, Henry St. John, Viscount, *The Works of the late Right Honourable Henry St. John, Lord Viscount Bolingbroke,* in five volumes, complete, published by David Mallet, Esq., (London 1754)

Boswell, James, *Boswell's London Journal 1762–3,* ed. F. A. Pottle, (London 1950)

———, *Boswell: The Ominous years 1774–76,* ed. C. Ryskamp and F. Pottle, (London 1963)

[Brown, John], *An Estimate of the Manners and Principles of the Times,* (London 1757)

Buchanan, George, *Opera Omnia,* Curante Thomas Ruddiman (Edinburgh 1715)

Burke's Landed Gentry, 1st edition (London 1846), 4th edition (London 1862)

Candid Observations on the Proposed Militia Law, and Plan of Arming the People. Addressed to a Gentleman in the Shire of Lanark. With an appendix containing all the Scotch Acts relating to a Militia, under the articles 'Weaponshawing', 'Host', 'Militia', and 'Levy', as abridged by Sir James Stewart (n.p., 1782) (Not found)

[Carlyle, Alexander], O. M. Haberdasher, *Plain Reasons for removing a certain great man from His Majesty's Presence and Councils for ever. Addressed to the People of England,* (London 1759)

[——], *The Question relating to a Scots Militia Considered. In a Letter to the Lords and Gentlemen who have concerted a form of law for that establishment,* By a Freeholder, Ayrshire, (Edinburgh 1760), (N.L.S.)

[——], *The Question relating... The Second Edition, to which is prefixed, A Preface by another hand,* (London 1760) (N.L.S.)

[——], *The Question relating... The Fourth Edition, with a Preface, in which some late objections against the establishment of a militia are considered,* (Edinburgh 1762) (E.U.L.)

[——], *The Justice and Necessity of the War with our American Colonies Examined. A Sermon,* (Edinburgh 1777)

[——], *A Letter to his Grace the Duke of Buccleugh on National Defence: with some Remarks on Dr. Smith's Chapter on that subject, in his book entitled An Inquiry into the Nature and Causes of the Wealth of Nations* (London 1778), *To which is now added, A Postscript, relative to the regiments of Fencible men raising in Scotland* (Edinburgh 1778) (N.L.S.)

——, *Anecdotes and Characters of the Times,* ed. J. Kinsley, (London 1973)

Clerk, Sir John, of Penicuik, *Memoirs of the Life of Sir John Clerk of Penicuik 1676–1755,* ed. J. M. Gray, *Scottish History Society,* Vol. XII, (Edinburgh 1892)

Commons Journals, Vols. 28(1757–61), 35(1774–76), 38(1780–82)

The Complete Baronetage, 5 vols. (Exeter 1900)

Craig, Sir Thomas, *De Unione Regnorum Britanniae Tractatus,* ed. with a translation by C. S. Terry, *Scottish History Society,* Vol. LX, (Edinburgh 1909)

[Cromarty, George Mackenzie, Earl of Cromarty], *Parainesis Pacifica; or, a perswasive to the union of Britain,* (Edinburgh 1702, repr. London 1702)

[——], *A Letter from E. C. to E. W. concerning the Union* [Edinburgh 1706]

[——], *A second letter, on the British Union* (1706)

[——], *A Friendly Return to a Letter Concerning Sir George Mackenzie's and Sir John Nisbet's Observations and Responce on the Matter of the Union,* (n.p., 1706)

[——], *A Letter to a Member of Parliament upon the 19th Article of the Treaty of Union between the Two Kingdoms of England and Scotland* [Edinburgh 1706]

——, *Synopsis Apocalyptica: or, A Short Plain Explication and Application of Daniel's Prophecy and St. John's Revelation, in Concert with it, and Consequential to it, by G. E. of C. Tracing in the Steps of the admirable Lord Napier of Merchistoun,* (Edinburgh 1708)

Dalrymple, Sir John, *An Essay towards a general history of Feudal Property in Great Britain,* (1757, 3rd edit., London 1758)

——, *Considerations upon the Policy of Entails in Great Britain. Occasioned by a Scheme to apply for a Statute to let the Entails of Scotland die out, on the demise of the Possessors and Heirs now existing,* (Edinburgh 1764)

[——], *Reflections Upon the Military Preparations which are Making at Present in Scotland,* (Edinburgh 1778)

[Defoe, Daniel], *Some Reflections on a Pamphlet lately Publish'd, Entitled, An Argument Shewing that a Standing Army is inconsistent with a Free Government, and absolutely destructive to the Constitution of the English Monarchy,* 2nd ed., (London 1697)

[——], *A Brief Reply to the History of Standing Armies In England. With Some Account of the Authors,* (London 1698)

[——], *An Argument Shewing, that a Standing Army, with Consent of Parliament, is not inconsistent with a Free Government,* (London 1698)

[——], *A Fourth Essay at Removing National Prejudices,* (n.p. 1706)

——, *The History of the Union between England and Scotland,* (London 1786)

[Dempster, George], *Reasons for Extending the Militia Acts to the Disarm'd Counties of Scotland,* (Edinburgh 1760), (N.L.S.)

Edinburgh Club, *The Book of the Old Edinburgh Club,* Vol. III, (Edinburgh 1910)

English Historical Documents, Vol. VIII, 1610–1714, ed. A. Browning, (London 1953)

[Erskine, David Stewart, Earl of Buchan], *Letters on the Impolicy of a Standing Army, in time of peace, and on the unconstitutional and illegal measure of Barracks etc.,* 'Albanicus' (London 1793), (N.L.S.)

The Faculty of Advocates in Scotland 1532–1943, ed. Sir Francis Grant, *Scottish Record Society,* Vol. 74, (Edinburgh 1944)

Ferguson, Adam, *A Sermon Preached in the Ersh Language to His Majesty's First Highland Regiment of Foot, commanded by Lord John Murray ... on the 18th Day of December 1745,* (London 1746)

[——], *Reflections Previous to the Establishment of a Militia,* (London 1756), (N.L.S.)

[——], *The History of the Proceedings in the case of Margaret, commonly called Peg, only lawful sister to John Bull Esq.,* (London 1761), (N.L.S.)

——, *An Essay on the History of Civil Society* (1767), edited with an introduction by Duncan Forbes, (Edinburgh 1966)

——, *Institutes of Moral Philosophy,* (Edinburgh 1769)

[——], *Remarks on a Pamphlet lately published by Dr. Price, entitled, Observations on the Nature of Civil Liberty, the Principles of Government, and the Justice and Policy of the War with America, and co., in a letter from a Gentleman in the country to a member of Parliament,* (London 1776)

——, *The History of the Progress and Termination of the Roman Republic,* three vols., (London 1783), new edition in five vols., (Edinburgh 1799)

——, *Principles of Moral and Political Science: being chiefly a retrospect of Lectures delivered in the College of Edinburgh,* two vols., (Edinburgh 1792)

[——], *Minutes of the Life and Character of Joseph Black, M.D.,* Addressed to the Royal Society of Edinburgh, Hallyards, Tweeddale, 23 April, 1801

——, *Biographical Sketch, or Memoir, of Lieutenant-Colonel Patrick Ferguson: originally intended for the British Encyclopaedia,* (Edinburgh 1817)

[Fletcher, Andrew, of Saltoun], *A Discourse Concerning Militias and Standing Armies; with relation to the Past and Present Governments of Europe and of England in particular,* (London 1697)

——, *The Political Works,* (London 1732 and 1737; Glasgow 1749)

——, *Selected Political Writings and Speeches,* ed. D. Daiches, (Edinburgh 1979)

——, 'Letters of Andrew Fletcher of Saltoun and his Family 1715–16', ed. Irene J. Murray, *Scottish History Society Miscellany X,* (1965)

[Fletcher, Andrew, Lord Milton], 'Civicus', *Queries, humbly offered to the Consider-ation of the Public*, [Feb. 1760], (N.L.S., Saltoun Papers, Ms. 17506, ff. 20, 21)

Glasgow, *Extracts from the Records of the Burgh of Glasgow*, ed. R. Renwick, 11 vols., (Glasgow 1876–1916), vols. VII, 1760–80, VIII, 1781–95

Harrington, James, *The Commonwealth of Oceana*, (1756), in J. G. A. Pocock (ed.), *The Political Works of James Harrington*, (Cambridge 1977)

Heads of a Bill for the Better Ordering the Fencible Men in that part of Great Britain called Scotland, (Edinburgh 1783)

Henderson, Andrew, A. M., *Considerations on the Question: whether the Act of Parliament establishing a Militia thro England ought to extend to Scotland in time of war*, (London, Westminster Hall, 1760), (Bodleian)

Hodges, James, *A Letter from Mr. Hodges at London, To a Member of the Parliament of Scotland*, (Edinburgh 1703)

[——], *War Betwixt the Two British Kingdoms Considered, and the Dangerous Circumstances of Each with regard thereto lay'd open*, (London 1705)

Home, John, *The History of the Rebellion in the Year 1745*, (London 1802)

——, *The Works of John Home*, three vols., (Edinburgh 1822). Vol. I: *Douglas. A Tragedy*, and *Agis. A Tragedy*

Hume, David, *A Treatise of Human Nature*, ed. L. A. Selby-Bigge, 2nd ed., rev. by P. H. Nidditch, (Oxford 1978), Bk. III 'Of Morals', (1740)

[——], *A True Account of the Behaviour and Conduct of Archibald Stewart Esq., Late Provost of Edinburgh, in a Letter to a Friend*, (London 1748)

——, *The Philosophical Works*, ed. T. H. Green and T. H. Grose, (London 1882, repr. Darmstadt 1964), Vols. III and IV, *Essays Moral, Political and Literary*

——, *The History of Great Britain. Volume I. The Reigns of James I and Charles I*, (Edinburgh 1754), repr. ed. D. Forbes, (Harmondsworth 1970)

——, *The History of England from the Invasion of Julius Caesar to the Revolution in 1688*, 8 vols., (London 1778)

——, *The Letters of David Hume*, ed., J. Y. T. Greig, two vols., (Oxford 1969)

——, *New Letters of David Hume*, eds. R. Klibansky and E. C. Mossner, (Oxford 1954)

——, 'New Hume Letters to Lord Elibank 1748–76', ed. E. C. Mossner, *Texas Studies in Literature and Language*, IV, (1962)

——, 'Hume's Early Memoranda, 1729–40: The Complete Text', ed. with foreword by E. C. Mossner, *Journal of the History of Ideas*, IX, (1948), pp. 492–518

Hutcheson, Francis, *A System of Moral Philosophy*, 2 Vols., (Glasgow 1755)

Kames, Henry Home, Lord Kames, *Sketches of the History of Man*, 2 Vols., (Edinburgh 1774)

Kyd, J. G., ed., *Scottish Population Statistics, including Webster's Analysis of Population 1755*, The Scottish History Society, (Edinburgh 1975)

A Letter Concerning the State of Arms in Scotland, Addressed to Earl of Hadinton; occasioned by the Remarks of a country gentleman on the proposed laws for establishing a militia in Scotland, (Edinburgh 1782), (Goldsmith's Library)

A Letter to a Member of the Militia Committee at Edinburgh, from his friend in East Lothian, (Edinburgh 1782), (Goldsmith's Library)

A Letter to the Noblemen and Gentlemen engaged in planning a Militia for Scotland, by a Burgess of Glasgow, February 18, 1760, (N.L.S., Saltoun Papers, Ms. 17506, ff. 6–9)

A Letter to the Right Hon. Charles Townshend, Being Thoughts on the Militia Laws

— *and for extending them to North Britain, and for making the Militia more useful,* 2nd ed., (London 1762), (Bodleian)

Mackenzie, Henry, *An Account of the Life and Writings of John Home,* read at the Royal Society of Edinburgh, 22 June 1812, published as the Preface to *The Works of John Home,* Vol. I

Montesquieu, Charles-Louis de Secondat, *De L'Esprit des Lois,* (1748), ed. G. Truc, Garnier, (Paris 1961)

[Morris, Corbyn], *A letter from a By-Stander to a Member of Parliament. Wherein is examined what Necessity there is for the Maintenance of a Large Regular Land-Force in this Island,* (London 1741, i.e. 1742)

[Murray, Patrick, Lord Elibank], *Queries Relating to the Proposed Plan for altering the Entails in Scotland, in a Letter to —,* (Edinburgh 1765)

Mure of Caldwell, *Selections from the Family Papers Preserved at Caldwell,* Part II, 2 Vols., ed. W. Mure (Glasgow, The Maitland Club, 1854)

A Narrative of the Late Riots at Edinburgh; and a Vindication of its Magistracy, against the charges advanced in the Memorial for the Papists of Scotland, (London 1779)

Neville, Henry, *Plato Redivivus, or a Dialogue Concerning Government,* 2nd ed., (London 1781), printed in *Two English Republican Tracts,* ed. C. Robbins, (Cambridge 1969)

Observations on the New Militia Bill, now under the consideration of Parliament, wherein the material alterations are pointed out, (London n.d., [1762])

Observations tending to explain the principles of the intended Bill for the better ordering the Fencible Men in that part of Great Britain called Scotland, (Edinburgh 1782)

Oswald, James, of Dunnikier, *Memorials of the Public Life and Character of the Right Hon. James Oswald of Dunnikier, contained in Correspondence,* (Edinburgh 1825)

The Parliamentary History of England, from the Earliest Period to the Year 1803, printed by T. C. Hansard, (London 1806–20), Vols. XVIII, XXIII

Parliamentary Register, or The History of the Proceedings and Debates of the Houses of Parliament, during the Fourteenth Parliament of Great Britain. 1774–1780, (London 1802), Vols. II, III, X, XII, XV

Parliamentary Register, or The History of the Proceedings and Debates of the Houses of Parliament. 1780–1803, (London 1781–1804), Vol. VII

A Pil for Pork-Eaters: or, a Scots Lancet for an English Swelling, (Edinburgh 1705)

The Principal Heads of a Speech in P--t, concerning The Scots Militia by a Right Honourable M--r from a certain Country in N--H B--N. Being an extract of a part of a Letter from a Gentleman of rank at London to his friend in Edinburgh, (1760), (Aberdeen Univ. Library)

A Proposal for a Regular and Useful Militia, (Edinburgh 1745), (Signet Library)

The Public Catechised; or a Few Cool Questions to the People, (n.p. n.d.) [1761], (Signet Library)

Queries Addressed to the Serious Consideration of the Public, 26 April 1760, [Possibly by Andrew Fletcher, Lord Milton], (B.L. Addit. Mss. 33049, ff. 322–3)

Ramsay, John of Ochtertyre, *Scotland and Scotsmen in the Eighteenth Century,* edited from the Ochtertyre Mss. by A. Allardyce, two vols., (Edinburgh and London 1888)

Reasons Against a Militia for Scotland, (Edinburgh 1783), (Goldsmith's Library)

Remarks on the proposed laws for establishing a militia in Scotland. By a country gentleman, (Edinburgh 1782), (Goldsmith's Library)

[Ridpath, George], *An Historical Account of the Antient Rights and Power of the Parliament of Scotland. To which is prefixed, A Short Introduction upon Government in General,* (1703), (Aberdeen 1823). Wrongly ascribed to Andrew Fletcher

[——], *The Reducing of Scotland by Arms, and Annexing it to England as a Province, Considered,* (London, repr. Edinburgh 1705)

Robertson, William, *The History of Scotland during the Reigns of Queen Mary and King James VI,* (London 1759)

Royal Burghs, *Extracts from the Records of the Convention of the Royal Burghs of Scotland 1759–79,* (Edinburgh 1918)

[Saville, Sir George], *An Argument concerning the Militia,* [1762]

The Scots Peerage, ed. Sir James Balfour Paul, 9 vols., (Edinburgh 1904)

[Seton, William of Pitmedden], *Memorial to the Members of Parliament of the Court Party,* [1700]

[——], *The Interest of Scotland in Three Essays,* (1700, 2nd ed., London 1702)

[——], *Scotland's Great Advantages by an Union with England: shown in a Letter from the County, to a Member of Parliament,* (1706)

——, *A Speech in Parliament on the second day of November 1706. By William Seton of Pitmedden Junior, on the first article of the Treaty of Union,* (Edinburgh 1706)

Sibbald, Sir Robert, *Provision for the Poor in Time of Dearth and Scarcity,* (Edinburgh 1699, 2nd ed. 1709)

A Sketch of a Bill for the Better Ordering the Fencible Men in that part of Great Britain called Scotland, (Edinburgh 1782)

[Sinclair, Sir John], *Considerations on Militias and Standing Armies; with Observations on Lord Shelburne's plan of defence,* (London 1782), (N.L.S.)

Smith, Adam, *The Theory of Moral Sentiments,* (1759), Glasgow Edition, eds. D. D. Raphael and A. L. Macfie, (Oxford 1976)

——, *An Inquiry into the Nature and Causes of the Wealth of Nations,* (1776), Glasgow Edition, eds. R. H. Campbell, A. S. Skinner and W. B. Todd, two vols., (Oxford 1976)

——, *Lectures on Jurisprudence,* (1762–3 and 1766), Glasgow Edition, eds. R. L. Meek, D. D. Raphael and P. G. Stein, (Oxford 1978)

——, *The Correspondence of Adam Smith,* Glasgow Edition, eds. E. C. Mossner and I. S. Ross, (Oxford 1977)

——, *A Catalogue of the Library of Adam Smith,* by James Bonar, 2nd edit., (London 1932)

——, *Adam Smith's Library. A Supplement to Bonar's Catalogue with a check-list of the whole library,* by H. Mizuta, (Cambridge 1967)

[Lord Somers], *A letter, Ballancing the Necessity of keeping a Landforce in Times of Peace: with the Danger that may follow on it,* (1697)

A Source Book of Scottish History Vol. III, 1567–1707, eds. W. C. Dickinson and G. Donaldson, (Edinburgh 1954)

Somerville, Thomas, *My Own Life and Times 1741–1814,* (Edinburgh 1861)

The Surprizing and Heroic Atchievement at Ravenshaugh Toll, n.d., n.p. [Edinburgh 1760], (N.L.S.)

[Swinton, John], *A Free Disquisition Concerning the Law of Entails in Scotland. Occasioned by Some Late Proposals for amending that Law,* (Edinburgh 1765)

T[hornton], W[illiam], *The Counterpoise: being thoughts on a Militia and a Standing Army,* (London 1752)

[Toland, John], *The Militia Reform'd: or, an Easy Scheme of Furnishing England with a Constant Land Force, capable to prevent or to subdue any Foreign Power; and to maintain perpetual Quiet at Home, without endangering the Public Liberty,* (London, 2nd ed., 1699)

[Trenchard, J. and Moyle, W.], *An Argument, Shewing, that a Standing Army is inconsistent with a Free Government, and absolutely destructive to the Constitution of the English Monarchy,* (London 1697)

[——], *A Short History of Standing Armies in England,* (London 1698)

[Trenchard, J. and Gordon, T.], *Cato's Letters,* 4 vols., (London 1724)

[Tucker, J.], *The important question concerning invasions, a sea war, raising the Militia, and paying subsidies for foreign troops fairly stated...Being a new edition of the papers first published in the Evening Advertiser,* (London 1755)

Tytler, A. F., *Memoirs of the Life and Writings of the Honourable Henry Home of Kames,* 2 vols., (Edinburgh 1807)

Wallace, Robert, *A Dissertation of the Numbers of Mankind in Ancient and Modern Times,* (Edinburgh 1753)

——, *Various Prospects of Mankind, Nature, and Providence,* (London 1761)

Wortley Montagu, Edward, *Reflections on the Rise and Fall of the Ancient Republics, adapted to the Present State of Great Britain,* (London 1759)

Writers to the Signet, *The Society of Writers to His Majesty's Signet, with a List of Members,* (Edinburgh 1936)

Wyvill, Rev. C., *Political Papers chiefly respecting the attempt...to effect a Reformation of the Parliament of Great Britain,* 6. vols., (York, 1794–1802)

Secondary Printed Sources

Adair, Douglass, '"That Politics May be Reduced to a Science." David Hume, James Madison and the Tenth *Federalist*', *The Huntingdon Library Quarterly,* XX, (1956–7)

Barrow, G. W. S., *Robert Bruce and the Community of the Realm of Scotland,* (Edinburgh 1976)

——, *The Anglo-Norman Era in Scottish History,* (Oxford 1980)

——, *Kingship and Unity. Scotland 1000–1306,* The New History of Scotland, Vol. 2, (London 1981)

Bayley, C. C., *War and Society in Renaissance Florence. The De Militia of Leonardo Bruni,* (Toronto 1961)

Black, E. C., *The Association: British Extraparliamentary Political Organisation 1769–1793,* (Cambridge, Mass. 1963)

Brewer, John, *Party Ideology and Popular Politics at the Accession of George III,* (Cambridge 1976)

Butterfield, H., *George III, Lord North and the People 1779–80,* (1949, repr., New York 1968)

Campbell, R. H., *Scotland since 1707: The Rise of an Industrial Society,* (Oxford 1965)

——, 'The Anglo-Scottish Union of 1707: The Economic Consequences', *Economic History Review,* 2nd series, 16, (1964)

Campbell, T. D., *Adam Smith's Science of Morals,* (London 1971)

Clark, I. D. L., 'From Protest to Reaction: the Moderate Regime in the Church of Scotland 1725–1805', in Phillipson and Mitchison, eds., *Scotland in the Age of Improvement*

Coquelle, P., 'Les Projets de Descente en Angleterre', *Revue d'Histoire Diplomatique*, XV, (1901), pp. 591–624, XVI, (1902), 134–57

Couper, W. J., *The Edinburgh Periodical Press from the earliest Times to 1800*, two vols., (Stirling 1908)

Craig, M. E., *The Scottish Periodical Press 1750–1789*, (London and Edinburgh 1931)

Cropsey, Joseph, *Polity and Economy. An Interpretation of the Principles of Adam Smith*, (The Hague 1957)

Cullen, L. M. and Smout, T. C., eds., *Comparative Aspects of Scottish and Irish Economic and Social History 1600–1900*, (Edinburgh 1977)

Devine, T. M., *The Tobacco Lords*, (Edinburgh 1975)

Donaldson, Gordon, *Scotland James V–James VII*, The Edinburgh History of Scotland, vol. 3, (Edinburgh 1965, repr. 1971)

Duff, Duncan, *Scotland's War Losses*, The Scottish Secretariat, (Glasgow 1947)

Duncan, Douglas, *Thomas Ruddiman. A Study in Scottish Scholarship of the Early Eighteenth Century*, (Edinburgh 1965)

Dwyer, John, Mason, Roger, and Murdoch, Alexander, eds., *New Perspectives on the Politics and Culture of Early Modern Scotland*, (Edinburgh 1982)

Dwyer, J. and Murdoch, A., 'Paradigms and Politics: Manners, Morals and the Rise of Henry Dundas 1770–84', in Dwyer et al. eds., *New Perspectives on Early Modern Scotland*

Elder, J. R., *The Highland Host of 1678*, (Glasgow 1914)

Emerson, R. L., 'The Social Composition of Enlightened Scotland: the Select Society of Edinburgh, 1754–64', *Studies on Voltaire and the eighteenth century*, CXIV, (1973)

Fagerstrom, D. I., 'Scottish Opinion and the American Revolution', *William and Mary Quarterly*, third series, XI, (1954)

Ferguson, W., *Scotland 1689 to the Present*, The Edinburgh History of Scotland, vol. 4, (Edinburgh 1978)

——, *Scotland's Relations with England: a Survey to 1707*, (Edinburgh 1977)

Finer, S. E., 'State and Nation Building in Europe: The Role of the Military', in Charles Tilly, ed., *The Formation of National States in Western Europe*, (Princeton 1975)

Flinn, M., ed., *Scottish Population History from the 17th Century to the 1930s*, (Cambridge 1977)

Foord, A. S., *His Majesty's Opposition 1714–1830*, (Oxford 1964)

Forbes, Duncan, *Hume's Philosophical Politics*, (Cambridge 1975)

——, 'Sceptical Whiggism, Commerce and Liberty', in A. S. Skinner and T. Wilson, eds., *Essays on Adam Smith*, (Oxford 1976)

——, 'Natural Law and the Scottish Enlightenment', in R. H. Campbell and A. S. Skinner, eds., *The Origins and Nature of the Scottish Enlightenment*, (Edinburgh 1982)

Furber, Holder, *Henry Dundas First Viscount Melville 1742–1811*, (London 1931)

Giarrizzo, G., *David Hume Politico e Storico*, (Turin 1962)

Graham, Henry Grey, *The Social Life of Scotland in the Eighteenth Century*, (1899, new ed., London 1964)

Haakonssen, Knud, *The Science of a Legislator. The Natural Jurisprudence of David Hume and Adam Smith*, (Cambridge 1981)

Hamilton, H., *An Economic History of Scotland in the Eighteenth Century*, (Oxford 1963)

——, 'Scotland's Balance of Payments Problem in 1762', *Economic History Review*, 2nd series, 5, (1953)

Hayes, James, 'Scottish Officers in the British Army 1714–63', *Scottish Historical Review*, XXVII, (1958)

Hecht, J. J., *The Domestic Servant Class in Eighteenth Century England*, (London 1956)

Hexter, J. H., 'Republic, Virtue, Liberty, and the Political Universe of J. G. A. Pocock', *On Historians*, (London 1979)

Holdsworth, Sir William, *A History of English Law*, vol. X, (London 1938)

Hont, Istvan, and Ignatieff, Michael, eds., *Wealth and Virtue. The Shaping of Political Economy in the Scottish Enlightenment*, (Cambridge 1983)

Hont, Istvan, 'The Rich Country–Poor Country Debate in Scottish Classical Political Economy', in Hont and Ignatieff eds., *Wealth and Virtue*

Howard, Michael, *War in European History*, (Oxford 1976)

Jarrett, Derek, *The Begetters of Revolution: England's Involvement with France 1759–1789*, (London 1973)

Jones, Peter, 'The Scottish Professoriate and the Polite Academy 1720–46', in Hont and Ignatieff, eds., *Wealth and Virtue*

Keegan, John, *The Face of Battle*, (Harmondsworth 1978)

Kettler, David, *The Social and Political Thought of Adam Ferguson*, (Ohio 1965)

——, 'History and Theory in Adam Ferguson's *Essay on the History of Civil Society*: A Reconsideration', *Political Theory*, 5, 4, (1977)

Kramnick, I., *Bolingbroke and His Circle: The Politics of Nostalgia in the Age of Walpole*, (Cambridge, Mass., and London 1968)

Lieberman, D., 'The Legal Needs of a Commercial Society: the jurisprudence of Lord Kames', in Hont and Ignatieff eds., *Wealth and Virtue*.

Lloyd, E. M., 'The Raising of the Highland Regiments in 1757', *English Historical Review*, XVII, (1902)

Logue, K. J., *Popular Disturbances in Scotland 1780–1815*, (Edinburgh 1979)

Low, J. M., 'A Regional Example of the Mercantilist Theory of Economic Policy', *The Manchester School*, 21, 1, (1953)

Lythe, S. G., 'The Tayside Meal Mobs 1772–73', *Scottish Historical Review*, XLVI, (1967)

Macaulay, T. B., *The History of England from the Accession of James II*, 5 vols., (Boston and New York 1856–61)

McCahill, M. W., 'The Scottish Peerage and the House of Lords in the Late 18th Century', *Scottish Historical Review*, LI, (1972)

Macdougall, N., ed., *Church, Politics and Society: Scotland 1408–1929*, (Edinburgh 1983)

MacFie, R. A. S., *A Bibliography of Andrew Fletcher of Saltoun 1653–1716*, (privately printed, Edinburgh 1901)

Macinnes, Allan I, 'Scottish Gaeldom 1638–51: The Vernacular Response to the Covenanting Dynamic', in Dwyer *et al.*, eds., *New Perspectives on Early Modern Scotland*

Mackenzie, W. C., *Andrew Fletcher of Saltoun. His Life and Times*, (Edinburgh 1935)

Mackesy, Piers, *The War for America 1775–83*, (London 1964)

McLeod, W. R. and V. B., *Anglo-Scottish Tracts 1701–14. A Descriptive Checklist*, University of Kansas Publications, Library Series, 44, (Kansas 1979)

Mason, R. A., '*Rex Stoicus:* George Buchanan, James VI and the Scottish Polity', in Dwyer *et al.*, eds., *New Perspectives on Early Modern Scotland*
——, 'Covenant and Commonweal: the language of politics in Reformation Scotland', in Macdougall, ed., *Church, Politics and Society*
Meek, R. L., *Social Science and the Ignoble Savage*, (Cambridge 1976)
Meikle, H. W., *Scotland and the French Revolution*, (Glasgow 1912 and London 1969)
Mitchison, Rosalind, 'The Movements of Scottish Grain Prices in the Seventeenth and Eighteenth Centuries', *Economic History Review*, 2nd Series, 18, (1965)
——, 'The Government and the Highlands, 1707–1745', in Phillipson and Mitchison, eds., *Scotland in the Age of Improvement*
——, 'The Making of the Old Scottish Poor Law', *Past and Present*, 63, (1974)
——, 'Patriotism and National Identity in eighteenth-century Scotland', in T. W. Moody, ed., *Nationality and the Pursuit of National Independence*, (Belfast 1978)
——, *Lordship to Patronage. Scotland 1603–1745*, The New History of Scotland, Vol. 5, (London 1983)
Moore, James, 'Hume's Political Science and the Classical Republican Tradition', *Canadian Journal of Political Science*, X, (1977)
Morgan, Valerie, 'Agricultural Wage Rates in Late Eighteenth Century Scotland', *Economic History Review*, 2nd series, 24, (1971)
Morrison, M. Cotter, 'The Duc de Choiseul and the Invasion of England 1768–70', *Transactions of the Royal Historical Society*, 3rd series, IV, (1910)
Mossner, E. C., *The Life of David Hume*, (Oxford 1970)
Murdoch, Alexander, '*The People Above*'. *Politics and Administration in Mid-Eighteenth-Century Scotland*, (Edinburgh 1980)
——, (with Dwyer, John), 'Paradigms and Politics: Manners, Morals and the Rise of Henry Dundas 1770–84', in Dwyer *et al.*, eds., *New Perspectives on Early Modern Scotland*
——, '"Beating the Lieges": The Military Riot at Ravenshaugh Toll on 5 October 1760', *Transactions of the East Lothian Antiquarian and Field Naturalists' Society*, Vol. 17, (1982)
——, 'The Importance of Being Edinburgh. Management and Opposition in Edinburgh Politics 1746–84', *Scottish Historical Review*, LXII, 173, (1983)
——, (with Sher, R. B.), 'Patronage and Party in the Church of Scotland 1750–1800', in Macdougall, ed., *Church, Politics and Society*
——, 'More Reluctant Heroes. New Light on Military Recruiting in North East Scotland 1759–60', *Northern Scotland*, (forthcoming)
Nairn, Tom, *The Break-up of Britain. Crisis and Neo-Nationalism*, (London 1977)
Namier, Lewis, and Brooke, John, *Charles Townshend*, (London 1964)
Oestreich, Gerhard, *Neostoicism and the Early Modern State*, (Cambridge 1982)
Omond, G. W. T., *Fletcher of Saltoun*, Famous Scots Series, (Edinburgh 1897)
Parker, G., 'The Military Revolution 1560–1660: a Myth?', in *ibidem, Spain and the Netherlands 1559–1659*, (Glasgow 1979)
The History of Parliament, Sedgewick, R., *The House of Commons 1715–54*, 2 vols., (London 1970)
The History of Parliament, L. Namier and J. Brooke, *The Commons 1754–90*, 3 vols., (London 1964)
Patterson, A. Temple, *The Other Armada. The Franco–Spanish Attempt to Invade Britain in 1779*, (Manchester 1960)

Phillipson, N. T., and Mitchison, R., eds., *Scotland in the Age of Improvement. Essays in Scottish History in the Eighteenth Century*, (Edinburgh 1970)

Phillipson, N. T., 'Towards a Definition of the Scottish Enlightenment', in A. Fritz and D. Williams, eds., *City and Society in the Eighteenth Century*, (Toronto 1973)

——, 'Culture and Society in the 18th-Century Province: The Case of Edinburgh and the Scottish Enlightenment', in L. Stone, ed., *The University in Society*, II, (Princeton 1975)

——, 'Lawyers, Landowners and the Civic Leadership of Post-Union Scotland', *Juridicial Review*, 21 N.S., (1976)

——, 'Hume as Moralist: A Social Historian's Perspective', in S. C. Brown, ed., *Philosophers of the Enlightenment*, Royal Institute of Philosophy Lectures, XII, (Brighton 1979)

——, 'The Scottish Enlightenment', in R. Porter and M. Teich, eds., *The Enlightenment in National Context*, (Cambridge 1981)

——, 'Adam Smith as Civic Moralist' in Hont and Ignatieff, eds., *Wealth and Virtue*

Pocock, J. G. A., *Politics, Language and Time*, (London 1971)

——, *The Machiavellian Moment*, (Princeton 1975)

——, 'Virtue, Rights and Manners. A Model for Historians of Political Thought', *Political Theory*, 9, 3, (1981)

Prebble, John, *Mutiny. Highland Regiments in Revolt 1743–1804*, (Harmondsworth 1977)

Rae, John, *Life of Adam Smith*, (London 1895)

Riley, P. W. J., *The English Ministers and Scotland 1707–27*, (London 1964)

——, *The Union of England and Scotland. A Study in Anglo-Scottish Politics of the eighteenth century*, (Manchester 1978)

——, 'The Structure of Scottish Politics and the Union of 1707', in T. I. Rae, ed., *The Union of 1707: Its Impact on Scotland*, (Glasgow 1974)

Robbins, Caroline, *The Eighteenth Century Commonwealthman*, (New York 1968)

Robertson, John, 'The Scottish Enlightenment at the Limits of the Civic Tradition', in Hont and Ignatieff, eds., *Wealth and Virtue*

——, 'Scottish Political Economy beyond the Civic Tradition: Government and Economic Development in the *Wealth of Nations*', *History of Political Thought*, IV, 3, (1983)

Schwoerer, L. G., *'No Standing Armies!' The Anti-Army Ideology in Seventeenth-Century England*, (Baltimore and London 1974)

Sher, R. B., 'Moderates, Managers and Popular Politics in Mid-Eighteenth-Century Edinburgh: the Drysdale Bustle of the 1760s', in Dwyer *et al.*, eds., *New Perspectives on Early Modern Scotland*

——, *Church and University in the Scottish Enlightenment: the Moderate Literati of Edinburgh*, (Princeton 1985)

——, and Murdoch, A., 'Patronage and Party in the Church of Scotland 1750–1800', in Macdougall, ed., *Church, Politics and Society*

Skinner, A. S., *A System of Social Science. Papers Relating to Adam Smith*, (Oxford 1979)

——, 'A Scottish Contribution to Marxist Sociology?', in I. Bradley and M. Howard, eds., *Classical and Marxian Political Economy. Essays in Honour of R. L. Meek*, (London 1982)

Skinner, Quentin, *The Foundations of Modern Political Thought: I: The Renaissance*, (Cambridge 1978)

——, 'The Principles and Practice of Opposition: The Case of Bolingbroke versus Walpole', in N. McKendrick, ed., *Historical Perspectives. Studies in English Thought and Society in honour of J. H. Plumb*, (London 1974)

Small, J., *Biographical Sketch of Professor Adam Ferguson*, (Edinburgh 1854)

Smout, T. C., *Scottish Trade on the Eve of the Union 1660–1707*, (Edinburgh 1963)

——, *A History of the Scottish People*, (London 1969)

——, 'Scottish Landowners and Economic Growth 1650–1850', *Scottish Journal of Political Economy*, XI, (1964)

Stair Society, *An Introduction to Scottish Legal History*, The Stair Society, Vol. 20, (Edinburgh 1950)

Stevenson, David, *The Scottish Revolution 1637–44. The Triumph of the Covenanters*, (Newton Abbot 1973)

——, *Scottish Covenanters and Irish Confederates. Scottish–Irish Relations in the Mid-Seventeenth Century*, (Belfast 1981)

Stewart, Colonel David, *Sketches of the Character, Manners, and Present State of the Highlanders of Scotland, with details of the Military Service of the Highland Regiments*, 2 Vols., (Edinburgh 1822) (reprinted Edinburgh 1977)

Swinfen, D. B., 'The American Revolution in the Scottish Press', in O. D. Edwards and G. Shepperson, eds., *Scotland, Europe and the American Revolution*, (Edinburgh 1976)

Thompson, E. P., 'Patrician Society, Plebeian Culture', *Journal of Social History*, 7, (1974)

Timperley, L. R., *A Directory of Landownership in Scotland c.1770*, Scottish Record Society, New Series, 5, (1976)

——, 'The Pattern of Landholding in Eighteenth-Century Scotland', in M. L. Parry and T. R. Slater, eds., *The Making of the Scottish Countryside*, (London 1980)

Trevor-Roper, H. R., 'George Buchanan and the Ancient Scottish Constitution', *English Historical Review*, Supplement 3, (1966)

——, 'The Scottish Enlightenment', *Studies on Voltaire and the Eighteenth Century*, LVIII, (1967)

——, 'The Invention of Tradition: the Highland Tradition of Scotland', in E. J. Hobsbawm and T. Ranger, eds., *The Invention of Tradition*, (Cambridge 1983)

Venturi, Franco, 'Tra Scozia e Russia. Un Dibattito Settecentesco sul Feudalesimo', *Russia. Studi e Ricerche I*, ed. V. Strada, (Turin 1974)

Ward, W. R., 'The Land Tax in Scotland 1707–1798', *Bulletin of the John Rylands Library*, XXXVII, (1954–5)

Western. J. R., *The English Militia in the Eighteenth Century. The Story of a Political Issue*, (London and Toronto 1965)

——, 'The Formation of the Scottish Militia in 1797', *Scottish Historical Review*, XXXIV, (1955)

Whyte, I., 'The Emergence of the New Estate Structure', in M. L. Parry and T. R. Slater, eds., *The Making of the Scottish Countryside*, (London 1980)

Williamson, A. H., *Scottish National Consciousness in the Age of James VI*, (Edinburgh 1979)

——, 'Scotland, Anti-Christ and the Invention of Great Britain', in Dwyer *et al.*, eds., *New Perspectives on Early Modern Scotland*

Winch, Donald, *Adam Smith's Politics. An Essay in Historiographic Revision*, (Cambridge 1978)

Worden, A. B., Introduction to Edmund Ludlow, 'A Voyce from the Watch Tower', Part V: 1660–62, *Camden Fourth Series*, 21 (1978)

Wormald, Jenny, *Court, Kirk and Community. Scotland 1470–1625*, The New History of Scotland, Vol. 4, (London 1981)

——, '"Princes" and the Regions in the Scottish Reformation', in Macdougall, ed., *Church, Politics and Society*

Youngson, A. J., *After the Forty-Five. The Economic Impact on the Scottish Highlands*, (Edinburgh 1978)

Dissertations

McElroy, D. D., 'The Literary Clubs and Societies of Eighteenth-Century Scotland and their influence on the Literary Productions of the Period', Edinburgh University Ph.D. Thesis (1952)

——, 'A Century of Scottish Clubs 1700–1800', Typescript, National Library of Scotland (1969)

Robertson, John, 'The Improving Citizen. Militia Debates and Political Thought in the Scottish Enlightenment', Oxford University D. Phil. Thesis (1981)

Sher, R. B., 'The Road to Adam Ferguson: Ideology, Incentive and the Edinburgh Chair of Moral Philosophy', Unpublished paper

Timperley, L. R., 'Landownership in Scotland in the Eighteenth Century', Edinburgh University Ph.D. Thesis (1977)

Index

in the Kirk, 77–8, 80, 131, 176, 183–5, 188, 198;

attitude to Scotland's martial past, 78–81, 105, 135, 241;

their political connections, 82–4, 131, 142, 175, 185–6;

in the Select Society, 84–6;

in the Scottish militia agitations, 98, 106–7, 113–14, 117–18, 122, 131, 146–7, 157, 160, 174, 179;

in the Poker Club, 118, 131, 176, 185–8, 199;

hostility to political reform, 174–5;

their outlook contrasted unfavourably with that of Hume and Smith, 238–43

Monarchy, concepts of,
limited, 23, 64, 65, 126, 212;
mixed, 28–30, 37, 65, 208;
civilised (Hume), 64, 71–3;
modern (Smith), 219–20;
universal, 56, 64, 231

Monmouth, Duke of, 22

Montesquieu, Charles de Secondat, Baron de, 117, 126, 138

Montgomery, Col. Andrew, 191

Montgomery, Col. Hugh, 141

Montrose, James Graham, 1st Marquess of, 5, 7, 25, 54, 149

Montrose, burgh of, 107, 111, 119, 123

Moray, Francis, 9th Earl of, 141, 158

Moray, county of, 194

More, Thomas, 93

Morris, Corbyn, 92–3

Mossner, E. C., 92, 94, 95, 97, 228, 232

Mountstuart, John Stuart, Lord, 83, 130–2, 139, 152, 191, 196;
his militia bill (1775–6), 130–2, 133–4, 137, 139, 173, 176

Moyle, Walter, 27

Muirhead (or Morehead), William, 158, 191

Mull, isle of, 137

Murdoch, A., 19, 57, 96, 122, 123, 152, 193, 194, 195, 197, 198

Mure, William, of Caldwell, 83–4, 96, 118–19, 127, 131, 152, 190

Murray, James, of Broughton, 141

Murray, Lord John, 95, 171–2, 195

Murray, John, of Struan, 127, 171

Murray, Col. Robert, 190

Musgrave, Sir Christopher, provincial Tory, 36

Musselburgh, 56

Myrton, Sir Robert, of Gogar, 190

Nairn, burgh of, 111

Nairn, county of, 194

Nairne, William, of Dunsinane, 149, 189

Namier, L. B., 96, 122, 123, 125, 126, 152, 155, 195

Napier, John, of Merchiston, 4, 56, 58

Naples, 56

Naseby, Battle of, 24

Natural Law, 12, 58, 75

Navy, 27, 44, 83, 87, 99, 161, 234

Neville, Henry, 14, 20, 27

Newcastle, Thomas Pelham Holles, 4th Duke of, 106, 108–9, 112–13, 120–1, 122–7, 165, 167, 171–2, 243

New Galloway, burgh of, 111

Newton, Isaac, 212

Nicholson, Houston Stuart, 190

Nine Years' War, 15

Nobility, Scottish (also Aristocracy), 2–6, 31–3, 34, 40, 44, 79–80, 102, 105, 116, 135, 162, 165, 166, 168, 169, 172, 174, 182, 186–7, 240–1, 244;
see also Landowners; Peerage Elections

North, Frederick, Lord, 132, 137–8

North Berwick, 111, 127

Norton, Baron, 191

Ord, Robert, Lord Chief Baron, 125

Orkney, 194

Orr, Mr., of Barrowfield, 190

Ossian, 104, 122, 185, 238 243, 244

Oswald, James, of Dunnikier, 83–4, 95–6, 109–10, 112, 114

Oughton, General James Adolphus, C.-in-C. Scotland, 136, 154, 179–80, 193, 198

Paisley, 150

Pantheon Society, 130

Parliament, at Westminster (also House of Commons), 6, 27, 28, 29, 65–6, 86, 98, 103, 108–10, 112–14, 115, 116, 119–21, 122, 130, 132, 139, 150, 164, 165, 166, 168, 171, 178, 220, 231

Parliament of Scotland — *see* Estates

Patriotism — Patriot, 81–4, 85, 88, 90, 95, 96, 103, 120, 129

Patronage, ecclesiastical, 78, 84, 183–5, 198

Peace and War, Act of (1703), 38, 41, 44

Peeblesshire, 111, 119, 124, 194

Peerage Elections, 173, 195

Perth, 111, 175